ALSO BY BEN BRADLEE

A Life's Work: Fathers and Sons (with Quinn Bradlee)

Conversations with Kennedy

That Special Grace

BEN BRADLEE
A GOOD LIFE

NEWSPAPERING

AND OTHER

ADVENTURES

SIMON & SCHUSTER PAPERBACKS

New York London Toronto Sydney New Delhi

Picture credits appear on page 521.

Simon & Schuster
1230 Avenue of the Americas
New York, NY 10020

This Simon & Schuster trade paperback edition November 2017

SIMON & SCHUSTER and colophon are registered trademarks
of Simon & Schuster, Inc.

For information about special discounts for bulk purchases, please contact
Simon & Schuster Special Sales at 1-866-506-1949
or business@simonandschuster.com

The Simon & Schuster Speakers Bureau can bring authors to your
live event. For more information or to book an event contact the
Simon & Schuster Speakers Bureau at 1-866-248-3049
or visit our website at www.simonspeakers.com.

Manufactured in the United States of America

1   3   5   7   9   10   8   6   4   2

The Library of Congress has cataloged the Simon & Schuster edition as follows:
Bradlee, Benjamin C.
A Good Life : newspapering and other adventures / Ben Bradlee.
p.   cm.
Includes index.
1. Bradlee, Benjamin C.   2. Journalists—United States—Biography.
1. Title.
PN4874.B6615B73   1995
070.4'1'092—dc20
[B]   95-11361
CIP

ISBN 978-1-5011-9171-8
ISBN 978-1-4391-2885-5 (ebook)

For
Sally and Quinn
who light up my life

CONTENTS

FOREWORD

by Bob Woodward and Carl Bernstein

Two years after he published this memoir Ben Bradlee said in a speech, "The more aggressive our search for truth, the more some people are offended by the press.

"So be it," he added.

"I take great strength," he continued, ". . . knowing that in my experience, the truth does emerge. It takes forever sometimes, but it does emerge. And that any relaxation by the press will be extremely costly to democracy."

The central feature of his character: Bradlee was fearless. He knew that finding the truth required standing up to power, not getting pushed around by anyone, and setting that standard and requirement for his editors and reporters. Never relax in the search for the truth.

As a reader of this memoir will see, he pulled off being Bradlee because he was not afraid. Not afraid of presidents; of polio; of moneyed interests; of publishing the Pentagon Papers in 1971; of possible retribution or the likelihood that the government might strike at his newspaper with all its power; of going off in World War II on a Navy destroyer in the Pacific; of confronting conventional wisdom or pushing the journalistic envelope; of making a mistake.

Bradlee knew discovering the real story took time and often required both mundane and extraordinary effort: knocking on the doors of potential sources, showing up without appointments, and building relationships of trust with confidential sources. It even meant meeting with a source in an underground parking garage in the middle of the night—Deep Throat, later identified as Mark Felt, the No. 2 official in the FBI.

While we were covering the Watergate story, Nixon's campaign manager Clark MacGregor called Bradlee to complain and list five women he said we were hounding for information. "That's the nicest thing I've heard about them in years," Bradlee said. He insisted on persistence—dedication to finding what we call "the best obtainable version of the truth." But he insisted we be polite, straightforward, listen with respect to the people we were covering, and make clear our purpose as reporters for his newspaper.

He didn't once buckle or pull back.

Another formulation of his theory of newspapering and life he often expressed: *"Nose down, ass up, and moving steadily forward into the future."*

When we made mistakes (and we did) he was not happy, but forgiving if we could explain how we screwed up. He knew how to move on. "What have you got for tomorrow?" was a frequent refrain. Don't try to replay the last play, look to and plan for the next. He was not a man of regret, nor of self-righteousness.

The night President Nixon announced he was resigning because of Watergate on August 8, 1974, Ben issued a powerful order to the newsroom: "Don't gloat, don't gloat."

He was like the great general, calm in battle, who consistently won the love and affection of his troops. He loved moving through the newsroom trenches, restless and prowling for the latest malfeasance, surprise, or gossip.

As Style writer Martha Sherrill wrote in 2014, remembering Bradlee after he died, he often greeted her by saying, "Hey Tiger!" Sherrill added, "He said things like that. He had lusty greetings, exotic epithets, and obsolete profanities he got away with. He was unabashed, uninhibited . . . a Boston Brahmin but [he] enjoyed being an improper one."

In *All the President's Men*, our book about covering the Watergate story, we wrote that Bradlee was "an alluring combination of aristocrat and commoner" who would grind his cigarette out in a demitasse cup during a formal dinner party; would curse like a sailor but then greet some visitors from France "in formal, flawless French complete with a peck on each cheek."

Bradlee was not above seeking some theater to protect his newspaper and reporters. When the Nixon reelection committee issued subpoenas for our Watergate notes, Bradlee and publisher Katharine Graham agreed to declare that she was the legal owner and any court action would have to be directed at her personally.

"If the judge wants to send anyone to jail," Bradlee told us with palpable glee, "he's going to have to send Mrs. Graham. And, my God, the Lady says she'll go! Can't you see the picture of her limousine pulling up to the Women's Detention Center and out gets our gal, going to jail to uphold the First Amendment? That's a picture that would run in every newspaper in the world."

Ben transformed not only *The Washington Post*: his impact extended to the nature and priorities of journalism itself and the political culture of his country. The principles, energy, and commitment to that best obtainable version of the truth live on. He saw large purpose in journalism.

In 2013 after Jeff Bezos, the CEO of Amazon, bought the *Post* from the Graham family, he came to Washington and met with the staff and employees.

"We can't think small," Bezos said, echoing Bradlee. "We need to think big." He said that it was evident to him "that people are eager for a new golden era, one that leans into the twenty-first century." The model was Bradlee's: "All businesses need to be young forever . . . The number one rule has to be: Don't be boring," Bezos declared. Ben had said precisely that, hundreds of times; and even as he aged, his outlook was always youthful, never boring.

Three years later, in 2016—a presidential election year—Bezos returned to address the staff. "Any of us, any individual in this country, any institution in this country, if they choose to, can scrutinize, examine, and criticize . . . especially a candidate for the highest office in the most powerful country on earth. It's critical.

"The *Post* has a long tradition of examining presidential candidates [and presidents], as it should be, and there's no way that is going to change."

As we write this introduction, Donald Trump is creating an entirely new American presidency, breaking most rules and setting a wholly nontraditional course. The Trump campaign and his election as president has appalled millions and been embraced by millions. Reporting and trying to understand the great division would have enthralled Ben. He would have seen Trump's charge of "fake news" as just another round of the nondenial denial, an attempt to make the conduct of the media the issue, not Trump's own conduct.

The Bradlee tradition and heritage continues—all concentrations of power must be aggressively but fairly examined.

On the steps of the National Cathedral before the memorial service and mass at the National Cathedral for Ben in 2014, Bezos said, "What better future could you hope for than to have the DNA of Ben Bradlee embedded in your institution." The institution was not just *The Washington Post*. It was the institution of journalism itself.

In 2008, 17 years after Ben retired as executive editor of the *Post*, we sat down with him for a tape-recorded conversation that focused on the future of journalism. He reflected on the convulsions in the news media, the rise of the Internet, the impatience and speed of the news flow.

There was too much handwringing that newspapers would disappear, he said. "I am really appalled about that. I cannot envision a world without newspapers. I cannot envision it. I can envision a world with fewer newspapers. I can envision a world where newspapers are printed differently, distributed differently, but there is going to be a profession of journalism and their job is going to be to report what they believe the truth to be. And that won't change."

No one in the history of journalism did more to ensure that legacy.

August 2017

PREFACE

W hen I was a child, we had to read books in French at home, and I remember one called *Les Mémoires d'un Âne* . . . The Memoirs of an Ass (or Donkey). Except for that, I have always thought of memoirs as the province of presidents and prime ministers, explorers and four-star generals, plus maybe a Secretary of State or two, or a literary lion. It seemed a bit cheeky for a newspaperman to run with such a crowd, especially a newspaperman trained to stay off the stage and keep himself and his feelings out of the story, and especially a native Bostonian newspaperman, trained from birth not to talk about family, money, or sex.

But this is a memoir, pure and simple, memories of the events that have left their mark on me. It is nowhere near a collection of my thoughts on the state of journalism, or on the proper relationship between the press and public policy. I'm still collecting them—still changing my mind.

I dared try my hand at a memoir only when I began to realize that I really had been dealt an awfully good hand by the powers that be. A hand that gave me a ringside seat at some of the century's most vital moments. A hand that allowed me to make an adventure out of the Depression, illness, and war, and a romance out of newspapering. It is called A *Good Life* because that is what I've had—and because when I was desperate for a title, David Halberstam said casually, "You've had a good life, Bradlee. Hey, why not call it that: A *Good Life?*" I have thought hard about the role of luck in my life and come to the simple conclusion that I have been wonderfully lucky. To survive polio. To survive more than three years on a destroyer in the Pacific War from Guadalcanal to Japan. To land a job on *The Washington Post*, after skipping an interview with the *Baltimore Sun* only because it was raining so hard when my train stopped in Baltimore first. To buy a house in Georgetown a few months before Senator and Mrs. John F. Kennedy bought a house only a few doors away. To try to persuade Phil Graham to buy *Newsweek* at just the right moment. To find the emerging Katharine Graham looking for an editor at the precise moment when the *Post* was ready to fly. And most important, to find the most extraordinary collection of newspaper types eager to sign up for the flight.

These newspaper types, now graying, some even gone, are the people I would like to thank first and most for their contribution to this book and to my delight in my working life. Larry Stern, Dick Harwood, Bart Rowen, David Broder, Haynes Johnson, Shelby Coffey, Phil Geyelin, Meg Greenfield, Bill Greider, David Laventhol, Gene Patterson, Bob Baker, Phil Foisie, Barry Sussman, Harry Rosenfeld, Jack Lemmon, Nick von Hoffman, Mary Hadar, Dick Cohen, Len Downie, Bob Kaiser, George Solomon, David Ignatius, Mary McGrory, Mike Getler, Walter Pincus, Chal Roberts, Don Oberdorfer, Murrey Marder, Eleanor Randolph, Myra MacPherson . . . to name any of them is to risk leaving out someone vitally important to me.

And, of course, the one and only Sally Quinn.

It would be hard to overestimate the contributions to my newspaper and to my time as editor of that extraordinary reporter, Bob

Woodward—surely the best of his generation at investigative reporting, the best I've ever seen. With his sidekick, Carl Bernstein, and the job they did on decoding the Watergate scandal, they put the *Post* (and me) on the map in ways that no one could have predicted. And Woodward has maintained the same position on top of journalism's ladder ever since Watergate.

A newspaper is not referred to as the "Daily Miracle" for nothing. It takes the talents of a great many people working a great many hours at the top of their game before an editor can put his feet on the desk and accept congratulations. With this kind of talent, congratulations are inevitable.

It would be ungrateful of me not to pause here to acknowledge the role of Richard Milhous Nixon in furthering my career. It is wonderfully ironical that a man who so disliked—and never understood—the press did so much to further the reputation of the press, and particularly *The Washington Post*. In his darkest hour, he gave the press its finest hour.

Writing is an acquired skill, at least for me. I wrote for almost fifteen years before I felt reasonably sure of turning in a coherent, well-written story. But in the Washington Bureau of *Newsweek*, even one's most beautiful prose was rewritten by some faceless bastard in New York, and back at the *Post* I wrote so many leads and headlines that managing editor Howard Simons regularly belittled my writing skills by referring to me as a sprinter. "Benny gets lost after the first two hundred words," he said.

In writing this book I had special, quality help from two women who gathered and organized the paper trail—detritus—of a disorganized life and forced me to think as well as write. First came Barbara Feinman, until she moved on to concentrate on her own career as a writer. She got me focused with skill and humor. Next came Katherine Wanning, whose diligence and patience were awesome. Their help was essential. Tom Wilkinson, my longtime friend and colleague, devoted hours to re-creating with me the sense of excitement in the 1960s and 1970s, and I am especially grateful to him. The same goes for Carol Leggett, secretary and friend, who has been irreplaceable from day one.

I have been reading forewords all my life, never quite believing the authors when they come to the point where they thank editors. Deep down I used to think that writers have a natural contempt for editors, as unnatural obstacles between them and the readers. Well, I am now at that point, and I was wrong. Alice Mayhew, whose title is Vice President, Editorial Director of Simon & Schuster, seems to have edited almost every book any friend of mine ever wrote. And I was especially worried about her. Again, I was wrong. Never mind her title—she is an editor's editor, enthusiastic but strong, fun but tough, and wonderful company. She proved what I secretly suspected all the time, that no one needs an editor like an editor. Her sidekick, Liz Stein, was gracious, persistent, and full of sense. And a special word of thanks to Dick Snyder, the former Chairman and Chief Executive Officer of S&S. He decided that I would write this book, Mayhew would edit it, and he would publish it.

But for the last thirty years it is Katharine Graham who has so generously and unselfishly given me the chances to do what I feel I was put on this earth to do. And I thank her every day for those chances. Make no mistake about it: there is only one thing an editor must have to be a good editor, and that is a good owner. Kay says the only editor of *The Washington Post* she was ever in love with was Russ Wiggins. And I accept that. I love him, too. But I love her for her courage, for her loyalty, for her determination to commit the *Post* to excellence and to hold it unswervingly to that commitment. I love the joy she gets out of her work, and the joy she gives others. I treasure her friendship and confidence.

It is no accident that the best newspapers in America are those controlled by families to whom newspapering is a sacred trust. With Don Graham now in the driver's seat, the *Post* is deep into the third generation. He is probably the best-trained newspaper person in America . . . reporter, editor, ad salesman, circulator, production assistant, general manager, publisher, now CEO, and still barely fifty years old. When I walked out of the city room in 1991, I bequeathed Don Graham's loyalty to my successor, Len Downie. There was nothing more valuable I could have left him.

A GOOD LIFE

ONE

EARLY YEARS

_____

I t was a balmy fall day—October 2, 1940.

The scene was a large, messy living room, converted to an office in one of those big, Victorian houses that circle Harvard Square in Cambridge.

The sign on the door read "The Grant Study of Adult Development." Financed by W. T. Grant, the department store magnate, and run by Harvard's Health Services Department, the study proposed to investigate "normal" young men, whatever that might mean, at a time when most research was devoted to the abnormal. Dr. Arlie Bock, the first Grant Study director, was convinced that "some people coped more successfully than others," and the study intended to search for the factors which "led to intelligent living." The guinea pigs were drawn from consecutive freshman classes at Harvard, a total of 268 men.*

_____

* A similar study of women students was started in 1947 at Bryn Mawr, Haverford, and Swarthmore.

I was one of those guinea pigs, and we were presumed by our presence at Harvard to have shown "some capacity to deal more or less ably with [our] careers to date." The researchers included internists, psychiatrists, anthropologists, psychometricians, social workers, plus an occasional physiologist, biologist, or chemist.

On that particular afternoon, I was a sophomore, just turned nineteen, a sophomore who had only recently been laid for the first time, sort of. The Depression and a six-month siege of polio had been the sole departures from an otherwise contented, if not stimulating, life.

The news was dominated by the war in Europe. Churchill had just replaced Chamberlain. Some 350,000 British troops had been evacuated from Dunkirk in small boats. FDR had masterminded the gift to Britain of fifty American four-stack destroyers,* and was nearing reelection to his unprecedented third term. Joe DiMaggio was about to hit .350 and win the American League batting title. Gas cost 15 cents a gallon. A luxury car cost $1,400. And Ronald Reagan had just been picked to star in *She Couldn't Say No* with someone called Rosemary Lane.

The Grant Study's social worker later described a classic young WASP, whose family income was $10,000 a year ($5,000 from my father's salary, $5,000 from my mother's dress shop), and whose college expenses were paid for by a New York lawyer grandfather. She described my father as "industrious, hard-working . . . interested in nature, trees, birds, antiques, sports and civic things." My mother was listed as "ambitious and industrious . . . musical and artistic" (which she would have liked), and as "rather of the flighty and ar-

---

* Including the U.S.S. *Crowninshield* (DD134), named for Madison's Secretary of the Navy, Benjamin Williams Crowninshield, for whom I was named. She was a four-stack destroyer, commissioned in 1919, stayed in and out of commission until she was given to the British in 1940, and became H.M.S. *Chelsea*. She was loaned to the Canadians for much of the shooting war. In July 1944, she was transferred to the Russians and renamed *Derskyi*.

Crowninshield, with President Madison's support, won a big battle assuring civilian supremacy over the Navy, but otherwise seemed to have cast more shadow than substance as Secretary. Contemporary historians described him as "irresolute and vacillating [and therefore] barely competent to handle the Navy."

tistic type. Very charming and young in her ideas [at forty-four]; almost immature." That last would have enraged her.

After the physical exam, the doctors noted their guinea pig was 5 feet 11½ inches tall and weighed 173 pounds, with warm hands, cold feet, "marked postural dizziness," "moderate hand tremor," "slight bashful bladder," three tattoos—one on left arm and two on right buttock—"rather short toes" with "slight webbing" between #2 and #3, a double crown in his scalp, and without eyeglasses, freckles, or acne. Blood pressure was 112 over 84. Pulse was 81; respiration, 22. Hair: dark brown. Eyes: brown/green.

The psychometrist made 107 different measurements, including head length (210 mm), head breadth (151 mm), nose height (51 mm), wrist breadth (59 mm), sitting height (95.6 cm), trunk height (60.9 cm), and something called "cephalo-facial" (21.19: 88.9); and made 134 separate psychometric observations: mouth breather (yes), chest hair (absent), thighs (muscular: + + +), buttocks shape (+ +), Fat Dep. Butt. (+), Fat Dep. Abd. (sm), chin (pointed), nasal tip (snub), teeth lost (none), earlobe (free), hands shape (long, square), handedness (right), footedness (right); and concluding medical physical appraisal (normal).

One of the psychologists described her guinea pig as a "very good-looking . . . boy, well-mannered and cultured. He walked into the office with the confident manner of one who knows how to deal with people." She was especially impressed with how this "quite normal, well-adjusted, and socially adaptable" boy had adapted to four months of leg splints and crutches during his bout with what was then called infantile paralysis. "In spite of being unable to move his legs [for a couple of months] and in spite of one of his friends dying in the same epidemic . . . he never did consider he would be paralyzed. This is a very interesting fact in illness. Do those people who develop a permanent paralysis have as much confidence while they are ill as this boy had?"

But they weren't all that impressed by much else.

"My general impression of this boy is quite good," the anonymous psychologist noted. "He probably will not have any trouble socially here at Harvard. His trouble will probably lie in a conflict between his conservative Bostonian raising and his ideas and ideals which are gradually becoming more radical."

"This boy's emotional response to things" attracted psychiatrists' attention. " . . . he often cries rather openly in a movie . . . he often puts himself right into the shoes of the actors and actresses, and . . . he enjoys this. He states, too, that he has a strong desire and emotional feeling toward [the film] 'A Foreign Correspondent.' As a matter of fact, he has seen this picture four times and is looking forward to seeing it again. He feels that a foreign correspondent is one of the most 'romantic' and 'glamorous' persons that live today. He is looking forward to doing this sort of work. My general impression is that this boy has a rather immature, emotional, and romantic outlook on what he wants to do."

Six months later I returned for one of many required follow-up sessions, and a new psychologist described someone quite different. "When he came in," his notes read,

I could easily see that he is mixed up. His principal problem seems to center around the fact that before he came to Harvard he was living in a more or less materialistic world. He had been more a typical American boy—quite athletic, quite popular in school, and doing his work fairly well. But it was not until his freshman year at Harvard that he began to think, particularly in the abstract. Thus, he has more or less changed to a theoretical, philosophical, impractical person, whereas before he was quite materialistic and practical.

This new toy, the philosophical and abstract, has rather confused him. In his confusion, the boy has become rather restless and dissatisfied with Harvard. As a result, he did very poor work in his midyear examinations. Shortly after doing this poor work, he started making plans for stopping school. At three o'clock one morning, this boy suddenly decided to go to Montreal and join the R.C.A.F. He went to talk with those people, and they said they would accept him, but at that time he backed out and came back to Harvard.

However, his restlessness and dissatisfaction continued. He began to wonder why he was here at Harvard; he wondered what kind of a life he was going to lead; and he was generally mixed up with his new plaything—the dealing with the philosophical, abstract and theoretical. Recently, he has gone down to the Navy Yard and found that he can join the Naval Air Force when he reaches 20, which will be August 26 of this year.

The general picture is one of confusion and dissatisfaction with himself and with the results he has been attaining here at Harvard. Entering into this dissatisfaction is his restlessness. He has done several things to overcome his restlessness. There have been times when he has drunk too much alcohol, but this does not satisfy him.

Sixteen months later, on August 8, 1942, "this boy" graduated from Harvard by the skin of his teeth at 10:00 A.M. At noon, I was commissioned an ensign in the United States Naval Reserve, with orders to join the *Philip*, a new destroyer being built in Kearny, New Jersey. And at 4:00 P.M., I married Jean Saltonstall, the first and only girl I had slept with.

I was not yet twenty-one. I had never been west of the Berkshires or south of Washington, D.C., and I was on my way to some place called the South Pacific, which was not yet a musical.

The education of Benjamin C. Bradlee was finally under way.

As a family, the Bradlees had been around for close to three hundred years, but well down the totem pole from the Lowells and the Cabots. Proper enough as proper Bostonians went, but not that rich, and not that smart. Grandparents who were well off, if not rich. Nice Boston house, not on Beacon Hill, not even on the sunny side of Beacon Street overlooking the Charles River, but on Beacon Street still. One car, no boats, but a cook and a maid, and a stream of governesses before the Depression, plus old Tom Costello to lug firewood up three flights of stairs to the living-room fireplace and to shovel coal into the basement furnace.

Josiah Bradlee (married to Lucy Hall), described as "the poor son of a humble Boston tinsmith" (Frederick Hall Bradlee), was listed among the fifteen hundred wealthiest people in Massachusetts and a millionaire in 1851. One authority wrote: "In spite of his great wealth and standing as a merchant prince . . . never attaining a place among the Proper Bostonians."

It was said of him, heavily: "If he sent a shingle afloat on the ebb tide bearing a pebble, it would return on the flood freighted with a silver dollar."

One of his proudest boasts: "In all the 82 years of his busy life he never spent but one night away from Boston. That time he journeyed to Nahant."

My father was a Walter Camp All-American football player from Harvard, turned investment banker in the 1920s, busted by the Depression in the thirties. Frederick Josiah Bradlee, Jr., son of Frederick Josiah Bradlee, grandson of Frederick Hall Bradlee, all the way back eight generations to Nathaniel Bradley, born in 1631, who got the cider concession in Dorchester, Massachusetts, in 1673, and made sexton in 1680. His job was to "ring the bell, cleanse the meeting house, and to carry water for baptism."

My father was born at 211 Beacon Street in the Back Bay. After they married, my parents first lived in an apartment at 295 Beacon Street. They bought their first house, a brownstone, at 267 Beacon Street, lived there for twenty-three years, and then moved across the street, back into an apartment at 280 Beacon Street. These were not adventuresome people.

After football, "B" Bradlee rose quickly like all Brahmin athletes of that era from bank runner, to broker, then vice president of the Boston branch of an investment house called Bank America Blair Company. And then the fall. One day a Golden Boy. Next day, the Depression, and my old man was on the road trying to sell a commercial deodorant and molybdenum mining stock for companies founded and financed by some of his rich pals.

There was always the promise of some dough at the end of a family rainbow, as soon as the requisite number of relatives passed on to their rewards. Especially Uncle Tom, whose fortune was so long anticipated, and his wife, the long-lived Aunt Polly. Tom was some kind of cousin to my grandfather, and lived in some institution in western Massachusetts, dressed immaculately in yachting cap, blue blazer, and white flannels, looking through a long glass across green fields for God knows what. Aunt Polly lived at 111 Beacon Street. My father and his two brothers called on her regularly to check her pulse, until she died of old age in her late eighties.

Before the right people died, my father kept the books of a Canadian molybdenum mine for a few bucks; he kept the books of various city and country clubs for family memberships; he supervised the janitorial force at the Boston Museum of Fine Arts—for $3,000 a year. And all through the Depression we lived rent-free, weekends and summers, in a big Victorian house owned by the estate of some distant relatives named Putnam in the woods of Beverly, Massachusetts. Rent-free, provided we kept up the grounds and barns, which "B" did with a passion, and with me when I was around.

This was Beverly, a glorious by-product of the Depression, when my family had the use of two houses, plus two big barns in twenty acres of beautiful woods, on a hill overlooking the bays of Salem and Beverly, less than a mile away. The owners were the trustees of an estate, who wanted to sell when no one wanted to buy. We had lived there, summers in the big house, winter weekends in the cottage, from 1932 until one afternoon in the summer of 1945. "B" and Jo were having cocktails on the big porch which girded the house, when an unknown car drove around the circle by the front door.

"Who's that, for God's sake?" Jo asked, according to family legend.

"Beats me," "B" is said to have replied. "Probably someone looking to buy the place. Been for sale for fifteen years."

Now for the first time in years, Jo was feeling almost flush. An elderly relative, who had been long forgotten in some convent, had recently been gathered, leaving Josephine $5,000. She announced that she was going to call Harvey Bundy, one of the trustees, and a family friend (also the father of future national security adviser McGeorge Bundy), and offer him the $5,000 for the whole place.

And over my father's dead body she rose from her chair and she did it. Harvey wouldn't take $5,000, but by God he would take

$10,000, and all of a sudden this gorgeous place was ours. I have nothing but wonderful memories of Beverly, learning a love of the outdoors that has never left me, cutting down each giant beech tree that died in the blight of that time, on the opposite end of a two-man saw with my father and his friends. Burning brush for hours on end, still a uniquely calming and rewarding experience for me half a century later. Climbing trees, collecting butterflies, growing vegetables, playing doctor with my sister's friends. "B" and I built a backboard in the garage, even though the ceilings were only seven feet six inches high. It taught me to keep backhands and forehands low, and kept me busy on rainy days.

My family's house in Beverly burned down years later. There was one great loss: three huge red leather scrapbooks kept by my grandfather about my father's football career. Pictures (the original glossies) plus stories in all the papers, about a tough, fast halfback called "B" by his friends and Beebo in the sports sections, who played on a team that never lost a game.

I remembered one clip from the *Boston Globe*. Dated Monday, November 23, 1914, Coach Percy Haughton wrote about his Harvard team after they beat Yale: "From a photograph I have before me, it appears that Coolidge had not more than a three-yard start over two Yale men. . . . Bradlee is depicted a half yard behind [them], and yet in spite of this handicap, he succeeded in throwing first one Yale man, and then the other sufficiently off their stride to give Coolidge a clear field for the touchdown." (Harvard coaches spoke and wrote the King's English back then.) Coolidge was my father's best friend, T. Jefferson Coolidge, who had recovered a Yale fumble on Harvard's three-yard line, and ran it 97 yards for the score.

My father weighed less than 200 pounds, but he was tough, barrel-chested, strong, fast, and soft-spoken. Lying in his arms as a child and listening to that deep voice rolling around in his voice box was all the comfort and reassurance that a child could stand.

My mother was a little fancier. Josephine de Gersdorff, from New York City, daughter of a prototypical Helen Hokinson garden club lady named Helen Suzette Crowninshield and a second-generation German lawyer named Carl August (pronounced OW-GUSTE) de Gersdorff, who was a name partner in one of the swell law firms . . . Cravath, de Gersdorff, Swaine & Wood. My mother was the co-holder of the high-jump record at Miss Chapin's School for years, fluent in French and German, lovely to look at, well read, ambitious and flirtatious. She took singing lessons from a faded opera star.

She was called Jo, and when she sang "When I'm Calling You" during Assembly one morning at Dexter School in Brookline just outside of Boston—she forgot the words. I thought I'd die. Miss Fiske, the principal, whose motto was "Our best today; better tomorrow," thanked her much too profusely, but I never really forgave her, even if I was only ten. Jo was ambitious, but mostly for us children . . . not so much socially (we were about as far up that ladder as anyone was going to go), but intellectually. We had governesses as long as we had the money to pay them, mostly desiccated women who used a switch to keep us speaking French. Every Saturday, no one in the family was allowed to speak anything but French. We took piano lessons (I can still play "Ole Man River" with the knuckles of my right hand). We took riding lessons at Vignole's Riding Academy in Brookline. We were forced to go to the Boston Symphony's Children's Concerts (Ernest Schelling, conductor) on Saturday mornings. We were taken to the opera every spring, when the Met came to Boston. One day when I was twelve, I was taken to an afternoon performance of *Madame Butterfly,* followed after supper by four hours of *Parsifal* (starring Lauritz Melchior and Kirsten Flagstad). We hardly ever pretended to be sick and miss school, because that meant listening to Josephine practice her scales for two hours.

They made an odd couple, come to think of it. My father would get pretty well tanked when forced to host or even attend her musical evenings. My mother quickly learned to loathe afternoons burning brush in the Beverly woods. My father loved words, but talked only when he had a point to make or a story to tell. He had a great sense of humor and wit, but smiled more than he laughed.

My mother talked a lot, especially when she was nervous. She really had no sense of humor, but she laughed a lot. Great teeth.

But figuratively or literally he had his hand on her behind for most of half a century. Our sense of family was very strong, especially after the Depression, when the maids departed and we replaced them. Their life together was generally joyous and supportive. So was ours.

"Ours" was my older brother and younger sister, Frederick Josiah Bradlee III and Constance. Freddy dropped the "k," the "Josiah," and the "III" as soon as he could—when he opened on Broadway as Montgomery Clift's understudy in *Dame Nature*. Connie was born the belle of the ball, and without any real education learned the art of coping at an early age, settling into the system with grace and comfort.

We children ate early by ourselves in the dining room, except Sunday nights. We all remember only hamburgers for supper and prunes for dessert. For months I stacked the prunes on a ledge under the table rather than eat them. That worked fine, until the time came to put extra leaves in the table one night for company, when all the prunes fell to the floor, caked with dust. I remember the debate between my parents about whether I should be made to eat them, right then and there. The prunes were on the menu because my mother was preoccupied by our bowel movements. On Christmas mornings, for instance, we were forced to wait for the last child's bowel movement before we could go upstairs and open presents. That was always Connie, who couldn't bring herself to fake it, flush the toilet a couple of times, and announce her mission accomplished. The same bowel preoccupation required regular morning spoonfuls of Gorton's Cod Liver Oil, which tasted just the way it sounds. I finally got so that I literally gagged and barfed it up on the dining-room wallpaper. Years later, after God knows how many coats of paint, an oily stain the size of a man's face would always emerge, mute evidence of this early form of child abuse.

Freddy and I fought pretty much of a pitched battle for the first thirteen years of my life. And I mean fought. Down two flights of stairs, one night, landing on the second floor of our Boston house in the middle of a cocktail party my parents were throwing . . . Freddy on top. He pounded my head into the floor again and again, making me say "give up" before my brains spilled onto the carpet. "B" was so sick of the fighting that he didn't pull us apart.

Two and a half years older than me, Freddy won all the fights—until I took up golf. Then one summer day I took out after him with a five iron in my hand and blood in my eye. Fortunately, before I got close enough to swing, "B" came up the driveway to prevent bloodshed. And so when I was thirteen, the fights were over, replaced by silence. We simply didn't talk for years. We lived in separate worlds. Mine dominated by the outdoors—tennis, butterflies, chopping wood, girls. His dominated by imagination, actors and actresses, theater. I scorned his world, because I didn't understand it. He ignored mine, because it bored him.

The governesses varied greatly in form and substance. Mademoiselle Cahors was stout, to put it gently, and mean. She waddled when she chased down the Esplanade after Freddy and me with a freshly cut switch in her fat hand. Mademoiselle Bouvier, known as 'Zelle, was a prissy snob, inordinately proud of her perfect French from her native St. Pierre et Miquelon Islands. It would have been useful to know then that St. Pierre et Miquelon had been settled by French criminals. She concentrated on Connie, and left Freddy and me pretty much alone, except to endlessly correct our French and our manners. Whenever we spoke to my father on Saturdays in French, he would mutter "Jeezus," and go off to another room.

The governess situation took an extraordinary turn for the better with the arrival from Switzerland of the fabulous Sara Metin, known quickly as Sally, only eighteen years old, with bright red Alpine cheeks—and an absolutely spectacular body. Sally quickly spotted us children as tight-asses, and resolved to do something about it. Like roughhousing, at least once a day. Like getting us used to nudity. Ours and hers. I shall always be grateful to the highest authority that hers were the first breasts I ever saw—and forever remembered, even if I was only ten years old.

Sally had fallen in love with a man named Eddie Goodale, whose family owned apple orchards in Ipswich, Massachusetts, and who had gone to Antarctica with the first Byrd Expedition. On days when letters from Eddie arrived at 267 Beacon Street from New Zealand, Sally would dissolve in tears of love and anguish, and share with us stories about Antarctica from Eddie's letters. The return of the first Byrd Expedition from the South Pole coincided roughly with the arrival on Beacon Street of the Great Depression. Sally left us to marry Eddie, and help run the orchard where all the Eskimo Huskies from the Byrd Expedition were kenneled. We stayed close to her for a long time. I used to spend weekends with the Goodales in Ipswich, helping with the dogs and picking apples. I was given a Husky puppy, Skookum, who outgrew me quickly, and knocked me down regularly whenever he greeted me. He was part of the family, until he broke into my father's pride and joy, a chicken coop where he was trying to raise ring-necked pheasants, and ate them all. Skookum went back to the Goodales, and from there back to Antarctica on the second Byrd Expedition, where we were told he died a hero. Got sick one night, and wandered away from his team and froze to death. I was very proud.

Sally's departure was soon followed by the rest of the Bradlee staff, and overnight we were alone, making our own beds, cleaning our own rooms, cooking our own meals, fetching our own firewood like real people. The Depression was upon us, the first truly marking experience of my life. The biggest change came when my father lost his $50,000-a-year job, and with it some of the male dignity that went with the role of provider. To keep us children in private schools, my father and mother depended on the charity of still rich old relatives, whom they didn't really like, but to whom they now had to suck up. Relatives like Grandpa de Gersdorff, and like Cousin Frank Crowninshield, my godfather, who never worked a day in his life. He was the oldest living Crowninshield, known chiefly for his dislike of Franklin Roosevelt and anything British. He suffered from hemorrhoids, and when he had to have his rear end X-rayed, he turned to the nurse and said, "Make sure this is a good likeness, so I can send it to that son of a bitch in the White House." Visits to these benefactors were dreaded, like visits to make payments to loan sharks.

There were few matters of moment on the agenda of this family, beyond the Depression. A little light FDR bashing, some modest outrage whenever one of Boston Mayor James Michael Curley's bridges collapsed, a lot of family vacations, a few too many drinks.

At first, my father couldn't find a regular job; he started coming home before five in the afternoon. But he struggled at various odd jobs, with great energy and without false pride. He kept his membership in various clubs, in return for keeping the club books. Some of his friends had invested in a commercial deodorant called SANOVAN, and he tried to sell it to big Boston companies whose officers he knew. Once he mopped an entire Boston & Maine Railroad car, to demonstrate SANOVAN'S powers to B&M officials.

For what seemed like an eternity the family car was a four-door Chevy, painted the God-awfully garish blue that the Chevy dealer felt would attract maximum attention to his demo car. "B" was proud of the good deal he got, while we children, especially Freddy, were embarrassed by the unwanted attention. When "B" put the SANOVAN tire cover on the spare tire that sat on the rear bumper, we all suffered.

Family conversation centered on ourselves and our friends. And none of us was what might be called interesting yet. There was almost no anti-Semitism . . . maybe a couple of Izzy jokes in twenty years, because there were no Jews in my family landscape—except for Walter Lippmann, who had married the co-holder of the high-jump record at Miss Chapin's School. Lippmann never addressed the question of his religion, then or later, and my family was only too happy to play it his way. And by the same token, there were no blacks in our lives, literally, except for Amos and Andy, who were absolutely sacred in our house. My father would sooner give up his sacred Martinis—known as "yellow boys" because they were made with three parts Booth's Old Tom Gin to one part sweet vermouth—than miss a minute whenever Amos 'n' Andy, or Fred

Allen, Jack Benny, or Ed Wynn, were on the Atwater Kent radio.
I had never spoken to a black man until I introduced myself to my
classmate Ray Guild in Harvard Yard our freshman year.

We used to spend either Christmas or Easter vacations with
the New York grandparents, trips I never really looked forward
to, except when we took the train to Fall River, and the Eastern
Steamship Line's overnight boat to New York. I always felt like
an outlander in New York, underdressed, unsophisticated, and
unappreciated—partly because of the dimension of the monied lifestyle, with Eckman, the butler, and Jimmy, the chauffeur.

Carl A. de Gersdorff was a little man with a gray moustache,
and he relished the fact that life at 3 East 73rd Street in New York
City, and summers in Stockbridge, Mass., revolved around him. He
got the first—and sometimes the only—drink at lunch, served on
a silver tray. Everyone had to wait for him to talk, or finish talking.

In the mid-thirties, President Roosevelt asked the Cravath firm
to negotiate a settlement to the Black Tom case with Nazi Germany.* Grandpa de Gersdorff, with his German surname and his *Almanach de Gotha* tucked firmly under his arm, got the case, taking his
prize assistant with him, a man named John J. McCloy, who would
return years later to run Germany as U.S. High Commissioner. I
remember hearing of their audience with Hitler, who told Grandpa
he had checked the family name in the *Almanach*, and I remember
Grandpa describing Hitler in terms that would in due course seem
uncritical.

My grandmother was warm and selfless, untouched by most of
the mundane realities of life. She could have been the prototype
for the garden club women. But even if she didn't care much about
the Boston Red Sox, she put other people first, and I remember her
with love.

Granny's two brothers—my great uncles—were always the highlights of our trips to New York. First, Uncle Edward Crowninshield,
who also never worked a day in his life, except for the two times he

---

* In July 1916, German saboteurs exploded thirteen warehouses full of munitions on Black
Tom Island on the New Jersey shore facing the Statue of Liberty.

went into the antiques business just to dispose of the heirloom furniture he inherited from various relatives and parents. He didn't stay in the antiques business very long, because my grandmother always bought all the family heirlooms back, leaving him flush and out of business. He was conspicuously tattooed, with a square-rigged, four-masted schooner under full sail on his back (put there during a ninety-day voyage to China), and coiled around the full length of his right arm a snake whose tail was plainly visible whenever he shook hands or shot his cuffs. He was an accomplished tap dancer, once getting pitched off the bow of Harold Vanderbilt's yacht in Newport Harbor, in the middle of the night, in the middle of his dance. He smoked opium, although I didn't learn that until he died. He escorted various celebrity women—like Edna Wallace Hopper, the first cosmetic tycoon, and Helen Wills Moody, the greatest tennis player of her day. He escorted them, and no one knew what else he did with them, although the word "mistress" was whispered whenever Miss Hopper's name was mentioned. And he was an accomplished amateur magician. We children used to love it when he asked Eckman, the butler, for a new pack of cards, tore and folded five or six of them into a box, which he then filled with smoke from his foul-smelling Turkish Melachrino cigarettes, and flicked with his finger to produce endless smoke rings.

And then there was Uncle Frank Crowninshield, my grandmother's brother (and some kind of cousin to the other Frank Crowninshield), the urbane, witty founding editor of Vanity Fair magazine, raconteur, art collector, toastmaster, member of the legendary Algonquin (Hotel) Round Table (with Dorothy Parker, Robert Benchley, Alexander Woollcott), historian of New York's High Society, friend of people as disparate as sportswriter Grantland Rice and Mrs. Vincent Astor. As a child I was uncomfortable in front of some of his African statues, especially the angular, highly polished nude sculptures with breasts pointing at me like oversized arrows, and in front of some of his collection of Impressionist art. But I was impressed that he had sportswriter friends as well as just fancy friends, and he treated me as an adult. Once when I was about twelve, I was allowed to take my sister Constance alone from 73rd

Street to Uncle Frank's apartment on 66th Street for tea. When he answered our ring of the doorbell, he was saying goodbye to a spectacularly lovely young woman, to whom he quickly introduced us. "Benny, I want you to meet my mistress, Clare Boothe." The future Mrs. Henry Luce, then the managing editor of *Vanity Fair*, didn't seem at all bothered, but I turned bright red. I wasn't at all sure what "mistress" entailed beyond having something to do with sex, but we sure didn't use that word much in Boston.*

When I was fourteen years old and in the ninth grade at boarding school—or the Third Form, as it was called at St. Mark's School, in Southboro, Massachusetts—I got polio. St. Mark's was one of a dozen citadels of WASP culture that dotted the New England countryside, each giving absolutely first-class educations to young boys preparing to join a world that was slowly ceasing to exist. One hundred eighty boys from the finest (read richest) families, so WASP that the only Jew in the school was a practicing Catholic named Moore, whose mother was a Pulitzer from St. Louis.

Polio hit the school as an epidemic in the spring of 1936, striking more than twenty boys, killing one, permanently crippling three more, and paralyzing another half dozen, including me, for some months. The researchers at Harvard Medical School couldn't wait to get our blue blood into their white mice, convinced that the isolated epidemic gave them a perfect shot at isolating the virus. If you were not alive during the time when polio swept the country every year, it is hard to imagine the fear that came with it. Children—at least in my crowd—were not allowed to go to the movies, to eat raw fruit or vegetables, to swim in public pools. Mothers (at least my mother) were terrified.

After the first child was officially diagnosed to have polio, all

* Twenty years later, I found myself standing next to Mrs. Luce as we waited for an elevator late one night at the Beau Rivage Hotel in Geneva. She was then the American Ambassador to Italy and I was the brand-new European correspondent for Newsweek, and we were both in Geneva in connection with a Foreign Ministers Conference. When the elevators were slow in coming, and since no one else was there, I decided to introduce myself, and when the elevators still hadn't arrived, I started telling her how we had met once before. And then before I knew it, I was past the point of no return in the mistress story. She looked me in the eye just as the elevator door slid open, and disappeared without a word. I stayed put.

St. Mark's parents were informed, and asked to keep their children at the school—rather than risk spreading the epidemic by bringing infected children home to start new epidemics there, an argument my parents bought. At school we were told to sit upright on the edge of our beds twice a day, and bring our chins to our chest. If it didn't hurt, we were free of the disease. If we felt a sharp pain in the small of the back, we probably had it.

One Sunday a week or two into the epidemic, Fred Hubbell and I had spent all afternoon fooling around the track. We sprinted, we ran, we jumped, we threw the hammer and the discus. We showered, dressed, ate, and sat down on the edge of our beds. The pain for both of us was intense. Late that night in the infirmary, we both had high flulike fevers and aches. By noon Monday, we were side by side in an ambulance, headed for Boston thirty miles away, siren screaming.

My father and George P. Denny, the family doctor, were waiting for the ambulance outside our Beacon Street house, to save the expense of a hospital, and I went up two flights of stairs in my father's arms to bed in my sister's room.

The ambulance with Fred continued on to Massachusetts General Hospital, where he died two days later, his lungs paralyzed beyond help. He was more promising than most of us, a strong and open, trusting boy from Des Moines, Iowa, full of joy and friendship.

For the first two weeks, polio behaves like the flu—aches, pains, fever, and headache. And one morning the aches and pains are gone. The temperature was normal. And the polio doctor, Frank Ober, was summoned for his macabre task. He didn't know how to prevent polio, or even how to treat polio. (Nobody did, Sister Kenny to the contrary notwithstanding.) But he knew his muscles, and he started checking mine, as I lay flat on my back, my father and mother watching me with anguish in their eyes. First, wiggle the scalp, then frown, raise each eyebrow, shut each eye, wink, left eye, right eye, sniff, move your lips and tongue, swallow, clear your throat, breathe deep, cough, sneeze, wiggle your ears, and so on and on. Right arm, from fingers to shoulders. Left arm, from fingers to shoulders.

I was going like gangbusters until we got to roll-ups: I couldn't get my shoulders more than a few inches off the sheets. It didn't take a rocket scientist to understand that my gut muscles were not working right. The rest of the examination didn't take long. I could move my hips some, and I could pee. My father had to lift me up for damn near thirty minutes, and call upon the laws of gravity, but by God I could pee. The bowels worked, though not always at my command, and that was pretty much it. No action in the leg department.

The tear ducts worked fine. Everybody's. But before very long, we were all talking about what we were going to do. Braces would be needed, because without any feeling in the legs, they could end up in shapes that could never be straightened. The braces would need footboards on them to hold my feet up, so the weight of the top sheet wouldn't flatten the soles to the bottom sheet. Someone (All-American Dad) would have to lift me into and out of a hot bath twice a day. And there was even prayer.

Looking back so many years later on the sudden truths that come with paralysis, I find it almost impossible to believe I wasn't pre-occupied with the prospect of a life permanently impaired. I have never been known for the quality or quantity of my introspective thoughts, but I can honestly say that I spent no time worrying about my future. None. I never saw myself in a wheelchair, or on crutches with braces. I rarely saw myself anywhere in the future.

I had only recently discovered the joys of masturbation, and was encouraged more than somewhat when I learned everything in that department had returned to "normal."

The Grant Study shrinks—and their successors—were always impressed with what they called my ability to adapt to new realities. I wonder now whether I was adapting to them or ignoring them. In any case, four weeks after Fred Hubbell died, I was back in an ambulance (paid for by friends of my parents) with siren blaring again en route to the big house in Beverly. From my bed I could see the big spruce tree, where I had built my treehouse a few years before. I could hear the foghorn on Baker's Island, and I could eavesdrop on the comings and goings of summer life out the windows. My brother and sister would shake their heads as fresh raspberries and thick cream, along with a stream of delicacies from S. S. Pierce, would be brought to me on a tray—gifts from my mother's friends—while they reported eating hamburgers and applesauce for seventy-three days running. They grumbled constantly about my being spoiled rotten, and that was plainly an understatement.

May and June turned into real summer, and I was neither scared nor bored. I could move laterally, from one side to another, thanks to a pair of trapeze rings installed for that purpose in the ceiling above my bed. My mother taught me how to play bridge with one of those special teaching boards. My father advanced me a fictional $200 to bet on the horses at Suffolk Downs. I studied the entries and past performances for hours, carefully recorded my bets—mostly two bucks to show—and listened to the race results on the radio. I remember making a $25 profit by Labor Day, which my father paid me. I read the sports pages cover to cover (and not much else) and listened to the Red Sox games as described by Fred Hoey over radio station WNAC.

Visitors were scarce. A few adults trying to score points with my parents. My St. Mark's School roommate Bob Potter, the only one of my own friends old enough to have a driver's license, dropped by almost daily to my surprise and delight. The mothers of other friends were so terrified of polio they ignored their doctors' advice that polio was not contagious after two weeks, and kept their kids away.

And then there was Leo Cronan, a fireplug Notre Dame athlete who was scratching out a living running a playground summers on the North Shore of Boston, teaching groups of us boys how to throw, catch, run, slide, box, bat for five or six hours a day. Leo was maybe twenty-three or twenty-four years old, and spoke reverentially of the legendary Notre Dame football coach, "Mr. Rockne." Leo was too short to be a great athlete, but what there was of him was all muscle and heart, and he came almost every night, to watch over one of his fallen "players," and to eat. He would put away almost a quart of milk each time, and as many of those Huntley & Palmer Biscuits (they were actually cookies) as were left over from the night before. This was the Depression, and the cookies were his dinner.

It was Leo who got me thinking about walking again, wondering aloud when I was going to want to try to stand, when I was going to dare to try to stand. Nothing hurt, but I still couldn't wiggle my toes, and the braces kept my legs so rigid I felt no change in my legs. Each brace consisted of two steel rods, attached to either side of a vertical foot pad, running up either side of my leg. Leather straps every few inches kept the leg itself up off the bed. The bars were joined by a curved metal strip at the crotch. It was painful even to think of standing up with them on, but Leo announced to me—never my parents—that "we" were going to do exactly that before the end of summer. No ifs, ands, or buts.

By the end of June he had me interested, and he started holding me under my shoulders at arm's length. At first, no weight on the footboards. Then just the least bit of weight. That made the braces dig into my crotch a little, then a lot. But by now I thought I could do it, and Leo said he was going to let me go, and catch me when I fell. And by God, he did. The next night, he asked me if I was ready to stand by myself with my father and mother watching, and he called them upstairs from the living room, and there I was, grimacing from the pain of the braces, but standing.

We all cried our different tears of relief. Leo downed another quart of milk and another box of biscuits, and we started planning to do it next without braces. Eight weeks later, wearing a corset to keep my belly from sagging (still no real stomach muscles), and on crutches, I stood on the first tee at Essex County Club with Bob Potter, ready to try a few holes of golf. I drove the ball into the creek that crosses the fairway about 50 yards away, and hobbled off the tee to fish it out. Only one trouble: when I leaned over to retrieve the ball from about two inches of water in the creek, I didn't have the strength to straighten up, nor the strength to stay bent over, and so into the creek I plunged, cracking my head on a rock as I went down. Potter was there to fish me out, bloodied but pleased with myself.

When it was time to go back to school, I was "recovered." I couldn't run, but I could walk without limping. No muscle refused to work, and naively or not, I was thinking of returning to sports the next year.

St. Mark's School specialized in fitting round pegs into round holes, fine-tuning good students and good athletes into better students and better athletes, turning them on to new opportunities like social work, debating, and extracurricular activities in general.

Square pegs—like my brother Freddy—just wouldn't fit into those round holes, and they were miserable. They were known as the "Dry-Hair-in-Chapel" crowd. Since they avoided sports at all costs, they didn't have to take showers after exercising in the afternoon, and so they showed up for the mandatory evening chapel services—one lesson, two prayers, one hymn—with hair uncombed and dry as a bone. Dry hairs like Blair Clark, who went on to be president of the Harvard *Crimson* and vice president of CBS News, or like Robert "Cal" Lowell, the distinguished Pulitzer Prize–winning poet, were tolerated, but clearly classified as outsiders. And this was my first lesson in the whole complicated matter of insiders versus outsiders. I liked being an insider, and it was a long time before I found the courage to tolerate, then explore, then enjoy outsiders.

Returning to St. Mark's in a corset to contain my sagging belly curtailed my athletic career more than somewhat. Football was out, period. I gave hockey a try that winter, but you can't skate on your ankles. Baseball was a little better, but I could barely beat my mother down to first base. And so I turned to dry-hair activities, like debating, editing—even acting. Following a minor triumph the year before as the "femme muette" in Molière's *L'Homme qui épousa une femme muette*, I played a cop in a school play. I sold charter subscriptions—forty-eight of them—to an exciting new picture magazine called *Life*, and I can still remember how thrilling that first issue seemed, with Margaret Bourke-White's extraordinary cover picture of Fort Peck in Montana. I tried out for the highly desirable job of exchange editor of the *Vindex*, the school's monthly magazine, and

I got it. The only thing an exchange editor had to do was to write the editors at all the girls' schools on the East Coast, offering a free subscription to our magazine in exchange for a free subscription to their yearbook, the one with pictures of the juniors and seniors.

Intellectually, the school's most exciting presence (for one term) was the great British poet Wystan Hugh Auden, who was a friend of our English teacher, Richard "Dreamy Dick" Eberhart. My memories of Auden are two: he had a really large mole on his lower left cheek, and he didn't bathe often enough. No recollection of his poetry, nor any recollection of being embarrassed by having no recollection of his poetry. We all liked Dick Eberhart, who went on to become a renowned poet himself. He was the Congressional Poet from 1959 to 1961, known then as the Consultant in Poetry in English to the Library of Congress. He had written an ode to masturbation, a first for St. Mark's English teachers, and he returned one fall with a copy of D. H. Lawrence's *Lady Chatterley's Lover* which he had smuggled through Customs for us.

In the more traditional studies, such as history, government, and the classics, I was generally ranked second in my class—to Henry Munroe, who used to score a perfect 106 on the *Time* magazine current affairs quiz, and later became a big shot in the Vick Chemical Company. The only time I ever ranked first in my class was the week Munroe had mumps.

The summer after polio I spent two weeks as a student counselor at Brantwood Camp, which St. Mark's School ran for white Big Brother kids from New York—my first exposure to the underprivileged. I saw my first pistol, when fourteen-year-old "Nick" from New York tried to establish his territorial imperatives over my cabin with a Colt .45. (Not loaded, it turned out.) I fished nine-year-old "Joey" from Fall River from the bottom of a pond, after luckily spotting him as he jumped cautiously in. He couldn't swim a lick. I listened to small boys telling me how they stole lead pipe from abandoned warehouses. I smoked my first cigarette.

Back in Beverly, on the eve of becoming sixteen, I got a job (my father got me a job) as a copy boy on the *Beverly Evening Times,* circulation 5,000. I thought it might be fun and he knew the owner. He had to drive me to work on his way to work, until I got my license and the use of a car in midsummer. This was a $300 Chevy coupe, vintage 1930 or 1932, which had belonged to my father's bootlegger. No springs in back, no seat in the rumble seat, which had been removed (and lost) to make room for the booze. For most of the summer I fetched coffee for Clayton Creesy, the city editor, and Mr. Stanton, a nice old man with stooped shoulders, a kind heart, and a green eyeshade, who was chained to the obit desk.

Before too long Buddy Conley and I graduated to "City Locals," a daily column of one- or two-sentence paragraphs about local citizens.* Beverly was both the last industrial town and the first summer resort on the seashore north of Boston. Economically it was dominated by a big United Shoe Machinery plant. To collect City Locals, I went the length of Cabot Street, stopping in one store after another and asking the employees what was new in their lives. Any birthdays, new arrivals, deaths? Illnesses? Any visitors at home? Any vacations planned? Home alterations? Parties, retirements, confirmations? College acceptances? Dean's lists? I got paid $2 a column— on top of my $5 weekly wage—and I learned a vital lesson: People will talk if they feel comfortable. My last week, I saw my first body. A man had killed himself by sticking his head in front of a Boston & Maine train near Ipswich. I threw up when the coroner asked me if I had ever seen a brain before, as he leaned over and slipped this man's brain into a plastic envelope. And I wrote a feature story about model ships on exhibition at the Peabody Museum. Here's the lead to my first byline, "Model Boat Exhibit Draws Crowd to Essex Galleries," August 1937, just before my sixteenth birthday.

"In the quaint attic galleries of Stephen's antiques shop on Main

---

* "Edgar Main, of 2 Bay Street, Alfred H. Massary of 13 Cherry Street, Salem, and Nathan Davidson of 43 Bow Street, three local merchants, launched their newly acquired boat this morning."
"Mrs. Charles Callahan of 22 Mathies Street is visiting her brother in Nova Scotia for a week."
"Miss Charlotte Peabody of Rowley has returned to her duties at the Beverly Hospital after a three weeks' vacation at Plum Island."

Street, South Essex, the Essex Chapter of the American Red Cross is presenting an exhibition of ship models, most of which have been donated by the families of Essex, whose ancestors themselves were shipbuilders of renown." Where, who, when, what . . . in forty-seven words.

Proper Bostonians—at least halfway proper Bostonians—were sexually repressed if not inhibited in those days. Sexual experiences were pretty much vicarious, such as they were. Gypsy Rose Lee and the Howard Burlesque Theater in Boston were a couple of years away. A grainy foreign film called *Ecstasy* showed Hedy Lamarr in orgasm, but that was as scary as it was stimulating. There was no *Playboy* magazine, only Cal York's Gossip of Hollywood in *Photoplay*, to be read in the barber shop, and vague rumors of wild orgies involving comedian Fatty Arbuckle and unidentified starlets.

There were girls, however, and my sister Connie's friends constituted the perfect circle to fantasize about. I remember taking Jenny McKean, my first love—and a love all my life—to the movies one afternoon, determined, by God, to kiss her at least and at last. But I ran into a problem that has plagued me throughout my life. The movie was *Dark Victory*, starring Bette Davis. We had held hands, sweatily, for most of the time, but by the end of the movie, as I remember it now, Bette Davis goes blind, and slowly ascends a grand and endless staircase, as the music of angels singing grows to a crescendo. Suddenly the movie is over, the lights are on, and I am crying uncontrollably. No handkerchief of course (at sixteen?). No Kleenex. And I was left with only the bottom of my polo shirt to stem the flow. When I dropped Jenny at her house, I clumsily screwed up my courage to try to kiss her. She demurred. And when I got home, my sister was on the phone listening to Jenny laugh.

Back in boarding school for my junior year—tuition paid by Cousin Frank Crowninshield, the godfather whose only achievement in life had been to marry a du Pont—I had apparently decided on a life of achievement. My health, if not my speed, had pretty much returned. I played varsity football and hockey, without getting my letter, but in baseball I was the starting first baseman for the team that beat Groton. My mother and grandmother had cried noisily a few weeks earlier when I hit a home run against Milton and thundered around the bases like a freight train. George Palmer and I were the school doubles champions in tennis. My marks stayed up, and I ended up as a class monitor and editor-designate of the school yearbook.

Half a century later boarding schools like St. Mark's seem hard to explain, especially the single-sex boarding schools. Parents feel guilty about sending little Johnny away for the better part of such important years. And little Johnny is in no hurry to swap the permissive attitudes of today's culture for the isolated discipline of a boarding school. The education provided was top of the line, but the education *not* provided—about race, poverty, anti-Semitism, crime, anything remotely counter-cultural—was extensive.

But still, I had a very positive experience away from home for five years, aged thirteen to seventeen, nine months a year. Was this the beginning of the "adaptation to life" which so interested the Grant Study researchers later? I knew my parents loved me. I really did. I was the original round peg waiting for the round hole—programmed to do well at schools like St. Mark's. Not yet comfortable with rebellion, cynicism, or complaint. I resent the inability of institutions to cope with different, distinctive children far more today than I did then.

During the summer of 1936, I spent six weeks at Brantwood Camp, and I spent my first night in jail, on the Fourth of July. The evening in question started at the staid and proper Dublin Inn, in Peterborough, New Hampshire, where I was importuned by my peers to find out what rye whisky tasted like. Old Overholt, or "Old Overcoat," as they called it, tasted perfectly dreadful, and it effected an awesome change in me. After dinner we all adjourned to the Keene (N.H.) State Fair . . . full of ourselves, full of booze, and full of thoughts about the upcoming football season. Bill Parsons, a fellow polio veteran and a future clergyman, and I got down in our three-point stance and charged off in various directions, whenever our buddies shouted, "Set!"

Eventually we started tackling people, and inevitably one person we tackled was a state trooper who was totally unamused. He marched four of us off to the clink: me, Parsons, Henry Allen, who later became Dr. Henry F. Allen, the chief of ophthalmology of the Massachusetts Eye & Ear Infirmary, and my childhood friend Herbert Sears Tuckerman. We were released in the custody of the camp chief the next morning, and had to greet one hundred kids in the scorching heat a few hours later. I have always wondered whether that night is part of my formal record, waiting to be found by the Feds when I run for high office.

Booze and my family have often been incompatible. My brother is a recovering alcoholic, who struggled with impressive courage—and ultimate success—to overcome his addiction. I doubt that I have ever had to fight so hard. My father just plain drank too much, and none of us could ever convince him how much his personality changed when he did.

The first real job my father found after the Depression was at the Boston Museum of Fine Arts, where he was the supervisor of the museum maintenance force that hung the art works and kept the galleries and the statues—and the toilets—clean. His salary was $3,000 a year. And then the job that took him through the tough times, until the family fortunes improved with some critically important deaths, was as a member of the Massachusetts Parole Commission. His pal, Leverett Saltonstall, had become governor of Massachusetts and appointed him, and he took the job with great seriousness. "B" loved the parole decisions less than he loved the rogues, who dominated Boston and Massachusetts politics, as rogues always have. He was particularly taken with one Patrick J. "Sonny" McDonough, an elected member of the Governors' Council, and a person who represented more than his share of the men who appeared before the Parole Commission in search of freedom. I'll never forget "B" 's report of a commission meeting at the Bridgewater (Mass.) state prison, where he had arrived a few minutes late. Sonny McDonough was sitting next to a client when "B" took his seat, and heard Sonny tell his client: "That's Bradlee. Look out for him. He pisses ice water."

My mother also went to work during the Depression, in a dress shop on Newbury Street in Boston, called ADEM, after her friends, the proprietors: Adelaide Sohier and Emma Lawrence. This impressed all of us, and all of her friends, because Jo was not exactly everyone's idea of your typical working woman. Bright enough, surely. Certainly pretty enough, and gregarious enough, but she had no calluses anywhere. She didn't seem tough enough. But she was. In a couple of years, she bought out her partners, with a loan from her father, and ran the shop herself. Running it included two buying trips a year to cloak and suit headquarters on Seventh Avenue in New York.

Christmases during this time in our lives were on the lean side. Our stockings were filled with more necessities—like socks, underwear, and combs—on top of the traditional orange in the toe than luxuries. As the family fortunes improved, I remember five-dollar gold pieces showing up, and I remember Connie getting a family ring. I got a Flexible Flyer sled one Christmas as my "big" present. My father walked me down to the Boston Common to go coasting on Christmas afternoon, but crossing one street, a taxi cab ran over the rear runner, twisting it into a shape that made coasting impossible. I could draw the shape of that twisted runner today.

The worst present experience of my life came a few years later, on my birthday. I had asked for golf clubs, since polio had forced me to take up golf over tennis, and mine had become too short. I got the golf clubs, but they were hand-me-downs from my brother, the non-jock, and *he* got new golf clubs. *On my birthday*. I didn't understand that then. And I don't understand it any better now.

In the summer of 1937, the New York grandparents gave us a six-week trip to France. We sailed over—it took almost ten days—on the S.S. *Champlain*, one of the first ships that would sink in World War II, and sailed back on one of the early voyages of the S.S. *Normandie* in less than five days. Tourist class. With my mother, my aunt Alma Morgan, and her husband, Tick, their daughter Tudie, and the three of us. I remember falling in love, and exchanging diaries with the beautiful Katherine Adams from Albany, New York, but unable to get up my nerve to kiss her. I remember riding the Ferris Wheel at the Paris World's Fair, suffering from acute lack of Boston Red Sox news in the Paris *Trib*, seeing every château in the Loire Valley, and winning the coveted Most Cooperative Child Award ($10).

TWO

HARVARD

By my senior year—1938-39—the winds of war were felt even in remotest Southboro, and in between trying (unsuccessfully) to get laid, and trying (successfully) to make admission into Harvard automatic, we talked nervously and hesitantly about Hitler, the Greater East Asia Co-Prosperity Sphere, and communism. At Princeton, someone had started the Veterans of Future Wars, which we felt was extremely sophisticated and convinced us that college would be cool. I participated in as many extracurricular activities as possible: I won four letters (in football, hockey, baseball, and tennis), was on the debating team, choir, and glee club—where I stayed even as my voice changed from alto to bass—and was yearbook editor and monitor. In retrospect, I seem to have been building a résumé without knowing what I needed a résumé for.

In any case, I got into Harvard with highest honors in English, French, and Greek, plus a pass in physics. There was never a question that I would get into Harvard, or go to Harvard. My father had gone there. My grandfather had gone there, and many genera-

tions of Bradlees before him, a total of fifty-one, all the way back to
1795 with Caleb Bradlee. No alternatives were suggested, or contemplated, much less encouraged. My brother, after being "asked
to leave" St. Mark's, and being kicked out of Brooks School for
smoking two days before graduating, had just as naturally gone to
Harvard.

But Freddy quit Harvard after only a few months. Unknown to
any of us, he had gone to New York and landed a role in a Broadway
play, by God. From his early years, he had play-acted, speaking aloud
to himself in different accents, perfecting a talent for mimicry that
astounded us all. He could then—and still can—make me cry with
laughter imitating my mother, my grandmother, my Uncle Sargent,
and later various in-laws, never mind Noel Coward, Mrs. Roosevelt,
Tallulah Bankhead, and Katharine Hepburn. He had done summer
stock in various locations on the East Coast while still in boarding
school, and there he was on Broadway, barely nineteen. My mother,
the "artistic" member of the family, was slightly uncomfortable with
an actor son, while my father, the nature-loving jock, was proud as
could be.

The impact of the new freedom at Harvard blew my mind. I
was only a couple of miles across the river from the Beacon Street
womb, but I might as well have been on a different planet. There
was a story about the difference between the Ivy League colleges.
At Princeton, they showed you where the swimming pool was and
taught you how to swim. At Yale, they shoved you into the pool and
watched you swim. At Harvard, they didn't care if you swam—or
sank. Even attendance was optional in all but a few classes. I didn't
attend a single class in Michael Karpovich's course on the History
of Russia (got a D). You could take as many—or as few—courses
as you wanted to take in any semester. You could drink what you
wanted, when you wanted to. As far as an innocent could see, the
path ahead stretched invitingly toward discovery and excitement,
without consequences.

Except that Hitler had sliced into the heart of Poland the week
before we arrived on Harvard Yard. Britain and France declared war
on Germany on September 3, the week we registered as freshmen.

We were the first class at Harvard to know, really know, that we would be going to war. That knowledge colored our every action, and our every reaction. It led me and many of my friends into the Naval ROTC, which had achieved elite status at Harvard by promising its cadets only the choicest assignments—destroyers or cruisers—once they were commissioned. We never even thought about what life might be like on a destroyer or a cruiser. We hadn't even seen one, but the knowledge that we were headed for the glamorous and dangerous destroyers or cruisers put a spring in our step.

And so, before I really could enjoy my freedom not to *have* to do anything, I *had* to attend ROTC classes and Memorial Hall drills, or face the prospect of slogging my way through the mud of Europe as a GI.

The winds of war made it easy to succumb to an unattractive, self-pitying attitude of eat-drink-and-be-merry-for-tomorrow-we-go-to-war. Especially drink. I hadn't taken another drink for two years, after winding up in the clink at Keene, New Hampshire. But the card games, the rathskellers, the coming-out parties, and whatever the hell it was that pulled us into the Ritz Bar so often, changed all that.

Late one night in the lobby of the Ritz in Boston, it seemed like a good idea to grab the firehose out of its glass-enclosed niche and hose down my pals just for the hell of it. I got the hose out, and was reaching for the release handle, when a member of Boston's Finest reached for me, pulled me a foot off the floor, and carted me off to jail once more. After a night listening to my cellmate—a drunken, toothless Swede—vomiting again and again, I was taken before some magistrate, who apparently knew my old man. He took one look at me in my filthy tuxedo, and said, "My God, your father must be disappointed in you."

I was driving my parents' brand-new Plymouth four-door home from a date on Charles River Drive just across from Harvard Stadium when I went to sleep at the wheel and smashed into another car, head-on. Mercifully both cars were moving at exceptionally slow speed, probably because the driver of the other car, a baker on his way to work, was as drunk as I was. Neither of us was seriously hurt, although I was bleeding profusely from a broken nose, and a cut on my left knee.

I had another problem. I was in costume, coming home from the annual Hasty Pudding Club Dance. In fact, I was in a hula costume, complete with black wig, plus falsies under a Hawaiian shirt, and a grass skirt. At least I was in a grass skirt until I got out of the car. In doing that, the grass skirt caught on the window handle, and when the two cops walked up to me, I was in my skivvies.

This was obviously no prank, and I would have been in serious trouble had not the good sisters at St. Vincent's Hospital come to my defense. When the cops took me there to get me sewed up, a small girl was in a rage of tears, defying the efforts of an intern to saw a ring that had become embedded in the swollen flesh of her finger. Her astonishment at the sight of me apparently outweighed her fear of the doctor, but in any case she wound up on my lap, stunned into silence, until the ring was off. In gratitude, the sisters later supplied me with a critically important note, stating that "no trace of alcohol was present" while I was being stitched up.

In addition to drinking, there were some moments when my mind was exercised. Not many, for I often got lost in the ponderous lectures of William Yandell Elliott and Frisky Merriman, and I missed the personal contact with the best of the teachers at St. Mark's. But every so often contact was made and the rewards were wonderful. The great John Finley, making classical Greek literature as vivid as life itself. Ted Spencer taking three whole months to explore and explain *Hamlet*. Sam Beer refereeing fights between my hopeless, inherited and thoughtless conservatism and my soon-to-be longtime friend Adam Yarmolinsky's equally hopeless and inherited and automatic liberalism, and teaching us both.

I had arrived at college without a single independent thought about politics or anything else in my head. My family was solidly Republican; they'd never voted for a Democrat. My father had worked for something called the Boston Finance Commission, a theoretically independent, but essentially Brahmin organization formed to rout out the considerable corruption in the office of the legendary Democrat, Mayor James Michael Curley. I'd also been taken by the hand at an early age down to Boston Common to listen to Curley speak. I remember "B" saying something like, "Listen to this guy. He can charm a bird right off the branch of a tree."

I attended the Republican National Convention of 1940 in Philadelphia—by accident. My sister Connie had a boyfriend, Eckley B. Coxe IV, "Buzzy," who asked us to stay with him on the Main Line during the convention. Buzzy had a sister, Betty, and she had a boyfriend who was working for the candidacy of Wendell Willkie. Her friend was in charge of trying to pack the gallery for the utility executive and darling of Wall Street, and that's how I ended up in the gallery chanting, "We Want Willkie!" without wanting anything more than a good time. My first lesson in political manipulation was right there for the learning, and went sailing over my head.

I read the newspapers, but mostly to follow the Red Sox. My interest in sports—watching them and competing in them—was as strong then as it is now. In the fall of my freshman year, I had gone out for football, mostly because I thought it would please my father. I weighed only 165 pounds, and there was a little problem with my speed. The first week, the coach looked at me and said, "You better be fast, kid, because you aren't big enough for this game"—even as it was played at Harvard. So my football career was over almost before it began, and I took up squash, which was being coached by the great Jack Barnaby, who had taught me some tennis at the Essex County Club near Beverly. I loved squash, perhaps because I could move 10 feet fast enough to be competitive. It was 10 yards that gave me trouble.

Baseball was what I was waiting for, and I was the starting first baseman when the freshman team set off to tour the South in the spring of 1940. It was a trip so out of control that when it was over Coach Dolph Samborski recommended that Harvard cancel all spring tours for the duration of the war. We started out by getting shellacked by Navy at Annapolis, after spending most of the previous evening at some joint on Baltimore's famous Strip. By the time we left, the ladies were stripping to the strains of "Fair Harvard," to give you an idea about our priorities. We did nothing right for ten days. I don't remember winning a game.

We got beaten 23-2 by Staunton Military Academy, for example. A fly ball was hit to center field, where our captain, "Pooch" Haley, staggered around trying to decide which of the three balls he was seeing to catch. He guessed wrong, and when he reached down to pick the ball up, he kicked it by mistake. He did the same thing—with the other foot—when he tried again. This provoked our pitcher, Joe Phelan, into shouting, "Pick it up, Pooch. It ain't shit." Great laughter in the stands, filled by friends we had made during the previous evening's peregrinations. I've never forgotten Pooch, who was killed in the war, or Joe's admonition, when confronted with my own inability to get out of a jam.

When we finally got back to Cambridge, my baseball career was in trouble. First a pitcher named Mort Waldstein had thrown a baseball right at my head, almost killing me. Then I looked up from the dirt to hear the umpire calling it a strike. That was my introduction to the curve ball, and the curve ball was my introduction to the bench. The curve ball, and a reluctance on my part to follow Coach Samborski's instructions. I was hitting lead-off one inning, and the coach had told me to "look at a couple," but when the first pitch came up fat as a soccer ball, I crushed it to right field—long, but still an easy out. I have forgotten my excuse. I played in the Yale game, as a late inning substitute—and struck out against the son of "Smokey" Joe Wood, the legendary Red Sox pitcher. Curve balls.

In addition to baseball, I was trying out—heeling—for the *Crimson*. I remember more about the atmosphere in the seedy *Crimson* building on Plympton Street, wonderfully messy, hectic, and full of ink smells, than I remember the stories or the competition. My friend from St. Mark's, Blair Clark, was president of the *Crimson*, and that spring he told me it looked like a two-way race between me and Paul Sheeline for the job that would lead three years later to the top. (Sheeline got it, and went on to become the chief financial officer of an international hotel chain.)

At the end of my freshman year I went on disciplinary probation for cutting too many classes, and that barred me from any kind of extracurricular activity. I was totally unfocused on anything involving my brain, and whatever I was learning came from the casual social experiences of someone marking time. I had learned something about gambling, from my father. We had pretty much a permanent black jack game going on in the rooms I shared in Wigglesworth Hall with Potter and Tuckerman. I forget the stakes, except that they were higher than I could afford. But I won—a few hundred dollars. In fact everyone won, except Bill Haskell, who couldn't afford it either. And suddenly he owed everyone—a few thousand dollars. In varying degrees we began to feel sorry for him, but we had won it, and each felt sure we would have had to pay up had we lost it, or quit before our losses got too big.

Finally, my friends Potter, Tuckerman, and Dick Cutler decided that we creditors should ask someone older and wiser for advice. They chose my old man, and we all trooped into 267 Beacon Street early one evening to listen to the word. My father was as sore as he ever got. Quiet, but serious. First, he announced that I was no longer a creditor. Haskell owed me nothing, since I didn't have the money to pay him if I had lost that much, and he would not have bailed me out. He told Dick Cutler that he knew the stakes were too high for him, too. Potter and Tuckerman were better off than we were, but he let them have it, asking them if they enjoyed watching a friend squirm just because he wanted to be part of our crowd. We were all enormously relieved, truth to tell. Someone called Haskell with the news, and we adjourned to the living room for a big pitcher of Martinis—unaware of the importance of the moment in our lives.

The pursuit of girls took an awful lot of time and energy, and my lack of success in this department was extraordinarily frustrating. I felt sure that the beautiful "H" would be the one to put me out of my misery, especially when she agreed to accompany me and some others on a ski weekend to Vermont. We had even discussed what the French call "la disposition des lits," and the outlook seemed most promising. Pip Cutler told me his girl was going to spend the night with him, and we only had two rooms. . . . At the end of the day, Pip challenged me to a race down what was called—appropriately—Suicide Six. I thought I could beat him by going straight down, forgetting that a road crossed the slope about halfway down. At the last second I saw the road, and had to try to jump across it.

SPLAT. I spreadeagled against the bank on the downhill side of the road, and ended up in the hospital. Two tendons torn. Nothing broken, except my spirit. I lay next to "H" all night, burning with desire, but immobilized by pain.

If this skiing weekend was a disaster, most of them were great adventures, as New England landowners finally found something useful to do with their rocky hills. Ski tows were simple jury-rigged contraptions using tractor PTOs and endless ropes. You could sleep in somebody's barn for $1.50 a night. Even with the hot buttered rum recipe from Kenneth Roberts's *Northwest Passage* (a fistful of butter, a handful of, cinnamon, and a ski boot filled with rum), weekends cost about ten bucks a day plus gas. Your mittens sometimes froze to the rope tow, but there was no waiting in line.

That first college summer all freshmen ROTC had to go to sea on a training cruise. I ended up on some old tub of an escort ship, tagging along with a convoy bound for Iceland. Not really dangerous, but the North Atlantic seas were rough enough, and the news from Europe was ominous enough. Hitler had invaded the Low Countries. Dunkirk had been evacuated at the cost of thirty thousand British dead and wounded. The Germans were marching in the streets of Paris. Rough enough to concentrate the mind of an eighteen-year-old still groping for a sense of purpose, and beginning to understand that this was the last summer of our lives without responsibility.

I started my sophomore year in trouble, still on probation, but taking five courses instead of four, vaguely planning to speed up the whole college process and get going on my career as a warrior. I lived in Eliot House with a lot of other preppies, and roomed with Thomas Johnston Livingston Redmond, a.k.a. Red Bird, or just plain Bird. We were an odd pair. Our mothers had been old school pals and insisted we look each other up. That should have guaranteed we avoid each other, but we had become friends. He had a quick mind, didn't study too hard, played good bridge. And he had a car, which I didn't, but which I needed desperately to wear down the continued resistance of the beautiful "H" and her successors.

The standout among the others was Jean Saltonstall, one of a handful of pretty "older women" (she was eight months older than I) who came from good Boston families and ran together in a Junior League pack, dominating the social scene, if only because none of them went to college. I liked her especially because she was so comfortable to be with, unthreatening where I didn't want to be threatened . . . as in "When are you going to grow up?" . . . and uncritical. She passed muster with my parents, unlike any of her predecessors, and the Saltonstalls as a clan had it all over the Bradlees, financially and socially. The Brahmin politician was a special subdivision of the Massachusetts Yankee in those days: Lodge, Bradford, Peabody, Herter, but especially Leverett Saltonstall, a governor and a senator for a generation. With a face that was one of the great political assets of his time, Lev Saltonstall was said to be Irish on his chauffeur's side by those looking to explain his great political success. Leverett Saltonstall was a second cousin of Jean's father, John L. Saltonstall, who was wonderfully handsome, and a great shot from a duck blind. He had eight children, and no job, ever.

Jean and I slowly and clumsily groped our way from casual friendship to steady friendship and finally, despite incredible obstacles, to lovers. The obstacles began with three bratty stepsisters and a bratty stepbrother, and ended on the night in question with old John L. himself. Over the years he had established a signal—the loud flushing of the upstairs toilet, with door purposely left open to increase the sound—announcing that it was time for whoever was downstairs to leave the premises PDQ. And of course, on this fateful evening the toilet flushed noisily, just as our virginity finally ended, clumsily.

If Jean's father epitomized the conventional Boston aristocrat, who clipped coupons and shot ducks, her mother, Gladys Rice Saltonstall (later Mrs. Henry Billings and finally Mrs. Van Wyck Brooks), personified an unconventional New York middle class which lived in a world of culture. She was the daughter of a doctor who treated the throats of New York's top opera and concert singers, and artists. She walked into a kind of prison when she walked into John L. Saltonstall's life in Brookline and Topsfield, Massachusetts, both bastions of the stuffy respectability that stifled Proper

Bostonians. She gave him four children, and ran away to tryst in a garret in Paris with a disabled concert pianist—from Boston. Unfortunately for her—and Jean—she was followed to the Left Bank by private detectives in the employ of her abandoned and unforgiving husband. The private eyes came back with more than enough evidence for divorce on the grounds of adultery. All the seamy details came out during a custody trial in Salem, Massachusetts, where Jean, age nine, was forced to testify. The parents had reached one custody agreement, which awarded the three oldest children to John L. and his new wife, and Jean to her mother, then living in New York. But at the last minute, John L. reneged on the deal and went to court to keep Jean. He "won."

I knew Gladys was going to be different when I first laid eyes on her—both of us naked as jaybirds—on Roger Baldwin's stretch of South Beach on Martha's Vineyard island. For days before we were to go to meet her mother and her new husband, Henry Billings, Jean had been saying there was something "awful" she had to tell me, but only after we were on the ferry. If she told me before, she said, I probably wouldn't go. On the ferry, I had struck up a conversation with the "French Angel," a professional wrestler billed as the world's ugliest strongman, a completely cultured man named Maurice Tillet who had been a professional tiger hunter in Indochina. He had a huge underslung jaw at the bottom of a truly awesome head. I had seen him wrestle some years earlier, and was thrilled to meet him and talk to him in my schoolboy French. Jean interrupted us to finally tell me her great secret: in her Martha's Vineyard crowd, all swimming was done on the "Nude Beach." The custom started because there were so many small children swimming starkers, the parents had simply joined them.

I have not forgotten the sense of fear and adventure I felt descending a long, steep staircase to the beach and into the unknown. I could see a large group of nude swimmers and sunbathers off to one side, too far to be really threatening. As I took my bathing suit off, Jean announced she was keeping hers on, because she had just gotten her period. I could have brained her. But I couldn't see myself putting my trunks back on, and so I pressed on, heart beating, to meet Gladys—plus Billings; Max Eastman, the writer and expert on Bolshevism, and his wife Eliena, a former ballerina; Tom Benton, the painter, and his wife; Roger Baldwin, head of the American Civil Liberties Union; Michael Straight, the editor of the *New Republic*, and his wife Belinda, a child psychiatrist. I had never met a child psychiatrist, a ballet dancer, a political magazine editor, a painter, a philosopher, or a civil libertarian with their clothes on— much less with their clothes off. This was a long way from 267 Beacon Street, farther than I had ever been, farther than I had thought I would ever get and survive.

I was battling my way through this interesting ordeal without major disaster when Jean's older brother, Jock, joined the group, apparently determined to make my life hell. "Boy," he said with a leer in his voice, and looking me straight in the balls, "we've never seen anything quite like that on the beach before." My heart sank. The worst is happening. An erection is imminent. I am doomed.

But it was only my tattoos.

The previous year, for reasons that escaped me then, as now, I had been tattooed three times. First, really inexplicably, my initials—B over C over B on my right buttock. Then a snake, coiled through the initials. And finally, a rooster just under my left shoulder. I have always liked my tattoos, but I would have given anything at that moment to be rid of them, and stop what felt like hundreds of eyes staring at me.

After that opening episode, I had no idea what to expect, but Gladys and her much younger artist husband became joyous and important influences in my life, opening doors to new experiences. Their friends were artists, like Benton, and like Yasuo Kuniyoshi, the Japanese painter, Jo Davidson, the sculptor, and Willie Seabrook, who had written books about Haitian voodoo. Seabrook was convinced that sexual pleasure could be greatly increased if the woman's other senses were all shut down for a period of twelve hours prior to making love. Accordingly, he was said to suspend his girlfriend in a hammock off the ground (so her feet would not feel the earth), plug up her ears, blindfold her, tape her mouth shut, and allow her to breathe only through straws in her nostrils. That sounded weird, but different. He described the ensuing orgasm as cataclysmic. The thought of my father suspending my mother for twelve hours—ears plugged, mouth taped, and all that—was awesome.

My parents knew no artists, beyond Thelma Herrick, the lady who had painted sappy portraits of us children. And God knows they couldn't even imagine anyone who would want to do anything like what Willie Seabrook was doing to his girlfriend. The politics of my in-laws-to-be were knee-jerk left. FDR certainly, but after him, Henry Wallace and the Progressive Party, where many of their pals had landed. My parents never voted for a Democrat until JFK in 1960, and never again after that. Conversations that would make them shiver in discomfort—about relationships, behavior, people, and politics—enlivened dinner-table conversations from Martha's Vineyard to Rhinebeck, in Dutchess County, New York, where the Billingses had a lovely small farm, to New York City.

Henry and I baled acres and acres of hay in Rhinebeck. In Martha's Vineyard, we bought a silo, ordered from a Sears, Roebuck catalogue for $186 as I remember, and put it up on a concrete ring, a few feet from a small fishing cottage overlooking Menemsha Pond. It was 18 feet in diameter, and after we cut in one door and a lot of picture windows, we had a local carpenter build a curved staircase up into a fabulous room with drop-dead wrap-around views, and a pull-down ladder into a bedroom full of stars.

In my second year at college, I drifted into an involvement with the final clubs (I drifted everywhere in those days), even then one of the most pointless institutions on campus. Two of these clubs, the AD and the Porcellian, were the most exclusionary. But my father and grandfather had been members of the AD Club, and I had been selected by the AD brass to be what was called the "key man," the person in the sophomore class who was told early that he would be admitted, to help recruit classmates thought to be desirable. I had agreed to do this, in the belief it would please and impress my old man. My pal, Peter Saltonstall, was the Porcellian's key man, and we competed desultorily for a few chaps, who were thought to be qualified because they had gone to good prep schools.

Late one night, we came up with two modest ideas to ridicule the whole club system. First, we would get them their candidates, and then together refuse to join the clubs we had worked for. Alternatively, we could get them their candidates, and then join the other club, not our own. But at the last minute we ran out of nerve, citing our conviction that our fathers would have been disappointed. I wish we had stuck to our guns, as I wish I had told the AD Club that if they didn't take my roommate Tommy Redmond, they wouldn't get me. No guts. Small potatoes, but no guts.

I also drifted into a real jam with Dean Sargent Kennedy. I had settled on a combined English-Greek major, thanks to the only professors I had managed to get close to, John Finley and Ted Spencer. In those days, anyone involved in any way in an English major was required to take a special examination in the Bible, Shakespeare, and Greek Classics before graduating. I had gone to a church/boarding school where the Bible had been pounded into my brains once a day and twice on Sundays. I had taken one course already in Shakespeare, and I was all but majoring in Greek, so I felt no pressure to take this exam right away.

But my friend, and fellow AD Club member, George Endicott Putnam, later to become a high-ranking executive of some Boston bank, felt differently. Late one night at a party at the end of our sophomore year, he informed me casually that he had taken his Bible-Shakespeare exam earlier that day and it was a breeze. Such a breeze, he went on, still casual, that after he had turned in his own exam, he had returned to his seat, written another exam, and turned that one in *under my name*. I spent the worst weekend of my young life, knowing I was in trouble, and wondering how to get out of it without fingering my pal.

Dean Kennedy didn't let me wonder too long; he summoned me to his office for what was advertised as a "career talk" bright and early a few days later. I knew better. After some minutes of how-are-yous and blah-blah-blah, he came quickly to the point. "Have you gotten your Bible-Shakespeare exam out of the way yet, Ben?" He had me in his sights, about to trigger me right out of school and into the Army. I said something like, "You obviously know that I haven't, but I can explain." He interrupted to say he didn't think there was an explanation, and he guessed I wasn't going to be around Harvard much longer. I told him the whole story, without coughing up Putnam's name, but pleaded with him for a few hours to find "this guy" and get him to come forward. He gave me that, and I went looking for George, urgently. A few minutes after I found him, he was in Kennedy's office, and somewhat to the dean's surprise confirmed my story. To the dean's surprise, because whereas I was plainly a marginally interesting Harvard sophomore, Putnam was by way of being a Big Man on Campus, on the Dean's List, and all that.

In a few days, the verdict came in: Both of us would spend the next year on probation. It was tougher on Putnam than on me. I had already been on probation; in fact, I had just gotten off. As they say in my chosen profession, life was still pretty much on the come.

The evidence was piling up that I wasn't accomplishing much at Harvard, not to put too fine a point on it. I was playing a lot harder than I was working, but even the playing showed not much energy, and little creativity. The embarrassment, I realize now, was that I was not embarrassed. I was cautious, and conservative— behaviorally, if not politically. The modest impulses to change society that were stirring were internalized and became modest impulses to change myself, and the obvious change staring us all in the face was to get on with it and go to war . . . sooner rather than later. I had talked to a Royal Canadian Air Force recruiter, but he turned out to be a friend of my father, and they had both talked me into staying in Naval ROTC. I took two flying lessons, instead. But I did start exploring the possibilities of speeding up the process of getting a degree. If I took five and six courses per semester, instead of four; if I went to summer school; and finally, if the Navy would let me take Naval Science III and Naval Science IV more or less simultaneously, I could graduate in August 1942, one month less than three years after I started. *If* I didn't collapse under the heavy courseload, and *if* I didn't get too many Ds.

There wouldn't be much elegance to the degree. It takes time to educate a late bloomer. But Potter and I—and ten other preppies, all bored, anxious, and in a hurry—decided to give it a shot.

I moved out of the "rat house," where Redmond and I had ended up. Rat houses were group houses (ours was at 52 Plympton Street) rented by a bunch of students with shared goals and interests. Our group's goals and interests were pretty much limited to partying, trying to get laid, and beating Yale, and pretty much excluded the kind of studying I was thinking of getting involved in. Halfway through my junior year, I moved back into my parents' house, and in fact was there on the fateful first Sunday in December 1941. All members of my generation know where they were and who they were with on Pearl Harbor Day. My mother and father and I were in the family living room, crouched over the same Atwater Kent radio—the one with the round speaker on top of the heavy oblong metal box of tubes and tuners—that had made us laugh so hard with Amos 'n' Andy, Fred Allen, Jack Benny, Ed Wynn, and Joe Penner.

The radio voice I remember was broadcasting from the roof of a hotel in Manila, describing bombers diving and bombs exploding. And I was trying to figure out what it meant for me. It really wasn't an exaggeration to say that life as I had known it would never be the same. The "whether" had been pretty much out of the war equation for some time, but now it was totally gone, and the only real question was "when." And the inevitability of it all became strangely comforting. Gone were all the choices that complicate young lives. Never mind "What am I going to do when I grow up?" but even "What am I going to do next summer?" was no longer a problem. I was going back to summer school and I was going to war; that's what Benny the Boy Warrior was going to do. I was too close to a degree now, and to an ensign's commission—only eight months and a day—to chuck it and run off to war overnight. So Harvard had to be completed, rather than experienced or enjoyed.

The last eight months of college still make me dizzy when I think of them. I was taking six courses, to get enough credits to graduate. I'd given up almost all forms of entertainment. No all-night bridge games. No piquette with Joe Reed at the AD Club, no extracurricular activity at Harvard, because even if I had a shot at graduating in eight months, I was still on probation. Jean and I were going steady, even though she spent that winter and spring in New York, vaguely studying and vaguely working as a kindergarten teacher. We were even talking about getting engaged, and wondering if it made any sense to get married before I went off to war. I was four months past my twentieth birthday, and Jean had turned twenty-one the month after Pearl Harbor.

More than fifty years later, I wonder what we were wondering about: getting married, when we knew I was going to war in a destroyer in a few months, almost surely to the Pacific where destroyers were sinking like stones, when we knew I would be gone for months, if not for good. Even as we discussed marriage, one of Jean's best friends, Pat Cutler, had married a Harvard ROTC ensign named Bob Fowler and was carrying his child, when he was killed in action on a destroyer in the Pacific. We grieved, but we pushed on with innocent confidence, and, by God, one afternoon I walked into the Saltonstall house in Brookline, past a row of those bratty stepsisters chanting, "Benny's going to marry Jeannie. Benny's going to marry Jeannie," and there I was standing alone in front of old John L., asking him for his daughter's hand in marriage. No toilets flushing noisily in the night now. This was formal and scary. He knew all about the Bradlee finances, the way all proper Bostonians know about each other's finances . . . common knowledge around the dining-room table at the Somerset Club.

My father was heading slowly back into the chips. Aunt Polly had finally died. Freddy, Connie, and I each had a trust fund with about $100,000 worth of blue-chip stocks, producing about $4,000 a year in income. This was slightly higher than the salary I would be receiving as an ensign. Jean had a little more, and I was headed for places where money was unspendable. John L. was gentleman enough not to bring up the fact that I was so young I would have to go down to City Hall with my father to get a marriage license. And after a few smiling, ritualistic questions, he gave his permission and offered his blessings. The bratty kids were informed, and Jean and I had a deal.

What was the hurry? What convinced either one of us that marriage would resolve any of the uncertainties we dared not admit to, much less face? Was there some vaguely glamorous, vaguely patriotic sense that marriage would make each life more meaningful? Who knows? No parent ever voiced a concern. No concern was ever shared between Jean and me.

We pushed forward, frantically juggling all the things that had to be done before graduation, commissioning, or marriage could take place. My problem was that to get married, I had to have my commission (or else scrap three years of officer's training). To get commissioned, I had to graduate (ROTC commissions were for college graduates only). And to graduate, I had to overcome all the academic obstacles I had created for myself by screwing around for the first eighteen months.

By June 1942, the end of my junior year, I got off probation at last, with a minimum of As and Bs, a handful of Ds, and a slew of the most ungentlemanly Cs imaginable. It began to look as if I could make it if I took four courses in summer school, and passed them all, especially Naval Science IV. I moved into the Saltonstall mansion in Topsfield, Massachusetts, and commuted to Cambridge every morning along with all the businessmen in their Brooks Brothers seersuckers and straw hats. Jean's stepmother, Margie (hard "g"), was a pain in the ass, domineering and demanding, and endlessly long-suffering about the difficulties of arranging a wedding in wartime. Gas rationing made it impossible for wedding guests to travel outside of Boston.

And finally it was August 8, 1942, a day which has defined hectic for me forever. At ten in the morning I graduated . . . ten months early. At noon I was commissioned, Ensign Benjamin Crowninshield Bradlee, 183735, D-VG (for Deck-Volunteer, General), along with eleven other preppies from those infamous WASP boarding schools, the first of our class to make it to war as naval officers. The wedding at Lindsey Memorial Chapel, next to the Ritz Hotel, and the reception at the Chilton Club, the female equivalent of that male bastion of respectability (and money) known as the Somerset Club, was still a few hours away, and they were difficult hours.

At command headquarters—267 Beacon Street—my mother was going not so quietly out of control, dressing herself and my sister, and worrying about whether my brother, the PFC, would show up in time from Fort Riley, Kansas, where he was stationed. Things got so tense around lunchtime that my father let out a loud "Jee-zus," and announced that he was going to rent a suite at the Ritz in search of a little peace and quiet, and he did. My mother screamed at him not to drink anything and "ruin the wedding," and I decided to go along with him to keep him company, and sober. On the way down to the hotel in the cab, the old man screwed up his courage and asked me if there was anything I wanted to know about sex. The subject had never crossed his lips before. As a matter of fact, there was a whole lot I needed and wanted to know about sex, but I was as embarrassed as he was, and allowed as how I was pretty well checked out by now in that department.

August 8 was the hottest day of the year, maybe in history, and I remember sweltering in my new uniform—dress blues, because the dress whites were not ready. But the wedding was flawless, with trophy bridesmaids and ushers. Freddy made it. My mother smiled a lot, and got a pretty good grip on herself. The old man stayed sober. Jean's mother was asked to the wedding, and came—but John L. refused to ask her to the reception.

Jean and I survived that day, too. I seem to remember ending up in the Hampshire House in New York, but have no memory of how we got there or when we got there. The wedding night was more significant in itself than in its detail. We were young, under-educated, unexperienced, a little afraid of both the known and the unknown, but we were under way on this wondrous voyage. We had been given a house on one of the Thousand Islands on the St. Lawrence River for a honeymoon. We took the train from New York City to Clayton, New York. We were picked up in Clayton and taken to our honeymoon house in a boat by a caretaker, who prom-ised to be back in five days . . . the first five days alone we'd ever had, and the last we were to spend alone for twenty-seven months.

Hanging over those five days were the orders I had received from the Chief of Naval Personnel:

If found physically qualified . . . you will further proceed to the

Service Force, Atlantic Subordinate Command, Naval Operating Base, for temporary active duty awaiting first available transportation to the vicinity in which the U.S.S. *Wyoming* may be. Upon arrival proceed and report to the commanding officer of that vessel for further temporary active duty under instruction in 40 m.m. guns. Upon completion of this duty, when directed by the commanding officer of that vessel, you will regard yourself detached; proceed to a continental port of the United States via such transportation as may be arranged by the commanding officer, U.S.S. *Wyoming*. Upon arrival in the United States you will proceed to Kearny, New Jersey, and report to the supervisor of Shipbuilding, USN, Federal Shipbuilding and Drydock Company, for active duty in connection with fitting out the U.S.S. *Philip* and on board when that vessel is placed in full commission, reporting by letter to the Commandant, Third Naval District.

That doesn't sound so scary, now, fifty-two years later almost to the day as I write this. But then? Where was the *Wyoming*? Hell, what was the *Wyoming*? What was a 40mm gun? Where was Kearny, New Jersey, and above all what was the U.S.S. *Philip*?

Well, the *Wyoming* was an old tub of a World War I battleship, then in the Chesapeake Bay, fitted out with masses of 40 and 20mm anti-aircraft guns, so that people like me could learn how to shoot them, and especially how to teach others to shoot them. Kearny, New Jersey, was a long taxi ride from the East Side of Manhattan, and the U.S.S. *Philip* was a brand-new 2,100-ton Fletcher-class destroyer, headed for the Pacific battle area as soon as she was ready.

THREE

NAVY

Life on a destroyer—the Tin Can Navy, as we proudly described it—was intimate, noisy, informal, boring, exciting, dangerous, arduous, crowded, scary, and boring again. Three hundred and thirty men jammed into a 2,100-ton ship shaped like a steel greyhound. Long (380 feet), or longer than a football field. Narrow (32 feet, about as wide as an 18-wheel truck is long). And fast (36 knots, or 40 miles an hour). In a heavy sea, a destroyer can easily roll as much as 90 degrees—45 degrees to either side. Handles were welded to bulkheads everywhere, to be grabbed during heavy rolls. And the decks bristled with a variety of offensive weapons. Five 5-inch guns, roughly equivalent to 105mm howitzers. Eight torpedoes, in two four-torpedo mounts amidships. A pair of four twin 40mm antiaircraft guns, plus another eight 20mm AA guns. And a dozen depth charges in racks along either side of the stern.

This was heady stuff for a Greek-English major whose only extended previous sea experience was aboard a 12-foot Brutal Beast sailboat, and whose only previous experience with weapons involved a Daisy Air Rifle. All I had ever hit was the side of a pig, a green-eyed vireo, and a passing car window. It was impossible to grasp, really, for a newly married, still twenty-year-old ensign, who had led—I was beginning to appreciate—such an insulated, sheltered life.

I served almost exactly two years aboard the *Philip*. Certainly the most important two years of my life, then and maybe now. I arrived excited and scared, a boy just turned twenty-one, at the Federal Shipbuilding & Drydock Company shipyard, on the Passaic River, where she was still under construction in September 1942. And I left her in September 1944, in Pearl Harbor, where she was en route to the Philippines to rejoin the war, fully repaired and modernized. A man just turned twenty-three.

That was a short time for so long a trip.

The trip really started in the East River at 72nd Street in Manhattan. The U.S.S. *Philip* (DD498) was finally off to war—weapons tested, compasses calibrated, tearful goodbyes completed—en route from the Brooklyn Navy Yard to Casco Bay, Maine, where we would pick up the battleship *Massachusetts*, and escort her some 10,000 miles through the Panama Canal, to Nouméa, New Caledonia. We had asked our captain, Tommy Ragan, for permission to give two short blasts on the ship's whistle at about 69th Street to alert Jean and a collection of *Philip* wives, who had gathered in our $100-a-month apartment with fourteen windows on the East River for one last wave farewell. Sentimentality still embarrassed me, and I felt only discomfort and embarrassment as my life and love receded slowly into the gray New York skyline. It was going to be almost two years before we saw each other again, and the next female person I saw was wearing a grass skirt and had a bone through her nose.

It took us about forty days to get to the former French penal colony of New Caledonia, through one of the worst storms in history off Cape Hatteras. So bad that one of the 16-inch gun turrets on the *Massachusetts* was staved in by the angry seas. (Think for a minute about seas strong enough to stave in a 16-inch gun turret on a battleship, and what they might do to a destroyer whose outer skin was three-eighths of an inch thick!) Just outside Nouméa we saw the U.S. carrier *Saratoga*, limping back into port after taking a torpedo hit a few hours before. I don't remember even going ashore in Nouméa. We were off almost immediately to join what was left of the American fast carrier task force off Guadalcanal.

For weeks we escorted one carrier as it launched strikes during the day, then raced as far as possible at flank speed during the night to launch more strikes the next day, trying to fool the Japanese into believing we had more carriers in operation than we did. The mission of destroyers in escorting larger, more valuable ships is to put themselves in harm's way. To find the enemy submarines lying in wait for the big ships and destroy them if possible, but to take the torpedo hit if necessary. To shoot down dive bombers or torpedo bombers if possible on their way to the big ships, but to take the hits in their place if necessary.

When escorting carriers, destroyers have one other job: during every launch and every recovery, one destroyer is stationed just aft and to one side of the carrier. If a plane doesn't get airborne and crashes into the water just after leaving the flight deck, the destroyer is there within seconds to rescue the pilot. And if a plane doesn't make it back to the carrier deck and lands in the water, same deal. Later in the war, the *Philip* got really good at this rescue procedure. We would steam up to the plane, reversing the engines when we were about 100 yards away. This would create a large turmoil in the water, which would move quickly toward the downed plane. Into this turmoil, a sailor would dive with one rope around his waist, and another rope over his shoulder to attach to the pilot. When all went well, the swimmer would almost surf right into the plane, the line would be around the pilot before the plane sank, and the pilot would be back aboard the destroyer, literally within two or three minutes.

Rescued pilots were prized possessions. Before returning them to their carriers—by breeches buoy, of course—we would strip them of all their fancy clothes—silk scarf maps, survival kits with great knives, compasses, and magnifying glasses, and their pistol. Then we would ask the carrier to send over all the geedunk (ice cream) they had, plus a minimum of two movies our crew hadn't seen. Only when they had complied did they get their pilot back.

The first time a man goes into battle—making eye contact with someone trying to kill him—is strangely like the first time a man makes love to a woman. The anticipation is overpowering; the ignorance is obstructive; the fear of disgrace is consuming; and survival is triumphant.

For me, that first time came near some forgotten island in the Strait of Bougainville, or "The Slot," as it will be forever engraved in the hearts of those who raced—or were chased—up and down it during most of 1943. We had escorted some LSTs filled with Marines to make an assault landing on . . . it could have been Vella Lavella, where the rats were said to be as big as dogs. LSTs were large, cumbersome, and slow transport ships, incapable of evasive action. We had gotten them ashore, when our radar operators reported "a mess of bogeys at 20, Angels 11." Translation: Enemy planes 20 miles away, flying at 11,000 feet. Someone else was directing the small group of F4-U Corsair fighters, flying cover for our little operation. So my job was to relay the changing range and altitude information (which were then cranked into an amazingly unsophisticated fire-control system) until visual contact was made. Then, my job was over, at least for a moment. When I heard the anti-aircraft guns of the other ships in our convoy, I ran out of the darkened Combat Information Center (CIC) onto the bridge. The first plane I saw was whizzing along the water about 100 yards away. Just as I recognized it as one of ours, and cheered as I saw him splash the plane he was chasing, I looked almost straight up, and there it was.

It was a Val, with its distinctive fixed wheels, covered with equally distinctive streamlined wheel covers. I could see the pilot. And worse than that, I could see the bomb he had just dropped arching lazily down toward us. How far away was the Val? Maybe 150 feet. How big was the bomb? Somewhere between the size of the Empire State Building and about 200 pounds, probably closer to the latter. Was I scared? Who knows? I was so exhilarated it didn't feel like any fear I had ever felt.

By the time I was sorting all that out, and noticing with some satisfaction that I had not wet my pants, the bomb smashed into the water so close that the towering splash soaked everyone on the starboard side of the ship—and never exploded. It was a dud. (I have felt strangely ambivalent about Japanese technology ever since.)

After a few weeks of trying to fool the Japanese into thinking we had a lot of carriers out there, instead of just the *Enterprise*, our squadron took up our semi-permanent assignment with three brand-new cruisers. The destroyers (*Philip, Sauffley, Conway, Renshaw, Waller, Sigourney, Eaton*) comprised Destroyer Squadron 22. The cruisers (*Montpelier, Denver, Columbia*, and *Cleveland*) made up Cruiser Division 6, and together we made up a Task Group, under the overall command of the flashy, charismatic Admiral William Halsey, or the brilliant, self-effacing Admiral Raymond Spruance, the admirals who taught our generation the art of "calculated risk." (We all preferred Spruance.) For the next nine months we alternated with a Task Group of older destroyers and cruisers in night raids up The Slot. We would leave Tulagi, an island about twenty miles north of Guadalcanal, in the brilliant sun of a late afternoon.

"Let's go get us some medals, Mr. Bradlee," said our commanding officer, Tommy Ragan. "Yes sir," replied Ensign Bradlee, hoping that his twenty-one-year-old sphincter would hold.

We would steam fast enough to be abreast of Bougainville by dark, and steam on more slowly in the dead of night toward Rabaul. Our official orders were to look for trouble. Some nights we found nothing, but not many. Some nights we would spot small coastal boats, transporting Japanese soldiers as they retreated up The Slot. Some nights we would be trailed by Japanese night fighters, who would suddenly bracket us in the phosphorous light of parachute flares—presumably to illuminate us for the Japanese submarines known to be in the area. Some nights we bombarded targets picked out for us by the Australian coast watchers, an extraordinary bunch of men, mostly former plantation superintendents who had melted into the jungle when the Japanese arrived.

And some nights our radars would spot a group of enemy ships coming down The Slot from Rabaul, looking for their own medals, and the two groups would shell each other in a blind slugfest for an hour or so. We worried more about Japanese torpedoes, fired from ships or submarines. Our torpedoes were nowhere near as good. Rabaul is where a young congressman, somehow a lieutenant commander in the Naval Reserve, flew over one night as an observer, and flew back to Washington immediately. Got himself a Silver Star for that single flight, as the world would learn later. His name was Lyndon Baines Johnson (D-Tex.).

Unless we were actually engaging the enemy, we would have to leave the waters off Rabaul by two or three in the morning in order to get safely out of range of the Japanese planes in Rabaul by daylight. We'd get back to Tulagi, refuel, and take on new ammunition, just in time to see the other Task Group start up The Slot to repeat the search and destroy mission. Of course, we would have to stand watch—four hours on, four hours off—until we went to General Quarters and started the whole process over again the next day.

Even without the constant concern for survival, it was an exhausting life that discouraged reflection, introspection, or anything more intellectual than reading. We slept in what we laughingly called our spare time—often in bunks that were only 18 inches above or below someone else, known as your fart-sack-mate. Always with a fan only a few inches from your face, since there was no air conditioning, of course. We played a little cards, mostly cribbage. We used to gamble—for high stakes because there was no place to spend money—but that had pretty much been outlawed by our skipper, Tommy Ragan. My favorite cribbage pigeon was Bill Weibel, from Detroit, the torpedo officer, hence known as "Tubes." Our games ended in a repeat of my college "21" games. All of a sudden "Tubes" owed me more than $4,000, which approximated a year's pay. When the captain heard about the debt, he ordered me to play double or nothing until I lost, and then quit playing for money. Took me three boards.

And we did read—when we weren't too exhausted or scared to read. Boswell's *Life of Johnson* was permanently in a book rack that had been welded to the bulkhead in the officers' head aboard the *Philip*. I got hooked on the anti-establishment works of Philip Wylie, like A *Generation of Vipers*. I remember particularly a book called *Love in America*, a scathing description of the basic relations between men and women by David L. Cohn. Both Wylie and Cohn questioned the soupy sentimentalism that dominated advertising and film. I read a novel by Gladys Schmitt called *The Gates of Aulis*. Bill Cox, an officer on the *Sigourney*, specialized in comics, especially "Terry and the Pirates." He had friends in the States who would clip comics from their newspapers, staple them together in sequences, and mail them out to him.

Bob Lee became my best pal and my model, probably because he was so many things I was not, at least was not yet. First, he was educated and motivated. He read books because he wanted to read books. Up to now, I had read books because I had to read books— except for *Lady Chatterley's Lover*. A couple of years older than I, he had been on a four-stack destroyer before coming to the *Philip*, and so the insignia on his cap had that tarnished look that separated the veteran sailors from the new kids on the ship. He had gone to Amherst on a scholarship, and really learned things. His father had been a carpenter in East Orange, New Jersey. His sister was married to a wholesale Amoco Oil dealer in East Orange, and I had yet to meet a wholesale oil dealer. He shared his destroyer knowledge gracefully and often. When we were still in the Brooklyn Navy Yard being outfitted with things like motor whaleboats, he had asked me one morning to go pick up the one consigned to the *Philip*. He quickly saw I didn't know what a motor whaleboat was (a motor launch), much less where it was, and we went off to pick it up together.

"General," as he was known, was just like the hero of Tom Heggen's great war novel *Mister Roberts*—relaxed, wry, hardworking, and loved by the people who worked under him. He was impressed by the way I had handled my first real people crisis. So was I, as a matter of fact. Before we sailed off to the Pacific, I was standing a night watch one night in the Brooklyn Navy Yard when a young sailor named Frank had pulled a Colt .45 pistol on me, maybe in search of a Section 8 discharge as a mental case. Since I was armed with my own .45, but would never have shot him under any circumstances, I had no choice but to talk him down quietly.

In thousands of hours of conversation at sea over more than twenty-four months, Lee and I shared each other's lives, peeling back layer after layer, until we didn't have to worry about our friendship: it had taken root and flourished.

Along about Christmas 1943, we got orders for Sydney, Australia, for a week of R&R. In conventional terms we hadn't had a day off for almost a year. We had not heard a female voice for the same length of time except in the movies. We talked a lot about Garbo nibbling on Melvyn Douglas's ear in *Ninotchka*. That's how bad it was. And Sydney was the answer to our prayers. As we steamed into Sydney Harbor, General and I were standing on the bridge together when Hoppy, the chief signalman, pointed to some flags waving from a distant hill and said, "You're not going to believe this." The flags were actually semaphore signals, and the closer we got, the more easily we could see that the signals were being sent by young persons of the opposite sex. Age sixteen, tops. In fact, they were asking if anyone might be interested in dates that evening.

Lee and I had volunteered to stand watch that first night, moored to the Woolloomooloo Docks, so the rest of the crew except for a skeleton force could go on liberty. I knew why I had volunteered: I wanted to put off for as long as possible the critical question, was I going to get laid after only eighteen months of enforced fidelity?

We were duly hailed for our generosity by the rest of the crew, and were sitting alone in the wardroom discussing the liberty we would take next day, when we suddenly realized that the ship was listing obviously and ominously to starboard—away from the dock. The reason for the list was not hard to find: thirty sailors were drooped over the railing talking to three young women who had rowed alongside looking for a little action. Pogies, at a glance. ("Pogies" is Navy slang for very young females, as in "pogey bait"—candy for use to lure "pogies" into the sack.) General and I couldn't come up with any regulation that was being violated, until one of the girls started scrambling aboard and the rowboat was being tied up. Plainly the pogies had accepted an invitation to entertain what was left of the crew, and the sailors looked to see what Lee and I were going to do about it.

General and I were widely respected for the wisdom of our decisions in disciplinary matters. This respect dated from an incident which had occurred one night a few months earlier, while the *Philip* was anchored in Iron Bottom Sound, Tulagi. We had rigged the movie screen forward and were showing a movie when another destroyer signaled for permission to come alongside. This was normally no big deal. We would stop the movie for maybe five minutes, while the other ship came alongside and moored bow to stern, allowing the new ship to rig its movie screen forward and show its movie alongside our stern. The whole process shouldn't take five minutes.

This time, though, the ship moored their bow to our bow. To make matters worse this was our new skipper's old ship, and Jimmy Rutter, our new skipper, was in no mood to ask his old captain for any favors. On top of that, damned if they didn't rig their movie screen forward and start showing their own movie, in competition with ours. Rutter, knowing when he was licked, threw up his hands, canceled our movie, and retired to his quarters. Not our crew, however. Some of them retired to the spud bin, the place between the smokestacks amidships where potatoes were stored—when there were any to store—and started throwing them at the new arrivals. Pretty soon one of our potatoes hit their commanding officer in the back of the neck, and pretty soon after that Jimmy Rutter was invited aboard his old ship for a tongue-lashing from his old skipper. Something about how important it was to take command quickly, and show his new ship who was boss.

Jimmy Rutter returned steaming and sent for General and me, immediately. He had never been so humiliated in his life, he told us. The worst behavior he'd ever seen, and in front of his old commanding officer. What kind of ship was this anyway? And he demanded that we find out who had done this dastardly deed, and tell them they were going to get their asses court-martialed. Lee and I left meekly, knowing we were on a fool's mission. Potatoes, we heard? "Mr. Bradlee, you know we ain't had no potatoes on this ship for months." We went from bow to stern. No one had seen any potatoes thrown. No one had seen any potatoes, period. Plenty of them told us they wished they had found some spuds, so they could have thrown them at those "bastids."

After delaying our report for an extra hour to enforce our claim of thoroughness, we told the captain we had found no culprits, and felt we had no chance at all of finding any. We wished his former skipper had not been hit by a flying potato, but we felt the *Philip* had been trashed, and some defense was explainable if not completely meritorious. Anyway he cooled off and we got credit from the crew for the lack of discipline.

Now we used the same strategy. We did nothing for about half an hour, then asked a chief petty officer buddy by loudspeaker to report to the wardroom. We were worried about the Sydney police, we said. These girls were plainly minors. We were worried about venereal disease, we said. These girls were also plainly pros. And we were worried about the number of Navy Regulations the captain could claim were being violated if he returned to the ship early. And so, we told him, we were going to stroll through the ship on an inspection tour in twenty minutes, and we sure hoped that we wouldn't find any extra passengers, or any rowboats. Right on schedule, we took our stroll. We found no stowaways, and the rowboat had disappeared into the Woolloomooloo night.

The next night was our turn ashore, one of the most memorable nights of my life—and I didn't even get laid. We started off in the (men's) bar of the Australia Hotel, downing glass after glass of the great, bitter Aussie beer. Next, we were flipping Australian pennies up over our heads into the large glass bowls, which hung on chains like lampshades under the hanging lights. We were quickly joined at this by a wonderfully tough-looking group of soldiers, a good deal older than we, and much harder. But just as thirsty. We had been told there were no able-bodied men in Australia; they'd all gone overseas to fight in Europe and North Africa. This, we'd heard, was why the women were so friendly. But these were able-bodied men, by God. These were the ragtag remnants of the Second Australian First. The First Australian First had been composed of the first Australians to leave to fight World War I. And these were the first Australians to leave to fight World War II. In fact, they had landed that very day, back home for the first time in five years, after fighting in Crete, fighting Rommel across North Africa, and after crossing the Owen Stanley Range in New Guinea to fight the Japanese. After these incredible battles, they wore no decorations other than the curved metal AUSTRALIA at the top of their shoulders. Despite our callow youth and comparatively limited battle experiences, we had at least one row of ribbons. After listening to their stories, we solemnly pinned our ribbons on them, and they wore them for the rest of the night, as we wore their hard-earned AUSTRALIAS.

As the night slowed into morning, and we slipped in and out of stages of oblivion, our new friends started slipping off quietly—except for one: the towering figure I can recall only as "Shag." "Shag" had taken a piece of shrapnel in his neck from one of Rommel's tanks at Tobruk, and he spoke through a hole in his throat. He'd been repaired and sent back into battle without home leave. He was pretty drunk by now, as drunk as we were, but it gradually dawned on us that he was scared, on top of everything else. Before long he told us why. He hadn't seen his wife for six years! And hadn't dared call to tell her he was home. She lived across Sydney Harbor in Manly Beach, but he was scared to go home to her alone, scared that she would think his new voice box would be a fatal disfigurement in her eyes. As the skies lightened he asked us, begged us, to go home with him. We pleaded that would be an intrusion; he insisted he needed us. Were we real mates, or not? What was friendship about, anyway? And finally, as the sun rose over this fabulous city, the three of us boarded the ferry to Manly Beach, Lieutenant junior grade Robert E. Lee, Ensign Benjamin C. Bradlee, and PFC "Shag," all three gloriously drunk, on the mission that scared him more than a desert battle. We wove our way slowly and noisily down this country road of cottages, each with gardens, fenced with rose bushes. And suddenly, "Shag" tottered to a stop, tears streaming from his eyes—and as tears streamed down our cheeks—we knew he was home. None of us said a word as a door quietly opened, a woman appeared, and they slowly walked into each other's arms.

Our next night was more selfish. We rented a flat for a week in Rosalyn Gardens, in a building that housed scores of pretty, friendly young secretaries, as willing to go to bed with us as we were desperate to go to bed with them. All it took was satisfactory answers to a few questions about VD, and since we were ashore for the first time in a year, we had satisfactory answers. So much for the fidelity problem. I felt such guilt, so fast, that it didn't happen again during our short stay. I tried one more time, but I found someone who preferred women to men, much to the amusement of General and his girl, who giggled all night in the next room. I remembered my mother and father talking about one of their friends being a "Lesbian" in the hushed tones reserved for all such matters, but in my innocence I had never thought that I might end up trying to seduce one.

Before I could wrestle my way through the subtleties of that particular moral quandary, we departed beautiful, downtown Sydney, waving sadly at our young nymphets, still in position on the hill, and headed back to more months up and down The Slot. We were involved in landings at Rendova, Vella Lavella, Bougainville, firing shots in anger, or being fired at, almost every time we looked for trouble.

Off Bougainville, under air attack, we clipped an uncharted coral pinnacle trying to dodge bombs, and had to steam down to Espíritu Santo to get a new propeller. The Navy had no way of making new charts, and so we had to make do with charts made by someone else, in some other time. Off Bougainville, we were using German charts. Our own private bit of coral lay uncharted 16 feet below the surface of Kaiserin Augusta Baie. Off Vella Lavella we got jumped by some twenty Japanese planes, which snuck in on us just over the water from the other side of the island. The first wave was over us so fast they couldn't release their bombs. When they came at us again, the *Philip* and the *Waller* were laying a heavy screen of smoke on either side of a column of fat-ass LSTs, trying to scramble to safety at 5 knots. Suddenly there was a deafening, shuddering crash, and I was sure we had been torpedoed, though I had seen no evidence of the much slower torpedo planes in the attacking force. Much to my relief, a voice broke radio silence, and the skipper of the *Waller* was saying something like, "I'm sorry. That was my fault. I was trying to bring my guns to bear on the bastards." Neither destroyer could see the other because of all the smoke, and the *Waller* had crashed into us amidships trying to get into a position where she could shoot her 40mm and 20mm guns against the Japanese planes. It was an historic admission. In all my time in the Navy, I never heard another open admission of error.

During some other landing our radar operators reported a "shitload of bogeys" about a hundred miles away. (In Navy parlance, an initial "shitload" could mean anything from two to a hundred; we would worry about details later.) We were particularly vulnerable, operating with the LSTs again, without any air cover this time and without the prospect of any air cover. I was in the Combat Information Center, sifting information from radars, SONAR, and radios to pass on to the captain when I thought they needed it. On the spur of the moment, I pretended I was a fighter director, vectoring nonexistent squadrons of F4S or F4US to attack this particular shitload of bogeys. Like "Code name for fighter squadron, this is code name for *Philip*. We have a mess of bogeys, bearing whatever, at about one hundred miles, or about ninety from you. Vector [whatever course, to intercept]." We kept this up for about five minutes, moving our "planes" up and down, right and left, when damned if the shitload of bogeys didn't suddenly change course and run off. I have no idea whether they even heard us. Lee and the skipper put me in for a Bronze Star for this particular scheme. Never got it.

Another time one stormy night we were fiddling with the fighter-director radio circuits in CIC, when we suddenly heard a distant voice singing "Bless 'Em All." And then a whole lot of different guys singing "Bless 'Em All," with especially good renditions of the final line, "Cheer up, my lads, fuck 'em all." They turned out to be a New Zealand fighter squadron, lost in the storm, getting their courage up to run out of gas and land in the drink. Our radar operators finally found them on their screen, and we interrupted their rendition of perhaps the finest Pacific War song, and sent them to the nearest friendly base.

My first important solo decision came just before dawn one morning, steaming in the middle of a line of the other destroyers in our division, off somewhere after a night in The Slot by ourselves. I was the officer of the deck, which meant acting captain since we weren't at General Quarters, when CIC reported an unidentified plane, closing on us fast, almost dead ahead. The blip on the radar screen lacked the pulse below the line on the screen (known as IFF for "Identification, Friend or Foe") which identified friendly planes, but we couldn't see it at first, and the gun crews on watch were tracking it. I was just about to give the signal for General Quarters and wake the captain, when we saw it, about 500 yards just off the port bow, lumbering along only a few feet off the water, easily identified as a "Betty," the code name for a twin-engined Japanese bomber. None of the ships ahead of us had fired, but when I saw it myself, I felt sure, and shouted, "Commence firing," just as the captain, the medal-hungry Wild Bill Groverman, popped out of his night cabin. (The flame from the 5-inch shots took both his eyebrows off, and he couldn't hear for a week.) We must have fired a dozen shots from the 5-inch guns, and a clip or two from the 40s and 20s, but we missed him. Later, the war historians identified this as a plane taking a high-ranking Japanese admiral to Rabaul.

This kind of responsibility was typical in destroyer war in the Pacific for its youngest officers. You start as J.O.D., Junior Officer of the Deck, helping the O.D. run the ship under way from the bridge. Eight months after I graduated from Harvard, I made Officer of the Deck. That meant that when we were not at General Quarters, ready for battle, I ran the ship on my watch—twenty-one years old, in command of a 370-foot warship, responsible for the safety of more than 300 people, four hours on watch, eight hours off, during which time you did your regular job running a department. Twenty-one years old, you are almost as scared of telling sailors what to do as you are of a Japanese bullet.

My regular non-battle job involved communications, the care

and feeding of the machines which provided raw information to the ship, and of the men who operated and maintained those machines. This responsibility was more educating than Harvard, more exciting, more meaningful than anything I'd ever done. This is why I had such a wonderful time in the war. I just plain loved it. Loved the excitement, even loved being a little bit scared. Loved the sense of achievement, even if it was only getting from Point A to Point B; loved the camaraderie, even if the odd asshole reared his ugly head every so often. For years I was embarrassed to admit all this, given the horrors and sadness visited upon so many during the years I was thriving. But news of those horrors was so removed in time and distance. No newspapers, no radio even, except Tokyo Rose, and of course there were none of television's stimulating jolts. I found that I liked making decisions. I liked sizing up men and picking the ones who could best do the job. Most of all I liked the responsibility, the knowledge that people were counting on me, that I wouldn't let them down.

Many of the reserve naval officers with no obvious technical qualifications were better at their jobs than the regulars. Naval Academy ensigns were mostly electrical engineers. They knew how steam turbine engines worked, but they weren't so sure when to start them or when to stop them. They were better doers than teachers, and in wartime they had to lead and teach.

The first night Jimmy Rutter was in command of the *Philip*, he had had to bring her alongside a tanker to refuel. Mooring a 2,100-ton ship to a stationary object—like a dock, or another ship at anchor—isn't all that difficult, even if you studied the fragments of Sappho more than seamanship. But only experience will teach you the exactly right moment to order the engines "All back, One" while the ship is still moving forward, or "All ahead, One" while she is still inching backward. Poor Jimmy Rutter had no such experience. Again and again, he was a moment late with his orders, and twice he snapped mooring lines. I suspect the boys in the engine room were answering the commands a second or two late, screwing the new skipper over just to let him know who was really the boss. But he finally endeared himself to everyone by shaking his head and saying, "Goddamn it, I can't stop this son of a bitch. You do it."

Barely seven months after our R&R in Sydney, we headed for another R&R session, this time in New Zealand. This one I was really waiting for. I had left the States with the title to a 1,000-acre sheep station on the North Island of New Zealand in my pocket. It seems that in the last part of the nineteenth century, one George Bradlee had so disgraced his parents by getting a young girl in a family way that he had been sent to live permanently in London, with a $50,000 stake. According to family legend, George had whistled through the $50,000 in no time at all, and returned to Boston. Next time, his father personally escorted him to New Zealand, bought him the sheep station, and left him there. George was said to have married a Maori woman. They both died—childless—at about the same time, and the title to the 1,000 acres returned to the Tremont Street vaults of Welch & Forbes, the Bradlee family trustees.

With Freddy in the cavalry at Fort Riley, Kansas, I was thought to have the best chance of getting to New Zealand, and so I was charged with reporting back to the family on the precise quality of this great asset. It was not to be. Two days out of New Zealand, we were turned around and sent to Eniwetok, where the biggest Pacific convoy ever was forming to bombard and invade the Marianas— Guam, Saipan, and Tinian. They were heavily defended, and critically needed, to serve as air bases for the planes that started to bomb the Japanese mainland in June 1944. The *Enola Gay*, which dropped the A-bomb on Hiroshima, took off from Tinian.

The Marianas campaign seemed endless. We had bombarded the shit out of Saipan for days before the 2nd and 4th Marine Divisions and the 27th Army Division had landed. Now, we were lying less than a mile offshore in direct radio contact with a young Marine lieutenant in a front-line foxhole. My battle job was to run the CIC—the Combat Information Center. One room crammed with all the radar, all the SONAR, all the radios, all the telephones, all the plotting equipment. All information came in to CIC, and CIC parceled it out as needed—to the captain, to the gunnery officer, and to the watch officer. When the young Marine and I talked he was so close to the Japanese defenders that I could hear them yelling, whenever he transmitted his request for a barrage of 5-inch gunfire from us. I've lost his name, unfortunately, but this guy was one brave son of a bitch. He would ask for gunfire in such-and-such a place—often within a few yards of his foxhole—and would relay the coordinates he gave me to the gunnery officer. First "Fire," then deafening explosion. Then pause, while the 57-pound shells streaked toward their target, followed by comments from our unseen buddy. "Fan-fucking-tastic"; "Bullseye" maybe. Often, even. And sometimes: "That was a little close, friends. Back off a blond one."

We had been at General Quarters doing this for more than fifty hours, when there was a lull while our forward area observer changed his foxhole. I told the captain I was out on my feet, and scared I would mess up. He told me to go down to the Radio Shack on the seaward side of the ship, and grab what sleep I could. I was in the middle of a deep, deep sleep, when I heard a strange explosion, followed by the noise of what could only be shrapnel hitting us. If it was shrapnel, it had to be from a Japanese shore battery and there had to be more coming. I burst out of the Radio Shack and raced forward back to my battle station. Halfway up the port side ladder, I felt a sharp sting in my right buttock. About what a squash ball used to feel like, traveling really fast, from really short range. I looked down, and by God there was a piece of shrapnel on deck, about two inches long, half an inch thick with jagged edges. Without thinking, I reached down and picked it up. Clearly it had ricocheted into me after hitting something else, because, though I could feel a small tear in my pants, I felt stung, not wounded. And it was extremely hot when I got it into my pocket and got myself back to my battle station.

The gunnery officer was now my special pal, Bob Lee. He and his team had silenced the shore battery before I got back to work, and I told him over the sound-powered phones that tied us all together in battle that my ass had got nicked. That word spread through the ship like wildfire, and by the time we eventually secured from General Quarters, it was widely believed that "Mr. Bradlee has been shot in the ass."

When the ship's doctor, Ralph Morgan, from Thomas Wolfe country in western North Carolina, saw that whatever had happened to me I was perfectly fine, he insisted that we go to the wardroom together. (Wardrooms on destroyers are normally where the officers meet and eat, but during battle they serve as temporary hospitals.) He made me lie down on the wardroom table, ass up, pulled down my pants to examine the "wound," a certain redness around the slightest, bloodless abrasion. Scalpel in hand, he announced that since there was no blood, there could be no Purple Heart, and damned if he didn't nick me, just hard enough to fetch a drop of blood. You have to apply for the Purple Heart, and—needless to say—I didn't. (But I did get sort of a Purple Heart—months later, when we had returned to the States for repairs to the ship and R&R for the crew. In the middle of a special ship's party, there was a roll of drums, and our new skipper, Wild Bill Groverman summoned me forward, asked me to bend over, and pinned a large purple velvet heart to my rear end, drawing blood for the second time.)

Once, when our forward area observer got a few much-needed hours off, we arranged over the fire-control radio circuit to meet. I went ashore in the *Philip's* motor whaleboat, armed to the teeth with a never-fired Colt .45 strapped to my waist, to pick him up. He turned out to be my age, and even younger-looking, all jerky gestures and haunted eyes. The crew cheered him aboard, and after the longest hot shower in the history of Destroyer Squadron 22, we gave him so much ice cream he threw up, and slept the sleep of the dead. I wasn't the only one crying when we cheered him off next day. I didn't know how to tell a man I loved him in those days, but I sure loved him.

He seemed so vulnerable, so much at the mercy of events he couldn't control.

Army units on the western side of Saipan were taking forever to get into position for the final push on the caves at the southern end of the island. One general was relieved of command of an infantry division because he was taking too long. The *Philip* was firing so many rounds of 5-inch shells, wherever our forward area spotter wanted them, that we were concerned that the barrels were deteriorating. We had been hit by Japanese shore batteries when I had been "wounded." We were doing our bombarding from as close as 1,500 yards off the east coast of Saipan, close enough to be swarmed over by the flies that we were told were attracted by the night soil used to fertilize the island crops. The stench was overpowering. At sunset, it was routine for destroyers to ask permission to proceed at flank speed into the wind, with all portholes and watertight doors wide open, to try to blow the damn flies out of the ship.

Finally, at the end of the campaign, the *Philip* was chosen to transport all the brass in the area from Saipan up to Tinian for a flag-raising there. Normally on a destroyer, if you saw a four-striper (captain) once a month it was a big deal. We never saw any kind of admiral, much less a general. Destroyers pride themselves on their informality, and flag officers are prohibitively formal. But now, here was all this brass down below in the wardroom, including the great man himself, Admiral Raymond Spruance. Spruance was both Commander, Central Pacific Force, and Commander, Fifth Fleet, at the time. Also the legendary Marine General Holland M. "Howlin' Mad" Smith, and a whole boatload of stars, bars, and braid. Our captain was in the wardroom with the brass, doing everything but stand on his head to occupy his guests. I was on the bridge, as Officer of the Deck, having been told only to "take her up to Tinian." No course, no speed, no nothing. Just "take her up."

It was one of those glorious tropical days that cost so much to enjoy in peacetime. Not a cloud in the sky. That incredible blue-green seawater. And so I thought we would take the brass on a real destroyer spin—like about 30 knots (33 mph). The water was so smooth you could hear only the big waves thrown off by the bow as the ship sped "up to Tinian."

Suddenly, the quartermaster snapped to attention (I'd never seen him do that before) and shouted, "Attention on the bridge. The Admiral is present." I saluted him (I was never awfully good at that), and asked him if there was anything he would like to see. He shook my hand with just the slightest smile, and thanked me, but he would just like to look around. We all watched him as he started thumbing through the file of ALNAVs (directives issued to all ships of the Navy and all the other Pacific ships). In this case, directives issued by Spruance to the *Philip*. Suddenly, he stopped, as if he'd found the one he wanted. As soon as he moved on, I rushed casually to see which one had been left for us to see, and I saw the one that ordered all ships to proceed no faster than 15 knots, unless specifically ordered otherwise.

I rang Jimmy Rutter in the wardroom and asked for instructions. We came up with a deceptively simple solution: every few minutes, we would decrease the *Philip's* speed by 1 knot, all but imperceptibly, and we steamed into Tinian an hour later making a steady 15 knots.

Once the Marianas were secure, most of our squadron was ordered back to the States. R&R for the crew, and repairs plus a complete overhaul for the ships. I had been twenty-one years old when the *Philip* steamed up the East River past our apartment on my way to war—scared of the future. As we steamed under the Golden Gate Bridge, en route to the Oakland Navy Yard, I was twenty-three years old—scared of different things. Like who would I find that I had married. And more importantly, who would she find that she had married.

But on the way from Saipan to San Francisco, our skipper received a formal envelope from Harvard College, addressed only to the Commanding Officer, U.S.S. *Philip*, FPO, San Francisco, California. In it was the long-deferred Bible-Shakespeare-Greek Classics examination, which I had never taken, with a letter from some dean asking the commanding officer to isolate me completely at some convenient time and get me to take it. I was not completely surprised because my father had written me that he had persuaded Harvard to let me take this exam and thus complete my degree (even though Harvard had eliminated the fucking exam from degree requirements a year earlier). And so I had been reading the Bible, some Greek plays, and a little Shakespeare in my spare time. The crew of the *Philip* was following this saga every step of the way, and cheered as I was escorted by the captain into his stateroom to take the exam, while the ship steamed home.

Half an hour later, there was a knock on the door, and a Seaman

First Class entered saying—apropos of absolutely nothing—"The Officer of the Deck [it was George Hamilton, an Annapolis engineer] presents his compliments, sir. The shortest verse in the Bible is St. John, chapter II, verse 35. 'Jesus wept.'" I finished the bloody thing, shipped it off when we landed in the States, and months later got a letter from my father announcing I had passed, with honors. Only a B, but honors.

Back in the States, and safely under that gorgeous Golden Gate Bridge, Lee and I started off home leave on the absolute worst foot, by missing the plane taking us back to our loved ones. We had used extraordinary pull to get us on a DC-4 to New York, leaving at 6:00 A.M. on the morning after we tied up in the Navy Yard. We had even gotten a room at the St. Francis Hotel, and then we had gone out to party. Next thing I knew, General was saying, "Jeezus, Beebo, it's six-thirty and we've missed our plane." It seems pretty obvious fifty years later, but I don't remember worrying about how come we missed our plane. I worried about explaining to Jean how come we missed the plane, and struggling to find another way back. Wartime trains from one end of the country to the other took forever—two and a half days—but that's how I Came Marching Home.

When we finally finished our first embraces, we each insulated ourselves with commitments that kept us superficially busy. Jean had been seeing someone to help her cope with the problems of marriage without a husband, after a family life that could easily be described as difficult, if not traumatic.

The "someone" turned out to be a Dr. Edward Spencer Cowles, a white-haired Park Avenue quack who dispensed feel-good concoctions to a variety of unsuspecting patients suffering from various forms of mental anguish. (Probably methamphetamines, according to one expert in this area.) I later learned that Cowles ran something called the Body and Mind Foundation, and had been investigated for violating medical laws.

But, damned if Jean didn't take me to see him on the same day I arrived in New York, and damned if I didn't go, meekly. I had no idea why Jean was seeing him, what relief he was providing her, or what the hell I was doing there instead of being greeted as some sexy war hero. We talked for maybe five minutes—the three of us—with Cowles telling me to be sure to keep my uniform clean and pressed: "You'll be needing it to fight the Russians before too long," then giving Jean her "cocktail" in a small paper cup, and we were out of there.

Soon enough we retreated to the comforting bosom of our families—anything to avoid being alone for too long. Neither one of us had developed any skills at being close, physically or emotionally, and our parents were so genuinely glad to see me, and find out what I had been up to, that it was relatively easy not to explore—much less understand—where our relationship stood.

My father wanted to know every detail of my life for the last two years, not that it was such a tough task. He yelled at my mother when she asked if I had ever faced danger. "Jesus Christ, of course he faced danger. What do you think he's been doing for two years?" He shook his head, and mixed himself another drink. He had become friends with Admiral Samuel Eliot Morison, the great naval historian and Columbus biographer. They had lunched together, at the common table in the Somerset Club's men's dining room. Morison, of course, knew in general what Destroyer Squadron 22 had been up to; he knew all about the nightly hunting expeditions up The Slot, all about the landings in the Solomons and the Marianas. Now, the old man's interest was consuming, and he wore his pride in me like a smile.

When he had gotten everything he could out of me about where I had been, he wanted to know everything about where I thought I was going. Morison had told him he thought the Philippines would be the next hot spot for destroyers and carriers. How soon would we be invading Japan? A particularly awesome prospect for destroyer types, for the destroyers would be taking the largest fleet of ships and men ever assembled to those unknown and scary shores. Sitting by the fire in that lovely Beverly house, we faced that prospect together.

Jean and I settled into a routine, insulated by family and friends, that left us in almost the same condition we had found ourselves at the beginning of home leave . . . cautious, not quite comfortable but perfectly pleased with each other, and perfectly willing to re-up for an unknown duration, despite the first signs that I was increasingly unsatisfied with my intellectual achievements and interests. If I had been able or willing at that time to describe a "trophy wife," I would probably have described Jean—pretty, sure to be a good mother, fine family and all that. Jean would be headed back to teach at the Dalton School in New York, sharing an apartment with my sister, waiting out the war. Unless she got pregnant. For without any real discussion or planning, that had become a possibility. I knew only that I was heading back out to the Pacific front, on the *Philip*, probably, until the war was over.

And soon enough, after four weeks leave, and two more weeks with Jean in Oakland, standing only one four-hour watch a day, as the ship's overhaul was completed and all the shiny new gadgets were installed, the time had come for those emotional farewells that I found so difficult. Other husbands got used to saying goodbye, dry-eyed and necking passionately in front of a hundred other people doing the same thing while the train was ready to pull out of the station, or while the ship was all but leaving the dock. Not me. I dreaded goodbye scenes then, as I do now. But this one was over, and I went back to war.

On the way back to Pearl Harbor, starting my third year in the Navy, we had begun to believe the end of the war was in sight. But instead of relief, we felt concern, and fear. It was one thing to be screwing around the Solomons, or the Marianas, but it didn't take a naval genius to look at the charts and see the Philippines and Okinawa ahead, closer and closer to the Big Casino, Japan. We didn't know about Kamikaze pilots yet, but we believed the Japanese would fight to the last American to defend their homeland; it was widely accepted that a landing on Japan would cost a hundred thousand American lives the first day.

When we got to Pearl, I was ordered to leave the *Philip* and report to the Commander of Destroyers and Cruisers in the Pacific, COMDESPAC. As his representative, I was to go from destroyer to destroyer communicating what wisdom I would accumulate about how to run Combat Information Centers to other destroyers in the ring of ships closing in on Tokyo. In the two years on the *Philip*, we had pioneered the theory of what a destroyer CIC should be doing during battle. CIC staff would monitor all incoming info, assess it, and distribute the information to the officers on a need-to-know basis. CICs hadn't existed when we put to sea in 1942, but they had grown so fast in concept and equipment that I was considered an expert at the age of twenty-three, even though I didn't have a clue how any of the machines worked. For eight months, from January through August 1945, I served on nineteen different destroyers—all of them under way and in battle, first in the Philippines, then with fast carrier task forces off Okinawa and Japan itself.

I reported to each of these ships by breeches buoy—an awesome contraption, which in its wartime version had become a canvas bag, attached by four short lines to a pulley. The pulley rode on a line stretched between two moving vessels. The pulley itself was connected to each ship by a line, so the breeches buoy—containing mail, ice cream, movies, or people—could be pulled from one ship to the other. A destroyer would pull up alongside a tanker, or a carrier, to refuel under way. I would transfer by breeches buoy from the destroyer to the mother ship. And transfer back to the next destroyer to refuel. Nineteen destroyers meant almost forty trips in this satanic device. Actually it got to be a piece of cake, when the ships got close to each other and stayed close and parallel to each other. Say 50 feet. All this with both ships making 15 knots. But destroyer skippers are human; they know that if they get too close, a surge of wind or water can slap their ships into a carrier—never mind who or what is in the breeches buoy—and there goes a career.

I had to land on the deck of a different destroyer every couple of weeks, scared shitless from the breeches buoy ride over, not knowing a soul, carrying only a single duffel bag, and aware that the last person anyone wanted to see was some young hot shot representing an admiral. I had to spend the first two days trying to break down that resentment. It helped when I offered to stand watch with all the rest of the officers, but that cut into my sack time seriously, and so I was always exhausted.

It helped enormously that I started my new outrider assignment
in the Philippines with my old squadron, and almost immediately
with my own ship. One day in the Philippines is still crystal clear
in my mind. It started in Subic Bay, on another sparkling morning. The crew was in dress whites, for we were headed for a special,
supervised liberty in Manila, which had been liberated a few days
earlier. As we steamed down from Subic Bay and turned left toward
Manila, there on our port side was the fortress island of Corregidor, where Lieutenant General Jonathan M. Wainwright and his
troops (the last forces of American resistance) had been starved
into surrendering in 1942. Corregidor was now officially in Allied
hands, but it was honeycombed by tunnels and caves, and the tunnels and caves were still hiding Japanese stragglers who had refused
to surrender. For a while, it was standard procedure for any American warship passing Corregidor in either direction—regardless of
any other mission, like making liberty—to check in with an Army
bombardment-control officer, get specific coordinates from him,
and lob fifty shells into some cave. We accomplished our mission,
even though the sailors handled the 57-pound shells like objects of
art, so as not to soil their dress whites.

I had volunteered to lead a small column of my crewmates
ashore. I wanted to walk to Santo Tomaso University a few miles
out of town, where recently liberated American prisoners were
awaiting relocation. My brave little band of sailors wanted to get
laid. Which turned out to be no feat at all. We had barely formed up
into a ragged column when we were besieged by little kids, shouting
the charms of their sisters, or mothers, and asking the guys if they
wanted to "zig-zig." As a matter of fact, they were extremely interested, and one by one they would drop out of line, for a remarkably
short period of time, and return to the column. We never made it to
Santo Tomaso, but we did make it back to the *Philip*, which had to
leave in time to get to Subic Bay before dark.

We had just finished sending another fifty shells into Corregidor
on our way back to Subic Bay, this time on our starboard side, when
a lookout spotted a head bobbing in the water about 100 yards away
between us and the island. Once we were sure it was not some *Philip*

sailor fallen overboard from booze or slaked lust, the captain asked me to go aft and take whoever it was aboard for later delivery to some intelligence types for questioning. I strapped on my .45, just in case he had some secret weapon, and went aft, with the crew offering such helpful advice as "Let's kill the Jap bastid." We threw him a line and reeled him aboard, the sorriest-looking SOB I ever saw. He was covered with sores, barely 90 pounds, clad only in a loincloth, and plainly more scared than I was. "Throw him back," one crewman suggested. Instead, I ordered him to strip. Very authoritatively. First in English, then—ridiculously—in French, in case he knew any words in my other language. Orders immediately repeated by the crew in Polish, Finnish, Greek, and Yiddish. He stripped, but just stared at us, until the doctor took him off to the infirmary, for further examination and incarceration.

Except for the Val pilot who had given me my baptism by fire in the Solomon Islands, this was the only Japanese person I saw during the entire war. Who was this forlorn figure, and where is he now? Was he wondering what the hell he was doing swimming half-naked off Corregidor, as much as I was wondering what the hell I was doing with a Colt .45 pistol in my hand, momentarily diverted from supervising an afternoon of street fucking and sightseeing?

This was the winter of 1945, and Desron 22 (Destroyer Squadron) was in on the tail end of the fabulously successful naval battles in the seas around the Philippines. After I straightened them out ("Smile," as the V-Mail letters home used to put it), I joined a destroyer squadron a few days before it fired torpedoes from a range of less than two miles at a huge Japanese Naval Force in the Battle of Leyte Gulf. The Japanese were caught steaming due north in a column in the narrow confines of Surigao Straits between the islands of Leyte and Mindanao. A successful torpedo shoot depends on knowing the course and speed of the enemy ships. In this case we knew their course, because they would run aground if they were on any other course, and their speed was not important because there were so many enemy ships: if you missed the one you were aiming for, you would hit the next one.

Or so we told ourselves.

One sunny afternoon, I found myself off the coast of Zamboanga on the island of Mindanao, in the southern Philippines where, as the old song that rang in my head went, "O, the monkeys have no tails in Zamboanga." In fact, I was off Zamboanga in a PBY, a clumsy two-engine seaplane, trying to take off for my next assignment, when the plane was scissored by Jap machine-gun fire but kept flying.

The early months of 1945 were the toughest of the war for me. I got almost no mail, which was more important to us all than food or ammunition. Someone kept pretty good track of where individual ships were, but no one could be expected to follow one brand-new lieutenant as he bounced on his own from ship to ship. I got almost no sleep, as I "taught" during the day and stood watch half the night. The problems I found, and tried to correct, were almost always the same, and therefore less challenging to solve. The noise level in the cramped CICs was always too high, with as many as six or seven voice radio circuits, plus the endless pinging of the SONAR, the submarine detection system, the reports of lookouts and radar operators, plus crewmen relaying voice messages they received by sound-powered telephones from all over the ship. The more imminent the battle, the louder the noise level, and the more important it was to hear everything. The other incredible challenge was to keep track of where your own ship was in relation to other ships: your own task force, your own fighter planes, enemy ships—surface and submarine—and enemy planes, at 20,000 feet, or at sea level on a torpedo bombing run. All this at speeds of up to 30 knots, in the dead dark of night as well as in the brightest daylight, in driving thunderstorms or in the fairest weather, in mountainous seas or dead calms.

We had been escorting some high-speed minelayers one night, trying to seal off an escape route used to ferry retreating Japanese soldiers. We had laid the mines, and were hauling ass at 37 miles per hour in a torrential rainstorm, when the captain came back into the CIC soaking wet and pleaded, "Bradlee, where the hell am I?" It was a good question, one I have often remembered at times when I felt I was in some jam, not entirely of my own making, and not entirely in charge of extricating myself. We were taught in Naval ROTC that if you asked an admiral where he was, he would put his hand on the center of the chart. If you asked a commander where he was, he would point at the chart. But if the skipper asked you where he was, you should be able to pinpoint his exact location. This captain didn't want to know latitude and longitude. He wanted to know he wasn't going to run aground at 34 knots, or collide with other ships. And thereby stop his career and his ship dead in the water. That was exactly what I wanted to know.

But each day of my naval life I had been learning perhaps the most important lesson of my life: You can't do any better than surround yourself with the best people you can find, and then listen to them. And I had done that. "We're one hundred yards behind the *Sauffley*, sir, in the middle of the channel, on the same course and speed. We're doing fine." I didn't know where the hell we were, but I knew where the best people we could find thought we were.

When whatever ship I was on during this winter and spring of 1945 went to General Quarters, everyone had a specific job, except me. It is one thing to accept or solicit advice from a visiting "expert" as you zigzag peacefully across the sparkling Pacific, but when a ship is attacking or under fire itself, a destroyer crew works together as a team, and strangers are tolerated with difficulty. I hated feeling helpless, but it is what I felt when one of the destroyers I was on fired a spread of torpedoes at a small column of Japanese warships in the middle of the night, using information produced by the team I was coaching but not leading. And I felt helpless as I followed the blip of a Japanese plane into our formation and was sent reeling as it crashed into the stern of another destroyer close by. This was my first encounter with the strangest of all Japanese behavior, the Kamikaze, or the Golden Wind. I could imagine myself in the heat of battle where I would perhaps instinctively take some sudden action which would almost surely result in my death. I could not imagine waking up some morning at 5:00 A.M., going to some church to pray, and knowing that in a few hours I would crash my plane into a ship on purpose.

Anyway, I boarded my nineteenth and last destroyer, the U.S.S. *DeHaven*, on July 23, 1945, some fifty or sixty miles southeast of the coast of Japan. She was the flagship of Destroyer Squadron 61, whose staff included my old friend Joe Walker, and she was commanded by my old *Philip* skipper, Bill Groverman. On August 7, I finished my inspection/instruction tour of the *DeHaven*, and was transferred (under way, of course) to a fleet tanker, the U.S.S. *Cacapon* (AO 52), to start a trip to pick up new orders in Pearl Harbor.

But on August 6, one atomic bomb was dropped on Hiroshima, killing 80,000 people in a flash, seriously injuring another 100,000, and leveling 98 percent of the city's buildings. All we knew came from a brief radio dispatch, and yet everyone knew it was the beginning of the end of the war. None of my new shipmates knew the first thing about atomic energy, much less atomic bombs. But I spotted an unused set of the *Encyclopaedia Britannica* in the modest library, and I volunteered to research the subject enough to write a small information bulletin for the ship's crew. Without knowing a thing, we sensed that this event was going to rival December 7, 1941, in importance to all our immediate futures.

Was this the first time I wrote in ignorance? Knowing way too little about my subject? Or the last?

I wish.

Memory has blurred my recollection of the last months of this assignment, but the opinion of my performance has been preserved, through the endorsements of the many commanding officers whom I served. Some of this evidence was provided by men whose future naval careers were not all that noteworthy, but it is all that I have that is tangible to show for those long months.

Life as an itinerant expert was incredibly busy and active on one hand—from battles to bull sessions—and yet isolated and lonely on the other. So I sustained myself with the life-saving mini-editions of *Time, Newsweek,* and *The New Yorker*—small *Reader's* Digest-sized publications without ads, but with proof that there was a world out there, beyond radar blips, endless horizons, and the uneasy cama-

raderie of friendships that would begin, flourish, and end in two
weeks.

I was sustained, too, by the fitness reports I received from each
commanding officer as I left one destroyer and headed for the next
one. These fitness reports were in the form of endorsements to my
orders, where my performance as a visiting expert was described
and evaluated. As a child, one looks for compliments. As an adult,
one looks for evidence of effectiveness, but that kind of evidence
was hard to come by in wartime, if you weren't a combat pilot, measuring enemy planes shot down, or a submarine skipper, counting
enemy ships sunk. My destroyer skipper bosses seemed to have spotted some things in me that appear almost more relevant to my later
life than to my life as a Navy lieutenant:

Lieutenant Bradlee is the first C.I.C. training officer [with]
practical experience and theoretical background equal to that
of ship's officers. . . . He is enthusiastic and knows how to put
his stuff over . . . he volunteered and stood watches with regular watch sections . . . he has increased interest of all hands in
C.I.C. work.

E. B. Grantham, C.O. of the U.S.S. *Robinson* (DD562). 14
March 1945

The services of Lieutenant Bradlee . . . are greatly appreciated.
More has been gained from his visit than from even the most
interesting publications. . . . It was pleasant as well as profitable
to have Lieutenant Bradlee on board. His manner and his constructive approach, which are such [as] to make others receptive
to his ideas, are worthy of note.

Chesford Brown, C.O. of the U.S.S. *Eaton* (DD510). 14
April 1945

Lieutenant Bradlee has done an outstanding job. His tact, friendliness, and obvious ability have been greatly appreciated. The
infectious enthusiasm and obvious competence of subject officer
have done much to revive interest and enthusiasm in tasks that

the same personnel have been performing for 18 months. The imaginative yet realistic approach that he makes on the difficult problem of casualty drills has been most valuable.

W. S. Maddox, C.O. of the U.S.S. *Mertz* (DD691). 5 June 1945

The report cards described the beginnings of an adult—still only twenty-three years old, but emerging with recognizable characteristics. Signs of a personality boy. A self-starter. Enthusiastic, tactful, hardworking, constructive, practical, diligent, consistent, resourceful, cooperative, realistic, able to inspire people below him, and to impress those above him—when he knows what he's talking about.

Without these generous endorsements, I would have been operating in a total vacuum, thousands of miles from superiors who were complete strangers. With them, I plugged away, almost convinced I was leaving each destroyer in better shape than I found it, and thus helping end the war which we all sensed was winding down. We were devastated by the news of President Roosevelt's death. No one in my immediate family had died by April 1945; FDR's death—almost personal—was the first. My last destroyers were operating with fast carriers and battleships off the coast of Japan itself. The giant 16-inch guns lobbed their shells over the destroyers I was serving, at targets on the Japanese mainland from about 25,000 yards offshore, only twelve miles. Escorting destroyers would station themselves between the battleships and the shore, to get torpedoed first in case there were enemy submarines around. Their guns flashed long before the deafening sound, and then what seemed like much later, we could actually see the 16-inch shells—big as Volkswagens—streak over our heads.

When August finally came with the world's first atomic explosions, I was on the fleet oiler U.S.S. *Cacapon*, waiting for a ride to Pearl Harbor. I got there on the escort carrier U.S.S. *Munda* (CVE 104) on August 17, 1945, three days after the fighting ended in the Far East. Two weeks later, on September 2, General MacArthur accepted the formal surrender of Japan on the deck of the U.S.S. *Missouri* in Tokyo Bay. And the war was unbelievably over.

I had more than enough points (which were earned for time in service as well as time in campaign battles) to be released from active duty. But I was stuck with orders keeping me in Hawaii to help rewrite the destroyer CIC manual before I got released, hoisted on my own fitness reports. I think it took me three weeks to finish the job. I hitched a ride on a cruiser back to San Francisco in October 1945, and back to the real world.

FOUR

NEW HAMPSHIRE

The excitement of coming home in one piece from the war that would really end all wars should have lasted longer. I found it hard to be anything but restless in New York. My fingers were always clenched. Jean and I were given a house in Boca Grande, Florida, to try to relax. But it was hard for me to enjoy doing nothing, as long as I didn't know what I was going to do with the rest of my life. My father's friend, Jack Stubbs, had always wanted me to work in his brokerage office in Boston, and reminded me of his long-standing offer. I was sure I wanted to do something that would make the world a better place, that would really make a difference. For a while in the Pacific, I had thought about teaching in the public school system somewhere, and making vital and creative contact with a handful of students who themselves would go out and make the world a better place to live. But that had come to seem too removed from the battles of history. And for the last years Bob Lee and I had talked about newspapering. While I was in the Pacific, the *Atlantic Monthly* magazine had run a contest, soliciting articles about the press in America. My father had sent me the contest announcement and arranged with *Atlantic* editor Ted Weeks to accept an article from me after the contest deadline. Without any current resource material, and without having read newspapers for a couple of years, my entry was in fact a criticism of what I remembered of the *Boston Herald*. Weeks didn't run it. I had nothing in my curriculum vitae to interest a newspaper editor, beyond my months as a copy boy on the *Beverly Evening Times*.

I couldn't find a job to save my neck, or at least I couldn't find a job of any substance. New York newspaper editors showed no interest in Navy lieutenants with a few ribbons. There were copy boy jobs galore, but all the reporter jobs were being kept for the men who held them when the war began. I wasn't scared of any kind of work, but after driving a destroyer around the Pacific Ocean, responsible for the lives of more than 300 men, I wasn't ready to settle for putting carbon paper between sheets of copy and fetching coffee for reporters. Anyway, I was so awed by the city rooms and by the city editors of the *New York Times* and the *New York Herald Tribune* that I was almost relieved when they turned me down. Same for the Boston papers, although I didn't want to work in my hometown. I wanted the suspense and challenge and excitement of another part of the world.

Finally, a man named George Frazier at the *Boston Herald* offered me a beginning reporter's job for $30 a week. The *Herald* publisher, Robert "Beanie" Choate, was a third or fourth cousin of mine, and he rescinded the job offer, saying that the *Herald's* nepotism policy made hiring me impossible. That was an extraordinarily lucky break. Going back to Boston would have been a dreadful mistake for me at that stage of Jean's and my life.

To keep from despair, I had accepted a job offer from Roger Baldwin, of Nude Beach fame, to catalogue the library of the American Civil Liberties Union and lick a few envelopes on the side as a $25 a week office boy. Lower than a copy boy, but not a career, and a chance to learn. Roger had noted that I "didn't know enough about civil liberties"—one of the great understatements of the early postwar period. I didn't know anything about civil liberties.

I knew a little about right and wrong, but mostly as they affected me. Roger figured if I went to work cataloguing the ACLU Library at 23rd Street and Fifth Avenue, I would probably have to read some of the books to figure out where they belonged. The library was small, and he could have hired a professional to catalogue it in a matter of days. It took me three months, but when I was through I knew something about the Sacco and Vanzetti case, about Elizabeth Gurley Flynn, future head of the American Communist Party, about the reactionary Reverend Gerald L. K. Smith, and Father Coughlin, the radio priest, and many other misfit extremists from all corners of the American political spectrum, all victims of some kind of restriction on their civil liberties. They flocked to Roger Baldwin for help in securing for themselves the rights they wished to deny others.

In time I was allowed to talk to some of the clients, to take down a first draft of the trouble they were in. I remember particularly talking to servicemen who had received what was known as a Blue Discharge, somewhere between an Honorable Discharge and a Bad Conduct Discharge. Many of them were homosexuals. Because of their Blue discharges they could not get performance bonds ensuring their honesty, and without performance bonds they could not get hired as truck drivers, electricians, salesmen, or a host of other trades. I was an innocent in matters of discrimination, as in so much else. But I'll never forget Roger Baldwin's tolerance, patience, and kindness to all. He dreaded meeting with Elizabeth Gurley Flynn. She smelled bad, he told me, and he disagreed with her on everything that mattered. He just shook his head at the hate preached by Smith and Coughlin, but he listened to them all, and he educated me.

I felt an overwhelming need to keep occupied while I waited for some opportunity to materialize, and so I enrolled in a couple of night courses in the New School for Social Research in Greenwich Village, one of them in fiction writing, taught by James T. Farrell, the author of the *Studs Lonigan* trilogy. Just in case the great American novel was locked somewhere between my belly and my soul. I was keeping all options wide open at that time in my life. But this option soon closed. Twice a week, our assignment was to write 1,500 words of fiction, and I couldn't write 15 words that I had to make up. I could exaggerate my own experience a little, but exaggeration made me feel untruthful. My "fiction" was without exploration of motive or emotion, and in a brief student-teacher session Farrell put me out of my misery. There was a certain facility for describing what I had seen, he said, but nothing interesting when it came to describing emotion. He was not the last to make that observation.

I began hearing about a group of veterans who were gearing up to start a daily newspaper in Manchester, New Hampshire, against the well-entrenched daily then owned by the widow of Colonel Frank Knox, who had been one of FDR's wartime Secretaries of the Navy, and later publisher of the *Chicago Daily News*. The man who picked Manchester as the site of this venture was one Bernie McQuaid, a New Hampshire native and a former *Chicago Daily News* foreign correspondent. The major financial angel was to be Philip Saltonstall Weld, fresh from a tough war with Merrill's Marauders in Burma, and another *Chicago Daily News* alumnus. He was a distant cousin of Jean's, though they didn't know each other. And the third putative founder of this newspaper was none other than Blair "Dry-Hair-in-Chapel" Clark, who had worked briefly for the *St. Louis Post-Dispatch* before going to war as a historian with the Third Army in Europe, under General Patton. The project was still a long way from reality when I talked myself aboard as the first staffer, and persuaded Jean to give Manchester a try. My salary would be $50 a week, half of which would be paid by the federal government under the GI Bill of Rights. My job, not to put too fine a point on it, was "office boy," although I was assured I would be a reporter when we actually started publishing. It was that assurance that made Manchester look better than New York. There certainly wasn't much about Manchester itself, a decrepit mill town, long since deserted by the textile industry for warmer climates and cheaper (non-union) labor.

Jean and I moved up to New Hampshire in February 1946, into

an old schoolhouse, with a one-room cobbler shop attached—in Candia, a few miles east of Manchester. The house cost $2,700, probably because it lacked both running water (no indoor plumbing) and heat of any kind. It would be six months before we actually started publishing, and during that time I swept the office, almost daily, tackled such odd jobs as looking for black market newsprint, and began learning something about this strange little state, which was struggling to find a new identity in the areas of new technology and tourism. There was plenty of spare time, and I spent it fixing up the house. As soon as I could, I put in a heating system and a Franklin stove. Bob Lee spent one of his vacations helping me put new clapboards on the side, plus a new roof. I dug a trench 4 feet deep and 50 feet long from the well to the cellar for running water. Only to be confronted with the very distinct possibility that the new paper would never see the light of day.

Phil Weld suffered from recurring bouts of malaria, contracted in Burma, and during one of them he decided that the losses projected for the new venture were too heavy for him, and he pulled out, taking most of our financing with him. McQuaid didn't have a nickel to invest. Clark had some thread and sewing machine money lying around under the tightfisted control of New York City trustees. I had scrounged up $10,000, half from my great uncle Frank Crowninshield, the magazine publisher, and half from my mother, who had finally inherited some funds, plus my own wartime savings. When we put it all together we had the grand total of $57,000. You haven't been able to start a daily newspaper for that kind of money since the eighteenth century, and our choice was to fold our tents quietly and sneak out of town, or to publish weekly. We came up with the concept of an independent Sunday newspaper, the *New Hampshire Sunday News*, a four-section paper, wrapped in a four-page comic section, the only Sunday paper in New Hampshire. In those days there were successful independent Sunday papers in Wilmington, Delaware, Newark, New Jersey, and Bridgeport, Connecticut.

And we were quickly successful—in circulation. We wrote about illegal stills, missing children, empty mills, polluters and pollution, and farm problems like brucellosis, since I was also the farm editor.

Before long, we were selling more copies on Sunday than either the *Union* or the *Leader* sold daily. That should have produced lucrative advertising, but the advertisers took a decidedly dim view of our crusading spirit, and stayed away in droves. We called ourselves independent, but in the good old Granite State "independent" meant leftist if not Commie in those days.

The editorial success of the *Sunday News* was largely due to Ralph M. Blagden, an extraordinary, intellectual man, then in his early forties, a sometime Christian Scientist, a voracious reader, a great wit, who smoked so much his rimless eyeglasses were always clouded with nicotine residues.

Blair Clark had found him, recuperating from a nervous breakdown, working as a night clerk in an upstate New Hampshire summer resort hotel. He had been the prize-winning managing editor of the *Star-Times* in St. Louis, battling the vaunted *Post-Dispatch* story for story, and winning his share. He was restless, intellectually and physically, skeptical, inquisitive, and enormously energetic.

With only $57,000 in working capital, we could not afford anything like presses or composing-room equipment, so this great young newspaper was created every Saturday in the composing room of the *Haverhill* (Mass.) *Gazette*, some thirty-five miles southeast of Manchester.

We were only seven, working under Ralph Blagden to put out a 64-page newspaper, each of us out of some division of Central Casting:

Ralph "Deak" Morse, from St. Johnsbury, Vermont, was our sports editor, a raw-boned, taciturn man in his mid-forties, who never met a cliché he didn't like—warm, kind, and loved by every jock in New Hampshire, and by me. He referred to his weekly column as "this pillar," and on some Saturday nights he let me sit in for him and cover the Nashua Dodgers in the Class B New England League for the *Sunday News* and the Associated Press. They had a promising pitcher and catcher who were both attracting a lot of attention: Don Newcombe and Roy Campanella.

Elias McQuaid, Bernie's younger brother, and a great reporter and a natural writer under pressure. Elias eventually became a diplomat and got me the job as his successor years later as the press attaché in the American Embassy in Paris. Elias was a born journalist, and a frustrated boulevardier. In the middle of a tough investigative story, he would indulge in flights of fancy that would do Walter Mitty proud, strolling in the Bois de Boulogne, hobnobbing with rogues and royalty, conversing with artists and poets on the Left Bank in Paris. Oblivious to the fact that his charming wife was marooned at the end of a country road, carless and coping with diapers. He was great company then, and again some years later in Paris, where he made his dreams come true.

His older brother, Bernie, whose idea for a new daily had brought us all to New Hampshire, was something else. The son of a Hearst rewrite man in Boston, Bernie had followed Frank Knox to Chicago, when the Colonel had joined the *Chicago Daily News*, and as a protégé of the Colonel had spent some time in Europe as a war correspondent. His view of himself and his importance lay somewhere between inflated and unrealistic. He had a terrible temper; he cheated at golf; he bullied people he felt were below him on the many ladders he occupied. And he resented people with more of anything than he had . . . from money to brains to friends . . . and there were many of them.

"Zeke" Smith, sixtyish and as bald as an eagle whenever he took off his gray fedora, toothless while he worked, fully toothed when he got spiffed up and went prowling at night. Zeke was a born boozer, right out of *The Front Page*. He had written every news story in the world many times. Move Zeke 60 miles south or 600 miles west, change the name of the victim, change the nature of the crime, give the governor a new name. Zeke had written them all. He was a godsend to us, particularly in the beginning, when he would churn out a dozen stories a day without a false start, while the rest of us, particularly me, were en route to sixteen rewrites for treatises on Veterans' Housing.

Norma Oboler was our women's editor; cheerful, educated, bright as can be, a lover of causes by nature and background, she was saddled with writing over and over again, "Given in marriage by her father, the bride wore blah-blah-blah," as she recorded every wedding she could find. She was my first Jewish friend and colleague.

Jay Gallagher was another journeyman journalist who could find an intriguing story wherever he looked, make it interesting, and get it in the paper. I can see him now, pretending to be Hank Luisetti, practicing his fade-away jump shots with crumpled-up copy paper into trash baskets spread about our "city room," an empty storeroom over Abe Machinist's department store.

Chet Davis was our photographer, who could do a little bit of everything, including write a fine story. Chet was the guy you thought of when you read those *Editor & Publisher* ads looking for "Sober pro, must have own Speed Graphic, car. Go anywhere." I see him easily still, looking out of page one, with a bloody nose and a smashed camera, inflicted by some goons who ran an illegal slot machine operation in Derry, New Hampshire.

En route to Haverhill, we would stop by a small lake, get out of the car, and start throwing rocks for distance, and for money. We all *knew* we could beat Blagden, an out-of-shape intellectual, a Christian Scientist, and all that, but week after week we would leave the lake with our arms hanging limply by our sides, while Ralph just beamed.

Blagden had an almost contagious sense of how to find a story and where it might go. For every answer we gave him, he had fifty more questions, and I learned everything from him in two years.

Once he asked me if I had ever written a story for a newspaper before. I said I had, but didn't tell him it was a feature on model ships, when I was sixteen. As I drowned the reader in the complexities of veterans' housing, filtered through American Legion politics and the New Hampshire legislature, Blagden would tell me caustically that "the essence of journalism is superficiality." When I reacted by leaving out details he felt were important, he would remind me, "You can't beat a simple declarative sentence with a few facts in it." I was just about to kill him—and head for Jack Stubbs's brokerage house—when he suddenly said, "Not bad," as if he were reading it for the first time, and flipped it over to the copy desk.

As a group, we were close, united by shared uncertainties, but reveling in the knowledge that we were making a difference, that the establishment—the old boy networks that ran banks and businesses, and the lawyers who ran the politics—resented our intrusive attitudes toward matters which they had decreed were off limits to the press. We lunched together almost every day—mostly at the Puritan Cafe on Amherst Street, a Greek greasy spoon joint where the hamburgers were cheap and the waitresses were pretty (where are you now, Jo?). Blagden would hold us spellbound with stories, about L. Z. Roberts, his publisher in St. Louis, about the legendary O. K. Bovard, the *Post-Dispatch* editor, about sneaking out on the fire escape of the *Christian Science Monitor* for a cigarette. We would hear story after story of how newspaper reporters pursued crooks and scandals, and put politicians in jail, and we dreamed of doing the same thing in New Hampshire. He made newspapering so exciting. He gave such purpose to our lives. We couldn't wait to get to work, and we were in no hurry to get home.

When we did get home, more often than not Jean and I would get together with Blair Clark and his voluptuous wife, Holly. They had a fancier house than we did, a lovely old farm house in Pembroke, New Hampshire, but wherever we ended up for a bottle of Almaden Mountain Red and spaghetti, we talked shop all night. Jean was soon in the decorating business with a friend, Mary McCarthy, in an office in the corner of a paint store on Elm Street. We were trying to have a baby, but that was still some time off. Mostly, we just worked, solving old problems every day, and facing new ones the next morning.

One problem had to do with delivering the *Sunday News*. To keep Sunday newspapers—especially the Sunday *New York Times*—out of New England, the Boston newspaper publishers had come up with a cynical—plainly illegal—scheme. Six days a week, newspapers were delivered to New Hampshire readers by a Boston & Maine Railroad train, which went right up the spine of the state late each night to Montreal, carrying whatever freight anyone wanted to ship, including newspapers. But on Saturday nights, the same train was chartered by the B&M to the Boston Publishers Association, which chose what freight they wanted to take. They chose not to take the *New York Times*, and they chose not to take the *New Hampshire Sunday News*. Our lawyers told us this was a violation of the anti-trust laws, or something, but when it was brought to the attention of my "cousin," Beanie Choate, he just laughed, and said, "Those guys don't have enough money to sue us." Which was true.

In its brief time on this earth—twenty-five months—the *New Hampshire Sunday News* won AP awards for excellence against all the established New England newspapers, even the dailies. We had a regular menu of interesting investigative and feature stories, plus a great, local sports section, women's pages that were frankly women's pages, and four pages of color comics. In less than two years, we had more circulation than any other newspaper in the state. We had two great "crusade" stories, and we had our teeth in a third when we went belly up for lack of advertising.

Annie Reid Knox, the widow of Colonel Frank Knox, sold the well-established *Union-Leader* to the mercurial right-wing nut William Loeb, and Loeb was quick to feed the advertising community's feeling of discomfort with us. His father was Teddy Roosevelt's private secretary and TR was Loeb's godfather. To prove that, and to prove that he wasn't Jewish, Loeb once ran a picture of his certificate of christening in the Episcopal church in the *Union-Leader*. Loeb was bankrolled at first by the Ridder family from St. Paul, Minnesota, until they could no longer stand him. And the Ridder bank roll was replaced by Leonard Finder, son of a prosperous St. Louis match manufacturer. Finder had no background in newspapers, and would have had no place in history had he not written a letter to General Eisenhower, then SHAPE Commander in Europe, urging him to run for president in 1948 *as a Democrat*. Ike's answer, citing a soldier's greater duty, put Finder's name into history's footnotes.

In any case, confronted with carpetbaggers in control of both newspapers, New Hampshire's conservative business leaders chose the right-wing nut over the liberals, and I guess we were doomed.

But that was all for Blair Clark to worry about. That's what publishers are for, isn't it? To worry about money? I was too busy learning from Ralph Blagden—how to write, how to look for stories, how to recognize stories, how to develop stories, how to treat anybody's first version of the facts with skepticism, if not suspicion. I learned so much from that man that I never forgot. I have worked for three great editors, older men who went far out of their way to share their knowledge and insights with me, to encourage me to reach always farther than I had reached before, to listen to other people, to change my mind when necessary. Ralph Blagden was the first. Ken Crawford, the bureau chief and columnist of *Newsweek*, would be the second; and Russ Wiggins, the great editor of *The Washington Post* for twenty-one years, the third.

The first of our two exposés had to do with the New Hampshire state treasurer and his collusion with a Wall Street law firm on a turnpike bond issue, and with a Manchester, New Hampshire, contractor in cahoots with all three. The Wall Street law firm actually wrote the legislation which authorized the turnpike bond issue (which they underwrote, of course), and wrote it in a way that rewarded the state treasurer and the contractor. Both went to jail. Simple and sweet, pretty as you please, incredibly exciting, and what the hell—we did it, this small band of $50-a-week reporters. My first lesson in the First Commandment of investigative journalism: Follow the Money. I also learned that you don't have to be an expert to write expertly about complicated issues. Greek/English majors can write about turnpike bond issues just the way they can drive destroyers. This was enormously comforting, for when I had been assigned to cover a rate increase hearing before the New Hampshire Public Service Commission, I had almost quit journalism. Utility rate hearings defied Blagden's dictum about superficiality—then and now.

Our second classic newspaper story was a steamy, heart-rending saga of backwoods misery, lust, incest, and murder, which ended up as a key part of the Grace Metalious novel (and TV serial), *Peyton Place*. I worked only the sidebars on this one, about a murder case in a forlorn hole of poverty called Gilmanton Iron Works, near the center of the state. Barbara Roberts, a woman in her early twenties, had been sentenced to thirty-years-to-life for murdering her father, after only a one-day trial, in which her court-appointed lawyer had persuaded her to plead guilty to a reduced charge of second-degree homicide.

McQuaid found an older sister who was more than willing to give him the gruesome details, and later he had a gut-wrenching interview with Roberts herself from the jail. The father, a merchant seaman, regularly raped both his daughters, often chaining them to a bed for days. Before leaving on a voyage, he had warned Barbara to meet him at the train station when he came back or he would kill her. Weeks later, a telegram announcing his return arrived too late, so she waited at home with her eleven-year-old brother for their father to return. He arrived in a rage, chasing both children around and around the kitchen table, shouting, cursing, and threatening to kill them both. She finally reached in a drawer for her father's pistol, and shot him dead. They buried him under the barn. Weeks later suspicious neighbors notified the police, and the body was found.

The court-appointed lawyer never raised the issue of self-defense, and somehow persuaded her to plead guilty. The story had everything a struggling newspaper could ask for: sex, violence, lust, human rights violations, and it was a *Sunday News* exclusive. We demanded a new trial or a pardon, or both, as the truth emerged. And Roberts eventually was freed, to the deafening noise of us congratulating ourselves.

Sandwiched between the super-stories, we produced just plain good stories, one after another, at the rate of five or six a week. I followed veterans' affairs, even wrote a Veterans Affairs column for a while. (The Associated Press distributed a weekly veterans affairs column under the byline of one "Major Nial." The major was a nom de plume for two cub reporters who became my good friends a few years later. One was Rowland Evans, who later became half of Evans and Novak, and the other was his assistant Phil Geyelin, who would become editor of *The Washington Post*'s editorial page.)

One night I covered a meeting in which veterans were clamor-

ing (it was a modest clamor; this was 1946) for new housing. One
William G. McCarthy of 788 Hanover Street, who was counsel for
the landowners whose property abutted a proposed veterans housing development, rose to voice his objections. "We're different in
Manchester," he was quoted in the *Sunday News* as saying. "We
don't want any housing projects. We just want to be left alone."
What he actually said, and very clearly, was "Fuck the veterans,"
but Blagden wouldn't let the F word into our family newspaper.
When we reported his objections to any veterans housing in the
story, I got my first libel suit: $10,000. In New Hampshire in those
days, the simple filing of a libel suit forced the sheriff to garnishee
defendant's wages and bank account up to the amount of the suit. I
was still making fifty bucks a week, and I had less than $300 in the
bank, but for weeks I couldn't cash a check and had to live on the
grocery store's credit and the generosity of friends.

I had joined the American Veterans Committee (AVC), largely
on the strength of its idealistic motto: "Citizens first, veterans second." It was conceived from a simple idea that we should forget
about any special privileges due us as veterans, and get on with
the business of building a new world. Chuck Bolte, who had lost
a leg fighting for the Queen's Royal Rifles in North Africa, was
the founder, and he had been joined by some of the young men
who were emerging as spokesmen for my generation. One was Cord
Meyer, whom I had known when he was at Yale (and who was to
become my brother-in-law ten years down the road). Cord had lost
an eye and a twin brother during the Pacific War. He was an aide to
Harold Stassen at the San Francisco Conference that gave birth to
the United Nations. He was soon to be president of the World Federalists, and if my generation was going to have a war hero leader,
Cord looked like a good bet.

As they did to all good organizations of that time, some Communists joined AVC and then tried to take it over. Nationally, that
is. In New Hampshire, we never had more than two hundred members, mostly young, idealistic, and Republican lawyer types. I tried
to recruit, especially on the west bank of the Merrimac River in

Manchester where the French-speaking population lived, descendants of the textile workers imported from Canada. My schoolboy French sounded great to me, but the French Canadian millworkers were unimpressed. It was one thing to speak their language—even with a funny accent—but I had no answers in French or English to their questions: where were the AVC's basketball courts, and clubhouse bars? Nowhere, of course, at a time when even the small towns of America boasted American Legion halls and Veterans of Foreign Wars bars. That's why we never had more than two hundred members in the whole state.

The idealism which had propelled my friends and me into the war was in full flower. As the war was winding down, I had started volunteering to my many different skippers to lead bull sessions with the crew about how the world we had known had changed, how we had changed, and what role we might play in changing it further. Nothing profound, nothing radical; I was neither. But the war had given me and many of my generation a sense of purpose, and a confidence that we could make things happen.

At the paper, of course, idealism came into play only occasionally. Most of the time we were scrambling for new angles to stories that had occurred during the week, and settling for whatever actually happened after the Saturday daily went to press. As in "Salem Liquor Store Broken Into," over eight columns. Or "State Liquor Store Embezzled." But more often than not we had some exposé working. There was the trap set by the Manchester Police Department for a rapist, using an eleven-year-old girl as "bait." The trap backfired; the girl was raped by a thirty-six-year-old man, and I was thrown down the stairs of the police headquarters by Chief James F. O'Neil for asking why.

I had covered O'Neil's successful campaign to become president of the American Legion as my first political campaign, and I had thought we were friends. But when the newspaper suggested that the trap would never have backfired if O'Neil spent more time in Manchester as police chief, and less time traveling all over the country as Legion chief, our friendship had been terminated.

O'Neil was succeeded by George Welch, the best mimic I have ever heard in my life, and a card-carrying practical joker. One morning on my way to work, a ring-necked pheasant had flown into my car. I had taken it to the local butcher to have it plucked, and told friends about the gourmet dinner I was soon to have. The next Saturday night, I had the duty in the Manchester newsroom, covering the state by telephone, and filing late-breaking stuff to the Haverhill newsroom. I got a call from a woman who asked me if I had killed a pheasant out of season earlier in the week. This woman became vituperative when I explained the accident. She said she was a founding member of the SPCA, and was going to report me to the authorities. When I hung up, "she" called back, and this went on for a couple of hours, during the busiest time of the week. Only after the paper had been put to bed did Elias McQuaid let me know I had been had by Welch.

Money was tight, even when my wages, now probably $55 a week, were not being garnisheed. I had landed a second job broadcasting the news on WKBR, a 250-watt radio station in Manchester, at 7:00 P.M. on Saturday nights. That was $25 more a week. At first I was petrified, knowing that I couldn't make the pear-shaped tones which those faceless announcers created so easily. I had a gravelly voice, like many male Bradlees. Later I got more comfortable. Too comfortable, one night. The "news" broadcast consisted of the first paragraph or two of stories that were to appear in next morning's *Sunday News*. My script was the quickly assembled carbon copies of the stories that reporters turned in to the copy desk. One night, when I hadn't even read the stories, I was sailing along, reading the lead of a story by Jay Gallagher. Timing was right on. Inflection was good. When I suddenly let my eyes wander a line or two ahead, as I read. There, like mines in a quiet field, lay the words "Fuck. Fuck. Fuck," signifying that the lead I was reading had been abandoned, but not crossed out. Still reading, I had to look for a place in the new lead to land safely, after leaping over the F-words. Tough on the heart.

On top of broadcasting one night a week, I had landed jobs as a stringer, for *Time-Life*, and less often for *Newsweek*. Stringing for

Life consisted mostly of arranging for photo sessions and then holding the lights for the superstar photographers. But the money was good—sometimes as much as $100 a week. My career as a stringer was cut short when I suggested a story to both *Time* and *Newsweek*. It concerned a new laboratory, the Babson Institute in Wellesley, Massachusetts, built by Roger Babson, a crusty oddball economist, to explore a way to lick gravity. To illustrate this important story, I had Chet Davis pose Babson, standing under an apple tree, holding a pencil at arm's length, point up. A few inches above the pencil point, we had hung an apple by an invisible thread to a branch of the tree.

I filed the same story and the same picture to both magazines, figuring that their legendary compulsion to rewrite everything sent in by their correspondents would keep me out of trouble. Wrong! *Time* loved it so much they decided to send their own correspondent and a *Life* photographer for the following week's book. *Newsweek* loved it, too. And as cheap an outfit as it was, they ran the picture and story without changing a word. *Time* called immediately, and I was off the Luce payroll.

Meanwhile, Jean was working for peanuts as a salesperson in the James W. Hill department store on Elm Street, and was making a few extra bucks as an interior-decorating consultant for a house-painting and upholstering company. She was also pregnant, after countless undignified visits to Dr. John Rock, Boston's pioneer fertility specialist. Our house now had heat, running water, new bathroom facilities, a new roof, and new clapboards. Our social life was still pretty much limited to the Clarks and Eliases and Lilian McQuaid. Visiting the McQuaids was especially fun in the snow. They also lived in Candia, but a mile down a dirt road which was never plowed in winter. Since McQuaid and I felt that putting chains on our tires was a direct insult to our manhood, we often spent more time going to and from the McQuaids than we spent there.

Elias's brother, Bernie McQuaid, had become increasingly depressed and difficult to get along with. He began to pick fights with Clark, his co-publisher, and almost dared me to side with him rather than with my old friend—for whatever my support was worth. Clark and McQuaid eventually split. Blair bought him out for $23,000, and two or three weeks later, Bernie went to work for Loeb, whom he had belittled for so long.

With Bernie in the enemy camp where he belonged, morale soared in the *Sunday News* newsroom. In August 1948, Jean produced a strange-looking baby boy, covered from head to toe with orange-red methiolate when I first saw him, and a small lump rising from one side of his tiny head, courtesy of the forceps at Eliot Hospital, Manchester. The methiolate had been used during blood transfusions, required by an RH incompatibility.

He was gorgeous. The thrill of a child, especially the first child, was like no other thrill in the world. He was Benjamin C. Bradlee, Jr., so named without much thought. Certainly no thought that years later he would say he would have preferred something like Archie. He was born during what felt like the hottest week in the history of Manchester summers, without air conditioning, of course. It was also the week when the *Sunday News* was finally doomed. With Bernie McQuaid pulling the strings, Loeb had begun to talk to advertisers about starting his own Sunday paper, and that put Clark between a rock and a hard place. Either he had to go out and raise a few million, to build a modern plant, and settle into a long, down-and-dirty battle with Loeb, daily and Sunday, or he had to get someone to convince Loeb it would be cheaper to buy us out than start a rival Sunday.

The paper was sold, and there we were, new parents, newly unemployed, and about to be back in the job market once more. But first, I had to get fired by the new owner in order to pick up my severance pay, which I needed to finance a job hunt. A few weeks before selling the paper, Clark had given me a giant raise to $75 a week, and the new title of City Editor. The raise would make it more costly for Loeb to fire me, and the title would dress up the ad I had decided to place in *Editor & Publisher*. Actually, Loeb could have saved himself my severance check ($450) by offering me a job. I would have had to quit, and thus lose my severance. The actual ax was delivered during an interview I had with him, as the stringer for *Time*, to whose good graces I had returned. As the questions got more and more detailed, he became more and more testy, until he finally cut me off with "We won't be needing your services, Mr. Bradlee," and that was that. A glorious, happy two and a half years, exciting, rewarding, unbelievably educational, and great fun from beginning to end.

FIVE

WASHINGTON POST: FIRST TOUR

CITY EDITOR of State's largest newspaper, 27, college graduate, news, feature, slot and make-up experience, will travel anywhere for good job on big daily. Available mid-October. Box 1694, Editor & Publisher.

Thus read my ad under "Situations Wanted" in the September 4, 1948, issue of *Editor & Publisher* . . . barely within the guidelines for truth in advertising. My title *was* City Editor, as if a weekly newspaper with an editorial staff of seven needed a city editor. I had been named City Editor only so I could use the title to find another job, not to direct a staff. We didn't have any full-time copy editors, so my "slot" experience was a bit of a stretch, and my make-up experience had ended abruptly when a union printer named Ike whacked me across the wrist with a column rule when I tried to put a stick of type into a page form.

While I waited for the answers to pour in, I wrote speeches for Dartmouth professor Herb Hill, who was running for governor as a Democrat. Jean and the new baby had moved down to her father's house in Brookline; we had sold our house for $10,000, but hadn't closed yet, and I needed the money. Speechwriting is an art form which I found extremely difficult. It was hard enough to figure out what I thought about the various issues of state government, never mind what the tweedy, pipe-smoking professor felt about them. He was a charming man with all sorts of brains, but no useful experience with voters. Sherman Adams, who was to go on to fame—and shame—as President Eisenhower's chief of staff, won the governorship, going away, and I was out of the Granite State for good.

My "City Editor" ad pulled maybe a dozen replies, most of them from trade publications like *Filling Station Daily*. Two came from real newspapers—one in Salt Lake City, and the other in Santa Barbara, where a man named Ed Kennedy wrote that he was actually looking for a city editor. My hormones weren't excited by Utah, but California did interest me, and Kennedy interested me a lot. He had been the AP war correspondent wrongly accused of prematurely breaking the release announcing that the war with Germany was over. History ultimately concluded that to be a bum rap, and he sounded like a young Blagden to me, as I went quietly crazy with my in-laws, a new baby, and no job.

After the 1948 elections wiped out my Dartmouth professor, I started making lists of where I might find work. One of these lists, titled "FUTURE BOOK," read as follows:

SUPER SERVICE STATION. . . . Want me; don't want.

NEW ENGLAND RETAIL GROCER. . . . Definite, but will refuse.

WASHINGTON POST. . . . Improbable, but want; working.

COWLES chain: Des Moines, Minneapolis. Good references, would want, possible.

Next two years probably don't matter geographically, if the job is good and the direction is up. Washington and foreign experiences could wait, and should, maybe.

I had two great letters from family friends—Edward Weeks, the editor of the *Atlantic Monthly*, and Christian Archibald Herter, the aristocratic Massachusetts congressman and former governor.

Weeks had written an editor he knew at the *Baltimore Sun*. Herter had written Herbert Elliston, who was the editor of *The Washington Post*'s editorial page.

Thus modestly armed at the end of November 1948, I withdrew all but a few dollars in my savings account ($825 sticks in my mind), bought a round-trip train ticket from Boston to Baltimore to Washington to Salt Lake City to Santa Barbara, and boarded The Federal at South Station . . . shaking in my boots.

The heavens opened up and it just plain poured as the train neared Baltimore early next morning. That lovely city was not so lovely in the rain. I decided on the spur of the moment to stay on the train until Washington, and start the job search at *The Washington Post*. I probably would not have gotten a job at the *Sun* that day, but my world might certainly have changed—and some other people's worlds—if the sun had been shining that day.

A few hours later, I had checked into my $6-a-night room at the Willard Hotel, crossed 14th Street, and walked nervously up the stairs of the Post Building to keep an appointment with Elliston. Trouble was, he had absolutely nothing to do with the newsroom, and couldn't have hired me if he had anything like that in mind. He was overtly uninterested in me, and I couldn't keep my eyes off the bust of himself right behind him. Very good likeness, it was. He did send me downstairs for my first encounter with the highly controversial—and able—city editor, Ben Gilbert. It is hard to re-create the fear I felt. This was the city room of a newspaper where every reporter I admired would die to work. *The Washington Post* was losing money. Everyone knew that. It was the third Washington daily in a field of four, in circulation. It was notoriously stingy with salaries, but it had a wonderful reputation for crusading journalism, fearing no man and no subject. To be specific about it, the true glory of its staff consisted of a powerful editorial page, the great Herb Block as the cartoonist, and the equally great Shirley Povich as the sports editor/columnist. Unmatched in their fields, and warm and generous men to boot. Forty-five years later, as this is written, Herb draws his cartoons at the age of eighty-five with the same bite he has always had. At the age of eighty-nine, when the baseball strike robbed readers of a World Series in 1994, Shirley re-created—from memory—the World Series of 1924, starring the long-gone Washington Senators.

The gods that had kept me on the train in Baltimore were still smiling. A reporter had quit unexpectedly the very day before, so there was a vacancy. Gilbert and the managing editor, Russ Wiggins, knew all about the *New Hampshire Sunday News*, much to my amazement (Gilbert had worked in St. Louis for the *Post-Dispatch* and for the *Star-Times* when Blagden was managing editor there), and before I could believe it, they were leading me to hope I was their candidate to fill the vacancy. Except that money was so tight, publisher Phil Graham had to sign off on every hire, in case he wanted to hold the vacancy and save a few thousand bucks. Next day, he didn't, and believe it or not, I had a job—at $80 a week, starting on Christmas Eve.

Before I actually went to work at the *Post*, I got a call from Ed Thompson, the managing editor of *Life* magazine. And damned if he didn't offer me a job—for almost twice the salary, $150 a week, in *Time-Life's* Atlanta Bureau. I could hardly believe that, either. As a Bostonian, I was leery (read ignorant) of the South, and I preferred writing and reporting to setting up photo assignments. Anyway, I had accepted a job, and couldn't in good conscience quit it before I put in a day's work.

By Christmas Eve, 1948, we had a small house and garden at 2911 Dumbarton Avenue in Georgetown (for $170 a month): a basement kitchen and dining room, one big living room on the street-level floor, and three small bedrooms and one small baby on the second floor. As the newest staffer, I drew the night shift—2:00 to 11:00 P.M.—and had to split my days off with at least one weekend work day.

A week later, on New Year's Eve, I had to do the obligatory day story, and there it was on the front page, two columns above the fold, my first byline in the big time:

Washingtonians Go All-Out To Welcome the New Year In

Washington said good riddance to 1948 in a multitude of ways
last night, and joined the rest of the Nation in welcoming 1949
with open arms and hopeful hearts.

I worked like a dog to make that story readable and I swelled
with pride at the results. Eighty bucks a week *and* a front page byline in a great newspaper? The byline was "By Ben Bradlee, Post
Reporter," which Walter Lippmann soon told me had to go. "That's
a sportswriter's byline," he said, with an inflection that suggested I
should aim a little bit higher.

Professionally, my first weeks were mostly spent rewriting handouts from civic associations, which ended up as little one-paragraph
items scattered throughout the paper, often for make-up purposes
only, to fill out a short news column. The very first day, I had handed
one in to the night city editor, John Riseling, with Phil Graham's
name misspelled. My first real break came when Russ Wiggins was
giving vent to one of his regular tirades against the evil and prev-
alence of gambling, which he regarded as a sin against common
sense, especially among the poor who gambled with grocery money.
Why not take the new reporter, he asked Gilbert, and sic him on
the bookies and numbers kingpins? No one in town knew me yet,
Wiggins figured, and I could poke around unnoticed. I had received
my first investigative assignment for the paper.

Not a betting man myself, I knew enough to start looking for the
answers in the Sports Department, particularly with my new buddy
there, Morris Siegel. Mo was great company, funny, disrespectful,
and warm. He was the particular favorite of Sara Bassin, who ran
the restaurant next to the *Post*, cashed our paychecks, and told us to
go home before it was too late. When I asked Mo for the names of
the ten biggest bookies in Washington, he grabbed a piece of copy
paper and started scribbling some names: Snags, who did numbers,
too. Gary, who ran the Atlas Club, an after-hours joint upstairs in
the building between Bassin's and the *Post*. Mo checked with his
pals and made one phone call, and gave me a list with ten names,

plus addresses and telephone numbers. I didn't feel I could go back to Russ Wiggins that fast. He had given me the assignment less than half an hour before. So I waited a day, typed the list out on regular *Post* stationery, and gave it to him two days later.

Wiggins looked at the list, shook his head in apparent admiration, and told Gilbert, "We got a damned good man in this new fellow, Bradlee. I've been trying to get that list for years."

Mo's kindness got me off rewriting handouts and onto an assignment to Municipal Court, where those on the lowest rung of the Washington ladder landed when they ran afoul of the law. Hookers, bookies, numbers runners, drug addicts, mashers, the victims and the perpetrators of the day's violence. A Washington institution was Police Lieutenant Roy Blick's Vice Squad, whose apple-cheeked young officers specialized in men's rooms. They would stand at public urinals around town—movie theaters, Lafayette Park, and others—wave their tallywhackers around until someone waved back, and bang: arrest for solicitation for immoral purposes. Pretty regularly, the cops would come up with some sad soul who could be described as important, maybe someone who worked for a senator, or maybe the CIA, and the desk would want a story.

The Circulation Department loved me in those days, first because our circulation was not that strong, maybe 160,000 ("and maybe some water in that," according to some experts), and because we had an early bulldog edition, which at that time had to have an eight-column banner every night, to attract buyers among the movie crowd. Harry Gladstein, the circulation chief, took to coming into the city room about six every night, wandering over to my desk to see what salacious junk I was working on, and then going over to Russ Wiggins just before story conference to report: "Bradlee's got a blind one picked up in Lafayette Park, works for the CIA." Sensitivity training was still a generation away. An eight-column banner in the bulldog might boil down to a few paragraphs inside in later editions, when the size of the headline reflected the judgment of the editors about the importance of the news, not the importance of street stand sales.

The best part of the Municipal Court beat was that I was in the paper with three or four stories a day, learning how to write tightly and I hoped with some flair. Unlike today, editors were stingy with bylines then. You started writing your stories only a couple of inches from the bottom of the copy paper to provide space for the copy editors to write the headline. We all became adept at leaving enough space for a headline and a byline, but the bylines were few and far between.

The real bonus of my Municipal Court experience came the very first day I was down there, when I was looking over the cast of characters for someone to have lunch with. A tall, muscular man with wavy hair and a rogue's grin stood out from the others like a preacher in a den of thieves. He was Edward Bennett Williams on *his* first day of legal practice under his own shingle, after years of trying damage cases for a large firm. We had lunch at some greasy spoon. We talked aimlessly, a little about New Hampshire, where his wife's family had a summer place, a little about the notorious Fifth Street Bar Association, an informal club of pretty much run-of-the-mill criminal lawyers. You wouldn't go to one if you were in real trouble, but they knew the cops, and the clerks and the judges . . . and thus, the stories. Ed and I would be best buddies for the rest of our lives.

Socially, our crowd consisted of young couples, around thirty years old, with young kids, being raised without help by their mothers, and without many financial resources. The Janneys—Mary and Wistar, who worked for the CIA; the Winships—Liebe and Tom, who worked for Senator Lev Saltonstall of Massachusetts; Sue and Nick Nikoloric, who worked for Abe Fortas's law firm; Scotty and Jack Lanahan—she was F. Scott Fitzgerald's daughter, and he, too, was a lawyer; Tony and Steuart Pittman, another lawyer. The men were mostly working at the lower levels of government, journalism, or law. We ate with each other at night, bringing the babies and one dish, or one gallon of Almaden Mountain Red or White at three bucks a gallon. We all had interesting jobs, or we thought we did. We were all involved one way or another with the events taking place in the sleepy southern town that World War II had made the capital of the free world, to quote Phil Graham. We had a confidence in ourselves and in each other that seems to have disappeared a half century later. We knew we were going to make a difference, and have a good time doing it.

We shared big-shot friends with each other. Ours were Walter Lippmann and his wife. They were our hidden assets as we started out in Washington. They would ask Jean and me to their famous cocktail parties three or four times a year, where we could rub elbows with everyone who had been or was going to be on page one. They all seemed extremely surprised to see *The Washington Post's* latest cub reporter in such heady company. Once or twice a year Lippmann would come to dinner, and a bunch of us would sit on the floor (Rowlie Evans, Phil Geyelin, or Bob Lee) and ask him questions about national and international affairs, searching for the historical perspective that he mixed with his insider knowledge. Lippmann was the star journalist of his time, a teacher, a student of the philosopher Santayana, a disciple of Colonel House, Wilson's *éminence grise* in the White House during and after World War I, and at the postwar peace conferences. Only a handful of newspapers could afford reporters who had anything like his expertise, and so for much of the newspaper-reading world, and for all of Washington, he *was* the foreign expert.

On one of these big-shot-sharing evenings we all ended up in the Bethesda house of Nick and Sue Nikoloric. He was a second-generation Yugoslav, who worked with the blue-ribbon law firm of Arnold, Fortas & Porter. Nick had been on the cover of *Life* magazine during World War II, illustrating an article on PT boats in Pacific combat. His big shot was Owen Lattimore, a State Department Far East Asian expert, then regularly on page one being bludgeoned by red-baiting Joe McCarthy as a Commie or a Comsymp. Lattimore was Abe Fortas's client, and Nick was Abe Fortas's ace assistant. That particular night Lattimore had brought along a Mongolian priest in flowing robes, who looked like the Dalai Lama or the Dalai Lama's cousin, In any case we peppered both of them with questions and Mountain Red, when Tom Winship surprised us all by asking the Dalai Lama (or his cousin) if he would sing us a Mongolian song. The wine had dissipated what had seemed unbreachable inhibitions, and suddenly he was singing in the high, whining monotone of Asian music. We were all amazed and grateful, until Tom told the priest he should learn some American songs, and much to our surprise—since Tom is completely tone-deaf—started singing a few bars of "Fair Harvard," and urging him to follow along, which he did.

Lattimore was the quintessential old China hand, many of whom had lived in China as children of American missionaries. Now they were charged by the McCarthyites with losing China. Several of them had already been run out of town. Lattimore would not talk about the fix he was in, nor did he crack a smile when his Mongolian friend tried to bend his vocal cords around "Fair Harvard."

In the summer of 1949, I graduated from Municipal Court to general assignment, the best reporting job on any newspaper, because you never really know what you will end up doing before the day is over. I was still concentrating on people in trouble, many of them on trial or on their way to the courthouse. Axis Sally, a cold fish from Maine who had broadcast Nazi propaganda from Germany to the Allies en route to Berlin. Judith Coplon, a low-level Justice Department employee who fell in love with a Soviet spy, Valentin Gubitchev, and slipped him a few secrets every so often. And then there was the great Bernice Franklin, the prototypical waitress with a heart of gold and dyed red hair at the People's Drug Store fountain on Thomas Circle, who was the star witness in the government's case against a major gambling operation.

Bernice had six children in various foster homes around Washington, and yet she was still joyous, cheerful, pretty, and when I met her, in love with a crippled newsstand operator named Till Acalotti. Just after midnight, one night, Bernice looked out the drugstore window and watched two police detectives beat the living daylights out of her boyfriend, leaving him unconscious on the sidewalk. Bernice knew Acalotti took numbers and horse bets on the side, and she knew he had to pay off the cops to stay in business at that choice location, but this was too much for her. Sometime after she got off work, she went down to the FBI and told her story to two agents, Downey Rice and Daniel O'Conor. The Fibbies poked around for a week, wondered whether it was big enough for J. Edgar Hoover's ego, and came to the *Post* newsroom for help.

Russ Wiggins was beside himself. This was the case that would crack big-time gambling once and for all, and embarrass the *Post*'s very own bête noire, Chief of Police Robert Barrett, who epitomized the essentially racist and selective law enforcement the *Post* was trying to change. Wiggins called for his newly discovered expert on bookmaking, and teamed me with Dick Morris, also known as the fastest typist in the newspaper business, and a future vice president of the Ford Motor Company. We interviewed Bernice Franklin, taking down her story from the time she was born. When we started hearing about bookmaking and numbers bets and paying off cops, we trotted her upstairs to Phil Graham's office. His secretary, DeVee Fisher, was a notary public, and she typed out Bernice's story as we dragged it out of her, put her under oath, and got her to sign it. Morris and I could then write her story, and source it "according to a sworn deposition received by *The Washington Post*." That sounded more bulletproof than it probably was, but it had enough authority to drive both the cops and the other newspapers crazy, especially *The Washington Times-Herald*, a jazzy, scrappy, and right-wing daily, owned by Eleanor Medill "Cissy" Patterson, a cousin of the legendary Colonel Robert McCormick of the staunchly right-wing, isolationist *Chicago Tribune*.

Morris or I checked in with Bernice once a day, whether or not we were doing a story. The U.S. Attorney had convened a grand jury, and the jurors heard Bernice's story with interest. Indictments based largely on her testimony were expected momentarily, when all of a sudden our star witness turned up missing. No rendezvous with Morris or Bradlee was kept, no one answered her phone. She wasn't living in Acalotti's apartment anymore. She had vanished, and one day we found out why.

". . . Star Girl Witness About Faces, Unfolds New Version of Gaming Probe": McCormick's *Times-Herald*'s eight-column banner announced, in two lines of 86-point type, that *they* had Bernice.

Wiggins, Gilbert, and everyone at the *Post* went ballistic. Morris and I were accused of carelessness, at the least, maybe more.

Had either of us showed more than a professional interest in Miss
Franklin, we were asked. I hadn't, thank God. Neither had Morris, he said. Anyway, we were told to get the hell out of the city
room and find her. And bring her back alive, ready to sing her song
once more for *Post* readers. We scoured the city without success. All
her old haunts. She wasn't at People's. Acalotti was a no-show at
the newsstand. The Washington cops were rooting for the *Herald*,
against the hated *Post*. We prowled the District's after-hours clubs,
where Bernice had hung out. Nothing. Finally the FBI found her.
We sweet-talked her back to DeVee Fisher in Graham's office. She
really did like us better, she assured us, but we had paid her nothing,
only bought her dinner a couple of nights. The *Times-Herald* had
done more for her, she said, but provided no specifics. Anyway, the
crisis was over. Wiggins was back in his chair, smiling. Indictments
came down. Her testimony forced the defendants to give up in
midtrial and plead guilty. And the caravan moved on.

Sometime during my first six months at the *Post*, our distinguished
Pulitzer Prize-winning White House correspondent Eddie Folliard
("Mr. Folliard" to me) asked me if I would like to visit the White
House some day, preferably Saturday, as his guest. I showed up that
morning, excited and nervous. I'd never been in the White House,
and I'd never met a president.

FDR was the first president I ever saw, only briefly and from
quite a distance. It was a cold, rotten, misting fall day in October
1944, at the Back Bay Station in Boston. I was on leave from the
Philip which was being repaired in Oakland, after getting sprayed by
shore batteries in Saipan. The president was in Boston, campaign-
ing for his fourth term, and I just happened to see him as he was
being handed down the step of a Pullman car in his wheelchair onto
the station platform. Manhandled down the step. I remember being
shocked to see how handicapped he was, since I, along with most of
America, had never seen him in his wheelchair. His upper body ca-
reened from side to side, awkwardly. His face looked gray, although
I was too far away to be sure. In five months he would be dead.

At the White House, Mr. Folliard and I were going slowly from room to room in the office space, when it became obvious from everyone bustling around that something unusual was going on. Apparently the president was about to receive a delegation of French big shots, led by the president of the French Senate, Gaston Monnerville, and no one could find the translator. Suddenly I heard Folliard tell someone that "young Mr. Bradlee here speaks French," and I was being asked if I would serve as the translator for Mr. Truman. I was much surer that I would serve than I was that I *could* serve. But in for a nickel, in for a dime. I figured some of the French politicians probably spoke some English, but I drew confidence from the conviction that none of the people around President Truman spoke any French. I made do, and we were out of there in less than fifteen minutes, and I felt wonderfully lucky.

The fact is, I was lucky. I was on a roll being in the right place at the right time, a luck that has stayed with me.

Luck was with me on one sunny afternoon in June 1949, as I came out of Bassin's restaurant and looked up at the Willard Hotel across 14th Street. I saw a soldier climb slowly over the rail on the ninth floor, grab it with both hands behind him, slowly getting ready to dive 110 feet down into the intersection of 14th Street and Pennsylvania Avenue, two blocks east of the White House and half a block west of the Washington Post Building. Without thinking really, I counted up from street level to the iron railing, and rushed across 14th Street into the hotel. Luck again when I saw an open window at the end of the hall, as the elevator stopped. I still find it hard to believe, but I crawled out on the ledge, between the building and the railing, and inched my way maybe 100 feet west toward Private First Class Paul J. McDuff, nineteen, from Bolling Air Force Base. For once, I had copy paper and a pencil with me, and as I got close, I could hear a voice talking slowly and carefully to him from a window around the corner, and I could see the cops, one floor up, getting ready to try to lasso him. I hadn't gone to shorthand school yet, but I filled every scrap of paper I had with the dramatic conversations, from start to finish.

"Let's talk it over, Mac. We got a lot to talk about. . . just talk it over with me for two minutes. That's all. . . . Don't jump now,

Mac. You've got your whole life to go. . . . Hey, son, don't jump now . . . you know that's a long way down there. . . . What would your mother think of you now? Me, I got no mother, but if I had I wouldn't hurt her for anything in the world." The voice belonged to Police Private L.A. Wallace.

Then suddenly another policeman sprang from a low crouch under a horizontal bar, wrapped his right arm around McDuff, and wrestled him back over the rail to safety as the gathering crowd cheered nine floors below.

As I crept backward on the two-foot-wide ledge to the window which I had climbed through, I knew I had one hell of a story, barely pausing to realize I had been a damn fool. Never mind the danger of falling myself, or scaring the GI into some act he never really meant to commit, but I could have interfered with the rescue attempt had the cops chosen to come my way after him, and found me between them and their target. But they didn't, the window was still open, and I had my page-one story. Hughie Miller, the legendary photo director of the *Post*—he was legendary because he was so tight he gave the photographers only a few exposures of 35mm film, not an entire roll—even snapped a picture of the whole thing from the roof of the Post Building, which ran 14 inches deep and four columns wide on page one. Only I could positively identify that figure crouched in the shadows behind the railing.

In June 1949, I covered the race riots in Anacostia with Jack London (named after the great novelist), who went to law school during the day and reported for the *Post* at night. Only the *Post* didn't call them race riots. Over the dead bodies of Bradlee and London, we called them "incidents," or "disturbances," or "demonstrations." The fight was over who could swim in what public pools. There were six such pools in the District of Columbia, all of them under the jurisdiction of the U.S. Department of the Interior. Three of the pools were for whites only (including the pool at Anacostia), and three of the pools were for Negroes only. My first encounter with "de facto" segregation. In Washington, the *Star* and the *News* still used the term "colored" to describe all blacks, whether or not race was germane to a story. At the *Post*, the rule was: never describe a person's race unless a description was necessary to make the story understandable. We used the term "Negro" then; the terms "black" or "African American" had not yet been born.

A bunch of young Wobblies from the Philadelphia and New York City branches of what was left of Henry Wallace's Progressive Party had decided that the integration of Washington's public swimming pools would be a worthy summer project. And thus they started to show up in the sweltering summer heat with young black kids in tow during the last two weeks in June. Once six black kids managed to get into the water briefly at one of the white pools, until they were booed and splashed out by about fifty whites. Lifeguards were asking to be relieved of duty, fearing disturbances they would be unable to handle. Crowds were getting bigger and emotions were getting hotter. And newspapers—the *Post* included—were scared to death of the story. Scared of telling the truth, and almost surely starting riots; scared of not telling the truth at a cost to their honor and reputations.

Washington was segregated halfway into the twentieth century. Restaurants could legally deny blacks service, and they routinely did. The black community was barely covered, even by the *Post,* which under Russ Wiggins and Ben Gilbert pioneered in this controversial area. Incidents were routinely not covered because they involved blacks. I remember listening to the police radio describe a crime soon after I came to work, and asking the night city editor if he wanted me to go out on it. "Naw," he answered, "that's black." A prize possession of one *Post* photographer of the time showed him sitting on his heels with the Capitol dome in the background holding the head of a black man, who had just committed suicide by throwing himself under a trolley. It had been taken by another city photographer. No story ever appeared about the man's death, which occurred in broad daylight on Pennsylvania Avenue.

At 3:00 P.M. on June 28, the police radio broadcast a "trouble call" in Anacostia, and London and I raced to respond. For the next six hours, we watched a pitched battle between whites and blacks in the field surrounding the swimming pool. Mounted park police rode their horses up and down the no-man's-land between the warring factions. Both sides were armed with homemade clubs, some of the clubs with nails sticking out of them. Waves of whites would periodically break out of the crowd to chase those whites they believed to be responsible for trying to integrate the pools, or to corner blacks. Blacks would go after isolated whites, wherever they could find them. In all, about four hundred persons were involved, equally divided by race. At least twenty cops were in the middle of the riots, with more in ready reserve.

London and I ran with each group. We covered it like war correspondents, close as skin to the action. We filed to the desk—the day city editor and the rewrite people—by telephone every half hour. When night fell, and the crowds dispersed, we headed back to the office, knowing we had a hell of a story, and knowing we had covered the hell out of it. In the cab, we wondered if anything else in the world had happened which might prevent us from leading the paper, at least in the bulldog edition.

We grabbed the bulldog edition as it came up from the press room. Our story wasn't on page one. Un-fucking-believable! Nothing in the rest of the A section. On the split page, the front page of the second section, usually the local or Metro Section in those days, still nothing. Not a goddamn word, and we started seething out loud. Things got worse when we finally found "it" inside the local section. Except that the story was not about the race riot we had just covered. The headline read: "G.S.I. [Government Services, Inc., overseen by the Interior Department] Will Run McKinley Pool/As District Board Withdraws." The first mention of Anacostia in the story was in paragraph 8: "No incident occurred at the Anacostia pool during the morning swimming period. . . ." The words "melee," "fracas," and "scuffle" showed up in paragraphs 9–11. And the events of the afternoon and evening were described as an "incident" near the end of the story.

Almost forty-three years later, Ben Gilbert wrote about the "incident" in a report on race relations at the *Post*, commissioned by publisher Don Graham, entitled "Lifting the Veil from the Secret City . . . *The Washington Post* and the Racial Revolution":

John Riseling, the night city editor, telephoned this writer [i.e., Gilbert himself, then the city editor] at home to brief him about what had happened to suggest that the day desk follow it the next day. Riseling related the complaints by Bradlee and London, saying they were "doing a rain dance" in the city room.

And that's exactly what we had done, full of indignation about how the great liberal *Washington Post* was scared to tell the truth, how the editors were so much a part of the establishment that we didn't dare talk about race unless we were running some sappy story about a black achiever, or some safe story about a white bigot. London was going to be a lawyer, so he wasn't worried about his newspaper career, but I had been at the *Post* only seven months and had nowhere else to go. But we were steamed, and let everyone know it.

Suddenly I felt this tap on my shoulder, and wheeled around to find myself facing Phil Graham, the publisher, in a tuxedo. "All right, Buster," he said, "come on up with me." He took me upstairs to his office on the fifth floor of the old Post Building. There—I couldn't believe my eyes—was Julius "Cap" Krug, the Secretary of the Interior, who was ultimately responsible for the city pools, his Under Secretary, Oscar Chapman, and representing the White House, President Truman's special counselor, Clark Clifford. All of them were in tuxedos, as I remember it.

Graham asked me to tell my story to these members in such good standing of the Washington power structure. Nervous at first, I turned myself on as I talked. When I was done, I was dismissed with a "Thanks a lot," and that was that. The story on page B2 did not change between editions, but the next day, it moved to the front page: "Anacostia Pool Is Closed/Until Further Notice." The story included the names of those wounded and those arrested, the number of police (100), and the number in the crowd (450). It was still referred to as a "disturbance."

Not until much later did I learn what went on in Graham's office. The publisher cut himself quite a deal with the big shots: Close the Anacostia pool immediately, and promise that all six pools will operate the following year on a totally integrated basis, or Bradlee's story runs on page one tomorrow. Krug and company had made the deal on the spot, despite the fact that meant one pool would be closed for the two hottest months in a sweltering city still largely without air conditioning.

That's a deal that no publisher would dare make today. First, blacks wouldn't stand for it. The days of whites making decisions involving blacks without their participation are long gone, and good riddance. Second, the deal could never be kept secret, and the deal depended on secrecy. Reporters would talk. Whistleblowers would blow their whistles. Journalism reviews would publish all the details. *Time* and *Newsweek*'s Press departments would put on a full-court press. Newsroom outrage, that new flowering of American democracy, would erupt.

But tell me how the world would be better if that deal had *not* been made? We would surely have had some kind of race riot that summer or the next. Instead, we had nothing like a race riot for nineteen years, until 1968, when riots were triggered by Dr. Martin Luther King, Jr.'s, assassination.

I am instinctively pro sunshine, against closed doors, pro let-it-all-hang-out, anti smoke-filled rooms. I believe that truth sets man free. I hate to yield even an inch of this high ground, but I am less sure today than I was when Phil Graham made his secret deal that the public is best served by knowing everything the second an incident happens.

After the riots were over, I returned to a steady diet of the abnormal, relishing the good stories, but beginning to chafe at the minor shadow these stories cast on the great issues of the day . . . like Senator Joe McCarthy, for instance, who was just starting down his infamous, Red-baiting path, never mind the rebuilding of Europe, and the Korean War. But for days at a time, dreams of replacing Walter Lippmann dissolved in that greatest of all joys: a good story.

I was on a trolley car going past the White House one November day in 1950, when two Puerto Rican extremists, Oscar Collazo and his confederate, Griselio Torresola, opened fire on Blair House, where President Truman and his family were staying while the

White House was being repaired. And thus I was the first reporter on the scene of that crazy assassination attempt, as I crawled on my stomach in plain sunlight east on Pennsylvania Avenue, with the body of White House Police Private Leslie Coffelt on my left, near the Blair House steps, and a body in front of me, the dead Griselio Torresola. That got me a page-one eyewitness story.

And there were others. Reuben Revens, a forty-one-year-old Army psychological warfare "expert," moonlighted as a sex therapist. He went to trial on charges of assault involving an attractive forty-eight-year-old woman who was having trouble in bed with her Veterans Administration husband. Revens's "treatment" was viewed by the government as assault: He had grabbed her head and forced her to fellate him in front of her husband. I couldn't figure out a way to describe this assault in a family newspaper, so I had to write two stories every night, after I got back from the courthouse. One for the paper, and one for the devotees of this genre of journalism—led by Phil Graham, who would check into the city room to read the latest Revens installment before he went home.

There was a disturbed young man who took his wife and baby on a picnic one sunny day, split the wife in two with an ax as she squatted to relieve herself, then buried the baby alive. I simply had no frame of reference to understand that kind of behavior, and I called a psychiatrist Jean and I had been seeing for guidance. Julius Schreiber was more interested in my weirdo criminals than he was in Jean and me, I think, but he told me to try to get into this chap's house. I talked his mother into letting me into the house and then upstairs into his bedroom. It was as strange as he was. Everything caked with dust, literally up to a quarter of an inch thick. He had forbidden his mother to enter the bedroom. Five dead goldfish lay in the upper left drawer of his bureau.

Jean and I had started seeing Julius Schreiber because our marriage had stalled. Ever since the war, the newspaper business had consumed me. I loved it. I was in love with it, I guess, and there was nothing comparable in Jean's life. The war had stopped in its tracks the discovery process, where young friends are supposed to mature into lovers, and where shared experiences are supposed to grow into common interests and common passions. We never really got much past being young friends. We were both so sexually inexperienced and culturally unadventuresome in that department, we never found ourselves as lovers. It depressed me to read that men reached their peak sexually at age eighteen. Since reaching eighteen I had been forced to abstain by war almost longer than I had been able to perform in peace.

As 1950 became 1951, I was feeling more and more frustrated by my assignments, gamey and entertaining as they were. My salary hovered on the wrong side of $100 a week. *The Washington Post* was still losing $1 million a year, and there was nothing on the horizon that looked like an expansion large enough to put me on the National staff, where I wanted to be. (The *Post* had no international staff in those years.) I felt appreciated, and my writing ability was improving, but there were two or three or four reporters on the city staff with skills and seniority greater than mine. Our friends were moving up in their law firms, or in the CIA, or on the various government staffs, and I felt impatient.

Just at this time, I got offered a job. This had never happened to me before. The offer came from Frank Pace, then Secretary of the Army, former Budget Bureau Director, and later the young president of General Dynamics. He had never heard of me, but he was married to Wistar Janney's sister, and one night at the Janneys' he mentioned he was looking for a personal assistant/press person, who would travel with him, write speeches, and generally spread the gospel according to Pace. One afternoon, I found myself in the Pentagon walking into the biggest office I had ever seen, with blue plush carpet as high as my loafers, for an interview with the Secretary. Pace had his back to me. He was hunched over, elbows on his knees, talking into a tape recorder hidden somewhere in what looked like a Magnavox record player. His message was cornball, inspirational, and I got the feeling this might have been the outline of a speech he would want someone to write for him. When he finally turned around, he did his best to put me at ease. The job would entail quite a lot of traveling, he said. (The first trip would have been to accompany President Truman and Pace to Wake Island, where the president was going to confer with General Douglas MacArthur six months before firing him for making persistent public demands for a bigger war against Red China, which was contrary to U.S. and U.N. policy, but of course I knew nothing about that.)

The money was good—almost twice what I was making as a reporter. And the idea of some travel was a plus (I had been as far as Pittsburgh once for the *Post*, covering a great train robbery), but I couldn't conceive of being someone else's alter ego. And so I turned it down.

One night I was sent over to the Statler Hotel, where Joe McCarthy was preaching to some group of the converted, not to cover his speech but to ask him a specific question, which I have long since forgotten. McCarthy's answer would be an insert in another reporter's page-one story, and I felt I was being told something important about my place in the pecking order. Anyway, I asked him the question. He answered by asking me if I minded revealing what newspaper I represented. I told him, and the whole room broke out in snickers, led by the snickering senator himself. I felt unarmed, unable to defend the paper or myself, playing too small a role to make a difference.

Just then, I got a letter from my old buddy Elias McQuaid in Paris. When the *New Hampshire Sunday News* had been sold to Loeb—and Bernie McQuaid had hired on to edit it—Elias had quit to work on a paper in Boston briefly, and then had joined the Foreign Service. By some miracle he had ended up as press attaché at the American Embassy in Paris, close enough to the boulevardier he had dreamed of becoming. He was going to be transferred in about six months, and he was writing to ask if I had any interest in coming over first as his assistant, and then as his successor—if he and his mentor at the State Department could arrange it.

I had zero interest in becoming a career diplomat. What little I knew about the Foreign Service suggested that the cover-your-ass crowd frowned on balls and initiative, especially at the lower levels. But the State Department was experimenting with journalists who spoke the appropriate foreign language to be press attachés. I hated to leave the *Post*, which had given me everything I wanted except assignments that touched on the great issues, or even an important issue. I was in irons. Jean hadn't really wanted to go to New Hampshire or Washington, and even though she spoke a little French, she was not at all keen on moving to Paris.

The whole question almost became moot when I flunked the oral exams, given by the United States Information Service (USIS). Press attachés were reserve Foreign Service officers, but administratively they were part of USIS. When I was asked if I was ready to serve as press attaché anywhere in the world, I said I was going to serve as press attaché in Paris. And that was the wrong answer, even though there was no way I was going to quit the *Post* to be the press attaché in Antarctica. That was straightened out when I got a second crack at the orals through the good offices of McQuaid's mentor, the Embassy administrative officer, Graham Martin. The same Graham Martin who became U.S. Ambassador to Thailand and Vietnam. The same Graham Martin who was to become the bane of liberals, as he fled Saigon from the roof of the American Embassy in April of 1975. I was ready to say I was panting to be the press attaché in Antarctica, but was not asked the question this time.

The USIS then offered me the job, and I had to decide. My salary was to be $5,400 a year, plus a modest housing allowance. Finally, I persuaded Jean—and myself—that this was still a time to be adventuresome. When and how would we ever get a chance to live abroad again? We could never get as good a place to live as Paris.

SIX

PARIS I—PRESS ATTACHÉ

We boarded the U.S.S. *America* in New York on a sunny day in June 1951, with all our worldly possessions. I was two months shy of thirty, and young Ben not quite three years old. I was excited and apprehensive at starting such a new chapter in such a fabulous part of the world, at such an interesting time in history. I was just developing a sense of who I was and what I was doing with my life, and now I was taking a right-angle turn. I had no great confidence in my skills as a diplomat, to put it gently, nor was I optimistic about how much the diplomats would appreciate me.

Jean was reluctant to leave a life that had become comfortable, even if it was not without its trials. Mostly me. The problems of finding an apartment, finding a school for Ben, finding a *bonne à tout faire*, finding new friends, all in a foreign language, and all on a shoestring, seemed formidable to her, as they damned well were.

Benny didn't care. On the boat to France, all he remembered was that I yanked him into the ship's swimming pool. It was years before he forgave me for trying to give him a crash introduction to swimming.

In the dining room on the first or second day out, we met Irwin and Marian Shaw and their young son, Adam. That chance encounter alone made the trip for me. Irwin had written The *Young Lions*, the first of the really good World War II novels, and had just published a second novel, The *Troubled Air*, about how the Redbaiters fragged the networks. The Shaws became the anchors for many expatriate Americans living in Europe in the fifties. Wherever they were—in Paris on the rue de Boccador (in the same building as Teddy and Nancy White, and Art and Ann Buchwald), in St. Jean de Luz near Biarritz in the Basque country, or in Klosters, in Switzerland—the sign said, "Welcome." The sports were incredibly competitive, the food was good, the wine flowed, the conversation was full of joy and laughter. Irwin was one of the few tennis players I ever knew who regularly shed blood during a match. I always felt he was trying to kill me, as he persuaded me to ski with him down the mountains above Klosters, and he wouldn't play you any game—like golf or squash—where he thought he would lose. I was always sort of in love with the beautiful Marian—warm, funny, and smart.

It took us forever to find an apartment, a forever spent with a small boy in a small hotel room with a smaller bath, until we landed a modern—for Paris—flat at 171 rue de l'Université, one block in from the river on the Left Bank, near the Eiffel Tower. Soon after we moved in, Benny broke out in hundreds of red spots, and that produced for the first time the great Paris doctor, Jean Dax, who looked him over, had two Martinis, and was willing to bet us he had chicken pox. In fact he had mosquito bites, since there were no screens on the windows, but Jean Dax became—and remains—a warm and wonderful friend, as wise about people as medicine (despite the mosquito bites).

At the embassy, as assistant press attaché, my first job every morning was to prepare the daily roundup of the French press—a dozen dailies and weeklies—for the embassy officers and for the State Department in Washington. Elias McQuaid had turned boulevardier with a vengeance with his Savile Row suits and his love of Paris. He was taking long lunch hours, for tennis or for food, and that left me to talk to the journalists about whatever was on their minds. The Americans were no problem. The good ones didn't bother with press attachés; they knew the ambassador and his top aides a lot better than I did. The bad ones had no good questions, meaning no questions that were hard to answer. The Brits were tougher, always showing off their shorthand skills and threatening to take down every bloody word you said. The French were tough for me at first, for I didn't know them and their political shadings, and I didn't speak French well enough to be sure I gave them the delicate nuances that had been given me by the policy wonks.

My secretary was the spectacular Marie-Thérèse Barreau, daughter of a French Army general from Versailles, smart, quick, sassy and fun. She delighted in teaching me about France, which I hadn't visited in fifteen years, and plunged me into conversation with people who spoke no English, smiling as I groped my way out of trouble. I could have brained her, but in a couple of months I began to master the slang and argot of journalism and politics.

Elias McQuaid left some months later, eventually to become the American Consul General in Edinburgh. I took over as the Attaché de Presse, auprès de l'Ambassade Américaine, and immediately started to get into trouble. The ambassador at that time was James Clement Dunn, one of a handful of career ambassadors in the Foreign Service. He had been Chief of Protocol, and Ambassador to Italy. I had met him some years before, when I was an usher at his daughter Cynthia's wedding to my friend Alexander "Budsie" Cochrane from Boston.

After Eisenhower was elected president in 1952, the new Secretary of State was the austere and joyless John Foster Dulles. He came to Paris for some conference, and I persuaded Dunn to persuade Dulles to give a background briefing over cocktails to the American correspondents. All the regulars came. Harold Callender of the *New York Times*, Walter Kerr of the *Herald Tribune*, Frank White of *Time*, Arnaud de Borchgrave of *Newsweek*, Bob Kleiman of *U.S. News*, Preston Grover of the Associated Press, Joseph Kingsbury Smith of the International News Service, and Ed Korry of United Press. Midway through the briefing, I could see Dunn was mad at something, and he took me aside to ask, "Who is that little shit who keeps calling me Jimmy? I've never seen him before in my life." I told him he was referring to David Schoenbrun of CBS, probably the savviest of all the American foreign correspondents, but a man whose ego made him hard to love. Ever the professional, Dunn said no more.

Sometime later, I got into real trouble, or rather Dunn got me into real trouble. The occasion was a *note verbale* about Indochina, delivered by Dunn to French Prime Minister Antoine Pinay, the little leather merchant from the Loire Valley, who died in 1994 at the age of one hundred two. Indochina in the fifties was a preview of Vietnam in the sixties. First the enemy was France, for trying to hold on to its colonial empire. And then the enemy was the United States for trying to prevent a Communist takeover. The effects were devastating to both countries. According to diplomatic protocol—Dunn's particular field of expertise—a *note verbale* is a message delivered orally, precisely so that the receiving government will get the message, but leave no written record, in order to avoid embarrassing anyone. The *note verbale* said something about how the French should not count on receiving U.S. aid for Indochina at the current level—around a billion dollars a year—unless France kept better track of where the money was going.

So far so good. The Elysée announced a visit from the American ambassador, and that was pretty much that. Until I got a call from Ed Korry, the United Press Bureau chief. Did Ambassador Dunn leave a copy of the *note verbale* at the Elysée Palace? I said he did not; it was a *note verbale*. No copy. Korry asked me to check. I did. Dunn repeated his story to me, and I repeated my story to Korry. Pretty soon, the UP ticker was tinkling. "The American Embassy today insisted that Ambassador Dunn delivered a *note verbale*," blah-blah-blah. I didn't like that "insisted." Then Korry called again and told me that Pinay's *chef de cabinet*, Félix Gaillard (later to become prime minister himself), had a copy of the message, in fact had read Korry the entire message, since the French didn't like to be threatened.

After I had checked again, the ambassador admitted he *had* left a copy of his *note verbale*. "Happens all the time among friends," he said. I had to call Korry to admit that I had misspoken and could not appropriately tell him that I had been lied to first. I already knew that newspapermen don't like being lied to, but Korry really let me have it. (He was mad at me to start with, because I had failed to introduce him to two visiting CIA biggies, whom Korry wanted to see about joining the agency.) The UP story read something like, "After insisting that he had not lied, Benjamin C. Bradlee, the American Press Attaché, late yesterday admitted that he had lied to the United Press," blah-blah-blah.

Almost as soon as I landed in Paris, the espionage trial of Julius and Ethel Rosenberg started showing up on page one of European newspapers. The Rosenbergs had been tried and convicted of espionage, in the landmark trial of the Cold War in 1951. They were convicted of giving the Russians information vital to the manufacture of atomic weapons. The trial, the verdict, and especially the death sentence had absorbed—then enflamed—France. As the architect of European recovery, the "Fire in the Ashes" in Teddy White's great phrase, America was easy to resent. The American presence was overwhelming; American cash was everywhere, and the Rosenbergs became the symbolic rallying point for everyone who had a bone to pick with our government. Not just the Communists, who lived on anti-Americanism, but the intellectuals, the Socialists, and everyone who worried about McCarthyism—and the death penalty.

Protests were staged all over France, and many of them turned into anti-American riots. One man was killed in a "Libérez-les-Rosenbergs" rally in the Place de la Concorde, a stone's throw from the embassy. We were severely handicapped in trying to counteract this wave of anti-American feeling. We had begged USIS for factual information about the case, and about the trial, so that we could at least respond intelligently to our critics. Before I knew what was happening I became, in effect, the Rosenberg attaché, charged with receiving delegations that came to the embassy to protest the verdict and the death sentence. This was an extremely difficult task. Contemporaneous newspaper accounts provided us with nothing like the detailed knowledge of the case that we needed to counter the emotional protesters. The last straw for me came when the blind mayor of Ivry, a worker suburb of Paris and a stronghold of the PCF (Parti Communist Français), showed up with his buddies, shouting questions, and we still had no material from Washington to answer them.

On a Saturday morning I went to my immediate boss, the embassy's public affairs officer, Bill Tyler, for help. Since we couldn't get any help from Washington, why didn't we send our own man—me, obviously—to New York to read the transcript of the entire Rosenberg Trial (and appeals), return to Paris as quickly as possible, and write a detailed, factual account of the evidence as it was presented, witness by witness, and as it was rebutted, cross-examination by cross-examination? Tyler thought that was a great idea. When could I—should I leave? Right away. Fine, but it was Saturday. The banks were closed and no one had cash for the air fare. "That's all right," said Tyler. "We'll ask Bobby for some francs."

Bobby was Robert Thayer, son of the founder of St. Mark's School, a longtime friend of my mother and father, and the CIA station chief in Paris. He reached nonchalantly into the bottom drawer of his desk and fished out enough francs to fly me to the moon, much less to the Federal Courthouse in the Southern District of New York, and I left that afternoon. This incident caused me some embarrassment years later, when a woman named Deborah Davis argued in a book about Katharine Graham that I had worked for the CIA as an agent. Her "evidence," obtained through a Freedom of Information request, was an internal CIA document noting that Bobby Thayer had advanced the cash for my air fare.*

It had been arranged that the D.A. for New York's Southern District, Myles J. Lane, would make a small office available to me, plus

---

* The book, *Katharine the Great*, was withdrawn from the Harcourt Brace Jovanovich list after I wrote a letter to Davis's editor pointing out thirty-nine errors concerning the thirty-nine references to me. Davis sued Harcourt Brace and the suit was settled. Her book was later republished by National Press.

a transcript of the entire court record of *United States* v. *Julius and Ethel Rosenberg*. I read it from A to Z, taking notes on the testimony of all the witnesses, almost around the clock. I left late at night for a shower and bed at my sister's apartment, and began again early Monday. Three days later I was back in Paris dictating a 7,500-word analysis of the Rosenberg case, which was translated into French and distributed to the French press in two days.

Not a whole lot changed, to tell the truth, even though at last we had some facts. In fact, the French president, Vincent Auriol, sent a top-secret letter over to the embassy to be sent to President Eisenhower, urging him to pardon the Rosenbergs, or at least to commute the death sentence. This was illegal under the French Constitution, which prohibits a French president from interfering in the internal affairs of another state. I felt I had been picked on enough already, without the help of President Auriol, so I called up my friend Blair Clark, who was now in Paris stringing for CBS as a kind of super-assistant to David Schoenbrun. Clark told Schoenbrun, who immediately ordered himself up on the CBS radio wire, and broadcast his "exclusive" about the French president's message to the American president. I was learning how to "manage" the news.

The Rosenbergs' executions left me depressed. I was convinced of their guilt after reading all that fine print, but I had trouble fitting the punishment to that crime, or any crime. I felt the State Department had treated it as an abstract incident with some diplomatic repercussions, rather than the vitally complicated drama it was.

This was the early 1950s. Eisenhower, elected president in November 1952, was staying aloof from McCarthy's Red hunts. In Paris, we had no U.S. television, no *Washington Post* stories, no real firsthand information until Charles "Chip" Bohlen came through Paris (and commandeered my office) on his way to become ambassador in Moscow. Bohlen was the star of the State Department's new generation of Soviet experts, and McCarthy had grilled him relentlessly while Secretary of State John Foster Dulles let him twist uncomfortably in the wind.

And then came Cohn and Schine—Roy Cohn and David Schine, Senator McCarthy's favorite investigators/hatchetmen—on their ludicrous, destructive crusade through Western Europe on behalf of McCarthy's witch-hunt, banning books from USIS libraries, berating Foreign Service officers, whose socks they couldn't hold, for insufficient zeal, threatening to investigate the British Broadcasting Corporation, and generally fragging a mess of intelligent people.

As soon as their itinerary was announced showing a weekend stop in Paris, correspondents started begging me to set up a press conference, led by the Brits, who were particularly outraged by the "little wankers thinking they were going to investigate the BBC." Some of the meanest bastards in all of journalism were drooling at the prospect of getting their hands on what an American official in Germany called "junketeering gumshoes." I could hardly wait to facilitate matters, but I had to think. If everything proceeded the way I felt sure it would, Cohn and Schine would be ridiculed, and they would seek revenge on everyone who had anything to do with it. I needed to involve Ambassador Dunn—who was to the manner born and all that, but a tough little monkey, at the end of his career and in no mood to be abused by types like Cohn and Schine. He gave a green light, but asked me to clear it with Graham Martin. Martin, smiling in silence, gave his nod.

Now, all I needed was Cohn and Schine, and they gave me the brush-off. They understood that the banning of Kay Boyle's books from the USIS library in Germany, and the ridiculing of her husband who was on that library staff, had not been well received in Europe. They were also trying to ban *Thunder Out of China*, Theodore White and Anna Lee Jacoby's book about the fall of China, and they knew White might be at any press conference in Paris. They absolutely refused on Friday, finally said no on Saturday, and only agreed at the very last minute to hold a press conference on Sunday afternoon.

We had prepared for just such an emergency by telling reporters to stay in town that Sunday, instead of lunching in some romantic *moulin* outside of Paris. We had collected fifty or sixty telephone numbers—homes, hotels, restaurants, and all that—and an hour after we had a green light for the press conference, we had fifty reporters sitting, nice as can be, in my office. Loaded for bear, with Art Buchwald of the *International Herald Tribune* in the front row, flanked by a pair of testy Brits.

Buchwald had just acquired a high-tech tape recorder, whose microphone was hidden in a regular-sized wristwatch, attached by a wire which ran up his left sleeve, around his back to the recorder itself, which was stashed in his right coat pocket. "You don't have to take notes," he told his colleagues. "I got it all, right here." I had less confidence than he had in his gadget, and my secretaries Margot McCloud and Marie-Thérèse Barreau were trying to take it all down in shorthand.

I was a basket case when the press conference finally started, after an inane introduction by me.

The first question came from the diminutive Reuter correspondent next to Buchwald, in a clipped British accent. "Mr. Cohn, Mr. Schine, are you happy in your work?" And things went precipitously downhill from there.

"How old are you, Schine?" barked Sy Freidin, who was then working for *Collier's* magazine, a dear pal (later revealed to have done the odd job for the CIA, unbeknownst to all of us).

"I wonder, sir, if you could tell us about your credentials in all this work?" This from another Brit, teeth clenched with anticipation. We all watched in amazement as Schine stood up, removed his wallet from his rear pocket, and produced a laminated ID card from McCarthy's committee. This exchange produced the great front page headline the next day in England's *Daily Mail*: "Look, Ma/We Got Credentials."

Throughout, Buchwald had his left hand up, pretending to want to ask a question, but really getting his wristwatch-microphone in position to pick up the Q and A. I would ignore him as I picked selected questioners, but from time to time Cohn or Schine would point at him, and he would have to come up with a question.

Most of the reporters were enjoying themselves too much to ask questions, content to sit back and watch the boy Commie hunters squirm. Halfway through the ordeal, the Reuter correspondent asked, "How *could* you be happy in your work?" and he closed the press conference with "Are you sure you're happy in your work?"

Cohn and Schine finally stormed out, glaring at all of us, and at each other. Most of us adjourned to the Crillon Bar across the rue Boissy d'Anglas, and waited while Buchwald disentangled himself from his high-tech equipment. Finally, he was ready. Silence fell, and Art turned on the machine.

Absolutely nothing, at first, then a low-pitched whine. For twenty minutes. And that was that.

Cohn and Schine decided to leave Paris as fast as they could, and start the final leg of their Midnight Ride in Britain. The British correspondents begged to know the flight number of their plane to London, but Cohn literally sneered at me when I asked him over the telephone later, and shut Schine up before he could tell me. The embassy had not made the travel arrangements, so I couldn't find out from our travel office. Finally I called Clem Brown, the resident meeter and greeter for Pan American Airways, and told him I absolutely had to have Cohn and Schine's flight number. Brown prided himself on his skills as a can-do type, and in fifteen minutes he had it, and we passed it along to the British press. More than one hundred British reporters met them at Heathrow, and their visit crashed around their ears. They took the next flight home.

We all felt we had made a contribution to the decline and fall of Cohn and Schine, which would finally occur in 1954, when Eisenhower finally got mad after the Army-McCarthy hearings, and perhaps through them, even to the gradual lancing of the whole abscess of McCarthyism.* Like most Americans abroad in and out of the diplomatic service, I had felt left out of one of the crucial battles of our time. I didn't like to miss any fight, especially that one, and

---

* Senator McCarthy accused the Army of trying to force him to abandon his anti-Communist crusade, after the Army accused McCarthy of using his influence to gain favorable treatment for one of his aides who had been drafted. The clash produced thirty-five days of televised hearings, after which the Senate investigated McCarthy and condemned his activities as unethical.

so I got a special kick out of helping them make fools of themselves.

As expected, one of the books Cohn and Schine had bullied USIS into banning abroad was Teddy White's *Thunder Out of China*. We all told Teddy to wear it as a badge of honor, until Teddy pointed out to us that the Book-of-the-Month Club was just at that time considering his new book *Fire in the Ashes* for a main selection, and was unlikely to have the balls to pick a book by a banned author. Teddy was starving as European correspondent for *The Reporter* magazine, and needed the money, although he never used that as an argument.

I had drafted a cable on White's behalf for the signature of President Eisenhower's new ambassador, Douglas Dillon. We got White's press card accreditation numbers from SHAPE, US AREUR, ECA, etc., and pointed out that in order to get them, Teddy had passed the stringent security checks instituted by Generals Dwight D. Eisenhower and the U.S. and Allied Air Chief in Europe, Lauris Norstad, plus Averell Harriman, who was then the national security administrator in Paris. Dillon, in the bravest ambassadorial gesture I know anything about, changed my classification from "Top Secret" to "Eyes Only SecState," and appreciably strengthened the recommendation that the book be unbanned ASAP.

And it was. *Fire in the Ashes* was selected by the Book-of-the-Month Club, and Teddy and Nancy could afford caviar at the goodbye parties, before he returned to a brilliant, pioneering new career as a political historian.

But that was braver and bolder than diplomacy usually got, in my experience. I was never really trusted by the diplomats, because of my belief that, all things considered, a press attaché ought to answer questions truthfully. This revolutionary theory got me in trouble when I realized that the Soviets were always calling in American reporters in Moscow whenever they delivered a note to the State Department, and filling their ears with a manipulated version of its contents. It was American policy at that time not to comment on these notes, and so for days the world knew only what the Communists had decided to tell it about their latest diplomatic maneuvering.

This policy of no comment seemed almost unpatriotic. I was reading these Soviet notes because the American Ambassador to the USSR, Chip Bohlen, made the AmEmbassy, Paris, an information addressee on the notes themselves, and on his own expert analyses. His cables invariably pointed out the crap in the Soviet notes, and put them into a perspective that contradicted the public Soviet version. I started mentioning this to reporters who asked. And reporters started asking me more often, as they started getting good answers. And so all of a sudden, dope stories about Soviet notes began appearing on the wires and in newspapers, datelined Paris.

The State Department complained. It didn't take a rocket scientist to figure out that the embassy was leaking, and it didn't take all that long for suspicion to center on me. I didn't volunteer anything, but when Ambassador Dillon asked me: "It's you, isn't it?" I admitted it, and gave my reasons. Dillon smiled, and even nodded, but said that perhaps we better knock it off, for a while. To say that initiative was discouraged in the embassy doesn't do justice to the cover-your-ass mentality that pervaded the joint. Diplomacy had taken me to Paris, but it was perfectly obvious it was going to take me no further—by mutual consent.

I loved Paris—and France—with a passion. Life was cheap, and even cheaper with black market francs. Life was different, exciting. Wining and dining were magnificent, and a fine lunch with a glass of wine in any of the hundreds of good small restaurants was affordable on my salary of about $8,500, costing little more than a dollar. I couldn't get over the French women, pretty or plain, in cafés, on the streets, looking you up and down with confidence and interest. My own inhibitions, bred into me over the generations, seemed so complicating, so dreary.

Every weekend Jean and Benny and I left Paris on a different road, for a picnic in a parc, for a tour of Chartres, for the Loire Valley (and wines). We spent a summer vacation in Normandy with the McQuaids. We went to London, Geneva, Germany on weekends. I was sure I could still speak German, after saying my prayers in German for so long. I finally realized I couldn't when it took me an hour to rent a bicycle in some Rhine village from a guy who spoke perfect English.

We went skiing in the French and Austrian Alps. I couldn't believe those thrilling mountains of the purest snow, with lifts at last instead of rope tows. I was totally blown away by being able to stand on top of a mountain pointing my ski pole at a village thousands of feet below, and then skiing there. On one of these trips we made friends with a couple from Holland, and I became smitten with "M," the beautiful wife. I followed her up and down the mountains for days—and almost incidentally we ended up in bed one afternoon while others were skiing. New recklessness for me, and new thoughtlessness. I wondered why I didn't feel more guilty.

At thirty, I was still an innocent in the boy-girl department, not all that far beyond the teenager who had thought about getting laid a lot, but didn't get laid a lot. I certainly had extremely limited experience with women looking at me and thinking about getting laid. And when I finally did meet one or two, their success was virtually assured.

Jean and I were now more friends than lovers. We had missed growing together in our early twenties, when growth together is so essential to any relationship. Things were not improved in Paris, where I was so involved and Jean was somewhere between uncomfortable and unhappy. A few months before home leave in 1953, we opted for a trial separation.

She and Benny moved back to Washington, and I joined them a few months later. I spent most of my home leave talking to Dr. Julius Schreiber, with Jean and alone, and attending some McCarthy hearings on the Hill. When it was time for me to return to Paris six weeks later, the feeling of adventure that still overwhelmed me still underwhelmed Jean. While I was cooling on the Foreign Service fast, I was nowhere near ready to go home for good. And so we went back to France together, too scared to call it quits, without options for another way of life, and with a future that lacked definition.

I had kept my eyes and ears open for jobs back in journalism where I belonged, including the *Post*, which still had no international staff, but without success. The Paris *Trib* interested me, but they paid nothing, and they weren't interested in me. Bill Attwood, who had been the *Look* magazine bureau chief in Paris, was returning to a big position with Cowles, and I got short-listed for his job. But Ed Korry got it.

Back in Paris, Jean and I soldiered on. There was a modest amount of scut work to be done in the embassy. We had to attend certain cocktail parties, but to work, not play. We had to pick up guests at the end of a receiving line every so often, and guide them to the booze, and chat them up for a bit. One's chances of finding someone interesting were poor, unless you count as interesting the odd French countess, who turned out to have been born Irish in Chicago, and had come to Paris with Mummy between the wars to land herself a title. The really interesting people had better things to do than go to embassy functions.

Jean and I had moved from the rue de l'Université to the fourth floor of 42 Quai des Orfèvres, on the Ile de la Cité, with fourteen windows overlooking the Seine and the Left Bank, and across a square from the Palais de Justice. We gave a great New Year's Eve party there, with everyone in costume as Apaches. Ladies in black satin skirts, slit to the waist. Gents in horizontal-striped matelot shirts. We had gone up to Montmartre the night before, Claude de Kemoularia and I, to find the right music, and we did—a great accordion player, a drummer, and a sexy female trumpeter. Kemou was the special assistant and the brains behind Paul Reynaud, the wartime prime minister of France, a longtime Radical Socialist politician. He had arranged for the colorfully dressed guards from the Palais de Justice nearby to "raid" our New Year's Eve party, until they took mercy on us and confessed it to be a hoax.

On the job, work involved dealing with the French press first, then visiting American reporters, before adjourning at midday. Lunches, for me, often started at the Crillon Bar across the street from the embassy, where the great Sam White was more or less permanently installed at one corner. (When they eventually remodeled the bar, they cut off Sam's corner and gave it to him.) He was a colorful, handsome, hard-drinking Australian, the Paris correspondent for the *Evening Standard* (London), and a special favorite of Lord Beaverbrook, its famous owner. Sam was not good at politics. The rise and fall of the many governments of the Fourth Republic voted in and out at the Assemblée nationale, only a few hundred yards across the Place de la Concorde and the Seine from the Crillon Bar, essentially bored him. But a whiff of scandal would bring Sam to his feet, asking Louis, the bartender, to place calls to starlets, philandering statesmen, or the objects of the Beaver's latest interest. I can still see Sam turning, ever so slightly shaky on his feet just after noon, and saying, "Louis, donnez-moi la *Queen Mary* at sea," and the call went through.

And then there was Bernard Valery, the joyous and resourceful correspondent of the *New York Daily News*, who taught me everything he knew about Paris—or tried to—and France, and Sweden, and Russia, and Japan. He spoke seven languages, and had written books in Swedish, French, and English. I can still hear Bernard, working on the visit to Paris of a president of Mexico, accompanied by a Mexican actress, not his wife, turning to the concierge of the Crillon and saying, ever so gently, "La question qu'on me pose est la suivante: quelle est la disposition des lits?"

There was tennis in all seasons and at all hours. With Irwin Shaw, Peter Viertel, the novelist and screenwriter, George Plimpton, who was just starting the *Paris Review*, my old New Hampshire pal Elias McQuaid, before he left, and struggling novelist Peter Matthiessen. Peter and I had become totally caught up in one of the great French cultural events, a *crime passionnel*, involving the dashing and politically promising young mayor of Orléans, Pierre Chevallier, a doctor, and his faithful but slightly drab wife, Yvonne, a nurse.

The mayor-doctor had just been named to his first cabinet post in the government of René Pleven, and in fact was getting dressed in his formal clothes with decorations for the inaugural festivities, when his wife broke in on him to plead with him on bended knee to give up his red-headed paramour, and come back to his loving family which had been so desolate in his prolonged absences. He stood unmoved, looking down upon her, with eyes that were close to contempt. On and on she pleaded, without even recognition from the man she loved. Finally, in despair, she retrieved a small revolver from a closet in her bedroom, and started shooting. Four times she pulled the trigger, until her young son, barely eleven, called out, *"Maman!"* from the next room. Yvonne took the child by the hand and led him downstairs into the custody of the concierge for safekeeping. Then she returned to the bloody scene, and shot her husband once more for good measure, ruining, one would think, all chance of pleading lack of premeditation.

The French press went crazy, throwing caution to the wind with police reporters, court reporters, sob sisters, psychiatrists, novelists, the works. The French felt they invented the crime *passionnel*. They were determined to leave nothing unsaid and they left nothing unsaid. The whole country was either outraged, or outraged that anyone would be outraged. The venue of the trial was shifted from Orléans to Reims, although hardly for fear that Madame could not get a fair trial in her hometown. No jury in France was going to convict her of anything. After only two days of hearing evidence, the jury retired to a room in the Reims Palais de Justice, which just happened to face on the public square. Thousands of French citizens had gathered under the jury-room windows and were shouting, "Bravo, Yvonne, bravo!" and "Libérez-la!" (Free her!) for the short time it took the jury to acquit her.

"C'est peut-être un peu excessif," *Le Parisien Libéré* editorialized on the front page next morning about the shouting crowd, but the whole country generally approved of liberating Madame. Matthiessen and I felt this was perfect for The *New Yorker*'s "Annals of Crime," and we started writing it one weekend in my embassy office, with hundreds of clippings spread all over the floor. Perhaps rewriting is a better word. We showed the first draft to Irwin Shaw, and he volunteered with only the smallest hesitation to forward it to *New Yorker* editor William Shawn, with a personal letter: Two young friends of mine have written this story . . . or something like that. And that was that. Matthiessen went back to the States, and the whole project was dropped.

Years later, Peter wrote me that the story had been resuscitated through his agent, but there had been two problems. The *New Yorker* had a rule against double bylines, and the editors there wanted some more information. Matthiessen had to rewrite it umpteen times, and I had contributed only a modest amount of rereporting. It ran November I, 1958, as an "Annals of Crime," under the title "Peut-être un Peu Excessif." Peter got the byline and two thirds of the money, and he deserved both.

Despite the listlessness of our personal life, there was such an excitement to this life—so many new tastes and sights and emotions—that it was inconvenient to reflect on the fact that I was still not engaged with the great issues of our time which I wanted to spend my life exploring. I had quit the *Post* because I was bogged down in a swamp inhabited by gamblers, indecent exposers, psychopaths, train robbers, racists, rapists, and the victims of all the above. The recovery of Europe, the rise of communism, the war in China, the excesses of anti-communism, the beginnings of the civil rights movement were all happening outside my field of vision. The great world leaders were leading, unobserved by me.

If my living conditions were now more glamorous, my involvement in history was not substantially different. All this made me vaguely discontented whenever I stopped briefly enjoying the glory of Paris in the early fifties to think about it. And to further complicate matters, I had fallen clumsily into an absorbing affair. Before that the sum total of my extramarital sexual experiences had been a few one-night stands. A single night in Sydney, Australia, the accident with a Bendel's saleswoman in New York, and an incident on the slopes of Ober Lech in Austria. Now with someone full of joy, humor, and adventure, I became overwhelmed by sex itself, and the sexual excitement that gave my relationship with her a vitality I had not known before.

From her I discovered the glorious truth that to be wanted by a woman was as consuming and thrilling as to want a woman, and as rewarding physically and emotionally. All those cumbersome Puritan legacies about sex and joy—laid on me by my heritage—slipped from my shoulders, and the world has looked different to me ever since.

My involvement with another woman made a mockery of our marriage, but I stayed put, guilty and unhappy, but unwilling to stop seeing her. I think Jean and I both doubted our chances of success in the long run, and both understood that each of us would inevitably find someone else. Selfishly, I never seriously thought of remarriage. The difference in religion and nationality, plus the preoccupation with sex, made it easy for me, typically, to sweep the whole matter under the rug. Although we never talked about marriage directly, my very Catholic friend had talked to a Vatican representative who specialized in annulments. He and I talked once, when he explained the various conditions under which annulments were possible. Had my marriage been consummated? Well, yes. Had promises been made that were never meant to be kept? Not that I could identify. Had my wife gone insane? Maybe I had; certainly not she.

The questions reminded me how unfinished, how incomplete a man I was. I had done what I had done, but I was a father. I had accumulated more experience than wisdom. The episodes of my life had not been woven into anything I was particularly proud of.

I felt generally miserable, as guilty about Benny as about Jean. I often wonder now whether I felt miserable enough. For the first years of my son's life, I had worked the late shift at the *Post*, which meant he slept while I worked and I slept while he was ready to bond. Benny, who was about five, spoke a lovely, accentless, sing-song French, even spoke English with a French accent. I had already disrupted his life by moving him to Paris and forcing him into a new culture and new language, and now it seemed that I was on a course to do it again.

Arnaud de Borchgrave put my private life on something of a back burner in the fall of 1953 by wondering out loud one day whether I might be interested in succeeding him as the European correspondent of *Newsweek*. There was nothing coy about my response: I would kill for it. Arnaud was a piece of work then as now, slight, perpetually tanned, jumping with nervous energy and ambition. The son of a Belgian count, he had enlisted in the British Navy three months shy of sixteen years old, landed a job as the United Press correspondent in Belgium after the war, and married an American secretary in the American Embassy in Brussels. He was attractive, mischievous, conspiratorial, and tended to exaggerate both the insidedness of his knowledge of important events and the importance of his own role in those events. A bullshitter, and a player among the insider group of foreign correspondents with a host of sources, not scared to peg even with the expertise of any one of his peers, and ready to work harder than almost all of them. But it takes one to know one, as the saying goes.

Arnaud would be leaving by the first of 1954 to become assistant foreign editor, and he said there was no obvious *Newsweek* candidate. He was prepared to recommend me to the foreign editor, who would make the decision. *Newsweek* in the early fifties was much less of a magazine than it has become, owned by Captain Vincent Astor, and managed for him by an American businessman, Malcolm Muir, who aspired to rub shoulders with the world's rich and famous without offending any of them with his magazine. People spoke of *Time*, in those days, never *Time* and *Newsweek*. The foreign editor who had to approve of me was Harry Kern, whose interest in foreign affairs was pretty much limited to Japan, Germany, Middle Eastern oil, and an Egyptian belly dancer named Tahia. He didn't really care much about France, except as a place to buy lingerie and drink vintage wines, as de Borchgrave had spent hours briefing me. I liked French wine fine, but I had just spent the best years of my life fighting the Japanese and the Germans, and knew next to nothing about oil, the Middle East, or belly dancing. Kern seemed to like me well enough when we finally met, but he positively loved me when he learned that Mrs. Vincent Astor, the famous Brooke, had been a childhood friend of my mother and her sister, Alma Morgan. When I was eventually offered the job, I never doubted for a minute that Brooke Astor was responsible, and I have thanked her often, for that, and for much more.

The embassy was something less than heartbroken when I told them I would be leaving, and secretly pleased that they didn't have to pay to transport me and my family back to Washington, just as *Newsweek* was delighted to avoid paying for our passages to Paris. *Newsweek* was notoriously chintzy then. My new salary was $9,000 a year, and I couldn't wait to get started. In fact I started on Christmas Eve again, taking a train to Montpellier to interview the author of a new biography of Lawrence of Arabia.

Why did I always start work on the eve of holidays when no one had to work, I wondered. Because there was no place else I wanted to be, and nothing I wanted to do more.

Frederick Josiah Bradlee as a twenty-four-year-old Army second lieutenant stationed on Governor's Island in New York. Two years earlier, he had been an All-American halfback at Harvard. Two years later, he was a runner for a Boston bank.

Josephine deGersdorff Bradlee at twenty-eight, with Connie on her lap, surrounded by Freddy, RIGHT, and me. She was only twenty years old when she married—beneath herself, according to her half-German father, but he was wrong, way wrong.

1

2

Josephine, known as Jo, was a real beauty. She was also co-holder, with Walter Lippmann's wife, Helen, of the girls' high-jump record at Miss Chapin's School in New York.

Dressed to the nines, just before the crash in 1929. Blue blazers and white duck shorts, from a visiting British clothier, and a stocking at half mast from God knows where.

3

4

Freddy as a young actor. He left Harvard in the winter of his freshman year and landed three straight Broadway parts in his first year. Theater critic Wolcott Gibbs named Freddy and Montgomery Clift the year's best ingenus.

5

Me as a senior at St. Mark's School—three years after a siege with polio, en route to Harvard with three highest honors and a pass in physics, and still unfamiliar with curve balls.

6

LIFE

PARTY TIME

DECEMBER 23, 1940 **10** CENTS
YEARLY SUBSCRIPTION $4.50

Freddy, the boy ingenu, on the cover of Life.

That's me in a breeches buoy, being pulled from a tanker to a destroyer, both going 15 knots, in the Pacific war zone. After two weeks on one destroyer, I'd be hauled back to the tanker for further transfer to the next destroyer to come alongside for refueling.

Jean Saltonstall Bradlee and I in a different war zone (note the clenched fist)—a Vogue story on home leaves. We had been married for more than two years, and had seen each other about two months.

My father, known as "B," and Connie (and cigarettes), at her wedding in 1947 on
the lawn of the house in Beverly, Massachusetts. He looks proud that he hasn't had
too much to drink. She looks relieved—and lovely.

The first edition of the New Hampshire Sunday News *goes to press in the summer of 1946, as Blair Clark,* LEFT, *and Bernie McQuaid look over a page one proof. Their friendship brought Jean and me to New Hampshire. Blair's friendship kept us there.*

12

This is my journalist's accreditation card, the one the French government pulled when it booted me out of the country for trying to talk to Algerian rebel leaders in the mountains of Kabylia in Algeria in 1956. The expulsion order was rescinded before my expulsion.

13

The Israelis had captured an Egyptian submarine during the Suez Crisis. They blindfolded the sub captain and, to confuse him, drove him around Haifa for two hours before delivering him to Israeli naval intelligence headquarters, only 200 yards away.

14

One of the few times I remember actually interviewing
President Kennedy, pad and pencil in hand. The start of a
smile on his face suggests this was a set-up for a
Newsweek *promotion*.

President Kennedy
with the Pinchot
women on the
porch at Milford,
Pennsylvania.
Tony Bradlee and
Mary Meyer sur-
round JFK and
their mother, Ruth
Pinchot, who had
changed from a
Greenwich Village
liberal to an ardent
supporter of
Senator Goldwater.

15

The Bradlees and the Kennedys in the White House family quarters before dinner one night. Jackie thought she was showing too much leg.

A stuffy picture of two of the unstuffiest men I ever met: Phil Graham with Fritz Beebe, the Wall Street lawyer who presided over the Post Company after Phil's death.

I seemed to be spending a lot of time in courtrooms during the seventies and eighties. Here I am walking into the federal court house, pretending to be some Mafia don ducking photographers, with Phil Geyelin.

And here I am leaving another federal court house with Katharine Graham. It looks
as if we won, at least a round.

20   *Katharine getting a fix on the next day's Watergate installment from Bob Woodward, Carl Bernstein, Howard Simons, and me. Carl's hairdo was calculated to further his hippy image, and thus to irritate the Nixon White House—and me, a little.*

The movie All the President's Men *made folk heroes out of us all. Here are Dustin Hoffman (Bernstein), Robert Redford (Woodward), and Jason Robards (me) playing hardball with Jack Warden and Marty Balsam as caricatures of Harry Rosenfeld and Howard Simons.*

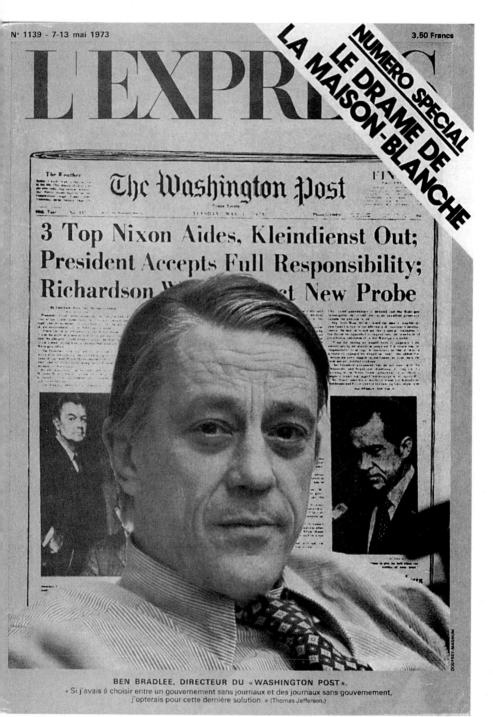

N° 1139 - 7-13 mai 1973

3,50 Francs

L'EXPRE

NUMERO SPECIAL
LE DRAME DE
LA MAISON-BLANCHE

The Washington Post

3 Top Nixon Aides, Kleindienst Out; President Accepts Full Responsibility; Richardson W... ...t New Probe

BEN BRADLEE, DIRECTEUR DU « WASHINGTON POST ».
« Si j'avais à choisir entre un gouvernement sans journaux et des journaux sans gouvernement, j'opterais pour cette dernière solution. » (Thomas Jefferson.)

22 *In the middle of Watergate, the French newsweekly L'Express used this picture of me to celebrate its twentieth anniversary. (I couldn't help feeling the cover it had planned fell through at the last minute.)*

23

In the composing room at the end looking at page one of the first edition, headlined simply, "Nixon Resigns."

A belly laugh from "Mums"— probably caused by Art Buchwald's "toast"—at the party she gave for my tenth anniversary in 1975.

24

SEVEN

PARIS II—NEWSWEEK

My new office was light-years from the press attaché's splendid suite in the American Embassy overlooking the Place de la Concorde. Now, I was in the wonderfully ratty Herald Tribune Building, on the rue de Berri, barely a block off the Champs-Elysées. In fact, I was on the fourth floor—close to the second "R" in the vertical H-E-R-A-L-D T-R-I-B-U-N-E sign, ten feet square—surrounded on three sides by drafty windows, directly across from the Hotel California. I have been colder standing watch on a destroyer in the dead of a North Atlantic winter, but nowhere else.

We had heat, but only sporadically, and almost never after five in the afternoon, which meant before lunchtime in New York where editors were either asking for copy or waiting for stories. Typing with gloves on is harder than it sounds, especially on the slim Olivettis we all carried along with the dirty trench coats as part of the foreign correspondent's uniform. Butagaz heaters (bottled gas) worked, if you were typing within their effective radius of four feet. We all prayed for inside, windowless offices, except on those not

infrequent occasions when there was some boy-girl action in one of
the hotel rooms across the street. Copy boys at the Associated Press
newsroom on the seventh floor were charged with keeping watch
on the street-front hotel rooms and alerting all voyeurs.

My "staff" consisted of Monsieur Jean, a sixty-five-year-old
garçon de bureau, already retired from at least two earlier jobs. He
worked only five mornings a week, getting the mail, stamping the
few outgoing letters, filing the French papers, and coughing. No one
I ever met smoked more . . . those musty, throat-closing, unfiltered
Gauloises. He would also deal with our moneyman, a seedy-looking
Algerian, who made daily rounds changing dollars into francs at the
black market rate. A salary of $9,000 a year didn't go far, but it went
considerably further at 450 or 500 francs to the dollar than it did at
the official rate of 350.

It was nothing to spend twelve hours in this grungy space, reading the papers, working the phones, filing—and playing gin rummy
from time to time with my pal Art Buchwald, who wrote "Paris
After Dark," a column for the *Trib*. Once I raced back from lunch,
late for an office rendezvous with my favorite aunt from New York,
who had made a special point of interrupting a European vacation
to see me. When I got there, only Buchwald was waiting for me
to play some gin. "I wish you'd tell your cousin, or your aunt, or
whoever the hell that was," he explained, "not to bother you in the
office." Apparently, I learned later, he had told her I had gone to
Germany suddenly, and wasn't expected back for two weeks.

Buchwald and I have different recollections of our gin rummy
games. I remember them as being extremely useful, given the miserable salary I was making. Frank White, the distinguished *Time-Life*
Bureau chief, had actually willed Buchwald to me as a special going-
away present, when he was reassigned back to New York. That's the
way I remember it. He has promised to tell his version in his own
book.

One of the sorriest-looking men I ever saw in my life walked
into the rue de Berri office one afternoon early in my *Newsweek* career, unshaven, his head swathed in bandages, and wearing a filthy
double-breasted gabardine suit, caked with blood. He walked in un-

announced, as so many people did in the afternoon, after the *garçon de bureau* left at noon, and handed me a plastic ID card for openers.

This was Frank Frigenti, and the card identified him as a graduate of Sing Sing Prison, where he had been incarcerated for murdering his mother-in-law, until he was deported to Sicily to hook up with other American undesirables like mobster Charles "Lucky" Luciano and Giuseppe "Big Mike" Spinelli. Frank was in mucho trouble, plainly, and being broke was only the beginning. If I could spare 10,000 francs ($20), he said, he could give me a story about how Lucky and his fellow undesirables were doing in exile ("Lousy— bored out of their goddamn minds"). Sounded like a story to me, so I "loaned" him the 10,000 francs while I waited for a go-ahead from New York. It took forever, and by the time I finally got it, he was into me for more than $150. Then old Frank started diddling me by holding back on the juiciest details until he got some more money. I finally finished my story, "Gangsters Abroad," but I couldn't finish with Frank. He just wouldn't leave the office, and I didn't feel like throwing him out, given the nature of the crime for which he had been convicted and then deported.

In despair, I told him I had a columnist friend who could help him more than I could, and that's how I dumped him onto Buchwald. Art came slouching into my office, took one look at Frigenti's still bandaged head and still bloodied gabardine suit, and turned right around to leave. But Buchwald is more commercial, if not smarter, than I am. He took Frigenti, got him a hotel room and a bath, sat him down, and debriefed him for ten days. The result was Art's first real book, A *Gift from the Boys* (the "gift" being a luscious blonde that the "boys" gave to their gangster pal, just before he sailed back to Italy as a deportee). He sold the book to the movies for $50,000, the first real money he ever made. Fifty thousand was real money in 1958, and I've been pissed off about Frigenti ever since.

In April 1954, with only a few months of "experience" under my belt as a foreign correspondent, most of which I had spent picking up accreditations, a Geneva conference was convened to try to arrange a truce and a peace between France and Indochina for the umpteenth time. I was told to get my ass down to Geneva and file an on-scener to go with the following week's cover story on Secretary of State John Foster Dulles, plus some quotes from the austere and colorless man. I was scared to death, since—unlike the other correspondents covering the conference—I knew absolutely no one in the Dulles entourage, and the Secretary was widely known as a cold fish, hard to warm up. I had met him only once, and knew he wouldn't know me from Adam's off ox.

To improve my chances for even an accidental contact with anyone who might help me, I went out to the Geneva airport to meet the Secretary of State's plane, and my heart sank even further. There to meet Dulles was my hero, James "Scotty" Reston, the *New York Times*'s best of breed. A few seconds later, Chip Bohlen, now Ambassador-designate to the Soviet Union, and who was going to be a critically important source for this conference, came down the ramp and greeted Reston, the way Damon must have greeted Pythias. "How are you, you old Scotsman?" I heard Bohlen ask, and cringed as Reston punched him playfully on the shoulder. These guys were buddies, and there I was, trying to get the attention of Carl "Mumbles" McArdle, the State Department spokesman, who never told anyone anything. The difference between, "Excuse me, Mr. McArdle, my name is Ben Bradlee, and I work for *Newsweek*," and the intimate camaraderie of Bohlen and Reston was discouraging.

Back at the Hotel Beau Rivage in Geneva, I sent a bottle of Old Overholt Bourbon up to McArdle's suite, at the suggestion of foreign editor Harry Kern. It worked—eventually—and Carl got me fifteen minutes with Dulles, exactly one hour before my filing deadline. I like to think I can get people to open up, especially when I am not prying into something sensitive. But I could barely get John Foster Dulles to move his lips, even when I asked about his trip over and his health. My file that night left no footprints at all on the next issue of *Newsweek*. But it did convince me that I should hang around the bars and see what I could pick up from anyone who would move his lips.

Hanging around for that purpose late the first night. I watched William Randolph Hearst, Jr., the young heir to the Hearst publishing empire, roll into the hotel with his INS (International News Service) stars, Joseph Kingsbury Smith and the legendary Bob Considine, in tow. This was the team that had just won a Pulitzer Prize for their interview with Joseph Stalin. But before I got too impressed, Hearst and Considine started wrestling on the hotel's polished marble floor, much to the amusement of the guests in the lobby bar. Lesson learned: there had to be more to getting Pulitzer prizes than I knew about.

It was here in Geneva that I got to meet my *Newsweek* colleague, Teddy Weintal, the magazine's longtime diplomatic correspondent in Washington. Teddy Weintal had been a diplomat in the Polish Embassy in the thirties, when he defected, long before defection was viewed solely through a Cold War lens. He had fantastic contacts, gathered after years as a professional extra man, swordsman, and correspondent. He was hardly a friend to beginning journalists, and he didn't write English particularly well, but years later, when I was about to replace the great Ken Crawford as Washington Bureau chief of *Newsweek*, and thus become Teddy's boss, Ken told me how to handle Teddy. "Don't tell him what to do. Don't even fool around much with his copy. Just bring him in Friday afternoons, tip him upside down, and see what falls out of his pockets. That's where you'll find the best stories."

I remember learning at the end of my first international conference that there was life after work, there was joy after fear. On Sunday morning I was invited to join the *Chicago Daily News*'s one and only Bill Stoneman, for his ritual Sunday breakfast of Aunt Jemima pancakes. Sunday afternoon, Crosby Noyes, the *Washington Star*'s European correspondent and a good friend, and I chartered a small sloop, and went sailing up and down Lake Geneva in a great breeze. And Sunday night, I got lucky with an old friend who had just separated from her Swiss husband. This was a different way of life.

Jean and I were still struggling along, even talking to a French psychiatrist about our troubles. That's not comfortable in any language, but tough in a language not your own. For me, I was on this perpetual high, more and more in love with my life, but Jean and

I were no longer in love. My adventure was consuming, and we were both at an impasse together, each of us increasingly vulnerable to someone who would share our needs and enthusiasms. My fling never had driven me to the point where life apart was unthinkable.

In the summer of 1954, Jean and I joined with Crosby and Tish Noyes, and Bill and Mary Edgar (he ran Press Wireless, the company we all used to file our dispatches), plus six or seven children, to rent an incredible nineteenth-century château forty-five kilometers east of Paris in the village of Boissy St. Leger. More than 800 acres, surrounded by a head-high stone wall, including a large pond, a working farm full of cows, pigs, chickens, ducks, and an odd, square swimming pool only four feet deep at its deepest point. The château itself had sixty-seven rooms, including a large ballroom, an antiquated kitchen in the basement, plus *salles* and *salons* galore. For this we paid 100,000 francs a month—less than $300.

Château Boissy St. Leger was owned by the Baron Rodolphe Hottinguer, a rich banker in Paris, whose title came through his Swiss banker forebears from Napoleon. We spent a summer there none of us will ever forget. Weekend parties that began Friday night, and continued all day Saturday through Sunday supper. Wives, especially Tish Noyes, cooked spaghetti. We jitterbugged in the ballroom, after endless lessons from Barbara Sulzberger. Her husband, Punch, later to become the publisher of the *New York Times*, was an intern in the Paris Bureau. We had long, wet picnic lunches, followed by long, wet or sun-filled walks. Noyes, Edgar, and I spent hour after hour cleaning the damn pool, which would be covered with green scum only hours after we scoured it. The inventive Docteur Dax cured the pool with a prescription of massive doses of *sulphat de cuivre*, or copper sulphate, which we learned later was some kind of poison.

The weekend that changed my life forever came in August of 1954, when our friends the Pinchot sisters hit town. Mary Pinchot Meyer, mother of three and wife of Cord Meyer, war hero turned World Federalists president and CIA biggie, and Antoinette Pinchot Pittman, mother of four, wife of Steuart Pittman, a Washington lawyer. They were both members of our Washington crowd—on the last leg of a European tour, to which they had treated themselves after seven years of diapers and dishes. And their lives were never the same, either. Mary and an Italian painter had fallen in love in Positano. Tony and I fell in love at Boissy St. Leger. I had picked them both up at their hotel in Paris on a Saturday morning, and taken them to the château, for sunlit hours of wine and food and talks and walks. Journalist friends, diplomat friends, French friends, British friends, children friends of all ages. A glorious time.

At night the feast started to move to a nearby *moulin*, where some other friends lived. Mary had hitched a ride back to Paris with someone. Jean went with others to the *moulin*. I took Tony with me. And we never got there.

Instead, we ended up in a little all-night café miles from nowhere, talking—shyly at first, then excitedly—about the state of our lives. As I left her at the hotel in Paris at five in the morning, I asked her to run away with me—for a night at a lovely *moulin* outside Paris. She made me wait until the next day, after she had talked with her sister. I think she sensed, as I certainly did, that there was a right-angle turn dead ahead, and once taken, there would be no turning back.

And, of course, there was a right-angle turn dead ahead, and there *was* no turning back. We ended up in a small, lovely room, overlooking a stream in what the *Guide Michelin* calls a *bel endroit*. And spent the next twenty-four hours exploring hungers that weren't there just days ago, and satisfying them with gentle passion, new to me.

We drove back to Paris in awe, and silence.

By the fall of 1954, I was hopelessly, falling down, head over heels in love with Tony. Never mind we had only seen each other a few days. I knew it.

After Tony and Mary returned to Washington, I moved out of the Quai des Orfèvres and into a series of what might have been the only dreary flats in that beautiful city. Everything I owned fit into an old Chevrolet coupe. Jean sensed that this was the end. In her sadness she had found someone else who was kind, if temporary. In fact she soon wanted out, and took Benny back to Boston for good. I was distraught and guilty about the end of my marriage and the loss of my son, yet desperate to see Tony again, to test the strength of our love. But, before I could do that, she had to decide what her future was going to be, and then give me the signal that there might be a place for me in that future. She did that by moving back into Washington with her four children from the lonely isolation of the Pittman family seat in Davidsonville, Maryland. By November, we had made plans for me to go back to Washington, make that *sneak* back to Washington, and start down a difficult path.

I don't remember what it cost to fly from Paris to Washington in those days, but I know I didn't have it. So to earn airfare for me to fly to Washington and for Tony to fly to Paris, I began a second career as a freelance feature writer and as an occasional broadcaster. First, as a replacement for David Schoenbrun, one of the stars that Ed Murrow had collected for CBS News, along with Charles Collingwood, Alex Kendrick, Richard Hottelet, and Dan Schorr. Each summer David would take off for Normandy to work on some book about France, and his one-month vacation would stretch into three. And I could replenish my bank account: $50 for one minute of air time, with $100 a week guaranteed, whether I broadcast or not. It was easy, David had told me. Just sit down in front of the microphone, rip your collar open, spit on the studio floor, and start talking. It wasn't easy. It was scary. But it was money.

At first I broadcast under my own name, but then Francie Muir complained to her husband, Malcolm Muir, my boss, that CBS was getting what she called "all that credit," when *Newsweek* was paying Bradlee "all that money" ($9,000 a year). So I had to come up with a pseudonym, which I eventually did. Ben Lenox. Or Anthony Lenox, when I freelanced for the *Washington Star* or other newspapers. "Anthony" sounded more authoritative, more Foreign Office, with even the suggestion of a Sir Anthony Lenox. "Ben," more eyewitness. But it was Ben Lenox who financed the first undercover trip back to Washington. (Later, after Schoenbrun returned from vacation, I had to finance my trips back and Tony's trips to Paris by writing travel pieces for Pan American's in-flight magazine. My fee, for one dynamite article exploring any place reachable by PanAm: one round-trip ticket between Washington and Paris.)

Except for the fact that we were virtually prisoners in the Congressional Hotel on Capitol Hill for fear of being discovered, our time together was glorious. I did meet the four Pittman children, who were to be part of my family for the next twenty years. Tammy was one and a half years old, and still in Dr. Dentons. Rosamond was three, and she just stared at me. Nancy, five, and Andy, six and a half, just looked uncomfortable. And I met Tony's mother, Ruth Pinchot, for dinner one night at Mary and Cord's. Given the circumstances, everyone was civil and on their best behavior, except for Cord, who was visibly pissed. What he could see that Tony and I were experiencing was plainly threatening to him.

Tony was ready to admit—in her words—that the plaster was off the walls in her marriage, but she had not envisioned tearing down the whole house to fix it. Instead, she went into analysis, and chose to make no major change in her life until she was through with analysis. That put some much-needed realism into our love affair: we weren't going to see each other for more than a week at a time, and we were going to get that week only when Tony could arrange for the peace and comfort of the children, when I could afford the trans-Atlantic flights, and when *Newsweek* and the news cooperated to provide consecutive days of calm . . . maybe four or five times a year.

Time together in France was pure joy, as we explored each other and the glorious corners of that romantic country. If the weather was cold, we would wander around the South of France, talking, taking picnics of local wines and cheeses into the fields, painting landscapes, believe it or not, living in castles one night, nondescript hotels the next. In Paris, we would walk the city from one end to the other, visit the barges on the Seine that doubled as restaurants or nightclubs. One special evening we took the redoubtable Janet Flanner, the *New Yorker* correspondent who wrote under the nom de plume of Genet, to Chartres, where the Boston Symphony under Charles Munch played an unforgettable concert in the thirteenth-century cathedral. Bats swooped and darted down from the vaulted ceilings, as the soaring music carried us miles and years away. At dinner and during intermissions Janet told us all about the castrati, young boys who were deballed in the eighteenth century to keep the soprano range of their voices. Janet Flanner wrote in *The New Yorker* more intelligently than any of the rest of us on French politics and French culture. I saw her often during the next year and a half, when I was trying to be a bachelor, and never spent a dull second listening to her restless, intelligent mind, just as I devoured every "Letter from Paris" she ever wrote for *The New Yorker*.

Time together in Washington was also joyous, but as long as our relationship was in the closet, it was also pretty much restricted to either an automobile or the four walls of a hotel room. Soon enough, though, I was asking Tony to marry me, and without her saying no— or yes—that gave us an awful lot to talk about. I don't remember spending too much time exploring the difficulties of doing it. That is not my style. I spent time trying to figure out how it could be done. I trusted Tony to determine the rightness—or wrongness— of a new life for the Pittman children, and for herself, with me. I missed Benny (it was only years later I understood how much) and I worked on finding a way to see him, now living with Jean in Boston, and integrate him into my new family, while working on the house-keeping details of a new life—housing, budgets, visitations—once I had decided that a new life with Tony was for me.

I had a small flat in the Place des Vosges that was even colder than my office. It was two rooms and a bath/kitchen so small that from the john you could easily turn on the tub faucet and the stove with one hand. These rooms were at the tail end of a very swell, if ancient, apartment, but it cost me only $100 American in cash each month. It had this fabulous view over the statue of Henri IV, but it had only Butagaz heaters, and they could not be left on when no one was home. That meant the temperature in the apartment was often below zero in winter when I got home. It got so bad once that my doctor, Jean Dax, put me in the American Hospital to thaw out. He gave me chest X-rays and a complete physical, even a Wasserman test, so that my stay would qualify under my health insurance plan.

Time in between, when I was "alone" in Paris, became suddenly tough for me. At first, I was like something out of *The Sorrows of Young Werther*, moping through any day I wasn't on the road reporting, daydreaming, reliving the last visit, punishing myself by going to bed early and alone. There I was a bachelor in Paris, living out every man's dream, but behaving like a moping monk. When I finally tired of that act and resumed a normal life, it was as if my determination was suddenly being tested, by strangers, and by wives of friends or acquaintances. A shared ride home would turn complicated. Sudden knee pressure could not be explained as accidental. Dinner partners would appear less interested in food than me. Eye contact across crowded rooms could develop in ways new to me. One woman, the wife of a friend, ambushed me one night in the shadows of the arcades under my apartment in the Place des Vosges. Even two of Tony's friends tested the waters, to my astonishment.

All my life, I have had an active fantasy life about sex, but always there had been insurmountable obstacles in the way of turning fantasy into reality. First, in my Boston, nice girls didn't fuck, and nice boys were taught control. We used to joke about how "they" put saltpeter in our food at boarding school, while suspecting it was true. Second, the sex life of a young naval officer on a destroyer in the South Pacific was the oxymoron to end all oxymorons. Third, a new marriage between the inexperienced and the inhibited was no place to learn, or it was no place to learn in our case. I thought of myself as a one-man dog, a one-woman man, and I was rattled to discover that under difficult circumstances I was not.

I didn't stay rattled, especially when all of a sudden Tony said yes to one of my once-a-visit proposals. I had a ring at the ready, specially made for me by my pal René Tupin, managing partner of Cartier, and a fellow member of an eating club called Bistro Anonyme. Conversation and energy now centered on the details of arranging for us to get married in Paris, and for her children to stay with us in France for one year. In return for having the children for the first year of our new life, we had to agree to return to Washington, and that meant I had to get a job in *Newsweek*'s Washington Bureau, or somewhere else. Suddenly there was a lot on my plate, but a decision had been reached and I could concentrate on the news, which I felt I had neglected.

The French defeat at Dien Bien Phu in 1954 and the subsequent French departure from Southeast Asia fanned the flames of nationalism in Morocco, Algeria, and Tunisia, and increased French determination to resist any further deterioration of their colonial power. The French attitude toward North Africans was incredibly condescending, even to someone not yet sensitive to all the evils of racism. The French "tutoyered" Algerians from Paris to Algiers, using the familiar form, much the way whites in the American South talked then to Negroes with whom they lived and worked. The French loved to argue with Americans about racism in the United States, and deeply resented any suggestion that racism was at the heart of their feelings about North Africa and North Africans.

All through the early 1950s, confrontations between whites and North Africans increased in frequency and severity fast enough to widen the responsibilities of the European correspondent of *Newsweek* to include regular trips to all three of the French "colonies" in North Africa: Morocco, Algeria, and Tunisia. I would leave Paris after deadline late Friday, catch the daily Air France flight to North Africa, getting off at Biarritz, renting a car for the quick drive to the Shaws in nearby St. Jean de Luz for a late supper. After a weekend of tennis, conversation, wine and spaghetti with clam sauce—maybe a bullfight in Dax, or even in Pamplona across the border—I'd catch the same plane coming through Biarritz on Sunday night, in time to spend a week, or two or three, in Rabat, Algiers, or Tunis. When reporting on a story was done, I'd manage to leave after deadline on a Friday night, on the flight that stopped in Biarritz for another wonderful weekend.

Reporting those trips was a bit tougher. The French lumped all journalists under. "Enemy." The *"pieds noirs,"* the ordinary French settlers in North Africa, many of them Corsican, were extremely conservative politically. They felt betrayed by the French intellectuals, and were terrified that France would abandon them. They would make you an honorary *pied noir* at night, while trying to drink you under the table, and then do whatever they could to make your life miserable the next day. My especial bête noire was French Army Colonel Jean-Baptiste Biaggi. His mission was to explain to me how determined the *pieds noirs* were to hold on to North Africa up to and including armed resistance to the French government. The native North Africans, especially the Algerians, were just as suspicious, but more inscrutable, and unless you spoke French with a Savannah accent, there was always the risk you would be mistaken for a Frenchman. And that put you behind a dangerous eightball. In the casbahs, as in the streets, a North African in a djellaba could be on a peaceful stroll, but he could also be carrying a machine gun, and your life could depend on which one it was.

Morocco with its casbahs and dancing girls and palaces was the most glamorous. I remember driving from Rabat to the Haute Atlas Mountains for a tribal feast one day, sitting in the back seat of a Citroën with John Wallis of the *Daily Telegraph* and Serge Bromberger of *Figaro*. To help pass the time on the endless drive, we had brought along one of the infamous dirty books in the Traveler's Companion series. Whoever was sitting in the right-rear seat read a page, tore it out, passed it to his left, and out the window it went after the man in the left-rear seat had finished with it. A special kind of pollution.

Tunisia was the most modern, despite the glories of ancient Carthage on the outskirts of Tunis. Habib "Bibi" Bourguiba, Jr., son of the prime minister, seemed a modern revolutionary, and determined to help his country achieve its independence within the system. He counted foreign journalists as his own particular preserve long before he joined his father's government, and went out of his way to guide them around.

But Algeria was always the toughest country in North Africa for me to decode, and thus the one I spent the most time trying to understand. Thousands of Algerians lived in France, working the most menial jobs. Many of them lived in the Goutte d'Or district of Paris at the bottom of Montmartre, a giant slum hostile to whites, not unlike Watts in Los Angeles came to be ten years later. Foreign correspondents would visit the area regularly looking for some rebel spokesman, some representative of the FLN (Fédération de la Libération Nationale), or fellagahs, as they were known. They were not so hard to find, but their bona fides were almost impossible to establish. No journalist—of any nationality—had done credible reportage about the FLN and its leaders.

It is in this context that I set off on a trip to Algeria in February 1956, ostensibly on an assignment to do a piece on the French Army's efforts to combat sporadic FLN attacks throughout the country. I had started on this assignment when I got into a taxi outside the Hôtel Aletti in Algiers at 11:00 P.M., February 6, a Monday. Here's what happened next, according to a letter I wrote six days later to Arnaud de Borchgrave, *Newsweek's* foreign editor;

There was another passenger in the front seat, next to the driver. We started talking, and I said something about for an American it was hard to get both sides of the story, to find a bona fide representative of the other side, the FLN, to know what it really was, how it worked in the field. They pulled off the road, and stopped. I was sure I had their interest, and started assuming they could do something for me. I started asking a lot of questions, and they kept interrupting me to ask me even more. Especially, how did they know I was an American correspondent. I gave them my conditions [for an interview]: I needed to be able to take pictures, I needed to see some guy who could prove to me he was "a big cheese" in the FLN, I needed to see uniformed troops with arms. I also needed to be able to ask any kind of questions, to say and write what I wanted. The car started up again. I gave them my card, with the hotel St. George's telephone and room numbers. They told me a Monsieur François Delorme would call me next day. Needless to say, I don't know these guys' names, nor could I possibly identify them.

Next day, sure enough, a Monsieur Delorme telephones, and asks me to meet him at the Café Le Paris, right near the Monument des Morts, in Algiers' main square. I told him I'd be wearing a brown sweater and red scarf. I go there, sit at the bar, and right on time in walk two Arabs, both young. One looking very natty, almost zoot-suitish, with wavy, black oily hair, a black moustache, and a thin, almost hatchet face. The other was about the toughest-looking dude I've ever seen, a fellagah for sure, I thought, with short stubby fingers so heavily ingrained with dirt they'll never be clean. I bought them each a cup of hot milk, while we talked about the weather, and then off we took, on foot, through the streets. We went into one bar, looked around and walked out, down the street to another bar, and sat down. Right away they asked me to prove I was an American, which I did. They told me I had been followed all day by the FLN, and would be for the duration. They told me if I squealed to the French, I would never leave Algiers. And they told me finally that they would take me to an FLN état-major, where I would be able to interview, photograph, and identify a rebel leader. I guess it is Krim [the vice premier]. They told me I would not know where I was since I would be blindfolded. They said I would be gone 48 hours or less. They said they didn't give a damn what I told French police when I was arrested, for I wouldn't be able to tell them anything which would compromise the FLN.

I still don't know anybody's name in this cloak and dagger *série noir*, and they very solemnly gave me their word I would be safe. I said how the hell could they promise that, and they simply said they could. They finally told me they would contact me Friday, and said I should bring only a toothbrush and a comb, after asking me "vous chaussez à quoi" [What size shoe do you wear?]. I told them to call between 11 and 4 because I thought I would be writing then. Actually since I learned Thursday of the Friday riots being scheduled, I wrote all Thursday night—till 5 A.M. Friday—filed early Friday morning, and spent all Friday on the streets. So I missed their call, but there was a message here at the hotel for me to meet Monsieur Delorme at 10 Saturday morning, again at Le Paris. I was there. So were they (same two). We got in the car and I thought we were off as we drove more than an hour into the countryside. But we finally stopped at some country café, and there I was told that the trip had to be postponed on account of snow. The pass was blocked, they said.

That brings us up to date. I'm just waiting.

I would like you to know why I decided to go ahead with this, and thus scrap our original idea to spend this week with the French Army.

In the first place, I know from a letter that you were interested in seeing if we could pull off such a story—and so am I.

Second, it is a thousand times better story. Everyone is out with the army this week—Grover, Clark, Stoneman, plus many British. So, it's already old hat, and it never was too much of a story. But no one (except Barrat)* has done the FLN, and even Barrat did it when there was little fat in the fire, and under completely undramatic circumstances. Here, then, is a worldwide exclusive, which will get us picked up all over the world, all for 48 hours, which if I don't run out of guts, won't be too difficult.

Third, I honestly don't think I will get kicked out of France, though I will almost certainly be arrested and questioned when I get back to Paris. But to avoid getting kicked out, I think we will have to proceed carefully—the timing has become more difficult because of the postponement.

a) Mitterrand is Minister of Justice, and he is a friend, or was.

b) I propose—presuming I get back to Paris Thursday—to rush the pictures to you, and then cable the story, as soon as I can stop shaking, either from Paris (via the less easily monitored commercial) or from Brussels if necessary. I feel that we must run at least one of those atrocity pictures (to convince the French—and the world—that we are not taking the position that these fellagah are nothing but national heroes), and I suggest we run the one of Allier, because he can be part of my story. It is the least ghastly and he is French.

c) As soon as you cable me the story is running—and the pictures—I propose to go to Mitterrand myself, tell him what I have done, how I did it, and tell him everything I saw. This procedure will make it utterly impossible for France to indict me for

---

* Robert Barrat, a French journalist who had been arrested after interviewing an Algerian outlaw leader.

"nondénonciation de crime contre l'état," which is the rap they arrested Barrat for. I won't get in trouble with the FLN, because I actually will not know the only thing that threatens them—to wit, the location of their headquarters.

d) When we appear, the press is surely going to come to me, and if you agree, I would propose to tell the press just what I have told Mitterrand.

There is only one more thing. I am going to end up with some wonderful pictures, pictures that I can sell for a hell of a price, pictures that we cannot possibly use. To reward myself for risking my peau, I would like your permission to do so. Of course, not until we are on the stands, and of course with *Newsweek* credit.

I sat in my hotel room for three days, waiting for the call that never came. To pass the time, I smoked some dope for the first time in my life—some hashish that I had been given by Jean's half sister in Geneva and carried halfway around Europe waiting for an appropriate occasion. I was completely nervous, scared that I might do things I would never do if I wasn't high. I bolted the door to my hotel room in the St. George, filled up my pipe with the hash, and fired it up.

Nothing happened. Nothing. And then I went to sleep. Woke up an hour later, reloaded the pipe, and went to sleep again. And that was that.

When it became obvious that Monsieur Delorme had disappeared, I flew back to Paris, and next morning went to see Ambassador Dillon to let him know what I had been up to in Algeria. As I was leaving the embassy I got a call from my maid, telling me that the cops were scouring the Place des Vosges for me. And when I got back to my office on the rue de Berri in a taxi, I was suddenly surrounded by cops and black Citroëns. Two cops got me by the elbows, lifting me off the pavement, and asked me to come along with them. I was protesting and asking for information, but just when I needed it I couldn't remember the French word for "warrant." It's hard to ask some burly French cop if he has a warrant when you don't know the word for warrant (*mandat d'amener*). In their car, the commissaire turned to me and said, "Bradlee, you are the object of an expulsion decree, and you must leave France within forty-eight hours." I kept asking them why, and got no answer, in the car, or later at the headquarters of the DST (Direction de la Surveillance du Territoire, roughly equivalent to the FBI).

For the next two hours. I sat in a small room, not allowed to use a phone, while one of my captors typed up a *procés verbal*, which added up to an admission that I had been arrested and served with an expulsion order. Expulsion from France didn't fit in with my plans at all. Tony and I were to be married in July, and had arranged to start off our new life with a year—and four stepchildren—in Paris. It would be tougher and less exciting in Chevy Chase. I left the DST headquarters with the expulsion order, plus the words, "In view of derogatory information received about Bradlee, Benjamin," but with no idea what the derogatory information was. Plainly it had to do with my abortive attempt to get to the FLN leadership, but since I had failed in that attempt and had written nothing, I was mystified.

When I went back to see Ambassador Dillon and enlist his help in getting the expulsion order canceled, he just laughed. "Best recommendation you could get as a reporter," he said, but he sent the deputy chief of mission, Ted Achilles, over to the Foreign Office to inquire and protest. The French press was strongly critical of the government and supportive of me, endowing me with qualities ("known and esteemed by his colleagues") that had gone unremarked for years. My biggest problem was John Denson, the crusty, irascible *Newsweek* editor. He wanted me to get kicked out of what he called "the cradle of liberty," and to "get into all the newsreels." Quai d'Orsay friends were telling me "this is madness," and urged me to shut up, while they made it go away. Finally, with Dillon and Achilles leading the way, we got the expulsion order "suspended." But that wasn't enough for Denson. Now he wanted the suspension "repealed," and it took another few days to get that done.

Despite the fact that I had failed to get the story, my arrest put me on the map. As a foreign correspondent I had been what I had been for two years. Except for my colleagues, and a few insiders in

Washington and Europe, no one had paid much attention to me or my work. But now I was enjoying my first fifteen minutes on page one. I had arrived professionally, in some strange way that I didn't understand. I failed to recognize this first example of how celebrity can change the meaning of events.

The day my arrest was on the front page of the Paris *Herald Tribune*, Susan Mary Patten asked me to lunch, somewhat to the chagrin of the scheduled guest of honor, United States Representative to the United Nations Henry Cabot Lodge. Susan Mary was married to Bill Patten on the American Embassy's political staff (and after Bill's death, to columnist Joe Alsop), and ran a "salon" on the rue Weber. I was just a bit scared, to tell the truth, unsure of what was going on, but her hospitality was a kind gesture, deeply appreciated. I didn't stop to think whether the invitation meant that I had arrived in some new, uncharted waters.

But never mind page one or guest of honor, no one would tell me exactly what the hell had happened to me, why I had been arrested (and haven't to this day). Only gradually did it emerge, a whisper at a time, that somewhere along the line in Algiers my North African contacts had changed from FLN rebels to agents provocateurs working for French intelligence. I sensed the presence of the fine Corsican hand of my "friend," Colonel Jean-Baptiste Biaggi, who was to become one of the leaders of the French settlers, and who would fight to the bitter end against President Charles de Gaulle and Algerian independence some years later.

The sheer joy and romance of being a foreign correspondent is hard to explain, even harder to exaggerate. Even when it's essentially boring—an interminable, no news foreign ministers' meeting in Geneva, for instance, or yet another new prime minister in France's Fourth Republic—the reporting has to be done. The story has to be filed, then one often partakes in some really creative bitching by the best bitchers outside the Army, followed by exhaustive discussions about what to eat and where to eat it. Expense account living encourages gastronomic risk taking, and imagination.

Even when it's dangerous—a war, a revolution, a plane ride

in an uninsurable vehicle, where the old bromide about the pilot wanting to survive as much as you do seems at least debatable— the adrenaline high is incredible, and long-lasting. Listen to a war correspondent talk about a night under fire in Vietnam's III Corps, and thirty years later it will sound like last night. Listen to a foreign correspondent who wandered in fear and consternation through the streets of Budapest in the fall of 1956, and you will hear passion forever, no matter how much the story is filtered through modesty, true or false. Listen to a man who will never be the same after seeing Rwanda and know the power of history, seen firsthand.

In between boredom and danger lie oceans of plain delight. And in those oceans you find stories like Grace Kelly's wedding to Prince Rainier of Monaco . . . the romantic love story of a beautiful Hollywood movie star and a real-life prince, regardless of the dubious quality of his princely lineage. On the luxurious Train Bleu overnight from Paris, Crosby Noyes of the *Washington Star*, Art Buchwald, and I formed a latter-day Three Musketeers—united against all enemies, sharing all risks and rewards, one for all, all for one. Our unity was quickly tested at the Monte Carlo railroad station when we couldn't find a taxi. We fanned out in search, seemingly forever, when Noyes finally found a Renault *Deux Chevaux* cab. These cars were smaller than Volkswagens, barely big enough for two passengers and two small suitcases, much less the Three Musketeers. But we were desperate. Noyes grabbed it, I jumped in, and off we went to our hotel, passing Buchwald en route, shaking his fist and shouting something about the Musketeers.

Actually, it was shortsighted of us to strand Art, because he was the only Musketeer with any connection to anyone involved with the wedding. He had seen Grace Kelly once, and he had actually shaken hands with Rainier, which was more than Noyes and I could say. My "connection," such as it was, was hardly promising. One of my St. Mark's School roommates had a brother, whom I barely knew, whose wife, whom I did not know, had been a classmate of the bride, and was now a bridesmaid. She was also born hostile to journalists, and this hostility had been honed to enmity by the creeps who were running the wedding.

None of us had a single credential to any of the parties whose guest lists and shenanigans an anxious world and impatient editors were waiting for. Between us we could muster only a single "pool" ticket, to some decidedly second-rate event. It was this moment when Buchwald pulled a rabbit out of his hat with what I have always believed was the best column he ever wrote, in a distinguished career of writing funny columns. The reason he didn't have a ticket, he wrote, was because the Buchwalds and the Grimaldis had been feuding for centuries, ever since the thirteenth century. According to Buchwald:

The reason for the feud is lost somewhere in the cobwebs of history, but it was a time when one of my ancestors, then working for the Viking News Service, covered a battle that Rainier Grimaldi fought against the Flemish Navy. Rainier I, then an admiral, decreed that only members of the Associated, United and International Press associations could accompany him into battle, but my ancestor, disguised as a Genoese sailor, hid on board the flagship and scooped the other three news agencies by four years. . . .

And so it's gone down through history. There was talk that Charlotte de Grammont, daughter of the Marshal de Grammont, who married the Duke of Valentinois on April 28, 1659, was in love with Rudolph Buchwald, then a court reporter for the News of the World. But we only have Rudolph's diary as evidence, and everyone in the family knows how unreliable he was.

Just last year, my Aunt Molly from Brooklyn was making up her guest list for my cousin Joseph's wedding to a nice girl from Flatbush.

I suggested she invite Prince Rainier, who was then in the United States.

"No Grimaldis," she said, "will be allowed at Joseph's wedding."

"But Aunt Molly," I protested, "this is the twentieth century. We've got to forget ancient family feuds. Prince Rainier's a nice fellow."

"I don't care for myself," Aunt Molly said, "but you know what a long memory your Uncle Oscar has. Besides, has Prince Rainier invited Joseph to his wedding?"

Of course, Art got his invitation—to the *church*, by personal courier from the palace, as soon as the Paris *Herald Tribune* hit the streets of Monte Carlo. And now Noyes and I were high and dry. I was able to dredge up an old acquaintanceship with Tom Guinzburg, whose father was the founder and editor of Viking Press. Tom was married to another bridesmaid, the actress Rita Gam, and I invited them to join Crosby, Art, and myself at some fabulously expensive restaurant overlooking the Mediterranean. But we got nothing. Zero. Miss Gam just sat there, staring moistly and silently ahead. Gorgeous, but mute. As a journalist, I always preferred my sources gorgeous and talkative.

But the food was incredible. That was one of the glories of France. When you start sucking air on a story, there's always a little one-star restaurant within easy reach where journalistic frustrations can be overwhelmed by food and wine. Suck air in Zagreb, and both you and the readers suffer. Suck air in Monte Carlo, and you can always eat at the three-star restaurant in Cap d'Antibes, and let the readers suffer alone.

The other great royal romance in Europe during the fifties, of course, involved Princess Margaret and Group Captain Peter Townsend. I didn't cover that, territorially co-opted as I was by our London correspondent, but watched in breathless awe as one of my colleagues—and pals—covered it in the greatest detail, although he was nowhere near Belgium, where Townsend was licking his wounds, or England, where the princess was being held in durance vile. In fact, my colleague was in the South of France with a female person not his wife. In fact, he was in the South of France with the wife of a colleague. Every morning and evening, he would call his Paris office. A loyal secretary would read him the wires, and the best of the French dailies' *exclusifs*. He would then hang up, write, call his office back, and dictate: "Dateline—Ostend, Belgium." Or whatever.

*   *   *

Tony and I were ready to get married long months before we actually pulled it off. First she had promised herself to complete analysis, before making any major move, and that took a full two years. Last, Jean Dax, the miracle doctor, moved heaven and earth to get a fast Wasserman certificate for Tony. In between there were the normal thousand things to do, complicated by small hurdles like oceans, divorces, and separation agreements and by the unforeseeable, all-powerful news. Algeria, for instance.

Jean and I were divorced in Paris, across the Place Henri IV from our apartment, in the Palais de Justice. Charlie Torem, from Coudert Frères in Paris, represented me, reluctantly. He knew and liked Jean. One afternoon in 1955, in a ratty little office in the very attic of the Palais de Justice, Jean and I showed up for the key moment in a French divorce, the *tentatif de réconciliation*, where the magistrate is charged by law with trying to bring the two litigants back together, to call off the divorce. "Monsieur," he addressed me with apparent interest, "quand est-ce que vous avez quitté le lit conjugal?" Literally, when did you leave the conjugal bed. Actually, when did you last make love to this woman? I couldn't remember exactly, and thought it was none of his business, but I'd been coached to say "at least a year," which was probably accurate.

And that was that. A few days later Jean and I were divorced. Thirteen years of marriage, tied with foreign string in a foreign land, and put away on a shelf. Two people out of love, never really in love, never recovered from the unseen scars of almost a four-year absence. And one child of seven, loving his father and needing his father, facing a future he didn't know or want, or cause. How is that a decent act? Can one man's happiness ever be worth causing that kind of misery? Even knowing, or at least truly believing, that after a better, wiser search your wife will find someone else with interests that are more shared and more enjoyed? Even hoping, but never knowing, that your child will remain a vital part of your life, or become a vital part of your life again? All but convinced that your child will gain more from the happiness and stability of his parents' new lives than he will lose from the unhappiness and instability of his parents' old life.

I think the conscientious pursuit of happiness by itself can validate decisions to change, to try again, especially when failure to change will lead to lives of duplicity, dishonesty, and deceit.

The answers will always be unknown, if only because roads not taken lead nowhere. Jean did in fact find the right man, Bill Haussermann, a Boston lawyer whose kind patience with my son would place him in my Hall of Fame, if he hadn't already been there. Ben was miserable for sure at what he felt was my treachery, but later he followed me into the newspaper business, after three months on the *Kabul Times*, such a strange place to start in the newspaper business, at the end of a two-year stint in the Peace Corps in Afghanistan. He returned to Boston, his beloved "Hub," and as an editor at the *Boston Globe* he has made me enormously proud.

As usual under stress, I put my nose down, and my ass up, and start driving toward the next goal. My next goal was to marry Tony, and I started driving toward July 6, 1956, with all deliberate speed. We were married in an ornate *salle* of the ornate Hotel de Ville, Paris's City Hall, a few blocks up the Seine from the Place de la Concorde, the Tuileries, and the Louvre. The ceremony was performed by a deputy mayor, a large, florid man who worked in the Renault factory in Paris. He spoke French with a heavy Russian accent, and paused in the middle of the ceremony to congratulate me on my obvious appreciation of the beauties of Paris, which I took to be a reference both to Tony's looks, to her maiden name, Antoinette Pinchot, and to my address in the priceless Place des Vosges.

Members of the wedding party included her sister Mary, and Mary's husband Cord Meyer, still together, however barely, Lionel and Toto Durand, the Buchwalds, the Torems, Jean Dax, and the *New York Daily News* correspondent Bernard Valery. Lionel Durand was one of the most remarkable men I ever met. He was my "assistant," which does him no justice at all, since he was twice as smart as I was about most things, certainly about all things French. In an uncharacteristic moment of largesse, *Newsweek* had given me my choice: a secretary or an assistant, provided he or she was French (and therefore could be paid less money, and in francs). I had chosen Lionel, as the absolute best of the breed. He was the son of a

French mother and a Haitian diplomat, married to a Jewish girl from Brooklyn. He was tall, dark, and handsome, incredibly well connected, especially to the cultural scene, where I struggled. He used the French familiar to Picasso, and was tutoyered back. He knew the leaders of the burgeoning French film industry, the literary shots, big and small. He was a fabulous asset to me and to *Newsweek*.*

Buchwald was my best man, stage-managing the ceremony while whining about Valery being late. We adjourned from the Hôtel de Ville to the Place des Vosges, trailing tin cans from our car, courtesy of Durand, who knew full well that the French had no such custom. And we drank bottle after bottle of champagne, toasting the miracle we had pulled off and the start of our great adventure.

In September 1956, Soviet Premier Nikolai Bulganin and Soviet Communist Party First Secretary Nikita Khrushchev made a rare trip outside the Iron Curtain—to Yugoslavia—and free world editors in their infinite wisdom sent a mob of journalists to see what they looked like, closeup. Including me. Trouble was my editors had just sent me to Turkey for one of those room-emptying "NATO's Southern Flank" stories that no one reads. I was intercepted at the Athens airport, and diverted to Belgrade via Salonika. More trouble arose when Bulganin and Khrushchev's plane from Moscow and my plane from Salonika hit Belgrade at the same time. Guess who had to wait 10,000 feet over the Yugoslav capital, while the Soviet leaders paraded through the city?

That meant that for the first time in my foreign correspondency I had to write a color story about an event I never saw—and this was before television showed things over and over again. By now, I was enough one of the boys so that I could get a "fill" that I trusted. A "fill" is a fill-in, and for news organizations who are habitually outgunned by the opposition, they are an absolute necessity. My fill came from Crosby Noyes, Alex Kendrick of CBS, and Sy Freidin, then working for *Collier's* magazine. When I had filed—after only a

---

* Lionel died unexpectedly in his sleep one night in 1961, shortly after he had been seriously tear-gassed in Algeria.

few hours on the ground—I had to face the question of lodging, since all hotel rooms had been sold for days. The senior American diplomat in Belgrade was Robert Hooker. He and his wife Dolly were old friends of my parents, but not yet of mine. They had turned down requests from their real press pals like Cy Sulzberger of the *New York Times* and were extremely reluctant to take me in, but finally Dolly agreed. She even drove me into Belgrade from #5 Pushkinova Pet the next morning, as we fantasized about the stir we would cause if the ambassador's wife was caught in an automobile accident, wearing only slippers and an overcoat over her nightgown.

The Soviets were eventually headed for a meeting with Marshal Tito on the fortress island of Brioni, but before they got there they visited Zagreb and then drove north from Zagreb to Bled, the fabulous lakeside resort in the heart of the old Austro-Hungarian Empire. The drive from Zagreb to Bled was hilarious, as the foreign correspondents were assigned four to a car driven by Yugoslav intelligence officers, who spoke at least some English since they would smile sometimes at various anti-Communist wisecracks. I was with Noyes, Ed Korry of the United Press, and Bill Stoneman of the *Chicago Daily News*. We kept getting stopped by Yugoslav soldiers, and with no help from our driver we had to talk our way through each roadblock. We finally elected Stoneman as our chief negotiator, after he lost his temper once. With a childlike smile on his face, and waggling his credentials in one soldier's face, he said with a gentle smile, "I guess you don't know who we are, do you, you dumb Communist son of a bitch." Our driver could barely stifle his laughter, but we were always waved through.

The phone call was from Dan Avni, the press attaché (and maybe more) at the Embassy of Israel, and a friend and colleague from my press attaché days.* It was early morning, October 28, 1956.

I could hear the tension in his clipped accent. (Like so many Israelis, he had served in the British Army as a young man.) The

---

* Dan is now Dan Vittorio Avni-Segre, dear friend and distinguished Israeli intellectual, who has taught in his native Italy as well as Israel, author of the wonderful *Memoirs of a Fortunate Jew*, about his incredible boyhood in Fascist Italy.

tension seemed reasonable. The headlines were ominous. In Egypt, Gamal Abdel Nasser had drawn a line in the sand when he nationalized the Suez Canal, and the British, French, and Israelis were about to react—with invasions. In Hungary, anti-Soviet sentiment had mushroomed into an anti-Soviet revolution. And in the United States, Eisenhower was in the last week of his run for reelection.

No one could have guessed what happened on October 24: a Russian army, including heavy tanks, had invaded Hungary to wipe out the anti-Soviet Revolution.

On October 29, Israel would invade Egypt "to eliminate fedayeen bases on the Sinai."

On November 5—after almost a week of bombardment and bombing—the British and French would invade Egypt, landing paratroopers at the mouth of the Suez Canal in Port Said and Port Fuad, respectively.

On November 6, Eisenhower and Nixon were overwhelmingly reelected, and Ike was going to withdraw U.S. support from the British and French, effectively forcing an early cease-fire.

Avni knew how much I wanted to make my first trip to Israel, he reminded me in that early morning call on October 28. We had talked about it many times. Now, he said, would be a particularly good time. Right now. In fact, he told me, there was a TWA plane leaving that very night, and if I hurried, he thought I could still get a seat. In fact, just in case I could go, he had reserved one for me.

In fact, it was the last commercial plane to land in Tel Aviv before the Israeli Army drove the next morning into the Sinai, Gaza, and eventually to the Suez Canal itself. I was alone in the Dan Hotel, surrounded as usual by an army of *Time-Life* scribes, photographers, and—toughest of all to compete against—the subarmy of gofers who rented the cars, made the reservations, filed the copy, fought the censors, and left the correspondents free to report. But we were comfortable at *Newsweek* knowing that we were competing with words actually printed in the magazine, not words filed to the magazine's rewrite staff.

This was my first shooting war since my destroyer days in the

Pacific. I was nervous, and I needed a story of my own that would outlast the Israeli Army's high-speed race to victory. My story was waiting for me at the head of the taxi line outside the hotel. I've forgotten his name long since, but when I asked the driver how I could get to the front, he said simply, "What about me?" Turns out he was on weekend leave from a unit that was fighting outside the Gaza Strip even as we spoke. He figured he could talk his way through the Kilometer 90 checkpoint, drive ten more kilometers to the front, watch the fighting, talk to the troops—"plenty of Americans," he promised—and get me back for a late supper.

And he was as good as his word. I filed the following story late that night, and it ran, word for word:

TO WAR IN A TAXI

Benjamin Bradlee, Newsweek European correspondent, is covering the Israeli front. A veteran of Arab wars and revolts* (once arrested by the French for getting too close to the Algerian story), Bradlee flew to Tel Aviv from Paris in time to eyewitness Israel's thrust which overran Gaza and broke the back of the Egyptian armed strength.

It's a strange war. From Tel Aviv, the Gaza battlefield is less than two hours away, down the main highway leading south through Jaffa. I drove down to the front in a seven-passenger DeSoto Taxi. (Israel's army command bars newspapermen from accompanying its troops.)

An hour and a half later, I watched the clash of Israeli and Egyptian armor in a fight that sealed the fate of Gaza. The battle unfolded literally before my eyes.

Overhead American-built Mustangs (World War II vintage) circled lazily before peeling off through moderate Egyptian ack-ack fire to attack selected targets with bombs, rockets and machine guns.

The scene of battle leaps suddenly from a countryside deceptively peaceful in the bright autumn sunshine: rich irrigated

---

* I had never covered an Arab war, and knew next to nothing about the Middle East.

guava and orange groves; children playing shoot the chutes in air raid shelters of the roadside kibbutzim (farm settlement).

Minutemen: As one nears the Gaza strip, fields are either deserted or farmers are at work in them with guns slung across their backs.

Five miles from Gaza, an Israeli garrison waved "hello" from a frontier hut. Around the next bend, at the crest of a hill 1.7 miles from the Egyptian city of Gaza, the fighting raged.

At first I could see nothing but the city, silhouetted against the blue Mediterranean. Then an orange flash, a puff of smoke and the sickening thud of mortar fire. There are answering flashes and the roar of artillery, and finally the chatter of machine-gun bursts.

As I faced Gaza, Israeli troops moved up under cover of an artillery barrage. I scrambled to a rise of ground—a solitary grandstand seat from which to watch the fighting at close range.

Four fighters roared in from the south, hedgehopping at a few hundred feet. From their flight direction, I thought they were Egyptian and looked anxiously for a nonexistent ditch. But they were Israeli planes, picking off objectives pinpointed by ground-to-air radio.

I looked back to check the position of my waiting taxi. An entire battalion suddenly materialized from the deserted countryside. A tank-led task force smashed its way into Gaza from another flank.

It wasn't much of a battle. Gaza, birthplace of the Biblical Goliath, showed few scars. Most of the fighting was on the outskirts, where Egyptians had been dug in.

Hands Up: An Israeli tank commander scoffed. The Egyptians, they were bad soldiers. They held their guns above their heads and tried to run. Then they threw away their guns and put their hands above their heads and surrendered. Similar cockiness, pride and contempt for Egypt is reflected all the way back to Tel Aviv.

In the cities of Israel, signs of war are hard to find. There are queues for buses (public transport has been requisitioned) and for gas. A few cars are camouflaged with a mixture of water and mud. An occasional window is striped with paper as a precaution against Egyptian air raids that never came. Old and faded curtains produce a relatively effective blackout. Automobile headlights glint dimly through blue-painted lenses. Newspapers show patches of white space, where censors got in their licks.

The Plain of Sharon was peacefully asleep beneath a starlit sky as I drove north from Tel Aviv toward Haifa. A single Israeli soldier guarded the highway junction where the road branches off to the Jordanian frontier, less than five miles away. Israelis note with satisfaction that their border with Jordan has never been more quiet in eight years of uneasy armistice.

These many years later that report sounds like a destroyer sailor talking, unfamiliar with military tactics, hyping the action just a tad, pleased with himself and the in-a-taxi angle.

A few days later, I was wandering around the docks of Haifa on another story, looking for details on the capture of an Egyptian submarine, when I suddenly spotted the submarine captain himself, sitting solemnly in full uniform in the front seat of an automobile, blindfolded. They had blindfolded him to make it difficult for him to figure out his destination. He was going to be interrogated at Israeli naval headquarters less than a mile away in the hills over Haifa, but they drove him around and around in circles for more than half an hour, trying to make it impossible to know where he was or where he had been. A picture of me, peering through a car window at the blindfolded Egyptian, appeared in the next issue of *Newsweek*.

I was and remain blown away by Israel and the Israelis, by their energy, by their arrogance, their condescension to those of us who are not accustomed to living within range of enemy guns, by their commitment, by their idealism. I never really understood it when Israelis told me how close their enemies were until I saw and heard those guns.

I was stunned by how American many of them were—in their

aspirations and values, and in fact. If you yelled, "Anyone here from the States?" hands always went up.*

The Israeli Army had overrun the Egyptians in the Sinai so fast that the world's attention was now focusing on Nasser's nationalizing of the Suez Canal, and what the British and French were going to do about nationalization. The place to be was obviously the canal, but how to get there was not so obvious. Those of us who had rushed to Israel felt cheated because, even though we'd had a good little war, we had missed Budapest and the Hungarian uprising, going on at the same time. We were damned if we were going to miss out on Egypt, too.

I had sent the following advisory to the New York editors: "My chances of getting to the canal from Tel Aviv are nil. The Israeli Army command tells me they are not going [as far as] the canal; they'll stop 10 kilometers short, and that looks like a mighty poor 10 kilometers to be walking alone."

When a ride to Athens came up, I decided to take it, because there were several flights from Athens to Cyprus, including one at 9:00 A.M. the next morning, and whatever action the Anglo-French force took would start from Cyprus. I was at the Athens airport before seven, and talked my way onto the 9 o'clock flight by persuading the captain to leave 60 kilograms of freight behind in Greece. Of course, when I got to Nicosia, the British and French commands had accredited all the correspondents they were going to accredit. But they took one more, and one hour after the French Army landed at Port Fuad (next to Port Said), I landed at the already secure airport between the two.

Both cities were a mess. In these situations, the number-one problem for a journalist is always transportation. How do you get around in a city you've never seen, filled with people speaking a language you cannot understand? Just as it was gospel among my foreign correspondent friends to tap an Israeli Embassy (if there was

* This is a standard time-saving procedure for foreign correspondents, especially when a deadline looms. The classic example of the genre can be found in Edward Behr's report of a BBC correspondent, Desmond Stewart, asking a group of nuns in the Congo who had just been assaulted by rampaging African tribesmen: "Anyone here been raped and speaks English?"

one) for the best skinny, it was also gospel in those days to join up with *Paris Match* magazine photographers if you needed anything material like a jeep, or a pistol, or a fine dinner (and fine wine). The *Match* photographer I found was young Jean Roy (pronounced "Roi," as in the French word for king), the cowboy to end all cowboys, married to actress Lola Montez. He wore French Army fatigues, and he had "liberated" an Egyptian Army jeep moments after it had been liberated by the French Army. Our crowd for the next three days consisted of Roy—the driver—David Seymour, the magnificent Magnum photographer known as "Schim," who was working for *Newsweek*; and my old buddy Frank White, the *Time-Life* Paris Bureau chief, joined occasionally by Howard "Handlebars" Handleman, the European Bureau chief for the old INS. Thanks to Roy, we had a fine dinner of sole, salad, and a chilled white (French) wine in the basement of a bombed-out house, hidden from scavengers picking over garbage in search of food.

Next day, we drove through a ruined city, teeming and deserted at the same time, looking in darkened, lightless morgues—and counting bodies until we puked. We watched trucks unload sacks of flour into crowds that hadn't eaten in three days. I can still see Schim, a wisp of a man, standing on the jeep silhouetted against the darkling sky, quietly photographing mob scenes of Egyptians ripping sacks of flour apart.

Two hours later he was dead, and so was Roy.

While White and I peeled off to write and file our stories, Roy and Schim had driven down the canal highway and out of friendly territory, into no-man's-land, and finally into Egyptian territory, where they were ambushed. White and I were writing when we heard the news. A different day—a day when we didn't have to file, a different hour, when we still had time to write—and White and I would have been history.

Filing was somewhere between hard and impossible. The French offered to take my copy by motorboat to the battleship *Jean Bart*, which was moored in the Mediterranean somewhere. There it would be censored, they said, sent by radio to Toulon or Marseille (someday), and from there, maybe to PREWI, Paris, and on to New

York. I figured there was no chance of that ever working. There were no civilian facilities up and working. So I bummed a ride on an Air Atlas plane to Akrotiri, in southern Cyprus, where the military had seized all communications. We finally found two spaces (there were no seats) on a four-engined York bomber-transport, WWII vintage, for a ten-hour, non-stop, non-pressurized flight to Hyères, in southern France, listening to the moans of a French admiral who had lost most of his balls in a jeep explosion a few hours earlier. From Hyères it was only three hours more to Paris, where I filed this dispatch:

Port Said is now an ugly, festering sore on the mouth of the Suez Canal. Its cemeteries are littered with hundreds of unburied dead, bloating fast under a scorching Mediterranean sun and black with flies.

The wards of the city's candlelit hospitals are jammed with moaning wounded. Its morgues are clogged chest-high with dead. Streets are blocked with rubble or awash with broken sewer and water mains. Low-hanging wires threaten decapitation.

Black-veiled women sit motionless, quietly weeping in the rubble. Men in dirty striped pajamas and barefoot children pick through ruins for pots and pans. Dead goats and donkeys rot in the streets, unnoticed except for the stench. There is a choking, inescapable smell of death, smoke, and sewage.

Even before ships and airplanes brought in British troops, Port Said was devastated by RAF Venoms and Hunters, backed up by a naval bombardment.

Yellow Hearse: Lt. Gen. Sir Hugh Charles Stockwell, commander of the Anglo-French army task force, told correspondents just in from Cyprus that only 100 civilians were killed in Port Said. As he said this, we who had been there for two days followed a yellow Coca-Cola truck full of corpses to one of the three cemeteries. Twenty-seven bodies were unloaded. Those strong enough to brave the odor counted another 100 awaiting burial under the bright purple bougainvillaea bushes inside. There are at least 2,000 dead.

Gen. Sir Charles Keightley, commander in chief of the binational forces, assured newsmen on Cyprus there was no "shortage of food" in Port Said. We had just watched thousands of Egyptians rioting for food. Ignoring tank guns trained on them and troop-filled trucks which roared through the streets, they pillaged stores and attacked any fellow citizen who clutched an edible morsel.

Ghost White: One morning I watched a mob break through a barbed-wire barricade around an open-air flour depot in the center of town. Like the flies buzzing around them, they swarmed over 200-pound sacks, then staggered away with more than they could carry. Barely did they get more than five yards before being set upon by others. Nervous British troops watched the mobs, then fired machine guns into the air. The paratroop major in command radioed for tank reinforcements but, before the Centurions arrived, an English-speaking Egyptian timidly approached him with a better idea: "Get your soldiers to split the flour sacks with their bayonets. Then the people can fill small containers." The major bought the idea. Egyptians plunged under human pyramids and came out with filthy baskets or aprons half-filled. Black-haired and dark-skinned men and women were powdered a ghostly white as they swept the streets for a last fistful.

I watched a small, ramshackle truck filled with barrels of stinking sunfish literally torn apart by a mob filling hands, pockets, even dust-stained fezzes.

In four days, only two hole-in-the-wall stores in the Arab quarter dared to open. I watched 200 people charge one of them and plunder its shelves clean in less than five minutes.

An Anglo-French communiqué announced: "The civil facilities of Port Said are being quickly normalized." Two days later there was still no electricity, no water and no police. At the Egyptian General Hospital, the principal medical officer, Dr. Elezdeine Hossny, said in halting English: "It is horrible. I have to operate by flashlight or kerosene lamp. I have to work in the most unsterile conditions, getting buckets of water wherever I can find them. Listen to those moans. We had only 500 ampules of morphine on hand and they were gone days ago. Many of these people have bullets in their abdomens and legs. But we have no anesthesia for them."

The doctor hadn't left the hospital grounds in 72 hours, but said he had counted more than 500 dead. He took me through two morgues. One was piled high with bodies. The other was temporarily empty as two masked attendants swabbed blood off the floor.

Crude Wiring: The countryside is littered with Egyptian equipment (mostly British made) and British landing force gear, marked with a big white "H" to distinguish it from the enemy's. There are many Russian T-34 tanks, mortars and guns. I watched a British Tommy shoot the lock off an abandoned Egyptian truck. It was empty, except for four Russian riot guns. The land surrounding Gamil Airfield is riddled with foxholes less than three feet deep (anything deeper strikes water) and a crude minefield of hand grenades, visibly wired.

The absence of any organized police generated terror in Port Said. One young Egyptian, spotting my green correspondent's badge, broke through a mob and begged: "Can't you get them to restore order? The jails were all emptied weeks ago and convicts were given weapons as soon as the bombardment started. Soldiers left more when they fled. There are thousands of guns hidden in houses today. Our homes and stores are being robbed. We are all helpless."

Every street is alive with people, but these are unlike other Arab mobs. They are unbelievably polite and friendly to Europeans. For two days, I roamed freely in a jeep amidst the riots and pillaging. Wherever I went, the jeep was immediately surrounded. In French North Africa, riding in that unprotected fashion, I would have been promptly killed. But here Arabs want to talk. And they beg for food with pathetic hand-to-mouth gestures or ask for medical supplies for their families. We had traded a commandeered Egyptian Chevrolet truck against three cases of French K rations, but they lasted only a few hours. Now there is nothing to give them.

Two wars in three weeks, separated only by the Sinai Desert. My new wife—and her four children—were in Paris, and I was somewhere in the Mediterranean, doing what I felt I was on earth to do.

There was no real down side to living in Paris in the fifties, but the people one worked for liked Paris, too, and every so often they would decide to drop in on you. "Touring the bureaus" it was called then—and now. A chance for big shots to travel abroad in search of contacts and anecdotes which they could use later to prove to their friends that they were in fact big shots.

Malcolm Muir, Sr., was a case in point. He was the editor-in-chief of *Newsweek*, a small man to whom status among the rich and famous was vitally important. He and his wife Francie, a large woman, to whom status among the rich and famous was equally important, generally came to Paris and London once a year to polish their status. For weeks before they arrived, the correspondent had time for little else but to prepare for the royal visit. Any failure, or even shortfall, in these preparations was likely to be fatal. An earlier European executive of *Newsweek* had bitten the dust solely because the limousine he had ordered to take the Muirs out to the Duke and Duchess of Windsor's *"moulin"* in Gif-sur-Yvette outside of Paris was too wide to fit between the stone pillars at the entrance of the mile-long driveway. The heavens had opened with rain, and Malcolm and Francie had been forced to slosh through the mud for so long that even curtsying was a challenge.

The correspondent was in a classic no-win situation during these ceremonial visits. If General de Gaulle, in self-imposed exile at Colombey-les-Deux-Eglises, was unwilling to receive Mr. Muir, it was because the correspondent had no influence, surely not because the general had been bored to death last time he had to listen to the American businessman. If General Eisenhower couldn't fit the Muirs into his schedule at SHAPE headquarters, it was because the *Newsweek* correspondent lacked clout. When the Muirs insisted on giving a cocktail party, either at our apartment or in a room at the Ritz, if their fellow big shots dropped by for a drink, it was to see the Muirs. If no one came, it was my ass. One of the longest forty-five minutes of my life came just before the first guests arrived for cocktails one night, while the Muirs and Tony and I tried to make polite conversation over the racket of four children under nine, and no one else. Finally, the doorbell rang and it was good old Paul Reynaud, age eighty, escorted by his assistant, our old pal de Kemoularia. "Ah! it's the President," Muir said with his hands outstretched, and face beaming, convinced it was he, not Claude de Kemoularia, who had produced the former prime minister. And I was alive for another year.

Sometimes, visiting firemen made less pretentious social demands. Harry Kern, the foreign editor, for instance. His major interests were good food and good wine, and he was knowledgeable about both, and the very finest exotic French lingerie. And if Kern himself couldn't find time for a quick trip to the lingerie store, the *Newsweek* Paris correspondent was expected to volunteer.

John Denson, the remarkable character who was *Newsweek*'s editor for eight years, had different hungers. Mostly, John wanted company, and American food. He wasn't remotely interested in seeing anyone new, much less any Frenchman. At lunch, even in the very best restaurants, he wanted hamburger, or scrambled eggs. At night, he would sit in the darkest corner of a nightclub, hiding behind dark glasses, drinking orange juice with a brandy chaser, and grunt every so often. But occasionally he would get horny and wonder aloud about what someone he was looking at would be like in bed. (Never mind, we all wondered, what the hell would *he be* like between the sheets?)

One night, late in some Left Bank joint, John found his eyes falling more and more on a tall, rangy, attractive blonde with broad shoulders, significant cleavage, and very theatrical makeup. A couple of brandies into the evening, John asked me to find out who she was. Well, I already knew. She was the well-known Coccinelle.

And she was a man.

"The hell she is," John said, when I explained Coccinelle to him. "Look at those tits." The tits were in fact impressive, but the papers were filled with news of Christine Jorgensen and her revolutionary sex change operation. I told John to take a look at her hands and especially her knuckles, but he would have none of it, and we asked her over to our table for a drink. I told Coccinelle that Denson didn't believe his eyes, and John began to think I was trying to protect him from some predator he refused to see. It took almost an hour to talk him out of the joint, and back to his hotel room.

Denson took some getting used to, with his full-time dark glasses, and his habit of chewing while he mumbled. After one session with Denson, a young female researcher asked my friend, Gordon Manning, "My God, what were those nuts he was chewing?" and Gordon answered, "I think they were mine."

EIGHT

NEWSWEEK, WASHINGTON

The prospect of returning to Washington in 1957 after six years plus in Europe filled me with trepidation. My territory stretched from the English Channel to the Sahara Desert, and from the Azores to Turkey, with a little Yugoslavia and a little Israel thrown in for good measure. But I had concentrated on France, North Africa, and the international conferences of Geneva, and in that bailiwick, the only real American players represented the *New York Times*, the *New York Herald Tribune*, *Time-Life*, *Newsweek*, U.S. *News*, whatever organization Teddy White was working for (ONA, *The Reporter*, or *Collier's*), plus David Schoenbrun of CBS. That made me a pretty big fish in a pretty small pond—maybe eight serious U.S. correspondents. But now I was heading back to be a small fish in a big pond—one Washington correspondent without experience covering national news, among 1,352 accredited Washington correspondents.

And I was scared. We had to go back to Washington to live up to Tony's separation agreement which allowed my stepchildren to stay in Paris for one year. So I was a beggar, not a chooser, delighted to have a perch even on the lowest rung of the job ladder in *Newsweek*'s Washington Bureau. (De Borchgrave had told me it would be a great "tactical mistake" to change from "The European correspondent" to "A Washington correspondent." He said my career would never recover from the demotion.)

Bureau manager Ken Crawford knew only that he had been told by the faceless "New York office" that Bradlee from Paris would be joining the bureau, never mind what reporter he might have had in mind for a vacancy he didn't even know he had.

But Kenneth Gale Crawford turned out to be generous, funny, tolerant, and a great teacher. Just a wonderful man. Like Ralph Blagden before him, Crawford spent hours explaining to me how Washington worked, who ran things and how, telling me who was important and why, and then who was really important. I could never repay him for half the kindnesses he showed me.

At least initially, my new colleagues were less generous. I had been assigned to a previously nonexistent beat, as a swing man to take up any slack in reporting diplomatic news, congressional news, and economic news. In practice that turned out to mean that I was given assignments that had been turned down by the regular beat men—Teddy Weintal at the State Department, Sam Shaffer on the Hill, and Bart Rowen in the field of economics. To establish their territorial sovereignty, newspapermen don't quite urinate around the perimeters of their domain the way jungle animals do. But they came close with me. Weintal gave me most stories—if any—involving Central America, most of Latin America, the Philippines, Morocco, Indonesia, and Antarctica. I figured that was fine to begin with while I learned my way around town, but I began to see the full dimension of my problem when Weintal went on vacation and I had to cover the State Department. When I called on Chip Bohlen, whom I had come to know in Paris, the first thing he asked me was "How come Weintal asked me not to talk to you while he was off on vacation?"

Same thing with Sam Shaffer. He had all of the Senate, where most of the action was. I could have the spit-backs, and I could have the House, except the Speaker of the House. The Speaker would hold an informal background session with reporters in his back office every noon, where the politics of the day's agenda were explained and the strategies outlined. It was inconceivable that a reporter could cover the House without covering those daily briefings. But I was supposed to. With Bart Rowen, matters were slightly different. Since I had never gone beyond Harvard's EcA, in which I had barely wangled a C, he felt less threatened. But he still owned the Treasury Secretary and Department, the Fed and its officers, the Council of Economic Advisors, and the Bureau of the Budget. It was agreed by all that the Central American Common Market was the perfect story for Bradlee: it was minor foreign, and minor economic, with minor congressional impact. No one understood it, no one cared a hoot about it, and it was a story whose time had not yet come.

The nominal bureau chief of *Newsweek* was Ernest K. Lindley, the columnist/lecturer and inventor of the infamous Lindley Rule, which allows public officials to talk to journalists with impunity. Reporters can use the information, but can cite only themselves as authority. Thus, under the Lindley Rule, the Secretary of Defense can tell reporters the United States is going to war Thursday with Trinidad, but the story must read, "The U.S. will declare war against Trinidad Thursday, this correspondent learned yesterday." It is the classic way to float trial balloons—by definition deceitful and duplicitous.

In fact, Lindley had nothing to do with the bureau. He wrote a weekly column on Washington and foreign affairs. He was one of the first journalists to hit the lecture circuit in a big way, giving more than 125 lectures a year in his prime. And he was in love with the new medium of television, especially Larry Spivak's "Meet the Press."

I, too, was in love with TV—watching it. I dared not aspire to appearances on television. But quite soon after I came back to the States, a friend of mine had the idea of a thirty-minute TV show, called "Briefing Session," where experts, including journalists occasionally, would chew on one of the day's topics. He wanted to do the first one on Algeria, and asked me to be on the panel since I passed for an expert, and would for the next few months. I jumped at the chance. Channel 13 broadcasting from New Jersey somewhere, a public service station, paying only $50, and no *travel expenses*. I still jumped to get my feet wet. When the word went around the office that I had gotten this TV gig, Lindley called me into his office for a little chat. How was I doing and all that stuff, and then the conversation turned to Algeria. He had been so interested in my dispatches "from the Magreb." I spent thirty minutes giving him a fill, as we say, and thought nothing of it.

Until my friend called me with the bad news. It seems that Lindley had called the producer to say that he had heard about "Briefing Session," and he was wondering if they would be interested in a name expert—like himself—to help the new show get off the ground. My TV debut was indefinitely postponed.

Lindley and I never did make it to friendship, but Weintal, Shaffer, Rowen, and I sure did. Crawford told me not to worry about their frailties but concentrate on their strengths. Teddy Weintal can't write worth a damn, he would say, but he picks up a lot of good information as an extra man on the Georgetown dinner circuit. All you have to do with Sam Shaffer is take out the self-serving quotes, Ken explained, and then he was the best man on the Hill. The quotes went this way: "'You've got to remember one thing, Sam,' Majority Leader Lyndon B. Johnson said in his private office Friday night...." Or even, "'Sam,' the Speaker of the House emphasized...."

I undertook to learn about power Washington with my new colleagues—and my guru was Ken Crawford. He gave me long hours of who's who, and who had been whom. He taught me to look for the good in people, and to find it before criticizing anyone. If someone landed on Ken's shit list, he truly belonged there.

The cast of characters who were my new colleagues included:

• Charles Wesley Roberts, the White House correspondent. Chuck Roberts had roomed with Tom Heggen at the University of Minnesota, and was in fact the model for Heggen's hero in his great war novel *Mister Roberts*.

- Leon Volkov, a former Soviet Air Force pilot, who had flown his MiG to freedom, covered Soviet affairs, when Weintal let him. Ken Crawford had ghost-written a series for Leon in the *Saturday Evening Post* called "Stalin Hates Me," and given him the $3,000 fee. Leon used the money to marry the beautiful Galina, then playing on Broadway in *Call Me* Madam.
- John Madigan, a journeyman journalist from Chicago, right out of *Front Page*, who constantly shuffled through his desk and his pockets, muttering, "We'll crack this case."
- Peter Wyden, a refugee from Berlin, who had been employed at sixteen by the U.S. Army when he told them, "I speek six languages, Heenglish, the bast." A good, commercial writer, with a good sense of humor. He and I wrote a play called *How Please?* while my wife was pregnant, and his wife was permanently pissed at him. Never produced. Great rejection letters.
- Dick Davis and his successor, the human vacuum cleaner Lloyd Norman, who was part of the Pentagon while it was being built.
- Ralph de Toledano, the darkly handsome house conservative, *Newsweek*'s anchor to windward with Nixon and the aggressive right.

Then there were "the girls," who consoled, cajoled, and comforted the male chauvinist egos around them:

- Charlotte Kennedy, whom Lindley drove to drink, but who ran the office despite him.
- Thelma MacMahon, Charlotte's right hand and successor, who held the place together with warmth and charm.
- Norma Milligan, a researcher-librarian, who became an expert on so many things, including Washington women and especially White House women, before there was a women's movement.

At home in Georgetown, Tony and I financed our house with meager savings, plus a mortgage, plus a $20,000 second mortgage from my father, who said the $60,000 price "sounded like the national debt" to him. And we started frequenting Sloan's Saturday morning auctions on 13th Street next to my office in the National Press Building.

At work, the strange rhythm of a newsweekly took over our lives. Slow Mondays, with few people even working in New York. Tuesday was planning day, with story suggestions and story conferences. Wednesday was a reporting day. Thursday, reporting and the first writing, as deadlines for back-of-the-book stories fell due. Fridays produced the major news deadlines, Saturday came Periscopes, and long pleadings with New York editors not to fuck with the stories we filed. Sundays off, unless the roof caved in somewhere.

As the low man on the bureau's totem pole, everybody's number two, I began to realize I was getting a crash course in what makes Washington tick. I feasted on the droppings from other reporters' tables, almost never bored. Sometimes frustrated, as I struggled to find something sexy or significant out of Romanian commercial delegations ("That's yours, Bradlee—foreign and economic"), Tunisian arms requests, flu vaccine shortages (only the CIA got everyone vaccinated, by appropriating the label "indispensable" before anyone else), the newsletters of senators and congressmen, foreign aid (man and boy, I must have written half a million words on foreign aid), starling shit on the Capitol, Philippine vice presidents, the occasional papal encyclical, the theft of two shirts by the Welsh poet Dylan Thomas while he was the house guest of Attorney General Francis Biddle, restless colonels in Indonesia, Voice of America broadcasts on U.S. race relations ("Little Rock City is in Arkansas State"), Inter-American conferences, UNESCO, Alaska statehood, and various and sundry border disputes in Asia, the Middle East, or wherever.

But I was hardly ever bored, as interviews would reveal fascinating facts that might lift a story out of banality into interest, maybe significance, or even . . . truth.

• For a story on the Washington Cocktail Party, Senator Theodore Green, the Rhode Island Democrat who chaired the Senate Foreign Relations Committee, revealed to me that in the course of twenty years, he had been to more than seven thousand cocktail parties.

- For a story on foreign aid, Louisiana Congressman Otto Passman reached into his drawer for a pair of scissors, snipped off the "Secret" label, and handed me a much-sought-after Government Accounting Office report on screw-ups in our aid program for Laos. He was bitterly opposed, and so happy to provide this "leak" (and I'd bet I've written another half million words on leaks).

- Jerry W. Carter, of the Florida Railroad and Public Utilities Commission, testifying before a congressional investigating committee, "I've tried to tell you the truth, but I've got to tell you one thing: I've been trying to quit lying all my life, and it's the hardest job I ever had."

- Senator Strom Thurmond, who took Turkish baths before starting a filibuster to make prolonged absence from the Men's Room relatively painless.

Good stories, but not yet any of those "dingers" that become the talk of the town.

I interviewed a lot of journalists for Newsweek's Press section. Years later, when I was interviewed by anyone from Newsweek or Time, I knew that the junior reporter in the bureau had drawn the assignment and behaved accordingly, with caution. But I liked the Press stories, because I like journalists, and the journalists I talked to were always some rungs above me on the ladder.

There were stories about Joe Alsop, later to become a good friend, until his commitment to an American presence in Vietnam became an obsession that made friendship almost impossible. Joe was an enormously stylish man with great taste in all things, a serious snob, wonderfully educated, and a man of conviction. My favorite story about him dealt with a field trip he took with Rowland Evans during the 1956 election, when President Eisenhower was running for a second time against Adlai Stevenson, and when Joe started his lifelong infatuation with polling. Dressed in a green tweed jacket, tailored gray slacks, and highly polished English Peal shoes, Joe set out in search of farmers in Minnesota, carrying a cane. When he found one, he would nudge him with his cane, and ask, "What do you make of it, old boy, eh?" Before Vietnam, Joe and his brother Stewart were apostles of gloom about American military strength, and especially the missile gap with the Soviets. Friends used to hear him mutter, "Roots. We'll all be eating roots in a few years. All is lost."

There were features about the powerhouse women correspondents, Marguerite Higgins of the *New York Herald Tribune*, and Doris Fleeson, one of the toughest and smartest political columnists ever.

Higgins was not admired by her colleagues, to put it mildly, especially her male colleagues, and more especially by the great—and popular—Homer Bigart, twice a Pulitzer Prizewinner for the *Trib*. Beginning in Korea, and later in Berlin, the men charged, she got more than her share of exclusive stories in ways not available to them. Maggie herself said, "When you're young and blue-eyed and baby-voiced, it's hard to stop people saying, 'Run along, little girl,' and get them to pay attention to you. I remember I used to wish I smoked a pipe and looked serious like Drew Middleton [the *New York Times*'s military expert]." Bigart felt so strongly about Maggie that once when he was told that Maggie had lost a child in childbirth, he stuttered, "Wh-wh-what happened? D-d-did she eat it?" (I never filed that anecdote.)

I had known about Doris Fleeson before I met her. She had been one of the few women war correspondents in Europe in World War II, and while covering the war she had taken up with Blair Clark's father, a controversial federal judge, then an Army colonel, later to become chief judge of the American Military Government in Germany. Blair remembers having breakfast with his father one morning during the war, when Doris showed up at the table, saying, "Okay, Judge. I'm packed." She had long been famous to me as the winner of a bet made among all the women war correspondents—Sonia Tamara of the *Herald Tribune*, Janet Flanner of *The New Yorker*, Helen Kirkpatrick of the *Chicago Daily News*, and Mary

Welsh (Hemingway's wife)—as to which woman would be the first to pee in the Rhine. Fleeson was known as "God's angry woman," and she called herself a "by God practicing liberal." She disliked Ike, because "he thinks 'politics' is a dirty word." She was the first to talk about the Senate Majority Leader as "Old Doctor Johnson and his snake oil," and early on described Vice President Nixon as "totally devoid of conviction and spontaneity . . . a complete calculating technician." She criticized Republicans, but said, "There are going to be a lot of dry Democratic eyes following my hearse, make no mistake about that."

In the summer of 1958 I finally found, at last, the story that propelled me out of the herd—and it was among the leavings unspotted and unclaimed by my colleagues. This was a story that would have the whole town by the throat, a story that the senior reporters wished they hadn't let slip into my hands, a story where I finally had a chance to strut my stuff, come up with some exclusive information that got me noticed by the pros, and got *Newsweek* quoted by the daily papers and the nightly news broadcasts. It was a congressional investigation into the regulatory agencies, particularly the Federal Communications Commission (FCC), starting with a couple of corrupt commissioners at the FCC and ending up inside the White House itself, in the lap of the president's chief of staff, Sherman Adams, costing Adams and two commissioners their jobs. Nothing can compare with the thrill of a good story, yours alone, slowly developing, slowly leaving its mark on history. Nothing.

The investigation was chaired by Representative Oren Harris, a country judge from Arkansas, with what seemed to me to be a mean, holier-than-thou spirit. The chief investigator was a bright but abrasive New York University professor named Bernard Schwartz. Together they nailed FCC Commissioner Richard Mack for accepting $20,000 in gifts and loans, an interest in an insurance company, and sole ownership of another business without investing a nickel from a man who represented Channel 10 in Miami, a subsidiary of National Airlines. "I been loaning Richie Mack money for twenty-five years," said Thurman A. Whiteside, a squat and deeply tanned Florida fixer. And Mack was out of there.

They nailed FCC chairman John C. Doerfer, too, for collecting full travel and per diem expenses for himself and his wife from the government and from various TV stations and TV trade associations for trips to Miami, Bimini, and Pinehurst, North Carolina, and other points north, south, and west. I relished these two stories of low behavior by high officials, apparently so much so that I failed to do much with two other bits of information I picked up about committee members themselves:

1. Democratic Congressman Morgan Moulder of Missouri had his teenage daughter on his own payroll, to the tune of $12,000 over a period of five years; and
2. Chairman Harris of the investigating subcommittee was the vice president and part owner of an Arkansas TV station which had an application pending at that time before the FCC, the very agency he was investigating.

Two FCC commissioners, even if one of them was a chairman, were small potatoes compared to one presidential chief of staff, especially when the chief of staff was Sherman Adams, former congressman and former governor of New Hampshire. Adams was the strong, silent type, holier than thou and full of himself, who felt journalists belonged at the bottom of society's structure. To watch those people fall is to witness one of nature's most entertaining and rewarding spectacles—special falling stars.

Adams's name first showed up in the Oversight Committee's files, during its investigation of a colorful and crooked New England textile manufacturer, Bernard Goldfine. The committee chairman wanted to investigate more regulatory agencies than the FCC, and when his investigators turned to the Securities and Exchange Commission (SEC) and the Federal Trade Commission (FTC), Goldfine's name popped up everywhere. His mills failed to file reports to the SEC as required by law. And contempt proceedings against

Goldfine invariably stalled, and somehow dropped. His mills misrepresented various products as "100% vicuna," "100% guanaco," or "pure camel hair" when the FTC claimed these products contained eighteen different fibers, including rabbit fur, and enforcement procedures always seemed to get stymied.

It didn't take the committee long to discover that Goldfine's fairy godfather was Sherman Adams. "Certain high government officials"—including Adams—"enjoyed unusually lavish and expensive favors, and hospitality, from Goldfine," said one report. Suites at Boston's old Copley Plaza Hotel, for Adams and his wife. An Oriental rug from Goldfine to the Adams family. A vicuna coat (with or without rabbit fur?). A gold watch. More hospitality. Subpoenas produced receipts. My own contribution to this great story was to persuade committee investigators to loan me the receipts for an hour so that I could get photostats made. Editor Denson loved the receipts, and pictures of them ran in the magazine. Not only were they exclusive, but they told the story so cleanly. "Entire bill to be charged to Mr. Bernard Goldfine" was written boldly across the itemized hotel bills for "Mr. and Mrs. Sherman Adams," including room service, tips ($1.50), and parking. Same thing for the $2,000 rug bill. More subpoenas proved that these expenses were all deducted by Goldfine as costs of doing business.

Witnesses testified that Goldfine had once drunk a very public toast to "my friend, Governor Adams [who] never lets his friends down," that Adams had arranged an appointment for Goldfine with President Eisenhower, and that Goldfine had given thirty-seven White House and congressional staffers treasurer's checks (drawn on his Pilgrim Trust Company) worth $25 to $150. And here was my first lesson in how little it often took to corrupt a Washington official. A free night at the Copley Plaza for the chief of staff to the president and his wife (not even his girlfriend) must have cost less than $200 then. But that was enough. Adams, in return, was making the desired phone calls—from the White House—to the FTC and the SEC. For the first time, I understood the clout behind a White House telephone call. "Just a minute, sir . . . the White

House is calling. . . . Governor Adams," concentrated the mind of the recipients. In September 1958, the heat got too great, and Adams was forced to resign.

Goldfine himself was a wonderfully colorful character. He thought of himself as the incarnation of the American dream. To flog his "success story," he even hired the best-known public relations man of his time, Tex McCrary, and his assistant, William Safire, whose own colorful career would take him to the White House as a speechwriter for President Nixon, and later to the *New York Times*'s editorial page as its most distinguished columnist.

Goldfine was a rogue, and I've always had a soft spot in my heart for rogues, especially those rogues who don't hide behind pretense. I did a profile of Goldfine, laced with stories in his own Yiddish dialect. You didn't see much dialect in newspapers at that time; editors were scared of it. But Goldfine loved it. In fact, I was having lunch with him a few days later in the main dining room of the old Willard Hotel, when he asked me how many children I had. When I said five, counting step-children, he reached for his wallet and pulled out five crisp fifty-dollar bills, and pressed them on me. When I demurred energetically, he was shocked, and asked me how I could say such things. Then I spotted Goldfine's lawyer, Sam Sears, sitting a few tables away, and went over to him, holding the five $50s at arm's length in full view of the lunch crowd. I dropped them on the table and said to Sears—in a loud voice—"Tell your tiger he just can't do this; he won't listen to me."

The first and last time anyone offered me money in this business.

Goldfine ended up in jail—for contempt of Congress, failing to answer questions—and he needed more firepower than he could get from his lawyers, like Sam Sears, or like Ralph Slobodkin, who ran errands for Goldfine. He needed the best, and the best was my friend Edward Bennett Williams, from my Municipal Court days. More than thirty years later, in his life of Williams, *The Man to See: Edward Bennett Williams: Ultimate Insider; Legendary Trial Lawyer*, *Newsweek*'s Washington Bureau chief Evan Thomas gave this version of their meeting:

In the winter of 1960, Williams went to see Goldfine as he sat in jail. . . . Williams found an old, gray-haired man with a heavy Yiddish accent. After making small talk for a few minutes, Williams raised the fact that Goldfine had not filed any [tax] returns for the years [1953 through 1957]. "I'm sorry," Williams said, "but you don't have a defense." Goldfine greeted this news stonily. A few minutes later, when Williams excused himself to go to the men's room, Goldfine turned to Sam Sears and said, "Who does that young *momzer* from Washington think he is, telling me I have no defense? Defense? If I had a defense, I'd still have Slobodkin!"

Ed loved that story, and told it often to remind his audience (and himself) of his prowess.

Just before Goldfine emerged from obscurity for his fifteen minutes of fame, the Legislative Oversight Committee had stumbled over a mess involving TV Channel 5 in Boston, and its owner, none other than my fourth cousin and old nemesis Robert "Beanie" Choate, the publisher of the *Boston Herald-Traveler*. He had nixed me for a job right after the war. The FCC had awarded Channel 5 to the *Herald-Traveler*, against the recommendation of its hearing examiner, with a push from Secretary of Commerce Sinclair Weeks, and a few telephone calls and a lunch for FCC commissioners from Choate. The Taylor family, which owned the *Boston Globe*, led by Davis and his cousin John I, cried "Foul." They accused Choate of threatening to use Channel 5 to wreck the *Globe*, and of trying to screw the *Globe*'s efforts to borrow money from Boston banks.

They sent a bright young reporter, Bob Healy, with the face of an altar boy and the legs of a long-distance runner, to keep the story alive, and whip up a little congressional indignation, with the help of his pal Thomas "Tip" O'Neill, soon to become the House Majority Leader. I wasn't mad at Choate, but the *Globe* types were my buddies . . . Healy, the Taylors, my old *Washington Post* colleague Tom Winship, and his father Larry, who were managing editor and editor, respectively. So I helped Healy where I could—generally when stuff I learned would not hold for my later newsweekly deadlines—and largely because of Choate's ex parte contact with FCC

Commissioner George McConnaughey, the FCC eventually took Channel 5 away from the *Herald-Traveler*. The *Globe* prospered—so did Healy—and the *Herald-Traveler* never recovered from its loss of the moneymaking TV station.

This was heady stuff for the low man on the totem pole. Maybe not as "important" as the European Defense Community, or SEATO. But the same kind of camaraderie, and closer to the people. I still struggled with the foreign and economic scraps left me by Weintal and Shaffer. Counterpart funds, convertible currencies, foreign aid, economic and military, trade offensives, codfish and pollack wars, the Voice of America, Quemoy and Matsu, a little Argentina and Venezuela, oil production and the Common Market. But along the way I was meeting hundreds of interesting people, all of whom educated me more than I educated readers, I'm afraid. Adam Clayton Powell, another rogue, and another Williams client; Hubert Humphrey; Madame Chiang Kai-shek; Bob Hope, introduced to me by his pal and my neighbor, Missouri Senator Stuart Symington; Abdul Wahab, known as the Arabs' Bing Crosby; Drew Pearson and his wife, Luvie; George Marshall, the owner of the Washington Redskins (*Bradlee:* "When are you going to hire a black football player?" *Marshall:* "When the Harlem Globetrotters hire a white basketball player"); a slew of senators—Thomas Kuchel and William Knowland from California, Leverett Saltonstall from Massachusetts, Everett Dirksen from Illinois, Ken Keating and Jake Javits from New York, Clifford Case from New Jersey, and some suits from the executive branch: Dillon again, Bryce Harlow and Malcolm Moos from the White House.

I was still having the time of my life, even though it wasn't yet quite as glamorous as the life of a foreign correspondent. But I was getting hooked on Washington.

NINE

JFK

Many of the most important events of my life seem to have occurred by accident. Like not getting off The Federal at the Baltimore train station for a job interview at the *Baltimore Sun*, and instead staying on to Washington for a job interview at *The Washington Post*. And like buying a house in 1957 in Georgetown on the north side of the 3300 block of N Street, NW, only months before the junior senator from Massachusetts and his wife bought a house on the north side of the 3300 block of N Street, NW. Our first contact as couples beyond handshakes came on a sunny Sunday afternoon walking slowly through Georgetown, wheeling baby carriages. Their baby was Caroline, and ours was Dino, born just after Christmas in 1958. It was a warm Sunday in early 1959, and we ended up in their back garden, looking each other over, while pretending to size up our respective children. Caroline was en route to becoming the world's most photographed child, and for good reason: she was irresistible. Dino wasn't bad, either. Before we were married, Tony and I had pretty much decided not to have children, but the more we were together, the more that decision seemed arbitrary, and finally, wrong. A child brings a unique blessing to a marriage, and Dino arrived suddenly, two days after Christmas, narrowly missing being born in the elevator of the Washington Hospital Center.

Living in Europe, I had missed Jack Kennedy's first flash across the American political firmament, when he wanted to be Adlai Stevenson's vice president in 1956, only to lose at the convention to Senator Estes Kefauver of Tennessee. I remember thinking how attractive he was, how gracefully he moved, despite his slight stoop. We discovered we were all going to the same dinner that night, a big bash given by the former Ambassador to Paris—and now Undersecretary of the Treasury—Douglas Dillon, and his wife Phyllis. In fact I sat next to Jackie, and Jack sat next to Tony. We came home together, and by the time we said good night, we were friends, comfortable together and looking forward to the next time.

My interest and involvement in domestic politics were slow in coming. I had never covered a presidential campaign, or any political campaign. I had missed the Eisenhower-Stevenson campaigns, and therefore knew none of the Stevensonian Democrats, and only a few people in Ike's administration. And so the choice political assignments went to reporters with more experience. But while covering the House, I had come to know a lot of people in Congress, and even more of their staff. When I got to know Kennedy, I kind of staked him out as part of my own territorial imperative, and as he prospered, so did I. Kennedy had decided privately right after he lost the vice presidency at the 1956 Chicago convention to go for Big Casino next time around. By the time I got to know him, he was writing magazine articles, making political speeches, barnstorming across the country, and spending little time in the Senate—especially after he was overwhelmingly reelected in 1958 by more than 850,000 votes, the largest total vote ever recorded by a Massachusetts politician. No politician anywhere running that year in a contested election ran up a bigger majority.

The earliest political trip I can remember taking was in 1959 with Kennedy, Jackie, and Tony in a small chartered plane. A short hop first from National Airport to some meeting of Maryland Democrats at an ocean resort, and then on to our first trip to Hyannis Port, where the Kennedy clan lived in a compound of summer homes. Jack plunged into the crowd, shaking a thousand hands, while Jackie stood frozen, staring resolutely straight ahead, daring anyone to make conversation with her.

The public signal that the Kennedy campaign was under way, the signal no one could deny, came in the fall of 1959 when the Kennedy family acquired the *Caroline*, a converted Convair, comfortably furnished with good chairs, desks, and a bedroom, and put it at the senator's disposition. More often than not, the passenger list on those early flights—generally to talk to small political gatherings—consisted of Kennedy and Ted Sorensen, or Kennedy and Larry O'Brien, his top political honcho, with no reporters. Sometimes one reporter (sometimes me), sometimes two, rarely more.

Little by little, it was accepted by the rest of the *Newsweek* Bureau and by New York that Kennedy was mine. If a quote was needed, I was asked to get it, and without really understanding what running for president entailed, or where it would all end, I was embarked on a brand-new journey. Nothing in my education or experience had led me to conceive of the possibility that someone I really knew would hold that exalted job. The field in front of him was filled with mines. His age—at forty-three, he would be the youngest man ever elected president, the first one born in the twentieth century. His religion—too much of America believed that a Catholic president would have to take orders from the pope in Rome. His health—he had been given the last rites several times, and had been referred to by India Edwards, chairman of the Citizens for [Lyndon B.] Johnson National Committee, as a "spavined little hunchback." His father—Joseph P. Kennedy's reputation was secure as a womanizing robber baron, who had been anti-war and seen as pro-German while he was Ambassador to Britain during World War II, and pro-McCarthy during the fifties.

Tony and I told Kennedy how strange it was for us that he should be a presidential candidate, and I asked him once if it didn't seem strange to him. "Yes," he replied, "until I stop and look around at the other people who are running for the job. And then I think I'm just as qualified as they are." And I remember asking him toward the end of 1959 if he really thought—way down deep—that he could pull it off. After an uncharacteristic pause he said, "Yes. If I don't make a single mistake, and if I don't get maneuvered into a position where there is no way out." That meant, he said, he could never finish second in a primary, never let himself get in a position where everything was riding on a single event—the way Harold Stassen had done in the Oregon primary against Thomas E. Dewey in 1948—and then blow it. Stassen had convinced himself and others that he could beat Dewey in Oregon, and that a Stassen victory in Oregon would stop Dewey cold.

I wasn't convinced. I was still new to politics, too new to trust my hunches, and the primaries were coming up soon enough to answer everyone's doubts. I trudged all through the snows of New Hampshire, my old stomping grounds.* Kennedy racked up a huge win there, even if he was running against the west wind, as my father used to say, in the neighboring state of his own. In the next primary, Wisconsin, he expected to beat Hubert Humphrey, a native of neighboring Minnesota and the personification of a midwestern Democratic leader, in nine of the ten districts, and barely beat him, 6-4.

After Wisconsin, *Newsweek* assigned me to cover Jack Kennedy full time as he traveled the country in pursuit of the presidency. It is hard now to re-create those early political trips, on the *Caroline*. I can still see Governor Abe Ribicoff of Connecticut, gray fedora in hand, alone on the rainy tarmac greeting him, on an early trip to

---

* In 1948, presidential candidate Thomas E. Dewey campaigned in Manchester, N.H., and I was part of a group of local reporters squeezed into a suite at the Carpenter Hotel to watch the candidate eat breakfast. If he said anything interesting I have long since forgotten it, but I have never forgotten how Dewey exploded at a nervous waitress who stumbled a fried egg into his lap. I remember thinking a president would need better manners than Dewey showed that morning.

Hartford, Connecticut. And Kennedy did not forget Ribicoff's early support. "Abe can have anything he wants," he said later.*

Kennedy had decided to enter the West Virginia primary next to prove he could win in a strongly Protestant state, against the advice of his father ("It's a nothing state and they'll kill him over the Catholic thing"). The decision was taken at a family meeting in Palm Beach, when Jack Kennedy said simply, "Well, we've heard from the Ambassador, but we're going to go into West Virginia, and we're going to win." The Ambassador was aboard in a second.

We had been invited to sweat out the West Virginia vote with the Kennedys in May 1960. To help pass the time, we decided to go to a movie. Jack had selected something called *Suddenly Last Summer*, but the film's publicity included a warning that no one would be admitted and no one could leave after the film had started. So we went across 14th Street to the Plaza Theater, which then specialized in porn films. Not the hard-core stuff of later years, but a nasty thing called *Private Property*, starring one Katie Manx as a horny housewife. (For the record, I later found out that *Private Property* was on the Catholic Index of forbidden films. I never reported anything about that particular night at the movies.)

When we got back to the Kennedys' house on N Street, the phone was ringing. It was Bobby Kennedy, the campaign manager, and it was a win. Big. After modest war whoops and a glass of champagne, Jack asked if we would like to fly with them to Charleston on the *Caroline* for the victory photo op. I knew it was the story of the political week, and I knew that the whole night (minus the porn film) plus the flight down would give me the personal detail and color that news magazine editors crave. I got exactly what I bargained for, especially in Hugh Sidey's expression, as my talented opposite number on *Time* watched me get off the plane at the Charleston airport directly behind the candidate.

Reporters, and particularly editors, are always afraid of being se-

* In truth, Ribicoff couldn't in the end have anything he wanted. He wanted to be the first Jewish Attorney General, but the new president with the smallest majority since 1880 (when James A. Garfield outran General Winfield Scott Hancock by only 7,000 votes) wasn't ready for that. Instead, Ribicoff became Secretary of Health, Education and Welfare.

duced by politicians even as they seek seduction, or at least some suggestion of intimacy. Once I arranged to have Kennedy meet formally in New York with Malcolm Muir and the editors of *Newsweek*, and then informally with some of the editors at the home of my friend Blair Clark, by then a CBS News correspondent. The editors slammed questions at Kennedy, openly skeptical of this man who was too young, too Catholic, too eastern, too urbane to fit their preconceptions. Hal Lavine, a boozy pro who had been writing about politics for twenty years, asked Jack what he was going to do that would convince the skeptics that he wasn't "just another pretty boy from Harvard." Kennedy was enjoying himself, and stopped Lavine cold by saying: "Well, for openers, I am going to fucking well take Ohio." Not only had none of the editors heard a presidential candidate talk their language quite that way, but all of them knew that carrying Ohio would in fact impress the skeptics, and they wound up the evening impressed with Kennedy.

That bit about "fucking well take Ohio" never appeared in print. The press generally protected Kennedy, as they protected all candidates from the excesses of their language, and from the sometimes outspokenly deprecatory characterizations of other politicians. This protection most definitely covered Richard Nixon, whose language "was worse than yours, Bradlee," according to Ken Clawson some years later, after he had quit the *Post* as a reporter to become a Nixon aide in the White House. When India Edwards called Jack Kennedy a "spavined little hunchback" in an effort to cast doubts on Kennedy's health, not a line appeared anywhere. Reporters tolerated then what they felt to be the excesses of partisan politics. That toleration has slowly disappeared with a new generation of reporters, and I am not sure who's the better for that. The rules changed about covering the private language and behavior of presidential candidates. And editors struggled to cope with them. (Gary Hart's campaign in 1987, for instance.)

I flew to Los Angeles the week before the Democratic National Convention in July 1960, and a week before Kennedy and his team arrived. If it's a close race, the pre-convention cover story is one of the toughest news magazine assignments there is. The cover should be the nominee, but has to be selected on Wednesday, at least five days before the nominee is selected. The story must be finished Saturday afternoon, two days before. If you pick the right candidate, the editors are geniuses. If you pick the wrong man, you have a big problem, like looking for work. Kennedy had won the big primaries that counted, and was not threatened by the other Democratic candidates. I had persuaded *Newsweek's* editors that Kennedy would be the nominee, primarily because Larry O'Brien, Kennedy's political wizard, was the best delegate counter in the business and I had checked his last best delegate count. And so Kennedy's picture was on our pre-convention cover. *Time* had selected Lyndon Johnson for its pre-convention cover. The lines were drawn.

Kennedy had arranged for Tony to fly out to L.A. on the same commercial plane with him early Sunday morning, and I had given her a list of last-minute questions for him. She had written them down with a blank space for Kennedy's answers, and gave him the list when she sat next to him for most of the five-hour flight. He was having throat problems, and to save his voice he took the list and wrote down his answers. The list and answers never survived the chaos of convention week, and I can remember only one Q and A:

"What about LBJ for VP?" in Tony's handwriting.

"He'll never take it," in Kennedy's handwriting.

I never was any good at keeping souvenirs, but I sure wish I had that one.

The convention was a blur. I remember Mrs. Roosevelt moving majestically through the gallery, trying to rouse last-ditch support for Adlai Stevenson—a ploy masterminded, I later learned, by my old pal from Paris days, Bill Attwood, the editor of *Look* magazine. I thought she was succeeding until Ken Crawford told me to look at the convention floor, where the delegates were sitting on their hands, rather than at the gallery packed with a Stevenson claque.

I remember Kennedy visiting the enemy camp, when he asked to address LBJ's Texas delegation. I remember the governor of California, Edmund "Pat" Brown, holding on to the California delegation, seemingly forever, long after he had told Kennedy he would release his delegates. I remember Bobby, literally sick with fatigue, going over the next day's first ballot with me at two o'clock in the morning, one last time, delegate by delegate. And finally, the ebullient Teno Roncalio, Wyoming's lone congressman, casting the fifteen votes from Wyoming that put Kennedy over the top.

The campaign was a kaleidoscope of enormous, young crowds, which no political reporter could remember having seen before. (In a typical use of self-deprecation for his own purposes, Kennedy told reporters his staff had developed a new foolproof way of estimating a crowd: "Count the nuns, and multiply by a hundred.") Vice President, now candidate, Nixon felt it was too risky to refuse to debate Kennedy, and the first debate was held on September 26 in Chicago. It was produced by Don Hewitt of CBS, later to reign over "60 Minutes" and still doing so. I was one of the pool reporters, actually inside the studio behind all the camera equipment. The candidates' small talk was awkward, carefully polite but bloodless. I thought Kennedy looked amazingly cool, and unrattled. And I thought that Nixon, who was sick with a severe blood infection, looked like an awkward cadaver. When it was over, I wanted to check my own feeling that Kennedy had wiped the floor with Nixon, and went to the press room to listen to what the big boys were saying. Marquis Childs of the St. Louis Post-Dispatch, the New York Times's Scotty Reston, Roscoe Drummond of the Christian Science Monitor, and columnist Joe Alsop were declaring the debate dead even. Perhaps, I realized only later, because they too were afraid of the consequences of declaring the debate a victory for an upstart they liked over a sitting vice president they didn't like.

I switched over for a couple of weeks to follow Nixon. I barely knew him, having missed the first six years of his vice presidency, but I was struck by his inability ever to be natural, or comfortable in his own skin as the French say, not at ease with himself or with others. Christian Herter had told me that when he led a congressional delegation to study postwar Europe in 1947, Richard Nixon, a freshman congressman, was the brightest man on the delegation, working harder than anyone else. I looked for the qualities that had made a Nixon admirer out of Herter, an urbane intellectual who succeeded John Foster Dulles as Ike's Secretary of State. When I couldn't find them, I redoubled my efforts to get close to Nixon, to interview him, to be part of the Nixon pool, to bump into him wherever he went. I can get along with a variety of people, from watermen in southern Maryland to Hollywood producers, from Arab shopkeepers to Israeli officials, from professional athletes to concert pianists, but I struck out with Dick Nixon. I could talk to Bob Finch, a Nixon friend and California politician, who years later was to become Nixon's HEW Secretary. And anyone could talk to his press man, Herb Klein. But after them, you had to first run a gauntlet of hostile elbows in the Nixon entourage, trying to put the pieces of Dick Nixon together, and later to hold them together.

When I went back on the Kennedy campaign trail after two weeks with Nixon's campaign, Kennedy peppered me with questions about what Nixon's operation was like. Different, joyless, strangely dull, almost hostile was my answer.

Finally. Election night was endless, as Kennedy stalled a few critical votes short of victory on Tuesday night. Illinois, California, Michigan, and Minnesota were still undecided, and it was well into Wednesday before his election was official. When Tony and I at last got back to the Yachtsman Motel in Hyannis Port, there was an invitation for supper that night with Jack and Jackie at the Kennedys' house in the Kennedy compound. It was just us plus Bill Walton, the charming former journalist (*Time-Life, New Republic*) turned artist turned Kennedy worker (he had run the Kennedy campaign in Arkansas).

We arrived early, Tony eight months pregnant, and were greeted by Jackie in the same condition.* Kennedy came downstairs a few minutes later, and before anyone could say anything, he smiled and said, "Okay, girls. We won. You can take the pillows out now."

Over drinks, we talked nervously about what we should call him. "Mr. President" sounded awesome, and he was not yet president. He asked modestly, "What about 'Prez,' for now?" (Later when he was

---

* Marina Bradlee was born November 23, 1960. John F. Kennedy, Jr., was born November 25, 1960.

in fact president, we called him "Jack" only when we were alone together or with his closest friends, and "Mr. President" whenever anyone else was present.) Over dinner Kennedy talked about his sweating things out the night before. He said he had called Chicago's legendary mayor, Richard Daley, while Illinois was hanging in the balance, to ask how he was doing. "Mr. President," Kennedy quoted Daley as saying, "with a little bit of luck and the help of a few close friends, you're going to carry Illinois."

That quotation has haunted Kennedy's reputation. Since the dinner was explicitly off the record, I didn't publish it until I wrote *Conversations with Kennedy,* almost fourteen years later. And when I did, some Republicans chose to read it as confirmation of their belief that Daley had stolen Illinois, and with it the election for Kennedy. They felt the quotation showed Daley promising Kennedy that he could, and would, produce enough votes—dead or alive—to guarantee victory. Me, I don't know what the hell Daley meant. If it was Irish humor, it seems peculiarly inappropriate, not to say dumb.

After he conceded the next morning, Nixon asked his friend William P. Rogers to investigate the Illinois vote, to see if there were any grounds for contesting the election. Rogers was a lawyer, whose clients included The Washington Post Company, and he was Ike's Attorney General and later became Nixon's Secretary of State. He concluded that the Republicans could well have stolen as many votes in southern Illinois as Daley might have stolen in Cook County.

After dinner, in a mischievous mood, Kennedy turned to Walton and me and said, "Okay, I'll give each of you guys one appointment, one job to fill. What'll it be?" Walton spoke up first, and told Kennedy he should replace J. Edgar Hoover, by then the head of the FBI for more than thirty-seven years—a man who we learned years later had tapped Kennedy's telephone when he was a young naval officer, and eavesdropped electronically on his affair with Inga Marie Arvad, whom Hoover suspected of being a Nazi spy.

I voted to express my worries about the lack of meaningful oversight of the CIA, based on my foreign correspondent experience, by suggesting the replacement of CIA chief Allen Dulles, the venerable godfather of the American intelligence community.

Next morning I was back in the Kennedy compound to begin reporting a story about Bobby Kennedy . . . "The New Man to See in Washington." I was waiting in a small room, only to discover that in the next room Kennedy was meeting with his closest advisers, already at work on the transition. Suddenly, Jack's friend, Lemoyne Billings, came out in the hall. I heard him pick up the telephone and say, "Operator, the President-elect would like to place two calls urgently. One to Mr. J. Edgar Hoover at the FBI, and one to Mr. Allen Dulles at the CIA." The next voice I heard was Kennedy's, and he was telling Hoover how much he wanted him, was counting on him, to stay during the Kennedy administration. A few minutes later the whole scenario was repeated for Allen Dulles.

The transition was exciting in the 3300 block of N Street, Northwest. Kennedy was running potential cabinet officers in and out of his house, only a few yards from ours, and holding sudden front-door press conferences to announce his choices. (He told friends he would announce the new Attorney General at 2:00 A.M. by opening his front door a crack and whispering, "It's Bobby.") The weather was cold, and from time to time chilly. Thirsty friends in the waiting press corps would drop by for a pop, and once I sent my nine-year-old stepdaughter, Nancy Pittman, down the street carrying an ice-cold dry Martini, for Bill Lawrence of the *New York Times* and ABC.

It is hard for a weekly news magazine to scoop the world on anything, much less cabinet appointments. Secrets have to hold for a minimum of three days, often longer for a weekly. I got only one during the transition, and I was lucky to get that. It was the newly named Secretary of Defense, the president of Ford, Bob McNamara, and *Newsweek* had put him on the cover for a story about the new cabinet. The trouble was, McNamara had been offered Defense all right (in fact, I later learned, he had been offered his choice of Treasury or Defense), but he hadn't told Kennedy he would take the job. He would not talk to me, but his friend, the chairman of the Michigan Democratic Party, Neil Staebler, had assured me he would take

Defense. On Sunday night, too late to change the cover, Kennedy told me McNamara wouldn't give him his reply until Tuesday. On Monday, McNamara's face appeared on the *Newsweek* cover as the new Secretary of Defense. And on Tuesday morning, McNamara called Kennedy to say he would be delighted to be his Secretary of Defense.

The experience of having a friend run for President of the United States is unexpected, fascinating, and exciting for anyone. For a newspaperman it is all that, plus confusing: are you a friend, or are you a reporter? You have to redefine "friend" and redefine "reporter" over and over again, before reaching any kind of comfort level. And that takes time, before you get it right. If the friend is actually elected president, it gets worse before it gets better—a lot better.

I felt a particularly high discomfort level a few weeks after Kennedy had been elected. I'm not sure we had it right on the night of November 23, less than three weeks after Kennedy was elected, when Tony suddenly announced that Marina Bradlee was on her way into the world. According to past experience, we had less than twenty-five minutes before she would arrive, and we had no baby-sitter; our au pair was not due back from night school for another half an hour. I called Jackie to ask if her maid, Provie, whom my children knew, might be available for emergency help, but she had just left. I was really desperate when the newly elected president called to ask if one of his Secret Service agents would do, a man whose name I have unfortunately (or maybe fortunately for him) lost. He came over immediately. We left immediately. Marina arrived immediately. And when I got back to the house, everyone but Andy, aged twelve, was asleep, and Andy was watching transfixed as the Secret Service agent took his service revolver apart for the umpteenth time for Andy's entertainment.

With both our wives in hospitals after delivering children, Kennedy asked me if I would like to bring two-year-old Dino with him and three-year-old Caroline for a drive to Virginia and tea with his mother-in-law, the daunting Mrs. Hugh D. Auchincloss. Dino was named Dino because Tony and I like that nickname. His formal name was Dominic, only because the book we referred to while considering possible names said that Dominic and Ferdinand were the only names where Dino was an appropriate diminutive. The trouble was that I had to walk with Dino through the gauntlet of reporters and photographers guarding the entrance to the president-elect's house, and the trouble with that was that poor Dino looked like a war casualty. The day before, while ostensibly under my care, he had taken a swan dive from the top rung of the playground jungle gym to the cement. It had taken five or six stitches to stop the bleeding, and the only jacket I could find that afternoon was still covered with blood. I was stunned to see how excited the TV types and the photographers were by the photo op of the new president with a bloodied child.

Life changed for me when Tony came home with the new baby, especially at night, but down on N Street life went on, with the naming of the new cabinet and planning of the various inauguration festivities. After a fire in the boardinghouse across the street from us and, more important, from the Kennedys, Teddy Weintal and I had bought the burned-out building (with a down payment from each of us in the amount of $4,000). We rented the living room of this hulk to CBS—at an exorbitant price, even though there was no heat or water—for its round-the-clock surveillance of the goings and comings at the Kennedys.

The inauguration festivities were marked by five Inaugural Balls for the first time, reminding someone of the Eisenhower Inaugural in 1953 when there was more than one Inaugural Ball for the first time. (CBS radio announcer Larry LeSueur sailed gloriously into the history books when he said, "And now we take you to Washington, where both presidential balls are in full swing," and broke into a guffaw before the engineers could cut him off.) I have frozen in my mind the sight of Hugh Gaitskell, leader of the British Labour Party, dancing in his overcoat and silk scarf with an aging actress, almost alone on the floor of the cavernous D.C. Armory, both sloshed.

History now will have us believe that once—or twice—Kennedy slipped away from an after-the-balls party hosted by columnist and friend Joe Alsop, ever so briefly with actress Angie Dickinson for

God knows what reason. We never saw them that night, but I can believe it now more easily than I can understand it. I can see how it is physically possible, but the taste for risk and the belittling of the women involved boggle the mind.

It is now accepted history that Kennedy jumped casually from bed to bed with a wide variety of women.

It was not accepted history then—during the five years that I knew him. I heard stories about how he had slept around in his bachelor days—unlike other red-blooded males. I heard people described as "one of Jack's girlfriends" from time to time. It was never Topic A among my reporter friends, while he was a candidate. Since most of the 125 conversations I had with him took place with Tony and Jackie present, extracurricular screwing was one of the few subjects that never came up, and in those days reporters did not feel compelled to conduct full FBI field investigations about a politician friend.

My friends have always had trouble believing my innocence of his activities, especially after it was revealed that Tony's sister, Mary Meyer, had been one of Kennedy's girlfriends. So be it. I can only repeat my ignorance of Kennedy's sex life, and state that I am appalled by the details that have emerged, appalled by the recklessness, by the subterfuge that must have been involved.

The inauguration itself took place on a day so cold, no one could have survived without special precautions. Cardinal Cushing's endless prayer warmed no one. And the cold froze Robert Frost's eyes shut as he started to read a new poem composed specially for the occasion. And then the inaugural address. Was Kennedy's voice really that high-pitched? I don't remember it that way.

Two days later, Kennedy's first Sunday as president, Tony and I were upstairs with the new baby, when Dino raced upstairs and seemed to be saying something about the president being downstairs. We had identified what seemed to be a little problem Dino was having with exaggeration, and so we paid no attention. Until a voice boomed up from downstairs, "Anyone home?" And there he was in the front hall (we didn't lock our front doors during daylight

in those days) with some of his pals, walking back to the White
House from mass at nearby Holy Trinity Church.

Presidents have to convince themselves that they are ready to lead
their country, that they know what lies ahead of them. And Jack
Kennedy was no exception. But no president really knows what he's
getting into, and Kennedy proved it.

Eight days after his inauguration, Kennedy first saw the so-called
Lansdale Report, in which a CIA general, Edward Lansdale, concluded that "the US should recognize that Vietnam is in critical
condition and should treat it as a combat area of the Cold War, as
an area requiring emergency treatment."

Two weeks and two days after the inauguration, the so-called
missile gap miraculously closed. Kennedy had run on the missile
gap, claiming that the Soviets had more nuclear missiles than America did—with vigorous support from Joe Alsop and the military-
industrial complex. Now his Secretary of Defense had investigated
and concluded that the gap had never existed.

In March, Kennedy was told by his Ambassador to Laos, which
Ike had told JFK was "the cork in the bottle" of Southeast Asia, that
Laos was hopeless. Ambassador Winthrop Brown let it all hang out:
The king is hopeless. The general the United States was supporting
had never been near a battlefield. Laos was barely a country, he said.
Fewer than half the people spoke Lao. "They're charming, indolent,
enchanting people," the ambassador told the president. "They're
just not very vigorous."

Laos wasn't the cork in the bottle that Eisenhower had feared,
though it was a vast problem, and it plagued Kennedy throughout
his administration because our involvement was spreading into a
larger involvement with Vietnam, and because the Ho Chi Minh
Trail, the main Communist supply line, ran through Laos. That
May, Tony and I dined at the White House, and Kennedy started
off the evening in a rage. "You want to read something fantastic?"
he asked, pulling out of his pocket a two-page cable, apparently
written by some American Army officer in the twelve-man U.S.

military mission in Laos. "We're still holding [the village of] Houei Sai, but no thanks to the Royal Laotian Army, whose performance is just plain gutless," the president read. "While the battle for the airfield was raging, Royal Laotian forces were swimming in a nearby stream." He broke off reading to add that two Laotian generals had evacuated Nam Sa, before the U.S. mission had evacuated. "General Phoumi is a total shit," the president concluded indignantly, referring to General Phoumi Nosavan, deputy prime minister of Laos. Kennedy never forgot his own military experiences, and often used the language he absorbed during those early years.

On April 12, 1961, Kennedy learned that the Soviet Union had won the race to put a man into space—Yuri Gagarin in the spaceship "Vostok."

A year before Kennedy took office, the CIA had begun training a group of Cuban exiles to overthrow Fidel Castro. As a candidate he had been briefed twice about these plans, but in February 1961, Kennedy was asking McGeorge Bundy, his national security adviser, "Have we determined what we are going to do about Cuba?"

At dawn on April 16, that question was answered: The invasion of Cuba was launched by the CIA-backed Cuban exiles, and in forty-eight hours it was clear that it was a disaster—"the worst experience of my life," Kennedy put it. He felt badly used—and that's an understatement—by the Joint Chiefs of Staff, especially General Lyman L. Lemnitzer, their chairman, and disgusted with himself, for he had finally authorized the invasion, but supported it halfheartedly. Richard Reeves quotes Kennedy as muttering, "Those sons of bitches with all the fruit salad just sat there nodding, saying it would work. . . . How could I have been so stupid?" The Joint Chiefs never trusted Kennedy in the first place, and he never trusted them again.

And so in his first one hundred days, Kennedy had his first glimpse of the Vietnam that lurked in the minefields ahead of him and the next two presidents. He was frustrated by the mess in Laos. He lost his best offensive weapon in his fight with Republicans, when McNamara yanked the missile gap out from under his legs. The U.S. space program was shown up as a poor second to the Russians. And he had authorized and presided over a genuine military and political disaster in Cuba.

The Kennedys had come to dinner at our house on N Street, once, early in 1961. It was a favor I had asked for my father, who had voted for a Democrat for the first time in his life, and was now basking in what little glow my friendship with Kennedy was giving off. The dinner wasn't a disaster. The company was good: in addition to my parents, Walter and Helen Lippmann, plus Eve and Harry Labouisse, who was being considered for a New Frontier job. Nobody drank too much; the food was good. The Kennedys were gracious to everyone. But having a president to dinner is not worth the energy and effort. I had to shovel a foot of snow off the sidewalk in front of our house before I went to work that morning, and then the D.C. police sent two guys over to shovel off the whole block. The Secret Service took over the house. The goddamn reporters wanted to know everything. The sightseers had to be roped off.

But my dad was proud as he could be, reminiscing about old Joe Kennedy, who had been the baseball coach of the Harvard freshman team on which the old man was the catcher. And that made it worthwhile. Once.

A few months into his presidency, Kennedy talked to me about how foreign affairs were dominating his life. During the campaign he had not dwelled on foreign affairs—except for using the so-called missile gap—because that was not his field of expertise and Nixon was claiming it as his. And because there just weren't that many foreign affairs issues kicking around. Quemoy and Matsu, two small Formosan islands of no strategic value but coveted by Red China, were perhaps the major foreign hot spots. During the campaign, plans for an invasion of Cuba to overthrow Castro were kicking around the CIA and the Pentagon, but candidate Kennedy didn't know about them, and Nixon couldn't talk about them. "In the entire first Roosevelt campaign," Kennedy said, "foreign affairs were mentioned only once, and then in one paragraph of one speech on the last day of the campaign." Now, the president was expressing concern about the national capacity to solve problems like Laos and Cuba.

"We can prevent one nation's army from moving across the border of another nation," he told me. "We are strong enough for that. And we are probably strong enough to prevent one nation from unleashing nuclear weapons on another. But we can't prevent infiltration, assassination, sabotage, bribery, any of the weapons of guerrilla warfare."

Kennedy said he had learned a new and discouraging math: "One guerrilla can pin down twelve conventional soldiers, and we've got nothing equivalent." He spoke to me several times of the "six or seven thousand guerrillas" poised in North Vietnam, ready and able to present him with his next foreign policy crisis.

The Bay of Pigs left him philosophical soon after he had taken personal responsibility. "Presumably I was going to learn these lessons sometime," he said, "and maybe better sooner than later."

Jacqueline Kennedy was an instant, smash hit in the White House, radiantly suited to the glamour of the New Frontier, and to the dawn of the celebrity culture that was going to sweep America.

After Mamie Eisenhower, who loved the isolation of the White House, where she could play cards with the girls, and have her cocktails; after Bess Truman, who spent most of her time at her home in Independence, Missouri, Jackie was an exciting change. Only thirty-one, incredibly, when they were inaugurated, Jackie was the first president's wife to have lived abroad and to speak a foreign language fluently. But her image was glamour from start to finish, and the country fell in love with her elegance—and his. Together they were glamorous in a way that no American leader and his wife had ever been. The country rhapsodized over their clothes, their looks, their style—and their children. Especially those children.

When I first met Jackie, I had no idea how much she disliked politics and the press. Both made her feel uncomfortable, invaded. Both robbed her of the privacy and control she cherished. And yet she had chosen a husband who lived for politics, and who thrived on friendship and the give and take with journalists. She and Tony were alike in these likes and dislikes.

When we had started friendship as a foursome, I first thought of Jackie as one of the Beautiful People—shy, perhaps careful, diffident, enormously attractive, and bright. And I was a little scared of her. Our friendship was brief, varying from conversations to drinks to meals in the White House, and weekends together in Hyannis Port, Palm Beach, Newport, and Camp David. In a matter of days I had felt comfortable with Kennedy, sure that he instinctively understood the complicated perimeters of our friendship and the conflict between friendship and journalism. But in all the time I was close to them, I felt Jackie never quite forgave me for trying to be a journalist and a friend at the same time.

Sometimes, in the middle of a conversation among the four of us, I would feel a sidelong glance from Jackie, signaling that she felt some bit of information should remain private: Sometimes she would actually say so.

She had been plainly uncomfortable one night, when (at Tony's insistence) I had told Jack that I was making notes of our conversations when I got home at night, and dictating a memorandum from these notes the next morning. I thought he knew it, even approved of it, given his special interest in history, but Jackie was appalled.

Kennedy and I agreed that he could keep anything he wanted off the record—until at least five years after he left the White House. He was much more apt to tell me what to put in my notes than what to keep out. Jackie was never comfortable with our deal. She sensed that gossip could become history, perhaps, and that gossip was harder to control.

It was the president, through his secretary, Evelyn Lincoln, who decided who got invited to dinner. He and Jackie rarely ate alone, and they rarely mixed guests. Tony and I, for instance, were never asked to dinner with Martha and Charlie Bartlett, who had introduced the Kennedys to each other. Jackie seemed to enjoy these foursomes. She liked to see Jack relax and laugh. She once asked Tony if we four could be "best friends."

Jack was particularly fascinated by our efforts to get Nancy Pittman into some fancy dancing school. She had been turned down by the powers that be at least twice, probably because of me. (I had already been kicked out of the social register.) Finally, we got Mrs. Gifford Pinchot (Aunt Leila) and Mrs. Bordan Harriman to write letters sponsoring Nancy, and she still didn't make it.

When Kennedy learned we had failed again, he shook his head and said, "That's the kind of thing that made Dad leave Boston."

NEWSWEEK SALE; JFK; PHIL

———

Soon after I had joined the Washington Bureau of *Newsweek* in 1957, stories had begun appearing that the magazine was for sale—first in the trade press, and then increasingly in the general press. I dreaded these stories, not so much because I admired the management (I did not), but because I felt the bastards I knew were bound to be better than the bastards I didn't know. In fact, Malcolm Muir, Sr., ran *Newsweek* as an adjunct of the Chamber of Commerce for his business friends, and Malcolm Jr., who had the title of Executive Editor, presided preppily over the editorial product without energy or idealism.

But the magazine was owned by the legendary Vincent Astor, the tall, leonine, multi-millionaire head of the famous Astor family, then in his late sixties, ailing and childless. When he died in February 1959, leaving the magazine to the Vincent Astor Foundation (for "the relief of human misery"), the flow of "for sale" stories, especially in *Time* magazine, it seemed to some of us, reached flood stage. We wasted endless hours worrying about, and researching, this or that potential buyer, none of whom we knew. Norton Simon, for instance, the chairman and CEO of Hunt Foods, and future husband of the actress Jennifer Jones, threw us into a particular panic. Without knowing anything about him, we started referring to him as the "goddamn ketchup merchant." The stories ruined morale, at least in the Washington Bureau. A few of us felt like pawns, helpless and without weapons in the boardrooms where decisions to sell or buy *Newsweek* would be taken.

In fact, we did have some weapons. One, two, and three layers down, below all the people with the fancy titles, there was a lot of talent, energy, and flair. Like Osborn Elliott. He had been the magazine's business editor, and in that capacity knew his way around a boardroom. He was now the magazine's number three, as managing editor, and he was still in his thirties. I knew three publishers (a little) who ran newspapers of conscience and quality. Phil Graham of *The Washington Post*, for whom I had once worked; Joe Pulitzer of the *St. Louis Post-Dispatch* (we had gone to the same prep school); and Marshall Field of the *Chicago Sun-Times* (Tony Bradlee was a friend of his sister). Oz Elliott and I kicked their names around longingly, and in the greatest secrecy.

One night, after a bad day of brooding, and a few shooters, I called Elliott in New York and told him I was damn well going to pick up the phone—it was almost 11:00 P.M.—and call Phil Graham right then.

It was the best telephone call I ever made—the luckiest, most productive, most exciting, most rewarding, totally rewarding.

He answered the phone himself. I blurted out that I wanted to talk to him soonest about the *Post* buying *Newsweek*. He said simply, "Why don't you come on over? Now."

I was sitting in his living room ten minutes later. I stayed there talking, and trying to answer his questions—mostly about people, who was good and who was bad and why—until just before 5:00 A.M. I was back at 9:00 A.M., as ordered, with fifty pages of thoughts, "just stream-of-consciousness stuff . . . no one's going to read it but me," Graham told me.

I scarcely knew Phil Graham. I had worked for him, at a time when the *Post* was small enough that everyone knew everyone. We had dealt with each other a couple of times. Once I asked him to support my application for a Nieman Fellowship, and he had replied, "Fuck you. You've already been to Harvard." Once when he used me to integrate Washington's swimming pools. And once when I asked him for a leave of absence to take the Paris Embassy job and he said, "You bastards are all alike. You get a few bylines, and you're ruined." But he then gave me fantastic letters of introduction to Jean Monnet, General Eisenhower, General Norstad, and others. I did not know that Phil suffered from severe bouts of manic depression, and that my late night telephone call had come during an up phase.

Essentially my pitch to him was that *Newsweek* could be made into something really important by the right owner, if only the right people were freed to practice the kind of journalism Graham knew all about; that *Newsweek* was about to be sold to someone (whomever) who wouldn't understand or appreciate its potential; that it wouldn't require a lot more money . . . maybe a few thousand bucks worth of severance pay, and maybe *Newsweek* was just the right property for *The Washington Post* to make a move toward national and international stature. He got my message long before I was through delivering it, and all he wanted to talk about was the cast of characters. Who was who—in the Washington Bureau and in New York, on the news side and on the business side. God knows what I said, I was so turned on by his interest and enthusiasm. Luckily, there is no written record of this conversation, and the fifty-page memo I gave him at nine that morning has mercifully disappeared. I'm sure I was indiscreet; he encouraged indiscretion with indiscretion, and before I left he was using "we" and saying "could."

I reported to Elliott that day, and let my boss, Ken Crawford, into the loop. Two days later Graham, Crawford, and I were on the train to New York, with Phil's secretary, Charley Paradise, to meet with Oz, Gib McCabe, the business manager, and the great Fritz Beebe, who would quit the Cravath law firm, where he had watched over the Meyer and Graham family interests, to run The Washington Post Company with Phil Graham. Just north of Baltimore, Phil asked me and Paradise to leave the stateroom while he talked to Crawford. Charley and I were pals from ten years earlier. He had been a secretary at the Cravath law firm, when it was Cravath, de Gersdorff, Swaine & Wood, and he had known old Grandpa de Gersdorff.

Beebe met the train at Penn Station, and I got my first glimpse of this man who would play such an important role in my life. If it weren't for the twinkle in his eyes and the cigar in his face, I would have said FBI agent. He was wearing a brown fedora and heavy blue overcoat, trying to be inconspicuous against the dirty tile wall. At a later meeting, Beebe looked me over with a quizzical eye, as Graham sized up Elliott. We both wanted to be loved so much our judgment turned to mush, but we felt we both had passed muster, so far.

It was Beebe who so quietly and so efficiently refined Graham's enthusiasm into a series of inquiries and a list of answers that were needed before anything could be translated into a plan of action. Was it really for sale? Fritz figured it was . . . a weekly news magazine is not the kind of investment favored by foundations charged with maximizing income for the relief of human misery.

Would the conservative Vincent Astor Foundation sell anything to the liberal *Washington Post?* The legendary conservative Colonel Robert McCormick had sold the *Washington Times-Herald* to Phil Graham seven years earlier, and Vincent Astor had started out a Roosevelt Democrat (and FDR neighbor on the Hudson River), even if he had turned conservative. Beebe figured it would.

I had had dinner with Vincent and Brooke Astor, arranged by *Newsweek's* former editor Harry Kern, who was so enamored of the Astors that he moved into their apartment building. When Beebe heard that story—and the fact that both Oz and Phil knew her—his eyes really twinkled.

Could the *Post* afford to buy *Newsweek?* Beebe said he would find out from "Uncle Harvey," which turned out to be a code word for the Prudential Insurance Company's chief loan officer, named for Beebe's real live uncle, a builder in upstate New York. At what price? Nobody knew.

Who else was trying to buy us? Oz had heard on Wall Street that the Muirs were going to make an offer, using *Newsweek's* cash on hand as a down payment. Beebe smiled again. Norton Simon, the ketchup merchant, was in fact interested. And so was Doubleday, the book publishers, a new entry in the bidding war.

On the way back to Washington, Crawford revealed what Graham had said to him: Ernest Lindley was out of there ("We'll find him another job"). Crawford would take over the Washington column ("You want it?"), and Bradlee takes over the bureau ("Can he do it?"). That stunned me. He wasn't fucking around, as the saying goes.

For the next few days, under the tightest security, most of the action was in New York, as Beebe checked with Uncle Harvey, Oz worked on persuading Brooke Astor that Phil Graham was as good as he looked, that he and her young friend "Benny" wanted this deal to go through more than life itself. In Washington, Phil was hard to find for a while and I started worrying that his enthusiasm was flagging. (In fact, for a while it was, as a depression moved in.) But Fritz assured us the pursuit was still active, and our chances were still alive.

And then all of a sudden, it was D-Day, March 9, 1961, the day the Astor Foundation was going to decide on the new owner of *Newsweek*. The *Post* delegation consisted of Phil; his wife Katharine, who was then raising children, running an active household; John Sweeterman, the smart and steely head of the business side, who had done so much to put the *Post* in the black; and Russ Wiggins. They had checked into the Carlyle Hotel in New York the day before, and I had been asked to join them for dinner that night. The grandfather of all snowstorms closed the airports, and I got on the overnight train only to wake up the next morning at 8:00 A.M. stalled in a huge drift just outside Baltimore. I was desperate—scared that I would miss all the drama—but I got to the Carlyle just after one o'clock and found them all huddled uncomfortably around the phone, still waiting for the call that would put them out of their misery from Allan Betts, who ran the Astor Foundation.

In the bosom of the *Post* family, only Phil Graham really wanted to buy *Newsweek*. Katharine was worried about Phil's health, and her own. She was hospitalized with TB a few days later. Sweeterman was worried about the impact of buying *Newsweek* on the *Post's* bottom line. To his core Russ believed that if there was enough money to buy *Newsweek*, it should first be spent on improving the editorial quality of *The Washington Post*.

A couple of Bloody Marys later, Graham couldn't stand it any more and went to take a shower. And of course the phone rang. Phil leapt out of the shower, barely wrapped in a towel to take the call. All we heard was a series of widely spaced "Yups." Then he hung up and said, "We got it," and I literally shivered in excitement. Without any real idea of how, I knew my life had changed—again.

I was delegated to call Elliott, and then the plan was for Graham to meet Allan Betts in the waiting room by the elevators on the newsroom floor. Betts would take Graham to a staff meeting, introduce him to everyone, and Phil would deliver himself of an impromptu, emotional and uplifting speech. I was tagging along, and we were waiting for Betts in *Newsweek's* reception room, when Mac Muir walked through, spotted Phil, and, totally surprised, asked him what he was doing there. He didn't have a clue, nor had his father until about three minutes earlier. But when the old man spotted me sneaking into the staff meeting, he snarled, "Up for the kill, eh, Ben?" and our acquaintance was mercifully terminated. I couldn't help thinking of the poor bastard who got fired for hiring a limousine too big to get through the gates guarding the Duke and Duchess of Windsor's "*moulin.*"

Phil's speech promised only the commitment we wanted so much, and assured us all we would have a good time. A slight understatement.

It turned out to be an incredible deal for all of us at *Newsweek*, especially me, but it was also a once-in-a-lifetime deal for *The Washington Post*. The price was $50 a share, for a total of $15 million. But *Newsweek* had $3 million cash in the bank, plus a half-interest in a San Diego TV station, later sold for another $3 million. So the real price was only $9 million, and Beebe's Uncle Harvey, the Prudential, came up with most of that. Fritz once told me that the actual out-of-pocket expenses of purchasing *Newsweek* were "about

$75,000," a figure I do not understand. *Newsweek's* profits have averaged $15 million a year for the last thirty years, a figure I do understand. My reward was *Washington Post* stock, as a finder's fee, and an extraordinarily generous expression of appreciation. It changed my life, as much as the *Post's* purchase of *Newsweek* changed theirs.

Just as my life had undergone a sea change through friendship with the Kennedys and through the acquisition of *Newsweek* by *The Washington Post*, the Kennedys were changing the face and the character of Washington. Nothing symbolized this change more than the parties, for the Kennedys were party people. He loved the gaiety and spirit and ceremony of a collection of friends, especially beautiful women in beautiful dresses. They liked to mix jet setters with politicians, reporters with the people they reported on, intellectuals with entertainers, friends with acquaintances. Jackie was the producer of these parties. Jack was the consumer. They gave five or six dances during their time in the White House, and that's where it all came together.

The crowd was always young. The women were always stylish. And you had to pinch yourself to realize that you were in the Green Room of the White House, and that that chap who just stumbled on the dance floor was no stag-line bum, but the Vice President of the United States, Lyndon Baines Johnson.

Sometimes, the very best friends were asked not to come until after dinner—or that's how we sometimes explained our absence to ourselves. "They" had to have some of their out-of-town friends to the White House for dinner. The guest lists rarely included members of the Irish Mafia, the Irish Catholic political friends and associates, generally from Boston, who were in many ways closer to Kennedy personally and professionally than the Beautiful People, or the intellectuals. There was a fundamental dichotomy in Kennedy's character: half the "mick" politician, tough, earthy, bawdy, sentimental, and half the urbane, graceful, intellectual "Playboy of the Western World." Only a few people crossed that dividing line.

In spite of the pageantry, I always had the feeling that the news of the day was never too far from the dance floor.

At one dance in February 1962, a half hour before midnight, the president came across the dance floor to say he had a helluva story for me, and to ask me if it was too late in the week to change the *Newsweek* cover. It *was* too late, but I trusted his news judgment enough to know that if he was talking about changing covers, he was talking about a story. As he walked away he told me to meet him in the Green Room, under the spectacular Peale portrait of Benjamin Franklin, at 12:30 A.M. I was there promptly, talking to Katharine Graham, when he took me aside and gave me the word: Francis Gary Powers, the pilot of the CIA's U-2 spy plane, which had been shot down by the Russians nine months before, had been swapped for Rudolph Abel, a colonel in the Soviet intelligence agency, and the highest-ranking Communist spy ever caught by the United States. Abel had been fingered by a defector and convicted of conspiring to collect military secrets.

The story would be announced in a couple of hours, the president told me, and asked again if it was too late for *Newsweek* to change its cover.

If it was too late for *Newsweek*, maybe it wasn't too late for what we loved to call, condescendingly, "our sister publication," *The Washington Post*. I went looking for Phil Graham to ask him if the *Post*'s next edition could handle a new lead story. It could, he said, and pulled me over to a telephone sitting on the sill of a large window facing Lafayette Park in the main entrance hall of the White House. He got the *Post*'s night managing editor on the line, and after a few minutes of conversation, he handed me the telephone, saying, "Okay, Buster, start dictating."

A moment from another world! Imagine a reporter dictating an exclusive story, a lead story, sourced from the President of the United States, from a telephone just off a White House dance floor to the strains of Lester Lanin's dance band. It was the kind of moment that made Kennedy nervous about me, and me nervous about my relationship with him. It now seems also a risky thing for the president to have done. But I was not nervous enough to sacrifice the professional challenge and thrill.

The *Post* would catch 165,000 copies of the home-delivered edition with my story leading the paper, without a byline. The *Post* would have a world beat on the story for a couple of hours, much to the discomfort of Pierre Salinger, Kennedy's press officer, who had planned to deliver this exclusive to the other reporters present— Tom Ross of the *Chicago Sun-Times*, Bill Lawrence of ABC and the *New York Times*, and Rowland Evans, the syndicated columnist. When Graham and I rejoined the party after the phone call, the other reporters looked at us edgily. They had seen the president disappear at least three times, and now Graham and I were obviously up to something. At 2:00 A.M., the president disappeared once more, this time (as he told me later) to an open line to Berlin, and assurance that the prisoner exchange had actually been consummated. When he had that assurance, he flashed Salinger the signal to tell Ross and the others, and rejoined the party.

My one short conversation with the president about this incident, which pissed off a lot of reporters, especially the wire services, came four days later when the Kennedys and Tony and I were having cocktails before dinner.

"By the way, who do you work for anyway?" Kennedy asked, out of the blue.

"Are you making any charges?" I asked, not wanting to admit anything I didn't have to admit.

"No." He smiled. "Do you have any statement you want to make?"

"Not at this time," I said, not knowing how sore he was, or if in fact he was sore at all. He said he was about to order an investigation of the leak, but he thought it over for twenty-four hours and concluded that he didn't have to. He had not considered the possibility that I might write something about Powers for the *Post*. I felt he was somewhat in awe that I must have dictated the story during the dance from a phone in the White House. But not mad.

And we moved on to rehash the party. Rehashing the Beautiful People parties was almost as much fun as attending them, especially for those of us who had trouble thinking of ourselves as Beautiful People. We changed diapers, worked on Harry Homeowner projects, and scrambled for baby-sitters. Tony was too private a person to be interested in the Beautiful People, and I was too much of a journalist to be trusted by them.

But the parties and the people were a once-in-a-lifetime chance to look at this part of the Kennedy lifestyle. It seems of less moment today than it did then. But these were heady times. Something always seemed to happen at these parties, but just outside the boundaries of normal social behavior. Once it was Godfrey McHugh's girlfriend (he was Kennedy's Air Force aide), who had reportedly been seen taking a dip in the White House pool *and* jumping on the bed in the Lincoln Bedroom. ("Get after McHugh," the president said to Jackie.) Once it was a dust-up involving Gore Vidal—who was Jackie's stepfather's stepson in addition to his more impressive accomplishments—Lem Billings, Kennedy's friend from way back, and Bobby Kennedy. Fisticuffs were suggested but averted. Once it involved the seating at dinner. Naturally, the prized seats were on either side of the president, and one of the night's toughest decisions was who would get the nod. At dinner before one dance, the president was flanked by the Pinchot sisters, Tony Bradlee on one side, Mary Meyer on the other. And the Beautiful People from New York seethed with disbelief.

We were invited to a birthday party cruise down the Potomac on the *Sequoia* in May 1963. Invitations had read, "Come in yachting clothes," which meant white jeans to me. Guests included Bobby and Ethel; Teddy and a "Last Hurrah" type from Boston named Clem Norton who had been a friend and coat holder for Honey Fitz (Kennedy's maternal grandfather); Sargent and Eunice Shriver; the Bartletts; Bill Walton and Mary Meyer; George Smathers and his wife; Anita and Red Fay, Under Secretary of the Navy; Jim Reed, Assistant Secretary for Law Enforcement at the Treasury Department; Fifi Fell; and actor David Niven and his wife Hjordis.

After cocktails on the fantail, with thunder and lightning as omens of the storm to come, dinner was served below. There were many toasts, including Red Fay's interminable rendition of "Hooray for Hollywood," which panics the male Kennedys and no one else. The boor of the evening was Clem Norton, with his endless imitations of Honey Fitz and his harelip that meant very little to anyone not involved in Boston Irish politics. Norton got drunker and drunker, until at midnight he was literally stumbling over the presents piled in front of the president. There was a moment of stunned silence as Norton lurched forward and put his shoe right through a beautiful and rare old engraving of Washington that was Jackie's birthday present to her husband. It had cost more than $1,000, and Jackie had scoured galleries to find it, but she greeted its destruction with that familiar veiled expression. When everyone commiserated with her, she said simply, "Oh, that's all right. I can get it fixed."

At one point during the toasts, George Smathers rose and delivered a particularly laudatory eulogy of the president that embarrassed most of the guests. First, because earlier toasts had been either gently or not so gently teasing, and second because the senator from Florida had been spending much of his time recently working against various New Frontier proposals on the Hill.

It took Bobby to pipe up and say what everyone else was thinking. "Where were you when we needed you, George? You weren't with us in 1962, that's for sure." Kennedy led the roar of laughter that followed.

Kennedy had not learned that the Twist was passé, and kept calling for more Chubby Checker every time the three-piece combo played anything else for long. He had ordered the skipper of the *Sequoia* to bring the ship back to the dock at 10:30 P.M.—in case he wasn't having a good time. But he ordered her back to sea (four or five miles down the Potomac)—toward Mount Vernon—a total of four times.

The next morning we gathered on the South Lawn of the White House about noon, a touch hung over, for a helicopter flight to Camp David—our first trip to the presidential resort that Eisenhower had named for his grandson. The Kennedys, the Nivens, Caroline and John and Miss Shaw, their nurse, Captain Taz Shepard, the president's naval aide, ourselves, and the Secret Service. It was the beginning of another extraordinary day. The Nivens, who had known none of us before, were charming, and it felt like a gathering of old friends.

When we arrived, each of us went to small individual cabins.

Ours was "Maple," with a living room, one very small bedroom, one large bedroom, and two baths. We rallied ten minutes later in front of the main lodge, and Kennedy drove us all to a skeetshooting range near the heliport. Kennedy shot first, and he was as lousy as we all turned out to be, hitting about four out of the first twenty. Niven made us all laugh as he explained his theory that the secret of skeet shooting lay in the voice one used to order up the clay pigeons. Whereupon he would whisper, "High tower, pull," and miss, then shout, "Low tower, pull," and miss again.

We then went for a swim in the heated pool, with the president in his skivvies, after giving Niven his own trunks. He wore his back brace even for the short walk from the dressing room to the pool. His back had been, giving him real trouble, he admitted, but was almost "miraculously better" last night and today. Jackie told us that she had asked Dr. Janet Travell, the back wizard, to give Kennedy a shot that would take away the pain, if only for the birthday party. The doctor had said there was such a shot, but it would remove all feeling below the waist. "We can't have that, can we, Jacqueline?" the president had decided.

As we swam, Kennedy, Niven, and myself, the president ranged over a variety of topics: political giving, the Olympics, and yachting among them. He remarked that only the Jews really gave during political campaigns. And that observation reminded him that Hugh Auchincloss, his wife's stepfather, had been approached for a political donation in 1960. His "gift," Kennedy said, had been a promise not to contribute to the Republicans that year, as he did normally. "Eventually, the old boy came up with a magnificent five hundred bucks," he added. Dick Dilworth (Richardson K. Dilworth, mayor of Philadelphia) had once asked his friend Harold K. Vanderbilt for a contribution when he ran for governor of Pennsylvania, Kennedy told us, and he, too, had come away with a whopping $500.

Vanderbilt's name led Kennedy to a discussion of yachting, particularly how impressed he had been by how the Soviets won the Star-class races in the last Olympics, even though they had raced them for only a few years. And this reminded him of a story about how the New York Yacht Club had forced the resignation of some British lord who had falsely charged the Americans with illegally ballasting their candidate in the America's Cup races.

After the swim, while waiting for the others to arrive, the three of us got onto the subject of a guest at the birthday party the night before, who had told Tony *and* Jackie that he had not slept with his wife for sixteen years. Then we casually adjourned for Bloody Marys on the terrace which overlooks a sloping lawn and a valley that extends forever to the south. All the presents rescued from the rain and ruin of the night before had been piled around the president's chair for him to open. The lovely old engraving, punctured by Clem Norton's clodhoppers, had in fact been ruined. The president just put it aside, saying only, "That's too bad, isn't it, Jackie?" She was almost as unemotional.

The president's presents varied from expensive, beautifully bound books to the junkiest gifts sent to the White House by strangers. The present he seemed to like the most was a scrapbook from Ethel, which parodied the White House tours, with their own Hickory Hill madhouse substituted for 1600 Pennsylvania Avenue.

After lunch Kennedy retired for his ritual nap, and Niven and I played golf on the front lawn. There is one green, with four or five tees tucked into different parts of the surrounding woods. The Nivens had to leave at 4:00 P.M., and we all went for another swim before cocktails and dinner. Instead of spending the night as we had planned, Kennedy announced he had to return, and we all flew back to Washington.

Days like that were rare, but magical.

Kennedy and the press were made for each other, using each other comfortably, enjoying each other's company, squabbling from time to time the way real friends squabble, understanding the role each played in the other's life.

Kennedy liked reporters because they shared a craving to know what was going on, and to know what people were like. Like reporters, he was always hungry for gossip, giving and getting the hints of what others were thinking and doing. Kennedy liked to talk shop with reporters—promotions, firings, office politics generally. They shared a sense of excitement over current events.

Reporters liked Kennedy for being instinctively graceful and natural, physically unable to be programmed or to be corny. He couldn't have delivered Nixon's "Checkers" speech if he had lived to be a hundred. As far as I can find out, he called his wife "Jackie" only once in a public forum. I never heard him tell an off-color joke.

Female reporters liked him, but they were older, and few and far between. Some reporters, especially the older males, were slow in succumbing to Kennedy's charms, and Kennedy was slow to succumb to the qualities of a few reporters, especially older males. Like Dick Wilson, for instance, the bureau chief of the Cowles newspapers, a "Meet the Press" regular, and Gridiron Club big shot. Once we were talking about which reporter, in Kennedy's term, was "the biggest SOB" in Washington. Wilson, said Kennedy, after only a few seconds of thought. But a few months later he changed his mind after Wilson wrote a column about the Kennedy family, and particularly how JFK was a fine family man. "Good man, that Wilson," Kennedy then said with an ironic grin. "Great columnist. Sincere."

Other candidates to get a call as "biggest SOB" included Roscoe Drummond, once bureau chief of the *Christian Science Monitor*, and later *New York Herald Tribune* columnist, and Arthur Krock, the Pulitzer Prize-winning Washington correspondent of the *New York Times*. Once a firm Kennedy family friend, Krock had written the introduction to Kennedy's Harvard thesis, and was influential in getting it published as the book *Why England Slept*. Kennedy told me that Krock had never forgiven him for the *Newsweek* story on the Washington press corps, in which I had quoted him as saying he never read Krock any more. "Old Arthur, he can't take it any more," Kennedy said, "and when you go after him, he folds."

Kennedy occasionally got mad at reporters, although after a short time he usually couldn't remember why. Once he got sore at the whole *New York Herald Tribune* and canceled the twenty-four *Tribune* subscriptions then being delivered to the White House. The straw that broke his back, the president said, came the day after Senator Stuart Symington's investigation of stock-piling policies had revealed the multi-million-dollar windfall profit arranged by Messrs. George M. Humphrey, Arthur S. Fleming, and Robert B. Anderson, all members of President Eisenhower's cabinet. Symington's investigation had revealed that the United States had lost nearly a billion dollars, and that some producers had made profits of 700 to 1,000 percent. "And those bastards didn't have a line on it," Kennedy growled, referring to the *Tribune*. "Not a goddamn line." "Old Jock," the president said, referring to John Hay "Jock" Whitney, the *Trib's* owner, and former U.S. Ambassador to Great Britain, "is just trying to keep it alive to help Rockefeller in 1964."

Kennedy got mad at me in August of 1962 when *Look* magazine published an article by Fletcher Knebel, entitled "Kennedy vs. the Press," and subtitled, "Never have so few bawled out so many so often for so little, as the Kennedys battle reporters." Something of an exaggeration, since everyone agreed Kennedy enjoyed better relations with the press than any president ever.

The objects of his displeasure were two paragraphs in the text of the story, plus some fancy graphics by *Look's* art director, entitled "They've Dueled with Kennedy." The graphics consisted of an old woodcut showing a bearded man in a three-quarter-length frock coat, left hand behind his back, right hand raised high with pistol at the ready.

The offensive paragraphs read as follows:

Even a good friend of the president, Benjamin C. Bradlee, Washington bureau chief of *Newsweek*, felt the presidential fire. Kennedy phoned him to take him to task for a *Newsweek* story about an old Massachusetts aide of Kennedy's being considered for a federal judgeship.

This was Francis Xavier Morrissey, a Municipal Court judge in Boston, whose legal skills were taxed by parking ticket cases, and whom Kennedy was in fact trying to slip unnoticed onto the federal bench. The presidential "fire" consisted of this one-way conversation: "Jesus Christ. You guys are something else. When I was elected, you all said that my old man would run the country in consultation with the pope. Now, here's the only thing he's ever asked me to do for him, and you guys piss all over me."

The article went on:

> Also ticked off later by Attorney General Kennedy for another story, Bradlee takes the rebukes philosophically and not too seriously.

There were two boxes containing names of journalists "Jumped on by Jack" and "Bawled out by Bobby." My name was the only one to make both lists.

> "It's almost impossible," [Bradlee] says, "to write a story they like. Even if a story is quite favorable to their side, they'll find one paragraph to quibble with."

The next morning the *Tribune* interviewed all the occupants of both dog houses. Hugh Sidey had the good sense to say that the Kennedys may whine a little but they are the best news sources in history. I felt I was probably in enough hot water, and was quoted by bureau chief Bob Donovan as declining to comment.

And that did it. From regular contact with the Kennedys—dinner at the White House once and sometimes twice a week, and telephone calls as needed in either direction—to no contact.

Then, in Newport, in September 1962, I received some FBI documents (from Salinger) dealing with how certain professional hate types were behind reports that Kennedy had been married once before his marriage to Jackie. The story, dubbed "John's Other Wife" by the reporters who knew of it, was pretty widely discredited. It was based on an entry in a privately printed genealogy of the Blauvelt family. The entry said that a twice-divorced Blauvelt descendant named Durie Malcolm had married JFK. Other Blauvelts said the genealogist had made a "colossal mistake." The FBI documents proved how various hate groups were fanning the flames with malice. To get the documents, I had to agree to show the finished story to Kennedy before it could run. I had never made that deal before.

I never did it again. When I showed him the finished story, he said, "Oh, how are you?", read it, and ended the conversation a few minutes later with "That's fine," and I was out of there.

After my "exile" ended, Kennedy remarked to Tony, "I sure was mad at him, but I forget why, now." He remembered all right the only time he ever brought it up to me. "Jesus," he started. "There you are really plugged in, better than any other reporter except Charlie [Bartlett], getting one exclusive after another out of this place, and what do you do but dump all over us."

But Kennedy had a good eye for reportorial talent. Jim Cannon, former national editor of *Newsweek*, who had joined me in the Washington Bureau, had quit to join Rockefeller's staff (he later became President Ford's domestic policy adviser). I told Kennedy that I was in the market for a couple of good young reporters.

"How much do you suppose Tom Wicker makes?" the president asked like a shot, referring to the *New York Times*'s rising star, "and how much could you pay? It would be a hell of a coup for you to stick it to the *Times* by getting him. He wrote a damn good story about my background briefing before Christmas . . . straight, simple, just the way I said it."

What about Tom Ross, then the number-two man at the *Chicago Sun-Times*, later an Assistant Secretary of Defense, and the man I really wanted? "He can be a bit of a prick, but he's good," the president answered. "I like him and I'd hire him." Translation: Kennedy admired Ross, and he had probably just written a story the Kennedys didn't like but knew was true.

It was common knowledge how much the Kennedy men depended on each other, especially how much the president depended on Bobby; but their private behavior reminded me of some rambunctious game, almost like roughhousing . . . full of wit, sarcasm, and love. The times I saw them together, they were relaxing, teasing each other, bantering, making each other laugh.

At a party given by Steve and Jean Kennedy Smith, Kennedy rose to toast his Attorney General, and started by talking about a conversation he had had earlier that day with Jim Patton, president of Republic Steel, part of a running feud he was having with the steel industry, which wanted to raise prices.

"I was telling Patton what a son of a bitch he was," he said with a smile, referring obliquely to his already famous remark that his father had told him all businessmen were sons of bitches. He paused with the true comedian's sense of timing, and went on, ". . . and he was proving it.

"Patton asked me, 'Why is it that all the telephone calls of all the steel executives in all the country are being tapped?' And I told him that I thought he was being totally unfair to the Attorney General, and that I was sure that it wasn't true.

"And he asked me, 'Why is it that all the income tax returns of all the steel executives in all the country are being scrutinized?' And I told him that, too, was totally unfair, that the Attorney General wouldn't do such a thing. And then I called the Attorney General and asked him why he was tapping the telephones of all the steel executives and examining the tax returns of all the steel executives . . . and the Attorney General told me that was wholly untrue and unfair." And then, after another pause, he said, "And, of course, Patton was right."

Bobby interrupted from his seat to explain in mock seriousness, "They were mean to my brother," referring to Big Steel's price increase. "They can't do that to my brother."

Time magazine had described Teddy Kennedy a few weeks earlier as having smiled "sardonically." After the toast to Bobby, the three brothers were talking about Teddy's smile when I joined the conversation. "Bobby and I smile sardonically," the president explained to me. "Teddy will learn how to smile sardonically in a couple of years, but he doesn't know how, yet."

Kennedy could be extremely defensive, if a relative came under criticism, especially his youngest brother. In March 1962, it came out that some ten years earlier, Teddy had persuaded an undisclosed friend to take a Spanish exam for him at Harvard. The dean had learned about it and kicked them both out, but with an option to reapply after a certain time. After two years in the Army, Teddy was readmitted and graduated in 1956. Kennedy talked about it philosophically, at first. "It was good to get the story out," he said. "He's got six months [before the primary vote in Massachusetts, where Teddy Kennedy had just announced for the Senate] to fight his way out of it. It's just like my Addison's disease. It's out, and now he's got to fight it. It won't go over with the WASPs. They take a very dim view of looking over your shoulder at someone else's exam paper. They go in more for stealing from stockholders and banks."

I went to Springfield, Massachusetts, to watch Teddy make his political debut at the Massachusetts Democratic Convention—an experience in ethnic excess that I will never forget. Two scenes remain particularly vivid in my mind. The first is of gubernatorial candidate Endicott "Chub" Peabody, who was on crutches from a leg injury. (When the legendary James Michael Curley was told he would be facing Endicott Saltonstall Peabody in some Democratic primary, he is said to have replied, "Jesus Christ, not all three of them.") Now, Peabody, a former All-American guard at Harvard who was elected governor that November, was swinging his crutches at the supporters of such stalwart Boston pols as Peter "Leather Lungs" Clougherty and Patrick J. "Sonny" McDonough. They were supporting Teddy's primary opponent, Massachusetts Attorney General Edward J. "One of America's Great Legal Minds" McCormack, Jr., nephew of John McCormack, Speaker of the House of Representatives in Washington.

The second thing I remember best is a young political page who searched me out on the convention floor with an urgent message to call Operator 18 in Washington. The urgent message was not a child in the emergency room or a house on fire. It was just the President of the U.S. of A., looking for "a fill" on how Teddy was doing, and offering his observations on everyone whose name came up. "Clougherty," he said, "he's a real bastard. . . . Took me for two or three thousand dollars once. Cashed some checks of mine during one campaign." Kennedy asked me if I had talked to Sonny McDonough yet. When I told him I hadn't, he said, "Their day is gone, and they don't know it."

I was whispering to the president on the telephone despite the convention floor noise, because I was worried about how my colleagues in the press section might react if they knew who was on the other end of my phone. And if they knew I had called him collect, at his invitation. It was one thing to have a well-placed source. It was another thing to flaunt it.

Kennedy wanted to know what the lead of my story was going to be, adding, "It almost has to be something about Teddy's First Hurrah, doesn't it?" That really bugged me because I had already written my lead in the plane on the way up to Boston, and it *did* include the play on *The Last Hurrah*, Edwin O'Connor's great novel about Boston politics: "For fledgling politician Edward Moore Kennedy, 30, the First Hurrah rose from a steaming, smoking auditorium in Springfield, Mass., at 12:25 a.m., June 9, 1962."

In the end it was always the Kennedys against the world, united by a love and loyalty that was thicker than blood. But I remember the president reacting to Teddy with a condescension he never showed to Bobby. Even after Teddy was a senator, he seemed still the very much younger brother. Once at a dinner dance given by Douglas and Phyllis Dillon, I saw the president and Teddy standing together, with Teddy doing all the talking while the president roared with laughter. "Some pipeline I have into the White House," Teddy, whose campaign slogan had been "He can do more for Massachusetts," grumbled as I joined them. "I tell him a thousand men are out of work in Fall River; four hundred men out of work in Fitchburg. And when the Army gets that new rifle, there's another six hundred men out of work in Springfield. And you know what he says to me? 'Tough shit.'"

For a *Newsweek* cover story on Bobby Kennedy in the winter of 1962–63, I asked the president why he thought his brother was so great . . . "and never mind the brother bit." This was his answer:

"First, his high moral standards, strict personal ethics. He's a puritan, absolutely incorruptible. Then he has terrific executive energy. We've got more guys around here with ideas. The problem is to get things done. Bobby's the best organizer I've ever seen. Even in touch football, four or five guys on a team, it was always Bobby's team that won, because he had it organized the best, the best plays. Those Cuban prisoners [from the Bay of Pigs episode] weighed on his mind for 18 months. And it's got nothing to do with publicity or politics. In Palm Beach now, I bet there isn't one of the [Cuban exile] leaders who hasn't been invited to his house and to be with his family. His loyalty comes next. It wasn't the easiest thing for him to go to [Joe] McCarthy's funeral. [Robert Kennedy had been the Democratic counsel to the McCarthy Committee, and liberals felt he had not been critical enough of McCarthy.] And then when Jean McCarthy's new husband needed a job, Bobby got him appointed to something."*

Kennedy also told me two stories about Bobby and the Teamsters that I had never heard before. The first involved an official of the Teamsters Union, allegedly a friend of Teamster chief Jimmy Hoffa, who had been indicted by Attorney General Kennedy for some crime, convicted, sentenced, then suddenly started to "sing." He was apparently beginning to tell all when he was suddenly taken ill and rushed to the hospital, where it was found he was suffering from acute arsenic poisoning. Kennedy said the Teamsters had apparently heard the man was squealing, and had quite simply tried to poison him into silence.

The second anecdote concerned the recent discovery by the Justice Department of some hoodlum who reported that he had been hired by the Teamsters, given a gun fitted with a silencer, and sent to Washington with what the president said were orders to kill the U.S. Attorney General.

When we went to check these stories out, Bobby begged us not to print the first story, for fear that it would so terrify all potential anti-Hoffa witnesses that the anti-Hoffa cause would collapse. He refused to comment on the second story. *Newsweek* ran neither one.

Jack Kennedy admired above all his brother's toughness. He told me once with relish about a collision between Bobby and Chester Bowles, former governor of Connecticut, and a Stevensonian liberal who was then Under Secretary of State. It seems Bobby had heard Bowles was saying that he wasn't sure he was with the administra-

---

* G. Joseph Minetti, appointed to the Civil Aeronautics Board in 1962, was married to Senator Joseph McCarthy's widow.

tion in their handling of the early days of the Cuban Missile Crisis. When they next met, Bobby apparently went over to Bowles, literally grabbed him by the coat collar, and told him, "I want you to know something: you're with us all the way in this, right?"

During the Cuban Missile Crisis, my access to Kennedy disappeared, reminding me (and others) that my memories of this president are primarily composed of days and hours in his company. During those thirteen days from October 16 to October 28, 1962, I was scrambling for information like everyone else. The closer the country comes to war, the less its leaders find time to relax with friends. After Khrushchev blinked, in Secretary of State Rusk's great phrase, and the Soviet missile-bearing ship turned back, Kennedy talked about the difficulty of deciding who would join him in the emergency government headquarters hollowed out of the Blue Ridge Mountains of Virginia, thirty miles from Washington. "I'm afraid neither of you made it," he told Tony and me.

Once at dinner Jackie told us a story about how Bobby had gotten so mad about something that he called the Kremlin to complain. This story had been kicking around Washington for some time without corroboration, but the president made no effort to silence his wife's corroboration. RFK had apparently called Georgi N. Bolshakov, the favorite Soviet diplomat of the Washington press corps and the New Frontier types. It was accepted by us all that Bolshakov was really a KGB operator, but he was a gregarious spy who could drink up a storm, tell funny stories, and beat everyone at arm wrestling. The White House operators, Jackie reported, had been told that there was no answer the night the U.S. Attorney General tried to reach Bolshakov in the Kremlin.

I saw President Kennedy with both his brothers *and* his father only once, in the spring of 1963, after "the Ambassador," as his sons called their father, had suffered a crippling stroke. It was at a small dinner party with the Kennedys, Bobby, Teddy, Eunice Kennedy Shriver, ourselves, and Ann Gargan, a Kennedy cousin who had made taking care of the Ambassador her life's work. The old man was bent all out of shape, his right side paralyzed from head to toe, unable to say anything but a few meaningless sounds, plus "No, no, no" over and over again.

The evening was most moving—sad and joyous at the same time, as the old man's children tried to involve him, while he could react only with the sparkle of his eyes and a crooked smile. They talked constantly to their father, asking him, "Don't you think so, Dad?" and, "Isn't that right, Dad?" And before old Joe had a chance to embarrass anyone with his stream of "no's," they were off to their next subject. Bobby and Teddy sang a little two-part harp harmony, after Bobby suggested, "Let's sing a little song for Dad, Teddy." The Ambassador leaned forward in his chair, tilted his head back to see them more clearly, obviously delighting in their performance. For an encore, Teddy did his imitation of "Honey Fitz," bearing down on the distinctive lisp, to much applause.

The ceremony making Winston Churchill an honorary American citizen had taken place that afternoon in the Rose Garden, and Joseph Kennedy had apparently caught a glimpse of it from a second-floor window. The president teased his father about how "all your old friends showed up, didn't they, Dad?" It was obvious the president was referring to people high on the Ambassador's enemies' list. "Bernard Baruch," the president started listing them off. "Dean Acheson . . . he's on both the offense and the defense, isn't he, Dad?" Caroline and John were careening around during the cocktail hour, oblivious to Grandpa's condition, and obviously delighting him. At one point, John bumped into the small table holding Joe Kennedy's drink, spilling it smack into his lap. Ann Gargan had it cleaned up in a second.

Going into dinner was a struggle. Jackie supported her father-in-law on one side with Ann Gargan slightly to the rear on the other side, so that she could gently kick the Ambassador's right leg forward between steps. When he ate, she fed him, and wiped his mouth quickly and easily. Stone crabs were served at dinner, and the president asked Teddy to crack his for him. Apparently his back was that painful. "There's one thing about Dad," the president said with his mouth full of crabs. "When you go with him, you go first class." There was a gaggle of agreement, and the Ambassador said, "No, no, no," jabbing the air with his left hand, much as the president jabbed the air with his right hand to make a point. Everyone knew what he meant.

Jackie had gone to great pains to introduce me as "Beebo" Bradlee's son, and she reminded old Joe that he had coached the Harvard freshman baseball team, on which my father had played. "You remember your friend Beebo," Jackie had said to him. "You said how much better looking he was than Ben." More "No, no, no's."

After dinner the Ambassador sank back into his wheelchair and stayed in the circle of conversation for another half hour. Then Ann Gargan announced that "Grandpa is going to bed," and for the first time the "No, no, no" sounded right. The evening made an indelible impression on me. My parents were still in good shape, and here was this powerhouse of a father reduced to a shell. The Kennedys were at their very best, it seems to me now, when the males were alone together, and united.

Except for his love of the sea, John Kennedy was about the most urban—and urbane—man I have ever met. A well-manicured golf course, perhaps, or an immaculate lawn doing double duty as a touch football field, but that was as far as he could comfortably remove himself from the urban amenities without wondering what the hell he was doing, and worrying about making a fool of himself. He was not an outdoorsman. He didn't like to fish, as Eisenhower had, and he didn't like to wear costumes. There is one picture of him in a feathered headdress, posing with some Indians on a reservation, but only one. He didn't like shooting and was appalled once when he visited the LBJ Ranch and was taken in a limousine to a carpeted blind to shoot deer that had been driven toward him. He was a product of big-city life, and of the comforts and conveniences that his family had provided for him in the big cities.

And so his trip in the fall of 1963 across the northern tier of the United States to honor the cause of conservation was the cause of much conversation from the start. His friends in the press had christened him "Paul Bunyan" for the occasion, and an unlikelier Paul Bunyan would be hard to imagine, in his well-tailored suits and his handmade shoes, walking through the fields and mountains of this land, dedicating dams and parklands.

Tony and I had been particularly involved in this trip, since his first stop was going to be at "Grey Towers," the family seat of the Pinchots, in Milford, Pennsylvania, where Tony had spent her summers as a child and where her mother, Ruth Pinchot, now summered. I was going the distance for *Newsweek*, and Tony and her sister, Mary Meyer, were going along to Milford as guests of the president. The occasion of the presidential visit was to accept, on behalf of the United States, the gift of the former Governor's Mansion and some land, from Gifford Pinchot, Jr., Tony's first cousin. He was the son of the late Gifford Pinchot, a former Bull Mooser, who had been the first U.S. Forester, and twice governor of Pennsylvania.* That in itself was hardly enough to command the presence of the president. But a chance to see where his friends the Pinchot sisters had grown up, plus a chance to chat up their superconservative mother, was apparently irresistible.

Ruth Pinchot and the president had met, even liked each other guardedly. But to say that they were from opposite sides of the political spectrum is putting it mildly. Ruth Pinchot came down from upstate to New York City as a liberal teenager from the Elmira Free Academy, but during the last years of the Roosevelt administration she and her husband had turned toward the hard right. Her affection for her daughters led her to be more than civil to their friend, the president, but it was assumed by all that every time she saw him, she assuaged her guilt by doubling her normal contributions to Senator Barry Goldwater, and to her Bible, William F. Buckley's *National Review* magazine.

---

* Tony's father was Amos Pinchot, the governor's brother. He had started in politics as a Republican, quit to join Teddy Roosevelt, quit TR charging that he had become "a prisoner of the steel trusts" to join FDR, and finally quit FDR to join various progressively nuttier causes. Among Teddy Roosevelt's papers is a letter to Amos Pinchot, which includes the sentence: "Dear Amos: When I spoke of the Progressive Party as having a lunatic fringe, I specifically had you in mind." Amos Pinchot died in 1944.

Tony and Mary had flown to an air base near Milford in New-burgh, New York, with the president and Agriculture Secretary Or-ville Freeman, and to Grey Towers itself in the president's helicopter. I had arrived earlier on the regular press plane. The ceremony and the president's acceptance remarks were brief and unnotable. After-ward, instead of touring the former Governor's Mansion, Grey Tow-ers, Kennedy insisted on visiting Ruth Pinchot's house, the younger brother's much more modest house a few hundred yards down the road. I couldn't jostle my way through to the porch, where we nor-mally, and faithfully, celebrated so many sacred cocktail hours, but could only stare while photographers snapped one of history's stiff-est sets of smiles.

After Milford, the trek of Paul Bunyan through the Northwest had little personal interest (except for a magical predawn walk-cum-lecture around the lake outside of Jackson Hole, Wyoming, conducted by Interior Secretary Stewart Udall). The president would call my hotel room every few days to hang out on the phone, and once—in Jackson Hole—he called to ask me to "a little party we're having" after a day's festivities. But later that same afternoon, Kenny O'Donnell called to uninvite me—without explanation.

In sober second thought, as my old Greek teacher liked to say, that second call has interested me more than the first one did. Ob-viously, someone had raised the question as to whether my presence was a good idea, and someone had decided it was not. I wondered why, but without the obvious thought that occurs to me now. I didn't think of investigating to see who might have been a special guest of the president. I figured someone had pointed out to him that he might risk alienating some reporter, if only one reporter was present. Is that so naive?

While the Kennedy magic was growing on the country, Phil Graham worked his magic on *Newsweek* quickly. In New York he wiped out both the Muirs, Senior and Junior, by giving them titles but not jobs. Oz Elliott was made editor, at just the right time for *Newsweek* and for Elliott, and with him came a new sense of hope and excitement. In Washington, out of nowhere, Ernest K. Lindley had been offered a job on the Policy Planning Council of the State Department. (I always suspected Phil enlisted Chip Bohlen's help to pull that off.) Ken Crawford took Lindley's column, and I became bureau chief, but it was the change in New York that started *Newsweek* on the road to commitment and achievement. All of a sudden the magazine shed its Chamber of Commerce, pro-business, pro-Republican establishment cast, and staked out new ground for itself. Younger, more creative, less cynically biased than *Time*. Fairer, less preachy, and more fun.

Perhaps Phil's greatest coup had been to persuade Fritz Beebe to leave a partnership in the prestigious Cravath law firm to run The Washington Post Company, and now he had him keep a special eye on *Newsweek*.

I hadn't known what to expect under *Post* ownership in Washington, which was Phil Graham's town more than mine. *The Washington Post* and the Grahams were beginning to dominate—culturally, institutionally—what Phil called the sleepy southern town that became the capital of the free world. They were in the process of replacing *The Washington Star* (and the Noyes and Kauffmann families) as the community's dominant force. And the Washington Bureau of *Newsweek* benefited from that dominance, and from the insider position that accompanied it. I remember feeling vaguely uneasy about what might happen when we were reporting stories where Phil's expertise was better than ours, and remembered vividly when Phil had kept news of the race riots over integrated swimming pools out of the *Post*. What might happen when the *Newsweek* Bureau tried to find out the truth about some organization close to Phil's heart?

Like the CIA, for instance. No one other than its chief, Allen Dulles, knew all that much about the CIA, and few believed what little information was made available. But Phil Graham knew all of the old boy network that ran the agency—Desmond FitzGerald, Frank Wisner, Tracy Barnes, et al.—and almost immediately after we had been bought by the *Post*, the Washington Bureau of *Newsweek* was working on a CIA cover story. Phil said he wanted to see the story before it ran, and that sounded like a reasonable idea to me. Our sources were all at the agency's lower levels, and they had to take lie detector tests every so often about their contacts with journalists. Even touch football contacts. Graham's sources were running the joint. Came the Saturday deadline for the cover story, and Phil was in my office, fine-tooth combing the copy, suggesting additions, but not demanding that anything be excised.

Phil dropped off our screen soon after the purchase of Newsweek, and we were so involved with ourselves and with Beebe, who was representing Phil, that we didn't worry about his absence. And we certainly didn't know the reason. We didn't know that Phil had suffered from severe depression since 1957, alternating between lows of withdrawal and dependency, and manic highs of erratic behavior and booze. It was his illness that had convinced many of his close friends that buying Newsweek would be ill-advised. Katharine herself had felt that way at first, then came to believe that the purchase would help assuage Phil's feeling that he was too much an overseer of her father Eugene Meyer's achievements, and not enough an architect of his own.

Phil had reemerged with a bang in 1962 when he showed up in New York, Paris, and Washington with Robin Webb, not Katharine Graham, on his arm. Webb was an Australian secretary/assistant in the Paris Bureau of Newsweek. She and Phil had stumbled from a fling to an affair when no one was noticing. But toward the end of 1962, Phil moved out of R Street and set up shop with Robin, and everyone was noticing. All of Phil's old friends remained resolutely loyal to Katharine. They would barely talk to Phil; they would not see him with Robin. His friends/colleagues at the Post went into a classic defensive crouch, attempting the virtually impossible task of running an organization for a man who was sick and whose sickness made him unpredictable and erratic. On his worst days, he would fire half of them, or hire others for whom there were no jobs. Phil was starved for friendship, and turned to his new Newsweek colleagues for relief. Including Tony and me.

One afternoon, near quitting time, Phil called from New York to ask if he could bring Robin to dinner at our house. I said sure, almost without thinking, because I felt sorry for him and because he had saved my life professionally. I knew Kay Graham and liked her, even was a little intimidated by her, but I didn't know her at all well and seldom saw her. I worked for Phil Graham. Phil urged me to check with Tony first, saying that he had been blackballed by most Washington houses. Tony okayed my invitation, and soon enough this strange evening was under way. Robin had showed up at the bureau office for a ride home, not unhappy with the consternation her visit caused. When Phil arrived he was very subdued, and quickly settled on the floor in front of a burning fire for a conversation with Dino, then aged four. This was not your standard where-do-you-go-to-school-young-man chat with a friend's son. This was a full-burn, adult conversation the likes of which I had not seen before. Forty minutes. No booze, no break. Everyone except Phil and Dino growing more and more uncomfortable. He told us he and Robin were going to buy a big house on Foxhall Road, and I remember thinking gloomy thoughts about where all this would end.

In fact we saw little of Phil in Washington after that, but met up with him from time to time at various *Newsweek* functions in New York, or in some restaurant's private dining room with a collection of news types, mostly with Robin Webb. I remember one evening in one of those private dining rooms, whose walls were the restaurant's wine cellar. A long table, with a dozen or more people. Phil sat at one end, with Tony on his right, and the gentle curmudgeon, Jack Knight, the editorial head of Knight Newspapers, at the other end. I couldn't hear what Phil was saying, but I could hear his voice rise, and I could see that Tony was uncomfortable. Suddenly, Jack Knight silenced the table with a firm, "Phil. Just shut up, will you?" And he did, but the hush that followed was deadly. It seems he had been teasing Tony about being quiet and shy, and the teasing was about to go a step too far.

I never felt I knew Phil Graham, the way a man ought to know a friend. His mind was so fast; his wit so keen; his charm was subtle, yet tangible; he was the friend we all dreamed of having. And yet before the discovery of drugs that could have controlled his violent mood swings, he was doomed.

That summer—1963—Tony and I were off on our first vacation without children. It was August, and we had rented a small farmhouse in Provence. We had driven south from Paris into the Rhone Valley, and finally through the goddamndest thunderstorm I have ever seen, man and boy. For miles, the road wound around the sides of hills, with vineyards stretching away from us and below us. The vintners, scared of the hail that might fall from the thundering clouds and ruin the grapes (still six weeks before they were ready to be picked), were firing shells into the clouds just above us to seed them with silver iodide, forcing them to disgorge their rain. The roar of the thunder, punctuated by the explosion of the guns, in the yellowing darkness of day's end made for an unforgettable drive.

The thunder was still rolling through the valley when the telephone rang at three o'clock in the morning. The telephone ringing at that time in that place could mean only disaster. But when I picked up the receiver, I could hear only endless static, overpowering an unintelligible male voice. We had to hang up, and wonder which child was how sick as we waited for it to ring again. And it rang every ten or fifteen minutes until six in the morning, when we finally had a voice on the phone we could understand. It was Larry Collins, *Newsweek*'s brand new Paris Bureau chief, calling from Paris, announcing what he described as "the most terrible news"—my heart sank—"Phil Graham has killed himself." And instinctively, because our children were safe, I turned to Tony and said, "It's okay. Phil Graham is dead."

Phil had returned to his family earlier in the summer, and entered Chestnut Lodge sanitarium in Maryland. Robin had returned to Australia, quietly, and a new beginning had started, when Phil talked the Chestnut Lodge doctors into a weekend pass and shot himself to death at the family farm.

And of course, it was the opposite of okay. It was so deeply sad to lose this bright light before he had lit up the world the way he was on earth to do. He was only forty-eight, with so much time left to do so much.

We flew that day to Marseille, and then to Paris, where Tony stayed with a friend and I went on to Washington for the funeral. The cathedral was jammed with friends and dignitaries, including the president, whose infant son had died only days earlier, as Phil's death brought everyone together. I went back to Paris right after the funeral service, and Tony and I completed this cursed vacation.

When I returned to Washington, Beebe was reassuring about the future of *Newsweek*, but he told me I had some fence-mending to do with Katharine: she was hurt that I had not paid my respects after the funeral, at a gathering on R Street. I had known of that gathering, but since I had not been asked to attend, I thought I should not barge in uninvited. Kay and I talked about it later, as I explained and apologized. She seemed mollified, but the fuss reminded me that if I had not known Phil Graham as well as I wanted to, I did not know Katharine well at all. I certainly was in no position to understand the conflict between her doubts about her own abilities as a businesswoman, and as a publisher, and her inclination to carry on the work of her father and her husband. She reached her decision with friends and colleagues in the newspaper business, most of whom secretly wanted her to sell them the *Post*.

She didn't really return to work to take over the reins until that fall, and it was months before she got the confidence to insist that she wasn't interested in being a figurehead.

ELEVEN

POST-JFK

By the early fall of 1963, Katharine Graham and I had made up, but the *Newsweek* Washington Bureau was the least of her worries. Fritz Beebe was dominating all our lives, telling each of us to tend to our business; everything would turn out for the best.

Tony and I went on with our old life, concentrating on children and their problems. When I got home at night, there was first of all time for the youngest: Marina, almost three, and Dino, almost five, both normal, healthy, spoiled children. And then there was what, seemed like interminable homework with Tammy, Rosamond, Nancy, and Andy Pittman. My cries of "Grown-up time," meant to signal the end of kids' time, would send them all scrambling up-stairs.

Our social life was limited to a few colleagues Tony liked. Polly and Joe Kraft, the columnist, especially; Art and Ann Buchwald; David Brinkley, then the king of NBC News, and his wife Ann; Ed and Agnes Williams; Rowland and Kay Evans. Not yet the Beauti-ful People. The celebrification of journalists was just starting.

And, of course, the Kennedys, who were recovering from the loss of their son, and going on about their complicated business of being President and Mrs. President. At dinner at the White House that fall of 1963, we talked about money. For a man who could afford to take no salary, Kennedy groused more or less constantly if good-naturedly about money. Jackie was spending him into the poorhouse, he would say, although there was little information available on their cost of living. We had a long-running, complicated bet about how much the new weekend retreat they were building in Middleburg, Virginia, would cost. The president bet $100 it would cost no more than $50,000. I said it wouldn't cost less than $75,000. No winner if it fell in between. It ended up costing more than $100,000, and I never got paid, but we went down there for a weekend, soon after it was finished in early November 1963.

It was a cool, sunny fall day, still warm enough to have Bloody Marys outside on the terrace, sitting on a stone wall overlooking fields and a new, still muddy, man-made pond. Caroline's pony, Macaroni, was wandering free on the terrace, munching grass. We were leaning against the side of the house, out of the wind in order to get the full sun. Captain Cecil Stoughton, the White House photographer, was milling around snapping still and moving pictures after a morning taking shots of Jackie riding Sardar, the Arabian stallion given to her by the king of Saudi Arabia. All of a sudden, the pony walked head down onto the front lawn, getting closer and closer, until the rest of us got up and scattered, but the president sat there, pretending to be fearless. Macaroni finally got so close to Kennedy that his nose was actually nudging the presidential rear end as he nibbled grass. And he wouldn't stop, pushing JFK over on his side, and then onto his stomach, and then onto his other side, in his search for more and more grass. We were all in hysterics, and the president was shouting to Stoughton, "Are you getting this, Captain? You're about to see a president trampled to death by a horse."

We spent the afternoon sitting on the stone wall reading the papers, and walking through the fields. At dinner we talked about his trip the following week to Florida, and the trip the week after to Texas. Florida was presenting no particular political problems, but

the political situation in Texas was fouled up with a feud between
Governor John Connally and Senator Ralph Yarborough, and Vice
President Lyndon Johnson a less viable mediator than he had once
been. The mood in Dallas was ugly; a month before, U.S. delegate
to the United Nations Adlai Stevenson had been booed, jeered,
hit with signs, and spat upon at a United Nations Day rally. Kennedy intended to use this "non-political" trip as an opportunity to
bridge the widening gap between liberal and conservative Texas
Democrats.

Talking about Texas led us to a conversation about Bobby Baker,
Lyndon Johnson's roguish aide, and Baker's name prompted Kennedy to suggest an elaborate practical joke. He suggested that I call
Torby MacDonald—his old college roommate, and now a Massachusetts congressman—without saying where I was, and tell him
that a story was surfacing about the FBI questioning of Mickey
Weiner, a Washington rainmaker of minor importance, and with it
the fact that when the FBI went looking for Weiner they found him
with MacDonald in Palm Springs. "Tell him you're going to have to
write a story about him," Kennedy said, as he asked the operator to
get him MacDonald.

"Lay it on old Torb good," he urged. The Signal Corps operators, who worked all Kennedy country retreats, got the congressman
promptly, and I laid it on him good, with the president and Jackie
listening on an extension.

"Listen, Torb," I began, "I'm afraid I've got a problem, and I'm
afraid it's a problem that's going to involve you."

Bradlee: "You know that time when the FBI questioned Mickey
Weiner about his role in the Bobby Baker case, and you were
with him in Palm Springs?"

MacDonald: "Yeah, well, what about it?"

Bradlee: "Well, the story's getting around, and I'm afraid I'm
going to have to write a piece about it. You know the Baker case
is big news, and Weiner is involved, and what I have to know is
what your connection with all of it is. What your connection is
with Weiner."

MacDonald: "Jesus, I've got no connection with Weiner. I just met him in the hotel where I was giving a speech and he sidled up to me and we talked, that's all."

Kennedy, with hand over mouthpiece: "Torb's hurting. Tuck it to him some more."

Bradlee, imagination now out of control: "Well, the FBI is telling us that there were some girls involved."

MacDonald: "What the hell do you mean, girls?"

Bradlee: "You know, girls, women?"

(Kennedy was now slumped over on his back on the sofa, he was laughing so hard.)

MacDonald: "I just barely know Weiner, for Christ's sake. What do you have to bring me into this for?"

Bradlee: "Well, you know everyone knows I'm a friend of Jack's and so I've got to be extra careful about anything that involves a friend of his. You know, if we don't write about you and Weiner and the girls, then people will say I'm on the Kennedy payroll, or something like that. So I'm afraid we really have to write something."

At this point the president, posing as me, asked a question of MacDonald, but there was something suspicious about the voice. MacDonald mumbled something, and Kennedy came on with another, meaner question, which I can't remember, but this time in his own voice.

"Oh shit," said the congressman from Massachusetts as he realized he'd been had, and by whom. I never heard Kennedy laugh harder than he did that night.

We left in the middle of the next day, after another relaxed morning, watching Jackie ride and jump, walking, and reading the Sunday papers.

It was the last time I ever saw John Kennedy.

I was on my lunch hour, browsing through the books at Brentanos, when the whispers started, faintly at first and then a chorus of "Oh-my-Gods," "Kennedy," and "shot." I raced into the lobby of the National Press Building and up to the *Newsweek* Bureau on the twelfth floor. Colleagues were crowded around the ticker, dazed, watching the deadly bursts of unbelievable, wrenching news, worsening every few seconds. Columnist Ralph de Toledano kept saying, "He's going to die, Ben," and I turned on him in inexplicable anger.

"Dallas, Nov. 22 (U.P.I.).—Three shots were fired . . ."

And then, so suddenly, he was dead.

Life changed, forever, in the middle of a nice day, at the end of a good week, in a wonderful year of what looked like an extraordinary decade of promise. It would take months before we would begin to understand how, but the inevitability of wrenching change was plain as tears.

The first change, thank God, involved work, and there was so much of it that grief was delayed. Kennedy died just after 1:00 P.M. Washington time, on a Friday. And Fridays are the beginning of the end of a week in the life of a news magazine. The covers have long since been printed, waiting for the rest of the book. All the features—the back of the book—have been edited and typeset. The leads of the news sections are being written, edited, rewritten, and rewritten again. The printed cover of the impending scandal involving Bobby Baker, LBJ's protégé, was scrapped. The entire magazine went out the window and we began all over again.

Our White House correspondent Chuck Roberts was with the president in Dallas, in the motorcade only a few yards behind his car. Whatever a journalist could do under those circumstances, Chuck would do and we all knew it, and so I wasted no time trying to make that one better. We just had to know he was on the case, and he called quickly to say just that. A new story conference was convened, with the Washington Bureau on the speakerphone. New assignments were made, and reporters scattered to complete them.

I had talked to Tony immediately, and talked to her soon again, starting to sort out our feelings, to wonder if there was anything we could do as friends that wouldn't clash with my role as a journalist. We concluded the clash was probably too basic. We wondered if we had any role to play in the next few days, except to mourn. Just then, Oz Elliott called to ask if I wanted to write something, an "appreciation," or a "tribute." I wasn't sure. I had only hours to deadline; I wasn't comfortable writing about myself, and my emotions; I didn't really know yet what I felt. I wondered how I could write anything without misusing the first person singular. But I said I'd try.

When I started to write, I started to cry. Never mind writing about emotions. I couldn't deal with them. In the middle of crying, reporters would burst in with new copy, editors in New York would call. And I didn't get very far. At about six-thirty that night, Nancy Tuckerman, Jackie Kennedy's social secretary, called to ask us to be at the White House about seven, to go out to Bethesda Naval Hospital, where the president's widow—alongside the president's body—was headed from Dallas. Tuckerman emphasized that she was acting on her own, and that I was being invited as a friend, not a journalist. Except for my own piece, the bureau's assignments were under control, and I thought I would be back in a few hours to finish what I had to do, or run up the white flag.

We drove out at breakneck speed with Jean Kennedy Smith, Tuckerman, and Eunice Kennedy Shriver, under motorcycle escort, sirens screaming. At one point, one of the motorcycles skidded out of control, and I was sure this night of violence had just begun, when the driver regained control, and we got there—only to wait for some hours in the large suite.

There is no more haunting sight in all the history I've observed than Jackie Kennedy, walking slowly, unsteadily into those hospital rooms, her pink suit stained with her husband's blood. Her eyes still stared wide open in horror. She fell into our arms, in silence, then asked if we wanted to hear what happened. But the question was barely out of her lips, when she felt she had to remind me that this was not for next week's *Newsweek*. My heart sank to realize that even in her grief she felt that I could not be trusted, that I was friend *and* stranger. Perhaps because of her warning, I remember almost nothing of what she said.

The rooms grew crowded with family and close friends, Charlie and Martha Bartlett, Kenny O'Donnell, Larry O'Brien, Bobby Kennedy, Bob McNamara. Small groups would form suddenly, confer seriously, break apart, only to re-form minutes later. There was a lot of talk about where the president should be buried. Some of the old Kennedy crowd argued for Boston. McNamara and others argued for Arlington, the National Cemetery. McNamara had already been there, and he described a "perfect site." There were decisions taken, changed, and taken again, on whether a wedding ring should be buried with the president. There were efforts to get Jackie to get some sleep, to change out of the pink suit. All unsuccessful. But mostly there were heads shaking in whispered disbelief. I remember no discussion of Lee Harvey Oswald, or of coroners' examinations.

Early in the morning, we left. I had a tribute to try to write. My first few sentences had been all wrong (I remember an "I" and a "my" which had to go, and went). I was back in my office just after dawn, and finally started out on the piece which ended up as "That Special Grace," a page in *Newsweek* a day later. Elliott literally pulled it out of me, encouraging, suggesting, wondering, showing the taste and patience which were his badges. Did I mean "careening" or "careering," he wanted to know, and I remember feeling so grateful for the question. I had so few answers that day, I welcomed a problem I could solve as I sought an answer in the dictionary to describe young John Kennedy's headlong rush through life.

"That Special Grace" was half elegy, half eulogy—written with an overdose of emotion. I was trying to capture the sense of loss felt by the entire world over his inexplicable death. I used words that he seemed to personify . . . graceful, restless, exuberant, hungry, blunt, profane, forgiving, gregarious, funny . . . about a thousand words, not enough to get him right.

Death triggers an introspective search for truth and meaning. The death of a president brings forth a rush of experts to help or complicate this search, and their work is never done. The violent death of John Kennedy played on the natural paranoia of Americans, and made it the most analyzed death in the country's history.

The evaluation, and reevaluation, continues unabated, thirty years after his death, with new books, films, and TV specials coming out yearly.

In the crowded hours after his murder, I wrote that "history will best judge John F. Kennedy in calmer days, when time has made the tragic and the grotesque at least bearable." I wrote about his humor, especially when it was directed against himself, about his hunger for life and the people in it, about his compassion, about his physical and intellectual grace. I described a Walter Mitty streak in him, where he slipped easily into heroic roles, like Arnold Palmer, maybe. I wrote of his exuberance, his easy profanity, born in his wartime experience, and his love of family. I ended my tribute by saying: "John F. Kennedy is dead, and for that we are a lesser people in a lesser land." A little flowery, maybe, but I was writing in tears, and I still believe that.

I included a few lines about Kennedy and Jackie, thusly: "John Kennedy loved his wife, who served him so well. Their life together began as it ended—in a hospital—and through sickness and loneliness, there grew the special love that lights up the soul of the lover and the loved alike." Also a little flowery. History has convinced me that Kennedy shared his love with other women, and he did so in a way that lit up very little except the sordid pages of the tabloid press. So be it. We can all wish he hadn't, but we cannot change history.

In midmorning on Saturday, friends and colleagues were invited to a special ceremony in the East Room of the White House. Ted Sorensen was staring into space, present physically, but locked alone in an awful grief. Robert Kennedy seemed almost catatonic, glued to Jackie's side as he was to be for the next days. Everyone wept when the "Navy Hymn" was played, the first of what was to seem like ten thousand times. I'll never forget any of it.

Newsweek closed early Sunday, and along with the rest of the world we stayed glued to the drama unfolding on television: the president lying in state in the Capitol Rotunda, the arrival of General de Gaulle, Emperor Haile Selassie, Queen Frederika of Greece, Prince Philip, and more dignitaries than I'd ever seen at one time.

And above all the faces of thousands of people, standing stunned, with tears in their eyes. Tony and I went to a small wake for some friends Sunday night, led by Dave Powers, the president's leprechaun, in the family quarters. Sargent Shriver told me I had been asked "by the family" to serve as an usher at the funeral in St. Matthew's Cathedral on Monday. I arrived early to get my instructions. I was to stand at the transept, the aisle that crosses the main aisle, and I saved two seats for Tony and Mary Meyer, who arrived together later than seemed possible, even for them.

When the funeral service was completed and the casket had been withdrawn, the parade of leaders inched slowly out of the cathedral down the main aisle, stopping in their tracks for minutes at a time, as photographers out front snapped everything to a standstill. The new president, Lyndon Baines Johnson, stood one foot in front of me, for almost five minutes. I remember thinking I had to say something, and so I mumbled, "God bless you," and some words about the whole country wishing him the very best in this awful time. He nodded almost imperceptibly, and then had to stay standing right there. The trip to the Arlington gravesite took forever, and Tony, Mary, and I ended up directly behind the imposing figure of General de Gaulle, staring into the brightest late autumn sunlight.

In the weeks after Kennedy was assassinated, Tony and I spent a couple of emotional weekends at Atoka, the Kennedys' country house in Middleburg, Virginia, with Jackie, trying with no success to talk about something else, or someone else. Too soon and too emotional for healing, we proved only that the three of us had very little in common without the essential fourth.

Only four weeks after the assassination, after the last of these weekends, we received this sad note from the president's widow:

Dec. 20

Dear Tony and Ben:

Something that you said in the country stunned me so—that you hoped I would marry again.

You were close to us so many times. There is one thing that

you must know. I consider that my life is over and I will spend the rest of it waiting for it really to be over.

    With my love,

Jackie

Jackie talked of staying in Washington, even enlisted Tony to look at houses in Georgetown for her, and eventually bought one. But by the time she had moved in, we felt she was not long for the city where her life had been ruined. Our friendship, which had always been a foursome, didn't work as a threesome.

The first months of the new Johnson administration suffered from an overdose of comparisons between Johnson and Kennedy, as LBJ struggled to right the country after the assassination. Johnson, and some of the Texans around him, resented the admiration in the press of Kennedy's style, interpreting that admiration as implicit criticism of his own style. The fact of the matter was that LBJ had just as much style as Kennedy; it was just different. If style is the distinct manner in which someone behaves and appears, LBJ was loaded. When he came into a room, that room was entered. When he put one hand on your shoulder and the other hand on your arm, you felt like you were being licked by a Great Dane. But he stayed suspicious of the people who had been Kennedy friends, even as he went out of his way to be courteous to Jackie.

    President Johnson's reservations about me were widely known. Once, in a memo to the president, McGeorge Bundy told LBJ that Kay Graham "has decided to move Ben Bradlee from *Newsweek* to the *Post* . . . to be Al Friendly's deputy. . . . Kay knows you have reservations about Bradlee, but she also knows that he has the respect of the professional press." Bundy continued with this interesting observation:

This may be as good a time as any for me to repeat my own judgment that while Ben Bradlee is a very determined and inquisitive reporter, he is not hostile to us. It is true that he was a great personal friend of President Kennedy. But he has never been close to Bobby—they are temperamentally opposites. What made Bradlee and President Kennedy friends was a shared coolness and irony and detachment, which was the side of JFK that does not appear in his brother.

Johnson persuaded Congress to enact most of the Kennedy legislation in 1964 and started off on his own vision of America, the "Great Society." New presidents mean new challenges for bureau chiefs, and I spent most of my time getting to know Jack Valenti, Bill Moyers, Marvin Watson, Harry McPherson—the Texas Mafia, who had replaced Kennedy's Irish Mafia. And before we knew it, President Johnson was on his way to Atlantic City, getting ready to run for the presidency that he had inherited by disaster.

National political conventions are like campaign ribbons for the military. Correspondents talk about them the way soldiers talk about battles, remembering—and polishing—their experiences like war stories.

Both conventions in 1964 were splendid examples of the genre, colorful, feisty, and fun: the Republican Convention in San Francisco, which nominated the wonderfully colorful Barry Goldwater in a thoroughly unpleasant but fascinating few days. And the Democratic Convention in Atlantic City, starring Fannie Lou Hamer and the warring Mississippi delegation.

The Goldwater convention gave most of us our first taste of the far right rank and file. No one in the Cow Palace that night will ever forget the booing thousands, jumping to their feet, and shaking their fists in approval, when President Eisenhower addressed the convention. Ike glared at the press gallery to his left and decried what he called "the sensation-seeking columnists" of the press. You could feel the hostility of the delegates. Later, they heckled Nelson Rockefeller off the podium. The liberal wing of the GOP was dying before our eyes. The hostility of the Goldwater entourage, with the exception of campaign manager F. Clifton White and key aide Richard Kleindienst, was close to hatred. It was years before

I got to know Barry Goldwater, and to love him, but then he was surrounded—and manipulated—by what seemed to be as mean-spirited, narrow-minded a bunch as I ever met.

News magazines routinely send a junior correspondent to the site of a political convention the week before, to write a scene-setter, describing wherever it was the delegates would convene. In 1964, we sent Philip Carter, a slightly erratic, wonderfully talented young reporter, to case the joint. Soon after he arrived, he called to say the only interesting thing in Atlantic City was some nut who was trying to break the flagpole-sitting record, 150 feet or so in the air. As a joke, I suggested he have a few words with him, and that night, watching the network news, damned if I didn't see Carter shinnying up the pole to do exactly that.

Since LBJ's nomination was foreordained, he tried to create suspense by pretending that he hadn't made up his mind about a vice president. No one really believed him, as he floated the names of Senator Tom Dodd of Connecticut, who was on the verge of being censured by the Senate for influence peddling and converting campaign funds for personal use, Senator Eugene McCarthy of Minnesota, and a few others, and then settled on the front runner, the one and only Hubert Horatio Humphrey, the senator from Minnesota. The only real news involved the two competing delegations from Mississippi. One, lily white, led by the political establishment. The other mostly black, led by Fannie Lou Hamer and Phil Carter's brother Hodding, son of the legendary antisegregationist editor from Greenville, Mississippi, Hodding Carter, Sr. Karl Fleming, chief of *Newsweek*'s southern bureau in Atlanta, was covering Fannie Lou, and I mean covering: hour after hour of interminable negotiating sessions. One day's session went on into the small hours of the morning, long after television's first team correspondents had called it a day. Close to 2:00 A.M. the delegation emerged from a meeting room like one large glob of fifty to sixty would-be delegates, with Fleming, white as can be, in the middle of this sea of black faces. The late night TV correspondent shoved a microphone in Fleming's face and asked him if he was a delegate.

"Yes, suh," Fleming replied.

"Well, what are you going to do now?" the second stringer asked, with innocence.

And Fleming rose to immortal heights, all cameras rolling, all mikes live, red light on: "Well, I don't know about my colleagues, but I'm going to get laid."

Even after more than forty months in a shooting war, after years as a police reporter, and after more years covering shooting wars in the Middle East, violence as a fact of my life had begun only with Kennedy's assassination. Even that monstrous act, my brain tried to convince my soul, was a random aberration. But violence came closer a few short months later with the murder of Mary Pinchot Meyer in the bright sunlight of a beautiful early fall afternoon in October. She was walking along the towpath by the canal along the Potomac River in Georgetown, when she was grabbed from behind, wrestled to the ground, and shot just once under her cheekbone as she struggled to get free. She died instantly.

My friend Wistar Janney called to ask if I had been listening to the radio. It was just after lunch, and of course I had not. Next he asked if I knew where Mary was, and of course I didn't. Someone had been murdered on the towpath, he said, and from the radio description it sounded like Mary. I raced home. Tony was coping by worrying about children, hers and Mary's, and about her mother, who was seventy-one years old, living alone in New York. We asked Anne Chamberlin, Mary's college roommate, to go to New York and bring Ruth to us. When Ann was well on her way, I was delegated to break the news to Ruth on the telephone. I can't remember that conversation. I was so scared for her, for my family, and for what was happening to our world.

Next, the police told us, someone would have to identify Mary's body in the morgue, and since Mary and her husband, Cord Meyer, were separated, I drew that straw too. There had to be two witnesses, and so I grabbed our family druggist and friend, Doc Dalinsky, for help, as I always did.

When I got home, the house was filling up with friends. A reporter from the *Post* showed up and I bit his head off, and slammed the door in his face. Later, I called managing editor Al Friendly to apologize, and asked him to send the reporter back. Teddy White showed up to keep a long-standing date for drinks, unaware of what had happened. He left when he saw we couldn't cope. The phones rang, the doorbell buzzed. Food and drink materialized out of nowhere.

Two telephone calls that night from overseas added new dimensions to Mary's death. The first came from President Kennedy's press secretary, Pierre Salinger, in Paris. He expressed his particular sorrow and condolences, and it was only after that conversation was over that we realized that we hadn't known that Pierre had been a friend of Mary's. The second, from Anne Truitt, an artist/sculptor living in Tokyo, was completely understandable. She had been perhaps Mary's closest friend, and after she and Tony had grieved together, she told us that Mary had asked her to take possession of a private diary "if anything ever happened to me." Anne asked if we had found any such diary, and we told her we hadn't looked for anything, much less a diary. We didn't start looking until the next morning, when Tony and I walked around the corner a few blocks to Mary's house. It was locked, as we had expected, but when we got inside, we found Jim Angleton, and to our complete surprise he told us he, too, was looking for Mary's diary.

Now, James Jesus Angleton was a lot of things, including an extremely controversial, high-ranking CIA official specializing in counterintelligence, but he was also a friend of ours, and the husband of Mary Meyer's close friend, Cicely Angleton. We asked him how he'd gotten into the house, and he shuffled his feet. (Later, we learned that one of Jim's nicknames inside the agency was "the Locksmith," and that he was known as a man who could pick his way into any house in town.) We felt his presence was odd, to say the least, but took him at his word, and with him we searched Mary's house thoroughly. Without success. We found no diary.

Later that day, we realized that we hadn't looked for the diary in Mary's studio, which was directly across a dead-end driveway from the garden behind our house. We had no key, but I got a few tools to remove the simple padlock, and we walked toward the studio, only to run into Jim Angleton again, this time actually in the process of picking the padlock. He would have been red-faced, if his face could have gotten red, and he left almost without a word. I unscrewed the hinge, and we entered the studio. Mary was part of the Colorist school of Washington painters, led by Morris Louis and Kenneth Noland. Her paintings and paints in the palest colors, and simplest shapes, pretty much covered the studio. We missed the diary the first time, but Tony found it an hour later.

Much has been written about this diary—most of it wrong— since its existence was first reported. Tony took it to our house, and we read it later that night. It was small (about 6" x 8")—with fifty to sixty pages, most of them filled with paint swatches, and descriptions of how the colors were created and what they were created for. On a few pages, maybe ten in all, in the same handwriting but different pen, phrases described a love affair, and after reading only a few phrases it was clear that the lover had been the President of the United States, though his name was never mentioned.

To say we were stunned doesn't begin to describe our reactions. Tony, especially, felt betrayed, both by Kennedy and by Mary. She knew Jack liked her. Jackie had once said in our presence, "Jack, you always say Tony is your ideal woman." She liked Kennedy back, but had never done anything to encourage more than friendship. Kennedy had obviously sought more than friendship with Mary, and had found it with her encouragement.

Like everyone else, we had heard reports of presidential infidelity, but we were always able to say we knew of no evidence, none. We were quick to say the obvious: that the Bradlees saw the Kennedys almost always as a foursome, and under those conditions, Kennedy's extracurricular carrying on did not come up as a point of discussion. Of course, I had heard reports of girlfriends. Everyone had. Even my father, who was trying to get up the nerve in 1960 to vote for a Democrat for the first time in his life, asked me about rumors circulating among his friends that Kennedy was a "fearful girler." Kennedy had once looked over the guests dancing at a White House party and said to me, "If only we could run wild, Benjy." Another time he said, "They're always trying to tie me to some story about a girl, but they can't—there are none." (This was during the time of the story known to the press as "John's Other Wife," a false report that he had been married once before Jackie.) And another time he referred to Mary Meyer as someone who would be "hard to live with." But it never occurred to me that these might be scraps of evidence of adultery. Maybe it was a simpler time, a naive time, but full field investigations required more evidence than that.

And so I was truly appalled by the realization of the extent of the deceit involved. I remembered, for instance, Kennedy greeting Tony often by asking, "How's your sister?", presumably including those occasions when he had just left her arms.

There is no comfortable way to cope with these incredible discoveries involving so many friends, even when most of the principals have died. By the time of Mary's death Jackie had disappeared from our lives, moving to New York eight months after her husband's assassination, but the memories of our times together were ineradicable. We were left to work out how the news had changed our opinions of President Kennedy and Mary Meyer. The answer for me was: not all that much. They were attractive, intelligent, and interesting people before their paths crossed in this explosive way, and they remain that way in my mind. There was a boldness in pulling something like that off that I found fascinating, and there was the realization that I had been fooled, misled. I resented the deception by Mary and Jack, but with both of them gone from my life, resentment seemed selfish. For Tony, I sensed a keen disappointment in both parties. She felt she was Jack Kennedy's friend, at least as much as Mary was, and all of a sudden she had come to realize that there was this difference. She had been kept in the dark by her sister and by her friend.

Mary's funeral was almost unbearable, as funerals always are for those who die too soon. I felt overwhelmed by the violence, magnified by Marina Bradlee, age four, who walked down the aisle holding my hand, her face bruised and cut, after crashing into the instrument panel of a car a few days earlier. I felt conflicted by the new knowledge that Mary and Jack Kennedy had been lovers, and that both now had been savagely, grotesquely murdered. My own world was somehow threatened.

Before we could sort it all out, we had to decide what to do with the diary, and we both concluded that this was in no sense a public document, despite the braying of the knee jerks about some public right to know. I felt it was a family document, privately created by Mary, privately protected by her thorough instructions to Anne Truitt, which should be followed. Those instructions called for its destruction. The next day, Tony gave the diary to Angleton, because he promised to destroy it in whatever facilities the Central Intelligence Agency had for the destruction of documents. It was naive of us, but we figured they were state of the art, and we got on with the business of mourning and memorializing.

There was only one eyewitness to Mary's murder, the driver of a pickup truck who was going west on Canal Road when he heard Mary scream. He identified a "black male," and police had found a black male, cowering in the watery shallows of the Potomac River below the canal, holding on to an overhanging bush. He told police he was fishing, had dropped his rod, and gone into the river to retrieve it. The homicide detectives were sure they had their man.

At his trial, the eyewitness identified the black man, but admitted that he had been looking into the afternoon sun, some 100 feet from the road, across the canal to the scene of the murder. The defendant was acquitted. (He was also escorted to the city limits, the cops reported to me, and told never to set foot in the District of Columbia again.)

It is important to say that I never for a minute considered reporting that it had been learned that the slain president had in fact had a lover, who had herself been murdered while walking on the C & O Canal. (Never mind the fact that the CIA's most controversial counterintelligence specialist had been caught in the act of breaking and entering, and looking for her diary.) Mary Meyer's murder was news, not her past love affair, I thought then, and part of me would like to think so now. The old-fashioned part of me, pre-prurience, pre-celebrification, pre-"Hard Copy."

I was extremely uncomfortable when the story of the Kennedy-Meyer affair became public years later, in the February 1976 issue of the *National Enquirer*. The troubled Jim Truitt, ex-husband of Anne Truitt, had given the story to the *Enquirer* in some spirit of revenge against his former wife, or against me.

With Truitt as the *Enquirer*'s only source, the story said that Mary and Jack had met twenty to thirty times in the White House during their romance from January 1962 to November 1963; that they had smoked grass (three joints) on one occasion; that Mary had kept a diary of the affair. On Sunday, February 22, 1976, the *Post*'s Howard Simons reached me in the Virgin Islands, where I was on vacation, and told me about the *Enquirer* story. And what did I suggest they do? I knew it was a story, now. Even stories consigned to silence for whatever reason, venal, compassionate, or otherwise, are public property as soon as that silence is broken. For the record, I shut up. Off the record, I gave reporter Don Oberdorfer as much guidance as I could. And even some of that was wrong: at the time I thought the diary had been destroyed.

But it turned out that Angleton did not destroy the document, for whatever perverse, or perverted, reasons. We didn't learn this until some years later, when Tony asked him pointblank how he had destroyed it. When he admitted he had not destroyed it, she demanded that he give it back, and when he did, she burned it, with a friend as witness. None of us has any idea what Angleton did with the diary while it was in his possession, nor why he failed to follow Mary and Tony's instructions. (Anne Truit and Cicely Angleton have disputed this version of the discovery and disposition of Mary Meyer's "diary." They say they "told" Jim Angleton "to take charge of this diary." They acknowledge Tony Bradlee gave the diary "and several papers bundled together" to Angleton "and asked him to burn" them. They say Angleton "followed this instruction in part by burning the loose papers," but "safeguarded" the diary itself.

Some years later, they say, Angleton "honored a request from Tony
Bradlee that he deliver the diary to her.")

One of the most intriguing stories of the day involved J. Edgar
Hoover, how long could he go on, and what president would have
the guts to fire him.

Hoover cordially disliked all but the most fawning journalists,
and all but the most fawning journalists disliked him back. The
slightest suggestion that he was going to call it a career would be
a big story. And so we had planned a *Newsweek* cover story on
Hoover, pegged to a firm decision that the search for his successor
was under way. I had persuaded Hoover's batman deputy, Cartha J.
"Deke" DeLoach, to talk Hoover into talking however briefly to Jay
Iselin and myself from the Washington Bureau, and writer Dwight
Martin from New York.

The interview was a disaster. First, "the director" did not want
to talk to Martin, believe it or not, because his wife's FBI file contained some information that offended the Great Patriot. She was
a Chinese national, and long before marrying Martin had worked
as a saleswoman for a Chinese tailor in Hong Kong. In that capacity, apparently, she had aroused the FBI's ineradicable suspicions by
looking for customers in places frequented by American military officers. I should have dropped the interview right there, but I wasn't
smart enough. After Iselin and I were ushered into "his" presence,
framed by two upright pistols wired as desk lamps, we asked him one
question, which he answered, uninterrupted, for twenty minutes,
and the interview was over. Total wipeout.

I stayed behind, at DeLoach's invitation, hoping to get something I could use, but without success. Instead, DeLoach wanted to
talk about Martin Luther King, some of his friends whom DeLoach
described as unsavory, and some of his "exploits." Pretty soon he
was talking about some King tapes, and asking me if I would like
to listen to them and read transcripts. I was so frustrated by the
non-interview, I never fully grasped what the hell he was up to, and
simply walked out. We bagged the cover story, and sat back to wait
for a sign that LBJ was going to move.

Some months later during a lunch with LBJ's special assistant, Bill Moyers, I got that sign. They were in fact looking for a new FBI director, Moyers told me, and went on to mention a few names. That's all I needed, and we went with the Hoover cover on the following issue, December 7, 1964.

The White House denied the story, as Moyers had thought they probably would, but no one expected what happened later in the week. LBJ scheduled a special Rose Garden briefing with Hoover in attendance, at which the president announced that he had "persuaded" Hoover to stay on as FBI director, apparently forever. On his way out to make his announcement in the Rose Garden, President Johnson muttered to Moyers under his breath: "Tell your friend Ben Bradlee, 'Fuck you.'"

TWELVE

WASHINGTON POST, 1965–71

By the end of 1964, only weeks without Mary, Tony and I were wandering innocently enough toward a crossroads in our personal and professional lives. Two murders had robbed us of significant anchors, who had made our lives meaningful and joyous. Their loss had made us less sure of ourselves, and of each other. Professionally, I still felt no involvement with the activist, inside politics of Lyndon Johnson, and had yet to come to know and respect the brilliant young men around him. If I didn't compare the Johnson presidency with the Kennedy presidency, *Newsweek* and others did, and I was the *Newsweek* Bureau chief. The piece I had written for *Newsweek* the weekend Kennedy died was published as a book, *That Special Grace*, by Lippincott in April 1964. The book seemed to brand me as hopelessly pro-Kennedy to the LBJ crowd, to my considerable annoyance. Hugh Sidey of *Time* magazine told me of a conversation he once had with LBJ on Air Force One. "What about that Georgetown crowd of Rowlie Evans and Ben Bradlee?" Sidey quoted the president. "How come when I say it, it comes out 'Horse Shit,' but when they say it, it comes out 'Chanel Number Five'?"

The *Newsweek* Bureau was running on automatic pilot. Each week as I made my rounds asking the reporters if I could help them in any way, they seemed to need less and less help. I was coasting, and I'd barely begun to worry about it. *Newsweek* had asked me twice to move to New York. First as National editor, and later as one of the so-called Wallendas (as in the great trapeze artists, The Flying Wallendas), as the top three editors called themselves. I had filled in a couple of times as National editor, and knew I could not stand the peculiar niche that *Newsweek* occupied in New York . . . the booze, the generally erratic hours, the impossible hours on Friday and Saturday, never mind an apartment big enough for all those children.

And so when Kay Graham called me for lunch in March 1965, neither of us suspected how susceptible I might be to discussing a change of scenery. She had chosen the F Street Club, a stuffy institution a few blocks from the White House, where the Washington establishment could entertain itself. (Much later I learned that she chose the club because she was worried about how she could arrange to pay for lunch without a scene. Since she was a member, and I wasn't, only she could pay.)

The lunch started off on the starchy side. I still didn't really know Kay well, and there was that lingering memory of how she had felt about my not calling on her after Phil's funeral, though we had gotten comfortable with each other. She wanted to know what I wanted to do when I grew up. She said she had heard that I had turned down two chances to move up the *Newsweek* ladder, and she seemed impressed both that I had been asked and that I'd said no. I was trying to explain my reasons, when out of the blue she asked if I'd ever given any thought to returning to the *Post*. I hadn't, because I hadn't seen any daylight over there—or looked for any. My *Newsweek* buddies were quite critical of the *Post*, and what they felt was its modest aspirations and undistinguished reporting. And they had spoken openly to Kay about their feelings, with no knowledge of the stifling impact of Phil's illness on the paper's managers and editors. I shared both feelings, and I thought *Newsweek's* Washington reporters were more energetic, more open, and less establishmentarian. But I was in awe of the paper's immediacy, its incredible impact on the community, and the shadow it cast on the government. A crook could be exposed, wrongs could be righted overnight. A victim could be extricated before a news magazine could make up its mind. And the urge to right wrong was the urge that made us journalists in the first place.

And I loved the *Post's* Sports Section.

Anyway, all of a sudden I heard myself say: "If Al Friendly's job ever opened up, I'd give my left one for it." I have wondered since if I really would have parted with my left one to be managing editor of *The Washington Post*. Attached as I am to it—and it to me—probably not, but having gotten that chance . . . if that was the price? In any case, I knew Al Friendly and Kay Graham were really close friends, and I couldn't believe his job was going to open up any time soon.

Phil Graham had told me that the Washington Bureau chiefs of weekly news magazines should stay put, working their way up to the top levels of the journalistic power structure, I told Kay. And I had gone along because I hadn't wanted to move to New York. But now with the bee in my bonnet, I could think of nothing else, and tried to pry out of Kay what, if anything, she might have in mind. She was not forthcoming, beyond suggesting that she had wondered if the *Post* might benefit by an infusion of some sort from outside. She had talked to Walter Lippmann about it, she said, and I felt a tingle of excitement in my arms and legs. Lippmann was my pal.

Lunch was over. Kay signed for the check, gracefully, and just like that I thought another life might be starting. I remember the next few weeks as interminable, waiting for the next signal. Kay remembers the next few weeks as an inquisition by me, pressing her to take the next step, whatever it was.

The next step turned out to be a proposal that I accept the title of Deputy Managing Editor for National and International Affairs, at the same salary ($50,000 a year), with an (unwritten) understanding that I would succeed Al Friendly as managing editor "sometime." The "sometime" lay there like a mackerel in the moonlight, its presence acknowledged but undefined. Kay had said to me, but to no one else, that sometime meant a year. I felt that one year was the outside limit, that the job of *Newsweek's* Washington Bureau Chief should not be abandoned for a deputy M.E. slot, unless one year was the outside limit. I shared my views with Russ Wiggins, the editor, who like all good administrators wished the problem would disappear. And I shared my views with Al Friendly. In a conversation at his house, I told him that I would give him 110 percent, and couldn't wait to get started, but I wanted him to know that I felt that a year in the bull pen was long enough. He was thinking more of three years as managing editor, he said. (He was on the ladder to become president of the American Society of Newspaper Editors in the third year.) And we left it at that, each of us knowing the unresolved difference between us. I wondered if I should take the job. He surely wondered if it should be offered me. We had never been close friends, but except for an incident early in my first incarnation at the *Post*, we had never been at odds. In fact, I had forgotten the incident until then.

I had come down out of the woods of New Hampshire at the end of 1948, convinced that Senator Styles Bridges was mixed up in a war surplus liquidation scandal of major proportions. My immediate boss, Ben Gilbert, and Russ Wiggins, had given me two weeks to see what I could do with the story in Washington, despite the fact that I was the lowest of the low city reporters. I paired up with my friend Ed Harris in the Washington Bureau of the St. *Louis Post-Dispatch*, who had won a Pulitzer Prize for the *P. D.*, and we pooled the few facts that I had with his expertise in Washington. I've never worked harder before or since than I worked for those two weeks. Twenty-hour days, one after another. We didn't tie Bridges to the war surplus scandal, but in checking the list of Bridges's political contributors, and cross-checking them with the Justice Department's list of lobbyists, I had come up with two interesting names: Alfred Kohlberg and William Goodman, both ardent supporters of Chiang Kai-shek. Kohlberg was a businessman who had made his money shipping Irish linen to be embroidered in China and sold in America as quality handkerchiefs. Goodman was a professional lobbyist and nut case, who had once run for mayor of New York City as the candidate of something called the American Rock Party—off the charts to the far right.

What I did write were the first stories ever written—I think— about the China Lobby, two of them, both on page one. Not the Teapot Dome, maybe, but very important to me, to prove to myself and my editors that I could play in this new league. My problem with Al Friendly came a few weeks later, when I discovered that the lead story in the Outlook Section was a long (and very good) profile of the man I had discovered, Alfred Kohlberg. It was bylined Alfred Friendly, not Benjamin C. Bradlee.

Much has been written about Bradlee and Friendly at this time in our lives. How I "got" him, if the story was written from Friendly's prism. Or how he was inhibiting the paper's great leap forward, if my prism was dominant. Al Friendly was a man of intellect, with an arch sense of humor, a wide circle of friends, and a ranging curiosity. He appeared to me from Day One as miscast in the role of managing editor, the job on a daily newspaper where all the thousand details of administration and production have to be coordinated before the paper can be in position to write the great stories. In fact, he had ceded those details to Ben Gilbert, the city editor, and in so doing had lost—or never found—the power to make great things happen.

A few things need to be said bluntly now. First, no one can imag- ine how difficult it was for the *Post*'s managers—editors and business types—to cope with Phil Graham's illness in the last long months of his manic depression. Many of them were fired, then rehired. Many were confronted with decisions taken by Phil—a new bureau here, a new executive there—pursuant to priorities and judgments that were at least erratic. A bunker mentality had understandably gripped the paper's managers, and a bunker mentality is not condu- cive to great leaps forward. The men who held the paper together during these trying times—specifically, Russ Wiggins, Al Friendly, and John Sweeterman, the head of the business side—made all fu- ture progress possible, and I knew it, and they knew I knew it.

Before I took the job as deputy managing editor with no commitments from anyone, only thoughts, I discussed it at length with Tony, knowing that the decision would change her life, too. I felt a new obsession coming on. I knew it would take thousands of extra hours just to learn enough to begin to know what to do—hours spent at *The Washington Post*, not at home. She knew I was aching to do it, and figured there was no point in objecting.

And so on Monday, August 2, 1965, I came home to *The Washington Post*, after an absence of fourteen years and six weeks, once again skipping my four-week vacation. My "office" was an 8-by-12-foot cubbyhole off the city room, tiled from floor to ceiling in Men's Room beige, in what once had been part of a photo studio.

However much I had, or had not, been badgering Kay Graham about getting on with it, I had not been exactly goofing off. From early May, I had been talking separately to two remarkable *Washington Post* reporters, Larry Stern and Howard Simons, both friends (though strangely never with each other), who felt that the *Post* was not living up to its potential. I pumped each of them dry about who on the staff was good, who was okay, and who had to be replaced if we were determined to have the best reporters on the key beats. Kay had kept her word, that five vacancies that she had kept frozen were mine to fill (not Friendly's), and I had a priority list of people to fill those vacancies. There was so much I didn't know—about presses, about composing rooms, about budgets—that I had decided to concentrate on the one thing I did know about: good reporters. And there was a bumper crop of them out there.

- Ward Just, who came over from *Newsweek* with me, bright, full of ideas and energy, and a wonderful writer, and the paper had plenty of room for those particular qualities.
- Bart Rowen, one of the very best business and financial reporters ever, who came over from *Newsweek* early in 1966. At that time, the *Post*'s business and financial staff consisted of S. Oliver Goodman alone, plus a part-time copy boy to handle the agate.
- Dick Harwood, of the *Louisville Courier Journal and Times*, one of the great reporters and editors of his generation. He was on some fellowship in New York, but when he heard I was back at the

Post, he called to say he wanted in. And it didn't take a genius to want him in your foxhole. I had known Harwood when we had adjoining offices in the National Press Club.

- David Broder, of the *New York Times*, well on his way to being the greatest pure political reporter of his generation. I had tried to hire him for *Newsweek*, but Malcolm Muir, Jr., was put off by David's wardrobe . . . brown shoes with blue slacks.
- Don Oberdorfer, then of the Knight Bureau, and a mortal lock to become what he became, a foreign affairs expert who could and did peg even with the very best foreign affairs experts.
- George Wilson, a future twenty-year Pentagon gold mine, then working for *Aviation Week and Space Technology* magazine. George succeeded the *Post*'s Pentagon reporter, whose nickname was "Black Sheet" (as in carbon paper), and who was paid by the Navy, while he was our correspondent (as a Naval Reserve captain).
- Stanley Karnow, an old Paris colleague, working for *Time-Life*. He was our expert on China—just ripe to open a *Post* Bureau in Hong Kong, and start the quality coverage of China for which he became so widely known and admired.

That was real firepower, and it was just the first wave! All in place within the first months of the new regime. The impact of these hires—on the outside world, as well as on the paper—cannot be overstated. Especially Broder, who was the first top rank reporter ever to quit the *Times* for the *Post*. The traffic had all been the other way. I romanced him like he's never been romanced—in coffee shops, not fancy French restaurants, because Broder was a coffee shop kind of man: straightforward, no frills, all business. I told him we had determined to get the best there was for every beat, that politics was the quintessential *Washington Post* story, and we wanted him. And we got him.

A quarter of a century later, in the easy remove of racial and sexual diversity, the hires seem awfully white and awfully male. Like totally white and totally male. The *Post* had pioneered in hiring any black journalists. Simeon Booker, in 1952, was the first black reporter on a white newspaper in Washington. More followed—slowly—but most of them, like Luther Jackson and Wallace Terry, moved on after comparatively short stays on the horns of their own painful dilemmas. Treated suspiciously by black activists, and denied the years of training and experience which would have made them truly competitive, Booker resigned in June 1953, and said later: "God knows I tried to succeed at the *Post*. I struggled so hard that friends thought I was dying, I looked so fatigued. After a year and a half I had to give up. Trying to cover news in a city where even animal cemeteries were segregated overwhelmed me."

In the summer of 1965, black reporters on the *Post* staff included only Bill Raspberry, the columnist and later a Pulitzer Prize winner, and Jesse Lewis, later a foreign correspondent and then a CIA officer in the Middle East. Dorothy Gilliam, a former assistant city editor and later a columnist, was on leave. As a *Newsweek* reporter and bureau chief, I had prided myself on knowing the best young reporters in the country, but none was black.

Women reporters had taken their place in city rooms during World War II, as the male reporters went off to war. Many of them excelled, but the majority had to leave because of the law that guaranteed returning veterans the same jobs they held when they went to war. News magazines were siphoning off good young talent, males and females, much as television had done in the decade from 1955 to 1965. This is an explanation, not an excuse. I was not sensitive to racism or sexism, to understate the matter. The newsroom was racist. Overtly racist, in a few isolated cases; passively racist in many places where reporters and editors were insensitive and unsensitized. This racism would slowly and painfully subside, if not vanish, over the next ten years.

But at the time, such racism at the *Post* (and other papers) stood in the way of excellence. Ten days after I arrived as deputy managing editor for national and international affairs, on August 11, 1965, the race riots in the Watts district of Los Angeles broke out. No *Washington Post* reporter was sent to L.A. for five days (there was no L.A. Bureau), and the first riot byline—the ubiquitous Chal Roberts, *The Washington Post*'s one-man band who could and did cover any story in the paper—plus the first mood stories from the riot scene from Bill Raspberry didn't appear in the paper until August 17. The delay was inexcusable for a newspaper which aspired to be judged as great. And I couldn't make anything happen, yet.

The trouble was threefold: the *Post* wasn't fast out of the box, period; the mind-set of the *Post* made editors ask how much an assignment cost, instead of how much the paper needed the story; and the *Post's* black reporters had had no chance to be tested under fire.

After scouting and signing new players, I spent all of my first few months trying to discover the secret of Ben Gilbert's power. He was one of the most interesting of my new colleagues, bright, able, extremely hardworking . . . but not appreciated by a remarkable number of reporters. Several of them sidled up to me early on to ask, almost hopefully, if it was true that I had decked Gilbert once in some fight we were supposed to have had back in the late forties. It was not true. In fact, he had hired me back in 1948, and given me way more than my share of his time and expertise. But my return put an end to his aspiration to succeed Friendly and Wiggins. He was still more than generous to me with his inside knowledge of where the power lay and what buttons to push to control the paper's inside politics. A considerable hunk of the power lay with him, because—it was soon clear—he did all the scut work that bored Al Friendly (with some justification): salary administration, scheduling, production coordination, deadlines, vacations, overtime, plus most of the assigning.

I decided to give myself a crash course in all that good stuff, especially production, about which I knew least. Every night, for one year, I would go home for a drink and dinner with Tony and homework with six children, and then come back down to the *Post* to watch the first, second, and third editions clear the composing room and then the press room. I'd get back home about 1:00 A.M., appalled by how complicated it was to bring everything together from typewriter to newspaper, and appalled by the power of the printers, engravers, stereotypers, and pressmen to bail the newsroom out when they wanted to cooperate, and to screw us to smithereens whenever they wanted to do that. "Bogus" type was explained to me twenty times before I understood what it meant, and I still can't believe it.

Bogus type (also known as "repro") was material set in type somewhere else—another newspaper, for instance. The *Post* was free to use this material, but under the existing labor contract, the *Post* had to pay its printers what they would have earned if they had set the type in the first place, even though the reset type would never be used. When this practice was eventually bargained away in the mid-1970s, more than 42,000 newspaper pages of bogus type, worth millions of dollars, were on the union's books.

My ignorance spilled out far beyond the premises at 1513-21 L Street, Northwest, with special emphasis on blacks. To be blunt about it, I didn't know anything about blacks, or the black experience, and I was about to become involved in the leadership of the number-one newspaper in a city that was 70 percent black, and a readership that was 25 percent black. I had had no black friends growing up. There were no blacks in my boarding school, only three blacks in my class at college, none of whom I knew at all. I had only one black friend as a grown-up . . . my *Newsweek* colleague, Lionel Durand, in Paris. He was Haitian and French, and he didn't know all that much about American blacks. At *Newsweek* I had known a handful of black leaders, like Roy Wilkins, A. Philip Randolph, Louis Martin, but I knew no ordinary black people.

Paul Moore, then the suffragan bishop of Washington, and a friend since I was nine, decided that it was his civic duty to expose me to Washington's black community before I became managing editor. And so he arranged with Father Bill Wendt, who was white but resolutely integrationist, and the rector of the Church of St. Stephen and the Incarnation, that I become the only white member of the Upper Cardozo Men's Council, an eclectic group of blacks—some former criminals, some solid citizens—who met Tuesday nights in Bill Wendt's church to talk about what was going on in the neighborhood, and what could be done about it. While Tony was teaching pottery to unwed teenage mothers in the basement, I spent almost fifteen months listening and learning upstairs. They dubbed me "the Hawk," because I pounced on their stories, investigated them, and got them in the paper whenever they checked out.

In the city room at night I bugged everyone for answers to a thousand questions. How come the night managing editor went home at 9:00 P.M.? Because he felt there was nothing to do after the first edition closed. How come we had an eight-column banner automatically, on the first and final edition front pages, whether or not the news justified such play? Because Harry Gladstein, the circulation chief, wanted one. How come the front page of the second, third, and fourth editions always had three or four small, one-paragraph stories, under headlines like "30 Missing in Ecuador Mud Slide"? To replace the space taken up by the eight-column banners in the first and final editions. How come we didn't cover fires or crimes in the city's black neighborhoods? Because the night city editors treated black and white victims differently. How come the production chiefs automatically approved our requests for page one color photos if it involved the pope? Because the powers-that-be on the business side were all Catholics.

I remember only a few fights. A couple with Dick Thornburg, the night managing editor, who felt I was usurping his role. He was right, and he left after a few months. One, a small one, with Al Friendly. I had decided to put some light story about Senator Bill Proxmire on page one of the city edition. Prox had called Friendly to complain. And Friendly had overruled me, which was certainly his prerogative. But I was down there six nights a week, way more than anyone else, and I was learning fast.

Out of the blue in the middle of October, less than three months after I had come back to the paper, Al Friendly went to Kay Graham and told her Bradlee could handle the M.E. job, and he was ready to do something else: the new ideas beat, which Al had dreamed up but could never find the right person to take over. Or an overseas assignment. Al had served the paper with distinction for more than twenty-seven years. He could and did write his own ticket. First, the new ideas beat, and later as European correspondent/London Bureau chief, in which capacity he proceeded to win himself (and us) a Pulitzer Prize for his reporting on the Six-Day War in Israel, in 1967. He eventually retired on his sixtieth birthday, as he had announced he would do years before.

Kay asked Wiggins if he thought I could do it, and when he said he thought I could, I became the managing editor.

And so, with the place barely energized, I was the managing editor. I had accomplished very little, beyond a few hires, and a good lead on a few more. There was not yet a steady diet of good stories. The paper still was hard to read. Production quality was a disgrace, with typos galore, with color so bad that the people in pictures regularly had four eyes and two sets of teeth. The design was just plain ugly, dominated by an Advertising Department more interested in the advertising revenue than the newspaper itself. Ink smudges, "see-through" (where ads were printed in such dark ink they could be read on the reverse page), were on every other page. I still knew barely more than my ass from left field about production. The staff was still small—303 people in the newsroom—and the newsroom budget was inadequate to say the least, around $4 million a year, versus close to $20 million for the *New York Times*, against which the world judged us, and against which I hungered to be judged.

To make matters worse, the budget for 1966 was incubating. Russ Wiggins had left budgeting to me, and I had been forced to lean heavily on Ben Gilbert, who knew everything, but had no stomach for the kind of fights we had to fight to make things better—and more expensive. The day finally came when the News Department had to appear before publisher John Sweeterman to justify its budget requests for 1966. John knew I had Kay Graham's support, but he wasn't about to turn over sincere money to the new boy on the block without making me explain what every dime was for. It was against his religion, and this religion had finally made the *Post* profitable after losing more than $1 million a year for twenty years. I couldn't believe it when he led me through every line of the newsroom budget requests, asking me why we needed however many thousands of dollars for everything from new positions to stationery. I didn't even know enough to say "product improvement," which is every editor's last-ditch justification.

And so in my first "clash" with the bean counters, in my first act of leadership, I got clobbered, not to put too fine a point on it. And I will always be grateful to John Sweeterman for that lesson. Never again did I go into a budget session knowing less than the holder of the purse strings. My father had always told me to move carefully when talking to someone who knew more than I did, if I couldn't or wouldn't shut up. But moving carefully or shutting up doesn't always work with publishers.

As managing editor, I started running the two story conferences: the first, at two-thirty in the afternoon when the section editors talk about their page-one stories in progress; and the second about seven, or whenever the night managing editor had produced the page-one dummy, or mock-up. That alone gave me a sense of responsibility for the paper that I had never known before, plus a sense of fear. Everyone in the newspaper business knew about the editor who had played the first atomic bomb as a small story inside along with the truss ads, and I was fearful of doing the same thing. I think that's what lies behind a lifelong encouragement of second-guessers, and a willingness to change my mind. Story conferences became *the* place to talk ideas, to express enthusiasms, to encourage initiative, to have some fun, to take chances, and generally to create the sense of excitement that seemed to be missing.

When the first wave of new hires showed up, a handful of real pros were already on board, of course, eager as I was for new blood. Men like Larry Stern. The one and only Howard Simons, eventually the managing editor, but before that the eclectic leader of the team he christened SMERSH, which stood for Science, Medicine, Education, Religion, and all that SHit. Pete Silberman, the soft-spoken genius who became an assistant managing editor of almost every department in the newsroom. The incomparable Carroll Kilpatrick at the White House, the most unflappable professional I ever met. Murrey Marder on the diplomatic beat, who had won his spurs covering Senator Joe McCarthy and gone on to be the *Post's* first, and for a long time only, foreign correspondent. Chalmers Roberts, an all pro whatever the assignment; sometimes the assignment process seemed to work best when Chal came to work, read the papers, and then decided on which story he wanted to do—local, national, or foreign. And of course the real pros like Herblock, simply the greatest cartoonist of his era; Shirley Povich, the nonpareil of American sportswriters; and Bill Gold, the local columnist, whose folksy prose ran six days a week on the comics page for over thirty-four years. Those disparate men, plus Herbert Elliston's editorial page, had been the main reasons to read *The Washington Post* for many, many years. And there was a serious young reporter named Leonard Downie—prematurely mature, they said, with a reputation as one hell of an investigative reporter. He was twenty-three years old then, nicknamed "Land Grant Len" because he was fresh out of Ohio State. He is the executive editor of *The Washington Post* today.

My first months were spent trying to be sure I didn't fall on my face. Russ Wiggins saved his thoughts for me personally, during private talks at the end of his day, when he would give me my nightly reading assignments. Literally. Had I read this book or that book? Well, I better read them, and let's talk about them tomorrow, he would say. I often ended up with three books to read, and it took me months before I dared remind him about all those children and their homework, and what used to be a private life.

The news was dominated by Vietnam, in a way that is hard to imagine today. Vietnam, and the many, many descendants of Vietnam, owned page one, it seemed, for years. Our correspondent in Vietnam was John Maffre, a solid journeyman reporter who had been chosen primarily because he was single and therefore thought to be capable of prolonged absences. The *Post* had no one in Vietnam for too long, and when Maffre got there he covered the war the way von Clausewitz might have covered it—as if there were armies facing each other across well-defined front lines.

But reporters like Neil Sheehan for the United Press, Peter Arnett for the Associated Press, and David Halberstam of the *New York Times* had written with perception and bravery and energy about the new realities of the war, where our allies were less committed than our enemy, and our soldiers were fighting a cause that increasingly lacked public support. I wanted a new Hemingway who could write like an angel, and who could explain the drama we were seeing on our TV screens in terms of the young soldiers who were sent off to change Vietnam, but in fact were changing America in the most fundamental ways.

And I found Ward Just, who came with me from *Newsweek* to the *Post*. The son of an Illinois publisher, Ward Just is one hell of a novel writer today. Then, he was just a wonderful young reporter/ writer, who found drama everywhere he looked—the drama that turned details into truth and isolated events into history. Sometimes Just would get a single quote that would tell an entire story. We spread one of those quotes, from a frightened GI surrounded by his enemies, eight columns over the top of the front page: "Ain't Nobody Here but Charlie Cong," as in Viet Cong. Sometime later, Charlie Cong threw a grenade in the general vicinity of Ward Just, spraying his head, back, and legs with shrapnel.

Under Russ, the editorial page was strongly for resisting tyranny wherever it ruled, and pursuing the fight against communism in Vietnam. President Johnson once thanked Wiggins for his support, saying that the *Post*'s editorials were worth two divisions to him. Many of the reporters—and a lot of their wives—thought the paper's editorial support of the war was morally wrong. I concentrated on trying to discover what was going on in Vietnam, on trying to determine who was telling the truth about Vietnam, before it occurred to me to find out where I stood myself. Tony Bradlee was marching in the streets with one of the many anti-Vietnam protest groups while I was trying to figure out who was organizing the protests, and how well—or poorly—they were reflecting American opinion.

At that time the Op-Ed page came under the jurisdiction of the managing editor, and at least theoretically that gave me a chance to run columns by writers who expressed my own views. But my own views were essentially non-political, and my theoretical power went unexercised. I was more interested in facts and people than in any one person's opinion about those facts. I was more interested in the press conference than in anyone's analysis of the press conference. And I still am. Early on I persuaded Joe Kraft—without the slightest difficulty, let me say quickly—to move his column from the *Star* to the *Post*. Joe was neither a bleeder nor a basher, just a thoughtful, hardworking intellectual, and a friend. But it was the friend part of the Op-Ed equation which made its supervision thankless. Walter Lippmann and Joe Alsop owned the top-left and the top-right spots on the Op-Ed page when they wrote. Who took their place on their days off, and who took the complaints when Kraft topped Rowlie Evans, or Evans topped Mark Childs? And how did you move some of the old-timers, like Roscoe Drummond or J. A. Livingston, a Philadelphia business columnist, up and out to bring in some new blood?

The solution, of course, is to have different persons editing the news columns and the opinion columns. When Russ Wiggins retired, his title had been Editor. When I succeeded him in 1968, I became Executive Editor, in charge of all non-advertising matters in the paper except the editorial and Op-Ed pages. My old pal Phil Geyelin took them over with the title of Editorial Page Editor.

I had been trying to get Phil Geyelin, even when I was with *Newsweek*, to leave the *Wall Street Journal* and join our modest crusade in some capacity. He fancied writing editorials, but I had nothing to do with the editorial page, where Russ Wiggins's intellect was in charge. They finally got together, and Phil joined up in February 1967 to write editorials for six months. If everyone still loved each other, Phil would take over as the editorial page editor, reporting to Wiggins, as I did. Six months later it happened, and almost the first thing Phil did was to hire Meg Greenfield, who was at liberty because Max Ascoli had folded the *Reporter* magazine. Mary Ellen Greenfield was one smart lady, with an irresistible sense of humor. I used to walk back to her office and schmooze until she laughed. That laugh would lift whatever was bowing my mind, and refresh my soul.

The hunt for talent on a newspaper never stops. The more we found, the hungrier we got. And as the newsroom budget increased slowly, and then not so slowly, this search for the best writers and the best reporters became an obsession. I was determined that a *Washington Post* reporter would be the best in town on every beat. We had a long way to go.

The second wave of stars brought us Jim Hoagland from the *New York Times*, first as a city side reporter, then as a Pulitzer Prize-winning foreign correspondent, foreign editor, assistant managing editor, and eventually primo columnist on foreign affairs. Nick von Hoffman from the *Chicago Daily News,* by way of the Chicago stockyards and activist Saul Alinsky's staff, was an irreverent intellectual who wrote like a dream. Peter Milius was the first of the Kentucky mafia, already lured from the Louisville papers by the time I arrived in August 1965. Nothing was too arcane for Milius. He could—and regularly did—make sense out of the federal budget. Milius was followed some years later by Bill Greider; although we were prodded by Harwood, we had been trying to get Greider for some time before we landed him. Greider had one of those attractive, restless, and inquisitive minds that led him easily from strip mining to the Federal Reserve Board. He had an open mind and a sense of humor. Everyone wanted to work with him or for him. Jonathan Randal quit the *New York Times* as its Warsaw correspondent to join Phil Foisie's fast-growing foreign staff. Randal is the last of the great foreign correspondents, glamorous in their storied trench coats, at home anywhere in the world. He could—and regularly did—file intelligent stories within hours of landing in a country he had never seen before.

Mike Getler joined up in 1970 and made it in leaps and bounds all the way up the ladder to deputy managing editor—an extraordinary reporter, and one of those editors whose people touch is perfect. Lou Cannon, the great political reporter and authority on Ronald Reagan, joined us later from the *San Jose Mercury News,* heavily backed by Harwood. Dick described him as the best political reporter in the country after Broder, and he was right.

Roger Wilkins, who had been an assistant attorney general in the Kennedy administration, had become an interesting, in-your-face, delightful, and useful friend. He never worked for me, but with my enthusiastic encouragement he worked for Geyelin on the editorial page during Watergate. He was quick to criticize me, but he convinced me that his criticism was an act of friendship and faith.

We never stopped recruiting.

The first wire service flashes from Memphis: "Dr. Martin Luther King, Jr., was shot outside a Memphis hotel Thursday afternoon.

His condition was not immediately known." It was 7:00 P.M., April 8, 1968. We had just approved the front page for the first edition when the newsroom came alive with that powerful buzz that precedes, then blends into, the disasters of history. The worst was soon confirmed: "Dr. Martin Luther King, Jr., was shot and killed late Thursday as he stood alone in the balcony of his hotel."

The very process of reacting to news like King's assassination spares journalists a lot of the immediate personal agony such events would normally inspire, as I had experienced when JFK was shot. At least initially, there is simply too much to do. Get reporters to the primary scene . . . that meant planes to Memphis. Throw out the page-one dummy . . . that meant finding another place in the paper for the stories that were not going on page one, or killing them outright. Get more space . . . that meant killing ads and stories. Tell the composing room—and the Circulation Department—that the first edition was going to be late . . . that meant holding trucks, rescheduling deliveries. Speak to the proprietors . . . it's their paper. Assign the sidebars . . . that meant a King obit, a story on what lay ahead for the civil rights movement, a profile of who shot him, for starters, plus local reaction . . . and that meant working the phones and fanning reporters across the city.

Outside, the streets of Washington were exploding in anger. Fires were set in downtown stores—mostly in the black sections of town. Looting started almost immediately and reached within a few blocks of the White House.

From the roof of the Post Building late that night, one could see the fires that pockmarked the northeast quadrant of the city. Smoke spiraled into the warm spring air, and sirens pierced the night. Sirens and the sound of breaking glass, as the looting began. I don't remember going home, hypnotized as the dimensions of the riot unfolded slowly, while an increasingly creative and adaptable staff of reporters went about the complicated task of separating fact from rumor, and harnessing their own emotions to the search for truth.

For the next ten days Washington lived under a curfew, and more than twelve thousand federal troops enforced it. More than a hundred reporters, editors, and photographers from the *Post* worked

around the clock, including twenty-four reporters and photographers assigned only to the streets, reporting from the Advertising
Department's radio cars. Fire and looting spread from the 7th Street
corridor—ten blocks from the White House—across the city. Bar-
ricades blocked off whole sections of the city. Tear gas penetrated
skin, and clothes. A dozen people were dead, close to four thousand
arrested. Never mind the kid stuff I had written about almost twenty
years earlier, this was an honest-to-God race riot, born of anger and
frustration, dedicated to a demand for attention.

The stars of the show were the black reporters and photographers, now more than a dozen. They instinctively shied away from
covering only "black" news. They knew they would be branded by
black leaders and rioters as Uncle Toms, but they had already faced
that nastiness. The black photographers, particularly, showed great
courage, for they were collecting "evidence" as they shot their stunning pictures of the looting, and the rioters knew it.*

The star of stars was Robert Maynard from the *York* (Pa.) *Gazette
and Daily*, who went on to a precedent-setting career as the first
black editor, and then publisher of a major American newspaper,
the *Oakland Tribune*.

The first time I ever laid eyes on Bob Maynard had been a few
years earlier, when he came to Washington for a week with the Nieman Fellows. They were hot-shot journalists in midcareer spending
a year at Harvard studying anything they wanted to study. They had
asked me to tell them what I was up to at *The Washington Post*.

He stood out in that crowd, not only because he was black in a
profession where there were damn few blacks, but because he was
confrontational, argumentative, mean, and skeptical, verging on

---

* During the riots, the D.C. Police Department asked us for permission to look through our
file of pictures (published and unpublished) for photographs where looters could be identified.
We had published 180 pictures during the riot's first week, and taken thousands more. We
declined, of course, pointing out we were in the news-gathering game, not the law enforcement business. We explained how the photographers' lives might be endangered, and the
newsgathering process sabotaged, but the government threatened us with subpoenas. With
my *Washington Star* colleague, Newbold Noyes, I met with Justice Department officials and got
them to agree to a "compromise." Each morning, we sent them over an 8-by-8-inch print of
whatever photo had appeared in the paper.

the obnoxious. Much of my ninety minutes with the Niemans was spent arguing with Maynard.

As I walked back to the *Post* from George Washington University, where we had met, I wondered about him and what the hell it would take to impress him, or even interest him. I doubted that I could impress him.

But there he was sitting in my outer office when I got back to work. He said he thought he might like to work at the *Post* much to my surprise. He would have to return to his paper in York, Pennsylvania, because he had promised to return for one year after the fellowship, but he wondered if we might be interested in him after that.

We damn well would be interested, and I told him so.

One year later to the week, he was back, and it wasn't long before he was the talk of the town, literally. He was a Metro reporter then, and a key building block in the *Post*'s belated commitment to attract high-quality black journalists to the newsroom. Bob Maynard had many qualities (he would be a national reporter, an editorial writer, an assistant managing editor, and the Ombudsman before he left the paper), but one of his most distinctive qualities was the rich, sonorous timbre of his voice. He spoke in pear-shaped tones, and by the second day of the riots he was in a radio car, crouched in the front seat, broadcasting back to the city room whatever he saw.

We all stood around the city desk radio bank as Bob "filed":

The flames are now rising, six, eight, now fifteen feet high. The entire store is being engulfed, while looters, mostly children, race in and out of the burning buildings, strangely unaware of the danger. . . .

My car is now being surrounded by four gentlemen, all of them apparently hostile. Now there are eight of them, bouncing the car up and down. I shall leave the air, momentarily, until things settle down. . . .

There are four policemen ducking for cover right beside my car. . . . They are down on one knee behind the hood and the trunk . . . with their guns drawn and cocked . . . aiming over

the car at the roof above us. . . . I am now getting onto the floor
under the dashboard as fast as I can. . . . Over and out.*

The city desk would ask for the exact address. A copy boy, taking it all down on a typewriter, would add the time, and we would
all cheer. NBC heard about Maynard's bravura performances, and
asked if they could send someone over to watch. We said, "Sure,"
and the network stayed to cover the riots by covering Maynard and
his gang. Same for the United Press.

A couple of days into the riots, I gathered up Howard Simons
and David Broder for a firsthand look at what was going on in what
we liked to call the capital of the free world. We ended up, about
3:00 P.M., in front of a big, burning warehouse in an overwhelmingly black section of the city. It was the biggest fire I'd seen since
Manchester, New Hampshire, when a whole block of Elm Street
went up in flames.

We were joined by two different groups of blacks, also sightseeing, and we all talked unself-consciously about the fire and the riots
in general. None of us felt the slightest bit threatened. Until we
were joined by a local TV crew, which took its time setting up and
shooting the fire. When they turned their cameras on us bystanders,
the blacks immediately started yelling at us, trashing us, even shaking their fists at us, creating enough of a disturbance to attract the
cops, and the next thing we knew tear-gas guns were going off and
the little aluminum canisters were rolling around the street. Broder
had apparently not seen or smelled tear gas before, and wanted a
better look, or smell. He walked over and bent down just as one of
the canisters popped, and he became a full-fledged expert in a matter of seconds. The TV cameras shot great stuff, full of action. Black
versus white, cops versus blacks, those slowly arcing tear-gas canisters, all against a raging fire. It didn't tell much about the truth, it
just made good television.

                    *   *   *

---

* As quoted in Ten Blocks from the White House, by Ben W. Gilbert and the staff of The
Washington Post (New York: Frederick A. Praeger, 1968), p.26.

It was three in the morning, less than two months later, when the violence that was at once so incomprehensible and so routine struck again with the assassination of Robert F. Kennedy. We were all still in the newsroom, waiting for the final edition of June 5, 1968, to come upstairs from the composing room, headlining Bobby Kennedy's victory over Eugene McCarthy in the California primary.

I heard those dreadful words, "Kennedy's been shot," just seconds before I watched Larry Stern pick up the telephone, blanch, and say, "I got Harwood."

Harwood was calling from the ballroom of the Ambassador Hotel in Los Angeles, only seconds after he had stared into the vacant, bloody face of the dying Bobby Kennedy. Dick Harwood, primitive in his search for the truth, impossible to deceive, and without peer in his ability to write a declarative sentence, had been assigned to cover Bobby Kennedy exactly because he was skeptical of Kennedy, and almost despite himself had grown to like Kennedy, then respect him, and finally to feel close to him.

The phone Harwood found was being used by a middle-aged woman who was trying to describe the chaotic scene to a friend. Harwood started to excuse himself, explaining why he felt his need was greater than hers. When she showed no interest in helping him, he helped himself. We told Dick what we knew, what the wires had said, and he told us what he knew. He had been by Bobby's side when Sirhan Sirhan's bullets struck. We told him we had stopped the presses and were going for an extra. He was to call us back with everything he had in thirty minutes.

In fact, I had already shouted, *"Stop the presses!"* (for the first and only time in my life), electrifying everyone in the newsroom, including myself. But the presses had not stopped. The emergency bell installed for just this purpose had been disconnected (by whom? we suspected the bean counters), and it took several minutes for the word to drift down to an indifferent press room that Bradlee really meant it.

Television shines its brightest in the first few hours after actions that are vivid and dramatic, when truths are hard to find and pictures give only clues. In these moments television doesn't have the time to sort out fact from rumor, nor the information to place events in context. That's the newspaper's vital role. What we can't achieve with immediacy, we provide with background and comprehensiveness. So, "extras" may not serve much purpose in the age of television, but we were determined to put out an extra anyway, maybe because the effort would keep us from facing the ugliness and the tragedy that was dogging this family. But also because there was news to be reported and we were newspaper reporters. The bean counters were slightly less enthusiastic, as they drifted into the newsroom asking, "What's all this about an extra?" and thinking of all that overtime money.

But we were determined. Katharine Graham was on the premises, and she wasn't telling us no, and before long Harwood was back on the phone to Stern. Together, they crafted the lead story, talking, listening, questioning. We added sidebars from the wire service, plus photos, rejiggered the whole A section of the paper, and finally hit the streets with our extra close to 6:00 A.M. It wasn't great, but we had been doing what we had been put on this earth to do, and we felt good about that.

And then I went home in the morning's early light, sat down at the kitchen table, and cried uncontrollably for an hour. I couldn't stop. I couldn't speak.

I was surprised at the intensity of my feeling. Bobby and I had seen each other socially from time to time, but not all that often. I had valued Bobby Kennedy as a source during the 1960 campaign. He was the hardest worker I have ever seen. But I felt he resented the access JFK and Jackie gave to Tony and me, and I had had one four-star battle with him in July 1964, when I was still working for *Newsweek*.

What role, if any, Bobby would play in the 1964 election had been a matter of great interest to everyone in town, including Bobby. President Johnson was saying different things to different people on the subject, and I had arranged to spend a long day with Bobby in the fall of 1964, starting at 6:00 A.M. at his home, Hickory Hill, for a trip to Kansas City, and Chicago, winding up after midnight in New York City. During the day, we flew commercial, and I probably spent four or five hours sitting next to the restless Kennedy, taking notes all the way, on a large, lined yellow pad. We spent two hours at the dedication of a Catholic Home for the Aged in Kansas City. Almost half of that time Bobby spent upstairs (away from TV cameras and other reporters) in a ward for the terminally ill, sitting alone at the bedside of a woman whose eyes were tight shut, whose death rattle was the only sign that life still existed in her frail body. I watched with tears in my eyes as the "ruthless" Bobby Kennedy stroked this unknown woman's hand, and spoke to her in a near whisper.

Later, en route to Chicago and New York, I asked him about the campaign, and about his interest in the vice presidency. He made no secret of his desire for the job, but was realistic about his chances: LBJ would never let him have it. My story for *Newsweek* stressed this particular revelation:

> "Actually," [Kennedy said], "I should think I'd be the last man in the world he would want. . . because my name is Kennedy, because he wants a Johnson Administration with no Kennedys in it, because we travel different paths, because I suppose some businessmen would object, and because I'd cost them a few votes in the South . . . I don't think as many as some say, but some."

The story was picked up by the wires, and other papers, and then inexplicably denied categorically by Kennedy and his aide, Ed Guthman, who were by then traveling in Poland. No such conversation ever occurred, went the first denial. After I provided enough details to disprove that, Kennedy and Co. came back with the explanation that the whole conversation was "off the record." This, too, was a lie, and I resented it. Such claims are tough for reporters to refute. There is no written record that can settle the disagreement. And the public is left at least in some confusion.

But that was four years before his death, and in the intervening years I had been slowly coming to sense this man's passion, his building rage at the persistent inequalities that plagued America, his readiness to embrace the hopeless and enlist in their cause. Vietnam was tearing America apart. Race was tearing America apart. Inequality was tearing America apart, and Bobby Kennedy's almost romantic determination to make a difference had deeply impressed me. There was no need to compare him with JFK; they were so different, except for that last name and that father. JFK was more intellectual, urbane, sophisticated, witty. RFK was more passionate, more daring, more radical.

And now, impossibly, they were both gone. What other country assassinates its leaders the way America does?

The journalist's reputation for being hard-boiled and cynical describes a self-defense mechanism. Without the pressure of the next deadline, a reporter could—and would—indulge his or her emotions. Sorrow, rage, despair, whatever. But with the next dead-lines—five of them every day—journalists must move on. We moved our energies on to, among other things, a problem that had been bugging us all for months: where in the paper were we going to cover the revolution in how people were living? Where and how would we cover what real people were doing, rather than criminals murdering or leaders leading?

There was no feature section, really. No regular place for profiles of interesting people. No place for wit or humor. No place for a look at social trends beyond the seasonal changes of fashion. And given the alleged imperatives of a cost-conscious Production Department, no one place in the paper where society's leisure activities could be explored. We covered television the way we covered congressional hearings, long on process, short on people, judgment, and motive. Our book and movie reviews jumped from one section of the paper to another, often ending up in different sections.

We did have a section called "for and about Women" (written in exaggerated, cursive type with a small "a" and a small "f") or the "women's section," as it was known. There, we covered fashions, parties involving embassies especially, and the wives of cabinet officials. A photo of Mrs. Dean Rusk, attending some country's birthday—with the ambassador often in native dress—was one of our specialties. We covered parties as if we catered them, but only if they were given by Gwendolyn Cafritz, or Perle Mesta, or maybe top military brass. We didn't cover parties as political happenings, with political as well as social purposes. We ran sewing patterns, and we ran recipes. My God, did we run recipes, few if any of which had ever been tested by us, and most of which required some mixture of hamburger (hot) and aspic (cold).

We did have a gossip columnist, the wondrous Maxine Cheshire, or "The Blue Max," as she was known in the city room. Maxine was the daughter of a Harlan County, Kentucky, coal mine manager, and she feared nobody. She was once described admiringly by one of her Harlan County editors as "pound for pound the toughest woman reporter I ever saw." The trouble with Maxine, if it was trouble, lay in her total involvement with investigative reporting. She would rather write about the foreign businessman's financial irregularities than his social behavior. I probably spent more time dousing fires ignited by Maxine than any other journalist except those that Woodward and Bernstein would ignite in 1972. But she was fun to work with and awesome to watch once she sank her teeth into someone's flank. "I'll get him," she'd say quietly. "I'll get him." And she usually did.

But the internal culture of "for and about Women" made me feel uncomfortable. Women were treated exclusively as shoppers, partygoers, cooks, hostesses, and mothers, and men were ignored. We began thinking of a section that would deal with how men and women lived—together and apart—what they liked and what they were like, what they did when they were not at the office. We wanted profiles, but "new journalism" profiles that went way beyond the bare bones of biography. We wanted to look at the culture of America as it was changing in front of our eyes. The sexual revolution, the drug culture, the women's movement. And we wanted it to be interesting, exciting, different.

By September 1968, we had all pretty much agreed on the concept, but it took us another three months to come up with the name. I would have opted for "Private Lives" if Noel Coward hadn't copyrighted those words, and if I could have brought myself to say, "Can I have the Private Lives Section?" I thought "Lifestyle" was a bogus word, suggesting the worst of Madison Avenue. "Living" was too passive, and essentially meaningless as a section title, like "Scene," "Panorama," "Trends," "Spectrum," or even "You." I liked the word "Style." I like people with style, with flair, with signature qualities, provided they have more than style and flair and signature qualities. And so three weeks before kick-off, Style it was.

The team that created the Style Section was an extraordinary group of journalists. The boss was David Laventhol, who went on to become managing editor, editor, and publisher of *Newsday*, and publisher and CEO of the *Los Angeles Times* and its parent company, Times-Mirror. With him worked Jim Truitt, who was trying to ensure we were thinking radically enough (Truitt once sat in front of a typewriter for 47 hours, making a list of more than 1,000 story ideas after I had asked casually, "Where the hell are all the ideas?"); David Lawrence, Jr., then on loan from the news desk, and later top gun at the *Palm Beach Post*, *Philadelphia Daily News*, and *Detroit Free Press*, before settling down as publisher and board chairman of the *Miami Herald*; Ben Cason, who wound up as senior vice president of United Press International and now runs a newspaper group in Ohio. And finally Elsie Carper, who brought grace and dignity to every job she ever held during her half century at the *Post*. Elsie wound up as women's editor, because we were scared we would forget all about women in creating something to replace "for and about Women."

We gave Nick von Hoffman the title of Culture Editor, for some unremembered reason. He took life much too lightly to be an editor, but he was a gifted, iconoclastic, and brainy reporter for the *Chicago Daily News*, and I had hired him as an investigative reporter after reading his stuff, especially a brave and perceptive series on the Catholic Church. A disciple of Saul Alinsky, the labor reform activist, Nick had worked in the Chicago stockyards, but had never been to college. He was a perfect hire for someone who was trying haphazardly to bring new excitements, new depths, new range to Washington reporting. He had written a stunning series for us in October 1967 about the drug scene in San Francisco's Haight-Ashbury District. A series so good that the *San Francisco Chronicle* had run all sixteen pieces on its front page. Nick had gone out there on an assignment from Larry Stern, then the national editor, and I used to listen to Nick's nightly telephone reports on the Hippie otherworld. I finally couldn't stand it, and flew out to San Francisco to see for myself—three of the most extraordinary days and nights of my life. It was as strange and unfamiliar to me as the war had been, watching those children—and adults—crashing after LSD trips, screaming from methamphetamines, and just mooning around under the influence of marijuana. Their domination by drugs and the need to get money for drugs was fascinating and frightening to me—as a man, as a father, as a citizen.

If we made a mistake in creating the Style Section, it was to steal too much talent from other sections and thus leave them feature-free, top-heavy with straight news. We had Phil Casey from the Metro Section, a quiet, warmly funny rewrite man who played the typewriter like a violin. We had Mike Kernan, another poet in newspaperman's clothing. And we had B. J. Phillips, who looked like a waif and wrote like some tough new kind of angel. She came to us from the *Atlanta Journal* and *Constitution*, hired by Gene Patterson soon after he became managing editor, in the vanguard of the new journalists, who looked at news with a novelist's eyes and a sociologist's insights.

BJ wrote the lead story in the first edition of Style on January 6, 1969. "Wanted by the FBI," a story about a twenty-six-year-old female kidnapper, was about as far removed as we could get from a normal "for and about Women" front page. We had debated amongst ourselves about how fast we should change the section, and as so often happens, had never really made that decision. BJ made the decision for us. An FBI Wanted poster of a young woman charged with kidnapping announced a major change. And some of the old-timers started griping. "Ben? Where are you hiding the Women's Section?" asked the headline in the local city magazine, *The Washingtonian*. Ladies in the locker room of one of the local golf clubs took us apart, and one of them told her husband, who just happened to be a top advertising wheel at the *Post*. It was Topic A at the next so-called vice presidents' meeting. Even Katharine Graham, who was an enthusiastic participant in many of the brainstorming sessions that created the section, voiced some concern. In fact, she voiced enough concern to lead to the only "fight" she and I have ever had. The only time we ever raised voices at each other.

"Damn it, Katharine," I heard myself say after one more expression of concern than I was programmed to take that day, "get your finger out of my eye. Give us six weeks to get it right, and then if you don't like it, we'll talk." It came out more harshly than I had intended, but it worked. We got our six weeks. In fact, we got twenty-five years, the best twenty-five years an editor ever had with an owner.

Style became a great hit in Washington, and widely imitated in the trade.

For a good part of 1969, a considerable part of my spare time was spent embroiled in a fight between Art Buchwald and Joe Alsop— unlikely combatants any way you cut it.

Buchwald has always been able to write his column in a couple of hours. Normally, he has his column idea before he has finished the front section of the paper, writes his column, and is looking for lunch partners by 11:00 A.M. He had already written umpteen books; he had his speeches down on 3 by 5 cards and could talk for three hours, easy. Now he wanted to try the theater; he wanted to write a play, and he damned well did. *Sheep on the Runway* was a farce about an arrogant, elitist Washington columnist, visiting an Asian country so small that sheep grazed on the only airport's only runway, totally disrupting the embassy, the ambassador, and the foreign country, while turning a minor dispute into a major war.

In the play, the arrogant, elitist Washington correspondent was named Joseph Mayflower, a wicked spoof on Joe Alsop, and the town was divided into two camps. For a while I tried without success to make peace between the two, but when Alsop forbade his friends from going to the opening night in New York, I wanted to be with Artie, and I was, for a splendid opening and a party afterwards at Sardi's. *Sheep on the Runway* ran for three months in New York, and then on the night that four people were killed on the campus of Kent State, the play opened in Washington—to a lousy review by the *Post*, of course. All my friends got lousy reviews in the *Post*. That was a given.

Anyway, Alsop never talked to Buchwald again, but of course, he never talked much to him before.

Actually, Alsop started talking less to me, too, about this time as he started measuring people and events on a scale that was calibrated solely to his feelings on Vietnam. Alsop thought that the Vietnam reporting from the *Post*'s young war correspondents, like Ward Just, was anti-war, and I was to blame.

Buchwald was on my side of that fight, and during many other moments of need in my life. He was even at my father's funeral in Beverly Farms, Massachusetts—maybe not the first or last Jew in that little enclave of WASP supremacy, but surely on that day the most welcome.

My father had died without warning or fuss in the spring of 1970, at age seventy-seven. In one of our regular weekly telephone calls, he told me he felt lousy, and thought he might even check into the Beverly Hospital for a day or so. He never complained about his health, so I told him I'd take the first plane up the next morning, but he died in his sleep of an aneurysm before I saw him again. I would have liked to put my head on that big chest one more time and tell him goodbye. Never a flashy man, and after his football heroics were behind him, never even a successful man the way success is measured by historians. He was a good and quiet man, though, filled with common sense and humor.

Every newspaperman worth his pad and pencil had mourned the passing of the *New York Herald Tribune* in 1966. Wherever they worked, journalists envied the *Trib*'s style, its flair, its design, its fine writing, its esprit de corps. No better sportswriter ever lived than Red Smith. Its columnists, from Walter Lippmann to Art Buchwald, from Dorothy Thompson to Jimmy Breslin, from Joe Alsop to John Crosby, were vital, original, top of the line. And its owner Jock Whitney was a gentle, graceful, and wealthy man, who loved newspaper people—the trait that newspaper people find most attractive in others, especially owners.

After the *Trib* folded, Jock kept the Paris edition alive because he loved it . . . the stylish, slightly eccentric Paris *Trib*, full of character and characters. It didn't make any money, didn't even try very hard to make money, but it had the kind of cachet that Jock Whitney loved and exemplified. But the *New York Times* had started its own full-fledged international edition in 1960. The European edition of the *Times* never made money, but its aggressive presence (and quality) in Europe was enough to push the Paris *Trib* into the red, and to force Whitney Communications into some serious thinking about survival.

Their solution: sell 45 percent of the Paris *Trib*—for less than $2 million—to *The Washington Post*, run *Washington Post* stories from the *L.A. Times-Washington Post* News Service, and put the *Post's* newspaper infrastructure behind the *Trib*, which currently had no supporting newspaper behind it. I knew (and cared) little about the quality of the investment as an investment, but I relished being asked to participate in a mano-a-mano battle with the *New York Times*. I mean, the *Los Angeles Times* wasn't being asked to join Whitney. Neither was *Le Monde*. Nor the *Manchester Guardian*. We were.

So we went mano a mano, and both papers started losing important money. The same desire to compete with the *New York Times* kept us from suggesting that we stop losing money and join forces. It was left to Sydney Gruson, the publisher of the international edition of the *Times*, to pull that off. I had been attracted to Gruson, mostly because of his newspaper talents and because he looked so much like my brother, but I was leery of him. He had been a distinguished foreign correspondent for the *Times*; his then wife, Flora Lewis, was a distinguished foreign correspondent for major newspapers and magazines. Together they knew everyone in the power structures of New York, Washington, London, and Paris, and I didn't. I knew young Arthur Sulzberger, Punch, who had been propelled to the top of the *New York Times* ladder by the sudden death of his brother-in-law, Orvil Dryfoos. Punch and I had been fellow reporters, and buddies, in Paris in the fifties, but I had trouble believing the mighty *Times* was going to give the *Post* anything like a fair shake in any merged enterprise.

I was wrong, of course, about the *Times*, and about Gruson. He became one of the delights of my life, funny, smart, not pompous, and a man who did not take himself too seriously (a quality which has always attracted me). Sydney wanted to be publisher of the merged newspaper, but the *Post* was scared of being gobbled up. Instead, he and I were put on the board of directors as editorial overseers of the paper,* and the new publisher was Bob MacDonald, a former McKinsey & Co. consultant and *New York Herald Tribune* general manager.

The new *International Herald Tribune* was a journalistic triumph, if not a financial success, and soon enough we began to consider an Asian edition. We felt we needed an Asian partner in a part of the world where none of us had any business experience. This presented us with our first potential conflict of interest, since the logical partners were either *Asahi Shimbun* or *Yomiuri*, the giant Japanese dailies, each with financially unsuccessful English-language editions. With its modest 10.1 million circulation in 1971, *Asahi* was the most valued client of the *New York Times*'s News Service, and the *Times* felt obligated to broach our idea of a joint venture to *Asahi* first. With a paltry 9.2 million circulation, *Yomiuri* was the most valued client of the *L.A. Times-Washington Post* News Service.

Gruson said it was *Asahi* first or nothing, and I had to yield, gracefully I'm sure.

If I live to be a thousand years old, I will never forget the four days we spent "negotiating" with *Asahi*, Bob MacDonald, Sydney Gruson, and Takashi Oka, the *New York Times*'s Tokyo Bureau chief, who served as our translator, on one side of an enormous polished boardroom table, and fifteen of the meanest-looking gentlemen I have ever seen on the other. ("Jesus," Gruson whispered to me early on, "they all look like that guy you rescued in your destroyer off Cor-

---

* We were both kicked off the *Trib*'s board of directors several times, to make room for various bean counters from the *Times*, the *Post*, and Whitney Communications, but we managed to survive in an honorary—if occasionally strident—capacity.

regidor.") I had been told repeatedly, by Gruson and others, about the Japanese penchant for ritual and ceremony, and I had been told specifically not to bring up the question of *Asahi* becoming our partner, which after all was why we had traveled across the Pacific Ocean. In fact, no one, repeat no one, brought up the subject for the first three days. Instead, we bowed to each other a lot, while we talked about the Japanese newspaper situation, about the New York newspaper situation, about the Washington newspaper situation.

By day.

By night, our new Japanese friends took us out to a series of geisha establishments, each more elaborate than the last. I didn't have a clue what to expect, and felt relieved when I realized that the issue of sex was not going to rear its complicating head. The geisha "girls" were in fact of a certain age, tasked only to keep our glasses full and our plates overflowing—glasses of warm saké and plates of indescribable foods. Every now and then a different geisha would stand up, go to one end of a bare room, and perform, playing a one-stringed musical instrument I had never seen before, or singing a song unlike any song I had heard before. Our hosts would applaud, and I tried desperately not to look at Gruson. At no time during the geisha dinners was any business discussed.

This went on and on, interrupted only once on a late afternoon, when Gruson and I visited some "baths" where we were bathed, and massaged within an inch of our lives, by professional bathers and massagers. At the end of these three days, we still had not uttered the words "Asian Edition" to our Japanese friends. I was en route to my first adventure in Vietnam, and ready to get started, and so we decided to bite the bullet next morning. Gruson brought it up early on the fourth day. Our hosts acted appropriately surprised, asked for a short recess, and returned quickly to tell us that such a merger would not be possible. I tried later that day with my associates at *Yomiuri,* came to the point quickly (much too quickly, I'm sure), and got the same answer. *Sayonara.*

After the collapse of our Japanese scheme, I flew on to Saigon for my first look at Vietnam, the impossible war that was scarring

America. (I had come within days of going there in the mid-fifties for *Newsweek* to cover the Guerre d'Indochine, which was then ruining France.) I landed at Tan Son Nhut Airport in February 1971, uncommitted politically as usual, a day ahead of schedule, an accident that saved Peter Osnos's life. Peter, who was part of our two-man Saigon Bureau, had planned to fly by chopper with *Newsweek* correspondent François Sully to take a look at the Cambodian border. He changed plans at the last minute so he could meet me at the airport. Sully's chopper had a bomb in it and blew up a few feet off the ground, killing all on board.

By instinct and habit, I was more interested in the whatness of the war than in the rightness or wrongness. I hated the idea that an authoritarian country like North Vietnam could wipe out a peaceful neighbor. But I didn't much like the idea that a corrupt country like South Vietnam in one hemisphere could be persuaded to ask the United States of America and millions of its citizen soldiers to come to its rescue, with never even an attempt to enact a declaration of war. I hated what the Vietnam War was doing to America, wasting our national energy and inflating our economy, dividing us between young and old, between rich and poor, black and white, generally alienating us all. But I had bought into the myth that America had a mission to come to the help of the weak, against the oppressors. I had tried too long to equate Vietnam with what I had seen as the justice of World War II, and I desperately wanted to see for myself, before I switched to the other side.

My guides were Osnos and the other *Post* correspondent in Saigon, Peter Jay, later a columnist for the *Baltimore Sun*. Our plan called for a week in Saigon and a week in the Mekong Delta, not exactly safe for the over-fifty set which I was about to join, but safer than some hellhole in I Corps. I saw as many of the players as would cram me into their schedules, including General Creighton Abrams, who was the commander of more than 500,000 troops in the Military Assistance Command in Vietnam; Ambassador Ellsworth Bunker; and a few Vietnamese leaders. I went to the "Five O'Clock Follies," where the correspondents were spoon-fed the information that the military wanted them to have that day, and where the correspondents expressed their distaste for this diet in a colorful but essentially meaningless ritual. I interviewed—and ate and drank with—other correspondents, particularly the spectacular Gloria Emerson of the *New York Times*, Kevin Buckley and Maynard Parker from *Newsweek*, and Peter Kann of the *Wall Street Journal*. And I walked the crowded streets. I am uncomfortable when I have no idea what's going on in the minds of people I see and talk to. And I was as uncomfortable in Saigon as I had been in Algiers.

My guide for a two-day trip to III Corps was Bill Colby, later director of the CIA, but then serving as director of CORDS (Civilian Operations and Revolutionary—later changed to Rural—Development Support, a CIA operation), the program which tried to identify Viet Cong agents who masqueraded in the Vietnam villages and persuade them to defect, or if they would not, get them killed. Colby impressed me as quietly confident, but a bit scholarly for such a blood-thirsty job. We flew down to III Corps in Colby's chopper, over seemingly peaceful, deep green land, but Colby quoted his pilot as saying we were shot at twice. Couldn't have proved it by me. We ate a remarkably good meal with the local ARVN (Army of the Republic of Vietnam) commander in the back room of a village house. Colby asked questions about how things were going, for my benefit as much as his own, I felt, and the ARVN commander answered with controlled enthusiasm—also for my benefit as much as Colby's. I felt like a sponge absorbing largely what others wanted me to absorb, but some of my own impressions were beginning to command attention. Like how well journalists and soldiers get along in the field, away from the politics of Washington. I never met a reporter who left Vietnam with anything but the greatest respect for the military—not the commanders of the Follies, but the guys in the field. God knows, the military saved our asses often enough.

The next day, General John Cushman took me on a kind of sampan, powered by the ever present Briggs & Stratton engine—just like the one on your average Roto-tiller—through a series of canals defining the rice fields. No action. Not even much movement among the natives. Our goal was an outpost manned by two young Army officers, both American, where I spent the night. Scared shitless. The two men weren't exactly scared, but they were preoccupied. This was a dark night, and darkness concentrated their minds. The VC knew exactly how many people were in this outpost, and our guys wouldn't have a chance if anyone else fired first. No one fired at all.

I was choppered back to Tan Son Nhut the following day, and flew west, toward Afghanistan, to spend a few days with my oldest son Ben, and his wife Cathie, Peace Corps volunteers, who were teaching English as a foreign language in Kabul. (When the Afghan students went on strike for three months, Ben volunteered as reporter/editor on the *Kabul Times*.)

I envied these two, starting out their lives together in this strange land, clear blue sky, brown land, and (in February) white snow blanketing the mountains. The concept of national service, especially the Peace Corps, seemed good for America, and better for those who served.

It took me another couple of weeks to get home, most of it spent in Israel, where I received the standard booster shot from Israeli friends, who wished to be sure that all American journalists were regularly exposed to their precarious condition and their valiant pursuit of independence. A few days of up at five in the morning to visit the Golan Heights, or the kibbutz on the Lebanon border, or the standard eighteen-hour tour of the West Bank, always guided by an Israeli citizen/warrior, marvelously convincing and just a bit condescending.

After an absence of almost six weeks, I dared hope that my return would have eased the personal strains that had been plaguing Tony and me. I distributed lush bolts of silk from Bangkok to the women in my family, while I filled the silence with one colorful anecdote after another from my trip. But I could see soon enough that presents were not going to be enough to wipe the slate clean. And before the night was over Tony had stunned me by revealing that she had wished I had stayed away. And I couldn't cope with that revelation.

My heart sank as I had a flash of what lay ahead: another failure, another agony. After I had returned to the *Post*, and devoted myself to it the way a man should devote himself to a woman—hours of shared commitment and excitement in the joyful pursuit of common goals—we came slowly and silently to realize that each of us was no longer the other's reason for being. Jack Kennedy and Mary Meyer had been murdered out of our lives, out of our reservoir of shared experience, and we had both changed in coping with their loss.

For Tony, the *Post* filled no need. What had once seemed like the promise of a fulfilling and exciting life, she now saw as a life dominated by a random series of more or less interesting headlines, unconnected to each other or to any meaningful philosophy. She was more comfortable with artists than with journalists or politicians, and she started studying sculpture at the Corcoran School of Art. She concentrated on developing skills in highly individualized pieces, which involved casting cement into various unique, womb-like, hollow shapes. Through her friendship with Anne Truitt, Jim's wife, she became first interested in, and later absorbed by, something called "The Work."

The Work is a self-awareness movement founded by a Russian-born philosopher/guru named Gurdjieff, and his disciple, Ouspensky, another Russian mystic.

The Washington group was led by a Gurdjieff disciple named Hugh Ripman, an Englishman who was the World Bank's director of administration. Ripman believed that people were sleepwalking through life. "We are prisoners of our own past," he said before his death in 1980. "Our conscious state is semi-hypnotic sleep. Our attention is not under control. Our sense of self is constantly lost in all kinds of different things. . . . You've got to set up a silent witness in yourself, not judgmental, just aware. . . . We have different 'I's,' and they are contradictory."

And just as Tony was unable to find any fulfillment in my life at the *Post,* I was unable to find any place for myself in The Work. Our common ground was a small space, filled with children, somewhere between the two things that interested each of us most. Sex, which had been overwhelming, became incidental, even accidental. And my six-week absence and a few bolts of silk were not going to change any of that.

At this point, I had no interest in falling in love with anyone else, even when some months later I found someone who made me laugh, and who liked sex—with me.

That relationship was satisfying, if aimless, but it pretty much ended during the winter of 1973, when Tony and I were seeing a shrink. The shrink was an asshole. A child psychiatrist we had consulted about some child's problem, or about our problem with some child. For the life of me, I can't remember a single insightful observation he ever made about any child, or about us, and I have no idea why we settled on him to lead us out of the darkness which was surrounding us. He wasn't close to being up to the task.

THIRTEEN

PENTAGON PAPERS

Sometime in the early spring of 1971 we had begun hearing rumors that the *New York Times* was working on a "blockbuster," an exclusive that would blow us out of the water. News like this produces a very uncomfortable feeling inside an editor's stomach. Getting beaten on a story is bad enough, but waiting to get beaten on a story is unbearable.

We heard the *Times* had a special task force at work on its blockbuster. We heard the task force was working in special offices away from the newspaper's 43rd Street offices. But we never found out who was part of the task force, much less what they were taskforcing about.

And there was so much news in Washington, we were having trouble keeping up with it all. On May Day the city hosted yet another in a growing number of anti-Vietnam demonstrations. *Post* reporters described Day One in West Potomac Park this way: ". . . at dawn's light . . . about 45,000 people were dancing, nodding their heads to music, making love, drinking wine and smoking pot." More than twelve thousand demonstrators were arrested—a record seven thousand on a single day. Downtown reeked of tear gas. Helicopters chop-chop-chopped across the city at tree-level day and night, a strange new addition to the capital scene.

At the beginning of June, we paused for a few days to focus on Tricia Nixon's wedding to Edward Cox. The Nixons had refused to accredit *Post* reporter Judith Martin to cover the White House on the wedding day. They didn't like *Post* reporters in general, but they particularly did not like stories she had written about the family. Any other reporter, but not Judy, we were told. And because we weren't about to let the White House—much less the Nixon White House—tell us who could or could not cover any story, we insisted on assigning Ms. Martin. We covered it from the TV tubes—and nobody but us gave a damn.

On Sunday, June 13, 1971, the top half of the *Post*'s page one was devoted to the White House wedding, but the top half of the *New York Times* revealed at last what their long-awaited blockbuster was all about: Six full pages of news stories and top-secret documents, based on a 47-volume, 7,000-page study, "History of U.S. Decision-Making Process on Vietnam Policy, 1945–1967." The *Times* had obtained a copy of the study, and had assigned more than a dozen top reporters and editors to digest it for three months, and write dozens of articles.

The *Post* did *not* have a copy, and we found ourselves in the humiliating position of having to rewrite the competition. Every other paragraph of the *Post* story had to include some form of the words "according to the *New York Times*," blood—visible only to us—on every word.

On Monday, June 14, the next installment of the Pentagon Papers appeared in the *Times*: "Vietnam Archive: A Consensus to Bomb Developed Before '64 Election, Study Says."

While candidate Goldwater was calling for the immediate bombing of North Vietnam, the story said, the Johnson administration had privately concluded two months before the election that he was right. The sustained bombing—known as Rolling Thunder—began three months after the election.

At the *Post* we had gone to General Quarters, and were trying desperately to get our own copy of the Pentagon Papers, or any reasonable substitute, and getting on with the job of rewriting the *Times*'s Monday story for our Tuesday paper. At breakfast Monday morning, my friend Marcus Raskin, a former member of Kennedy's National Security Council, and then a part of the leftist Institute of Policy Studies (IPS), offered me the manuscript of a book by IPS scholars, "Washington Plans an Aggressive War," which he said was "based on" the Pentagon Papers, and which had been written after "access" to the Pentagon Papers, whatever that meant. We were so far behind the *Times*, I expressed an interest, but the manuscript was a polemic against the war, and it carried only the quotes from the papers that served the cause. We read it with interest, but felt it was a poor substitute for the real thing.

Phil Geyelin had a friend in Boston who offered him what was described as two hundred pages of excerpts from the Pentagon Papers. That is apparently exactly what they were, but we had no idea of their context, and before we could get any idea, the substance of those two hundred pages showed up in the *New York Times*'s third installment, on Tuesday, June 15: "Vietnam Archive: Study Tells How Johnson Secretly Opened Way to Ground Combat." We were going out of our minds, especially when we read that U.S. Attorney General John Mitchell had sent a telegram to the *Times* asking them to cease publishing anything from the Pentagon Papers, and to return all documents to the Defense Department.

That same Tuesday, the Justice Department went to court and got an injunction against the *Times*, restraining a newspaper in advance from publishing specific articles, for the first time in the history of the republic. At least the *New York Times* had been silenced, never mind how.

Wednesday night, the *Post*'s thorny National editor, Ben Bagdikian, was contacted by someone and given a telephone number, to be called only from a pay telephone, where he could reach his friend, Daniel Ellsberg.

Dan Ellsberg was a zealous Harvard intellectual, who had served voluntarily for two years in the Marine Corps before becoming a defense research expert for the Rand Corporation. He had volunteered for Vietnam, where he served as an "apprentice" to General Edward Lansdale. He had seen plenty of action in the Mekong Delta in 1965 and 1966, and actively supported the American pursuit of the war, until he returned in early 1969 to Rand, where he had been a colleague of Bagdikian's.

Ellsberg was also the source of the *New York Times*'s 7,000-page copy of the Pentagon Papers, because of his friendship with and respect for the *Times*'s legendary Vietnam reporter, Neil Sheehan.

Late Wednesday, the 16th, Bagdikian flew to Boston, and first thing Thursday morning, he flew back with two first-class seats, one for himself and one for a large cardboard carton full of Pentagon Papers. The *Post*'s package consisted of something over 4,000 pages of Pentagon documents, compared to the 7,000 received by the *New York Times*. At 10:30 A.M., Thursday, June 17, Bagdikian rushed past Marina Bradlee, age ten, tending her lemonade stand outside our house in Georgetown, and we were back in business.

For the next twelve hours, the Bradlee library on N Street served as a remote newsroom, where editors and reporters started sorting, reading, and annotating 4,400 pages, and the Bradlee living room served as a legal office, where lawyers and newspaper executives started the most basic discussions about the duty and right of a newspaper to publish, and the government's right to prevent that publication, on national security grounds, or on any grounds at all. For those twelve hours, I went from one room to the other, getting a sense of the story in one place, and a sense of the mood of the lawyers in the other.

With the *Times* silenced by the Federal Court in New York, we decided almost immediately that we would publish a story the next morning, Friday, the 18th, completing in twelve hours what it had taken the *New York Times* more than three months to do. For planning purposes, we had to take that decision so that we could re-thread the presses to include four extra, unplanned pages . . . an operation that cannot be done on the spur of the

moment. At 4:00 P.M., we stopped reading and arguing to hold a
story conference, to talk out what we had, and what we could get
written and laid out in the five hours left before the first edition
deadline. Our first choice was a piece to be written by diplomatic
correspondent Murrey Marder about how the Johnson administration had stopped and restarted bombing North Vietnam to influence American public opinion, not to further U.S. military goals.
But Murrey, one of the world's most thorough reporters, was also
one of the slower writers. As a precaution, Chal Roberts started
on a story about U.S. diplomatic strategy in Vietnam under the
Eisenhower administration. Chal had the fastest typewriter in the
business, and we knew he'd get it done. Don Oberdorfer was out-
lining his story for Day Three.

But things were a little stickier in the living room.

There the lawyers were marshaling strong arguments against
publishing, or at least urging that we wait for the injunction against
the *New York Times* to be litigated. The lawyers were Roger Clark
and Tony Essaye, two young partners in the firm of William P. Rogers, who had been the *Post*'s lawyer until he quit to become Nixon's
Secretary of State. In midafternoon, they were joined by our own
Fritz Beebe, now chairman of the board of The Washington Post
Company. My heart sank when Beebe announced that our deliber-
ations were not to be influenced by the fact that The Post Company
was about to "go public" with a $35 million stock offering. Under
the terms of this offering, the *Post* was liable for a substantial claim
by the underwriters if some disaster or catastrophe occurred. No one
wanted to say whether an injunction, or possible subsequent criminal prosecution, qualified as a catastrophe. Just as no one wanted to
mention the fact that any company convicted of a felony could not
own television licenses, a fact which added another $100 million
to the stakes.

The lawyers were throwing a lot of case law at me and my allies:
Howard Simons, Phil Geyelin, and his editorial page deputy, Meg
Greenfield (managing editor Gene Patterson was minding the store
on 15th Street), citing legal arguments that seemed curiously irrel-

evant in a Georgetown living room, where Marina was selling lemonade, Tony was serving sandwiches, and telephones were ringing off the hooks. It was bedlam.

Two decades later it's hard to figure out why the hell the Pentagon Papers had become such a *casus belli* for the administration. I knew exactly how important it was to publish, if we were to have any chance of pulling the *Post* up—once and for all—into the front ranks. Not publishing the information when we had it would be like not saving a drowning man, or not telling the truth. Failure to publish without a fight would constitute an abdication that would brand the *Post* forever, as an establishment tool of whatever administration was in power. And end the Bradlee era before it got off the ground, just incidentally.

But I wasn't winning with the lawyers. A federal judge had enjoined the *New York Times* from publishing the same material, they argued. Therefore we did in fact have "reason to believe publication would damage the United States."

"Bullshit," a reporter would comment, not particularly constructively.

"Maybe we should tell the Attorney General that we have the papers and are going to publish them on Sunday," a lawyer suggested, looking for a compromise.

"That's the shittiest idea I ever heard," said Don Oberdorfer, constructively. Chal Roberts announced he would quit, and make a big stink about it, if we did that.

I was getting painted into a corner. I had to massage the lawyers, especially Beebe, into at least a neutral position, while preventing the reporters from leaving him no maneuvering room during what we all knew was going to be the ultimate showdown with Kay Graham. She was getting ready to host a goodbye party for Harry Gladstein, the veteran circulation vice president, at her house about ten blocks away.

Suddenly, I knew what I had to do. I snuck out of the living room to an upstairs telephone and placed a call to Jim Hoge, then the managing editor of the *Chicago Sun-Times*. Would he please, urgently, send a copy boy down to whatever Chicago courthouse was trying the divorce case of president of McDonald's Harry Sonneborn, vs. June Sonneborn, starring Edward Bennett Williams for the defendant, and give Ed this message: "Please ask for a recess ASAP. Need to talk to you NOW. URGENT"?

I had known Williams for more than twenty years and trusted his common sense more than anyone else. He was the best in the business. Fifteen minutes later, he called back all business, with a curt "What's up?" Without loading the dice—really—I took him through everything: what the *Times* had written, how we had tried to match them for three days, how we had finally gotten our own set of the Pentagon Papers, what we planned to do *tonight*, what the lawyers were advising us, how Beebe was getting caught in a bind, the public stock issue, the threat to the *Post's* three TV stations, how we were headed for a Fail-Safe telephone call with Kay. Maybe ten uninterrupted minutes, and then I shut up.

Nothing from Williams for at least sixty seconds. I was dying. And then, finally: "Well, Benjy, you got to go with it. You got no choice. That's your business." I hugged him, long distance, and walked casually downstairs back into the legal debate. When I had the right opening, I told them what Williams had said, and I could see the starch go out of Clark and Essaye, and I could see the very beginning of a smile on Beebe's face. Such was the clout of this man. After another hour of argument, it was Show Time, and Fritz, Phil, Howie, and I went to the four different phones in our house and placed the call to Kay. I didn't want to think about what I would have to do if the answer was no.

Fritz outlined all of our positions, with complete fairness. We told her what we felt we had to, we told her what Williams had said, we told her the staff would consider it a disaster if we didn't publish. She asked Beebe his advice. He paused a long time—we could hear music in the background—then said, "Well, I probably wouldn't." Thank God for the hesitant "Well," and the "probably." Now she paused. The music again. And then she said quickly, "Okay, I say let's go. Let's publish."

I dropped the phone like a hot potato and shouted the verdict, and the room erupted in cheers.

The cheers were instinctive. In those first moments, it was enough for all of us—including, let it be said quickly, the lawyers who had been arguing against publication—that Katharine had shown guts and commitment to the First Amendment, and support of her editors. But I think none of us truly understood the importance of her decision to publish the Pentagon Papers in the creation of a new *Washington Post*. I know I didn't. I wanted to publish because we had vital documents explaining the biggest story of the last ten years. That's what newspapers do: they learn, they report, they verify, they write, and they publish.

What I didn't understand, as Katharine's "Okay . . . let's go. Let's publish" rang in my ears, was how permanently the ethos of the paper changed, and how it crystallized for editors and reporters everywhere how independent and determined and confident of its purpose the new *Washington Post* had become. In the days that followed, these feelings only increased. A paper that stands up to charges of treason, a paper that holds firm in the face of charges from the president, the Supreme Court, the Attorney General, never mind an assistant attorney general. A paper that holds its head high, committed unshakably to principle.

What was immediately obvious to us was the amount of work still to be done before we hit the street with a Pentagon Papers story. In fact, we missed the first edition, while Beebe and I argued—for the first time—about Ellsberg. Beebe had not realized Ellsberg was Ben Bagdikian's source, and when he learned it, he tried briefly to revisit Kay's decision, wondering if Ellsberg had stolen the Pentagon Papers, in fact or in law. But there was no steam in that last spasm, and finally we published . . . and waited for the Nixon administration's response and for a look at how the *New York Times* would handle our story—with an AP wire story, page one.

We didn't have long to wait. Just after 3:00 P.M., Friday, June 18, with Kay and some editors in my office, I got a call from Assistant Attorney General William H. Rehnquist. After a minimum

of I-guess-you-know-why-I'm-calling and I-suspect-I-do, the future
Chief Justice came to the point, and started reading what turned
out to be the same message he had read to the *New York Times* four
days earlier:

> I have been advised by the Secretary of Defense that the ma-
> terial published in *The Washington Post* on June 18, 1971, cap-
> tioned "Documents Reveal U.S. Effort in '54 to Delay Viet
> Election" contains information relating to the national defense
> of the United States and bears a top-secret classification. As
> such, publication of this information is directly prohibited by
> the provisions of the Espionage Law, Title 18, U.S. Code, Sec-
> tion 793. Moreover, further publication of information of this
> character will cause irreparable injury to the defense interests of
> the United States. Accordingly, I respectfully request that you
> publish no further information of this character and advise me
> that you have made arrangements for the return of these docu-
> ments to the Department of Defense.

My hands and legs were shaking. The charge of espionage did
not fit my vision of myself, and all I knew about Title 18 spelled
trouble. That's the Criminal Code. But with as much poise as I
could muster, I said, "I'm sure you will understand that we must
respectfully decline." He said something like he figured as much,
and we hung up.

Soon afterward, the Justice Department contacted Clark and
Essaye and told them to be in District Court at 5:00 P.M. The *Times*
editors and lawyers were in various courts, arguing appeals and appealing decisions against them. At no time did they—or we—consider violating court orders, damning the torpedoes and proceeding
with publication.

For the next eight days—until just after 1:00 P.M. on Saturday,
June 26, in the Supreme Court of the United States—we were almost full time in the U.S. District Court for the District of Columbia, the U.S. Court of Appeals for the District of Columbia, the
District Court again, the Court of Appeals again (sitting en *banc*

this time), or in various legal offices, researching and actually writing affidavits and legal briefs.

At 6:00 P.M. on the 18th, the government asked District Court Judge Gerhard A. "Gary" Gesell to enjoin the *Post* from any further publication of the Pentagon Papers. Two hours later, he ruled for the *Post*. It took the government only another two hours to round up three judges on the U.S. Court of Appeals to ask them to overrule Judge Gesell. That made it just before 10:00 P.M.—when we were desperately trying to get Murrey Marder's story into the paper and get the presses started. They were supposed to start at 10:15 P.M., but as luck would have it, this night they were late. Herman Cohen, the news dealer who used to take the very first copies of the paper off the press to newsstands in the major hotels, was waiting, waiting, waiting, and the three-judge appellate panel was deciding whether to reverse Gesell's ruling. We figured if we could get a thousand copies on the newsstands we could argue that we had effectively published, therefore any injunction could not affect that day's installment. In addition, we had put the story on the *L.A. Times-Washington Post* News Service wire, with a special warning to editors that the Appellate Court was deliberating even as they were reading.

Finally, after 1:00 A.M. on the 19th, the court enjoined us, but agreed with Roger Clark that we could complete the publication of that day's paper.

Scenes from the next chaotic days remain frozen in my mind like frames from a Cocteau movie:

- We defendants had to be given emergency security clearances before we could even attend our own trial on charges of publishing documents we had already published.
- Courtroom windows were specially draped with blackout cloth, presumably to prevent unauthorized lip-readers (Soviet spies? Comsymps from Hanoi?) from watching testimony.
- Reporters had to spend hours explaining the Pentagon Papers to lawyers who had never had to cope with the arcane Pentagon world of classified material, before the lawyers could decide what affidavits they wanted from editors and reporters, or what questions to ask.

- Many times, stories that had already appeared in either the *Times* or the *Post* were included in the Pentagon Papers, but now classified top secret by the government.
- Often *Post* reporters plainly knew so much more than government prosecutors and government witnesses about U.S. involvement in Vietnam it was almost embarrassing . . . until one remembered how high were the stakes. My favorite ludicrous moment came when Gesell asked some poor Deputy Assistant Secretary of Defense, Dennis J. Doolin, to identify the one thing in the Pentagon Papers that would most damage the interest of the United States, if published by the *Post*. The poor guy blanched. The government lawyers caucused furtively, and quickly asked for a recess. We were almost as worried, trying to figure out what they would come up with. (We had collectively read most of the Pentagon Papers, surely more than the government had read, but none of us had read them all.) Finally, the trial resumed. The last question was reread, and the witness responded (you could almost hear the roll of drums): "Operation Marigold."

The more studious defendants among us—Chal Roberts, Murrey Marder, and Pentagon correspondent George Wilson—had brought a dozen reference books with them to court, just in case, and damned if they weren't able to find quickly three already published, detailed explanations of Operation Marigold, a June 1966 effort by President Johnson to get representatives of Poland and Italy to explore possible peace settlements with Ho Chi Minh. The following week's edition of *Life* magazine—not yet public—featured a signed article by Britain's prime minister, Harold Wilson. It was headlined "Operation Marigold."

Later, in a secret session—closed even to us defendants—before the U.S. Court of Appeals for the District of Columbia, the government tried to supplement an affidavit by Vice Admiral Noel Gayler, director of the National Security Agency. Gayler wanted to describe as particularly dangerous to U.S. security a specific radio intercept reported in the Pentagon Papers, allegedly proving that North Vietnamese ships fired on U.S. destroyers in the Gulf of Tonkin in the summer of 1964. The remarkable George Wilson stunned everyone by pulling out of his back pocket a verbatim record of the intercept, in an unclassified transcript of Senate Foreign Relations Committee hearings.

As the Pentagon Papers bounced their way from court to court—in New York and Washington—on their way to The Supremes, I made a decision which now makes me blush.

In an effort to be prepared for any eventuality, we had assigned two reporters to go out to Chief Justice Warren Burger's house in nearby Arlington, after trying unsuccessfully to reach him by phone. If the U.S. Court of Appeals ruled for the *Post en banc*, we knew the government would apply to the Chief Justice for an immediate stay—to stop us from publishing—while they appealed to the Supreme Court. We didn't want the government to sneak out unnoticed to Burger's house, so we sent our own emissaries: Spencer Rich, who normally covered the Senate, and Martin Weil, a former CIA type, who worked nights on rewrite as a city reporter.

Together, they walked up the driveway to the Chief Justice's home and rang the doorbell. It was almost midnight. Marty Weil's memo describes the next few minutes better than I can:

> After about a minute or two, the Chief Justice opened the door. He was wearing a bath robe. He was carrying a gun. The gun was in his right hand, muzzle pointed down. It was a long-barreled steel weapon. The Chief Justice did not seem glad to see us. Spencer explained why we were there. There was a considerable amount of misdirected conversation. It seemed for a bit that people were talking past each other. Spencer, who held up his credentials, was explaining why we were there, but the judge seemed to be saying that we shouldn't have come. Finally, after a little more talk, everybody seemed to understand everybody. The Chief Justice said it would be all right for us to wait for any possible Justice Department emissaries, but we could wait down the street. He held his gun in his hand throughout a two or three minute talk.

Sometimes it was not visible, held behind the door post. He never pointed it at us. He closed the door. We went down the street and waited for about three hours. Then we went home.

I was at home when the desk called to report this brief encounter and ask where we should play the story—page one, or inside?

"What story?" I shouted. "Just because the Chief Justice of the United States comes to the door of his house in the dead of night in his jammies, waving a gun at two *Washington Post* reporters in the middle of a vital legal case involving the *Washington Post*, you guys think that's a story?"

Over the years, I have prided myself in recognizing a good story when I see one, even when no one else sees it. This is what I do best. But of course I had momentarily taken leave of my senses. All I could think of was how much Chief Justice Burger disliked the press in general, and the *Post* in particular, how ridiculous the alleged story would make him look (I could visualize the Herblock cartoon with clarity), and how much I wanted to avoid pissing him off a few days before he took our fate in his hands.

No story, I ruled, and there was no story, until after the Supreme Court had decided our fate, when Nick Von Hoffman slipped it into a column.

No story? I hereby apologize.

On Monday, June 21, 1971, Judge Gesell again ruled in favor of the *Post*, after the three-judge Appellate Court asked him to hold an evidentiary hearing on whether the publication of the Pentagon Papers would "so prejudice" U.S. interests, or cause "such irreparable injury," that prior restraint could be justified. On Thursday, June 24, the nine judges of the U.S. Court of Appeals ruled 7-2 in the *Post's* favor. On Friday, June 25, the Supreme Court granted certiorari and agreed to hear the case. On Saturday, June 26, the case was argued in the Supreme Court. And on Wednesday, June 30, 1971—seventeen days after the *New York Times* broke the story, and ten days after the *Post's* first publication—the Supreme Court ruled 6-3 for the two newspapers. The next day, both of us resumed our stories about the Pentagon Papers.

For the first time in the history of the American republic, newspapers had been restrained by the government from publishing a story—a black mark in the history of democracy.

We had won—sort of.

What the hell was going on in this country that this could happen? How could a judge of the highest Court of Appeals in the land, Judge Malcolm R. Wilkey, a Nixon appointee who had been general counsel of the Kennecott Copper Corporation, and an Eisenhower appointee to the Appellate Court, seriously argue that the Papers "could clearly result in great harm to the nation," bringing about "the death of soldiers, the destruction of alliances, the greatly increased difficulty of negotiation with our enemies, the inability of our diplomats to negotiate"?

How could a president (who was three years from resigning in disgrace) and an Attorney General (who was three years later sent to jail himself) and an assistant attorney general (who was fifteen years from becoming Chief Justice of the United States) rush headlong and joyous down this reckless path?

Why this persecution/prosecution when the Pentagon Papers dealt entirely with decisions taken exclusively by Presidents Eisenhower, Kennedy, and Johnson, and ended some months before the Nixon administration took office?

And how come there was never a peep out of any of the principals when the Solicitor General of the United States, who argued the government's case before the Court of Appeals and the Supreme Court, the distinguished former dean of the Harvard Law School, Erwin N. Griswold, confessed *eighteen years later* that the government's case against the newspapers was a mirage? "I have never seen any trace of a threat to the national security from the Pentagon Papers' publication. Indeed, I have never seen it even suggested that there was an actual threat," Griswold wrote in a brave—and almost unheard of—correction of the record.*

We had no answers to those questions beyond recognition

---

* It appeared in an Op-Ed piece in *The Washington Post* dated February 15, 1989.

that the Cold War dominated our society, and realization that the Nixon-Agnew administration was playing hardball.

We did know that the Pentagon Papers experience had forged forever between the Grahams and the newsroom a sense of confidence within the *Post*, a sense of mission and agreement on new goals, and how to attain them. And that may have been the greatest result of publication of the Pentagon Papers.

After the Pentagon Papers, there would be no decision too difficult for us to overcome together.

FOURTEEN

WATERGATE

———

Some stories are hard to see, generally because the clues are hidden or disguised. By accident, or on purpose. Other stories hit you in the face. Like Watergate, for instance.

Five guys in business suits, speaking only Spanish, wearing dark glasses and surgical gloves, with crisp new hundred-dollar bills in their pockets, and carrying tear-gas fountain pens, flashlights, cameras, and walkie-talkies, just after midnight in the headquarters of the Democratic National Committee (DNC).

The best journalists in the world could be forgiven for not realizing that this was the opening act of the scandalous political melodrama—unparalleled in American history—which would end up with the resignation of a disgraced president and the jailing of more than forty people, including the Attorney General of the United States, the White House chief of staff, the White House counsel, and the president's chief domestic adviser.

But you would have to be Richard Nixon himself to say this was not a story.

The Washington Post got off to a running head start on the story, early on the morning of June 17, 1972, thanks to Joe Califano, once special assistant to President Johnson, then counsel to both the Democratic Party and *The Washington Post*. Califano was Edward Bennett Williams's law partner.

Califano called Howard Simons, the *Post*'s managing editor, that morning to tell him that five guys had broken into the DNC a few hours earlier and were about to be arraigned. I was in West Virginia for the weekend, where the telephone didn't work, but Simons called Harry Rosenfeld, the Metro editor, and Rosenfeld called Barry Sussman, the city editor. Sussman, still in bed, called two reporters, finally getting to someone who could find out what the hell was going on. (It flows downhill at newspapers, too.) The two reporters, chosen by Rosenfeld and Sussman, were local reporters, for this was a local story, involving the commonest of local crimes— breaking and entering.

They were Al Lewis, the prototypical police reporter, who had loved cops more than civilians for almost fifty years, and Bob Woodward, a former Navy lieutenant and one of the new kids on the staff, who had impressed everyone with his skill at finding stories wherever we sent him.

Lewis arrived at the scene of the break-in in the company of the acting chief of police, sailing past other reporters who had been stopped by the cops. He spent all day behind the police lines, calling in to the city desk regularly with all the vital statistics. Woodward covered the arraignment. He was sitting in the front row (where else?) where he heard James McCord, Jr., whisper, "CIA," when the arraigning officer asked him what kind of a "retired government worker" he was.

Bingo!

No three letters in the English language, arranged in that particular order, and spoken in similar circumstances, can tighten a good reporter's sphincter faster than C-I-A.

By day's end, and on into the night at police headquarters after the final deadline had passed, ten reporters were working on different pieces of the story. On his regular shift at Night Police, after three in the morning, reporter Gene Bachinski was given a look at some of the stuff taken from the pockets of the arrested men. Including address books, and in two of these he found the name of Howard Hunt; along with the notations: "W.H." and "W. House."

Bingo!

Just the recollection of that discovery makes my heart beat faster, more than two decades later.

Carl Bernstein, the long-haired, guitar-playing Peck's Bad Boy of the Metro staff, spent most of Saturday sniffing around the story's perimeter as all good reporters do, and soon was told to "work the phones." We needed help in Miami, where all the defendants came from, and it turned out we already had a correspondent there: Kirk Scharfenberg, another Metro reporter, who had spelled our tireless White House correspondent, Carroll Kilpatrick, on the Nixon watch in Key Biscayne.

The next morning Woodward went looking for the mysterious Howard Hunt, and started by calling the "W. House," and asking to be connected with him. An extension rang and rang, and rang. No answer. And a wonderful White House telephone operator (all White House telephone operators, by definition, are wonderful) told Woodward to wait, maybe Mr. Hunt was in Mr. Colson's office.

Bingo!

Another rush of adrenaline, with that word "Colson," the high-profile hatchetman assistant to Nixon.

Hunt wasn't there, but Woodward and everyone else wondered why he might have been there, when Charles Colson's secretary told him to try Hunt at Robert R. Mullen & Co., a PR firm. Hunt was there, and Woodward asked him how come his name was in the address books of two burglars arrested at Democratic headquarters.

There was a long, long pause. And then only, "Good God."

Bingo!

Kilpatrick spotted McCord's picture in Sunday's paper, and immediately recognized him as someone who worked for the president's reelection committee. CRP, for Committee to Re-elect the President, as the Republicans called it, or CREEP, as it came to be known around town.

Bingo!

In less than forty-eight hours, we had traced what the Republicans were calling a "third-rate burglary" into the White House, and into the very heart of the effort to win Richard Nixon a second term. We didn't know it yet, but we were out front, never to be headed, in the story of our generation, the story that put us all on the map.

Now, twenty years after the fact, it is far easier to re-create this fabulous story than it was to report this fabulous story . . . thanks to the incredibly detailed record which emerged slowly from the dark:

- Transcripts of tapes of more than 4,000 hours of conversations involving all the key characters . . . Nixon, Mitchell, Haldeman, Ehrlichman, Dean, Colson, et al.
- The voluminous record of hearings held by the spectacular Senate Select Committee on Presidential Campaign Activities, known as the Senate Watergate Committee, or the Ervin Committee, for its chairman, Senator Sam Ervin, the colorful North Carolina Democrat. Eighty-three days of testimony (most of it televised) from thirty-three witnesses.
- The record of the House Judiciary Committee's hearings on the impeachment of the president.
- The record of all the trials, which led to more than 40 guilty pleas or convictions.

But for six weeks after the break-in, we were flailing, searching everywhere for any information that might shed any light, unaware that we were up against a massive cover-up being orchestrated by the White House. We were picking at the story, knowing it was there but unable to describe what "it" was, finding what looked like pieces of the puzzle but unable to see where—or even if—these pieces fit. For instance, we soon learned that burglar Frank Sturgis had another name, Frank Fiorini—the same Frank Fiorini I had met some months before, with Tony's much older half brother, Gifford Pinchot.

Giff was a genuine original, tall, gaunt, and handsome, about sixty years old and a bachelor, living in Miami then, having been kicked out of Castro's Cuba. In Havana, he had lived with a Cuban woman, known only as La China, taught rhumba dancing, managed a couple of Cuban lightweight boxers, and worked as some kind of an engineer on the side. When I was in New York late one afternoon in 1971, he had asked me to meet him and a friend in an East Side bar for a drink. He thought I'd be interested. Fiorini was tall and well muscled, with oily, wavy black hair, and ham hands. He looked and talked like a hood, as he went about trying to persuade me and "Pinchot, here" to come up with the wherewithal for 1,500 gallons of Diesel fuel, so he could take a boat to Cuba, make trouble for a few days, and get out. I felt sorry for Giff, because his hatred of Castro was clearly going to be money in Fiorini's pocket.

After we'd identified Fiorini as Sturgis, I tried to see him for weeks after the Watergate break-in—through his lawyer, and through federal marshals—without success.

Bernstein finally broke into the clear with a story on August 1 about the origins of the money found on the Watergate burglars when they were arrested. It was a critically important piece of information. "Cherchez la femme" is good advice for investigative reporters. "Follow the money" is even better advice. Carl understood that instinctively, and persuaded us to send him to Miami to talk to the prosecutor there who had started his own Watergate investigation. He found Martin Dardis, an investigator who had traced the serial numbers on the crisp new hundred-dollar bills to the Republic National Bank of Miami. Did any of the burglars have a bank account there?

Damned if one of them, Bernard Barker, didn't have two. Dardis had Barker's telephone records and bank accounts subpoenaed, and found five cashier's checks, totaling $114,000, which had been deposited in one account in April 1972. Four of those checks, totaling $89,000, had been issued by a Mexican bank to a Mexican lawyer. The fifth check, for $25,000, was even more interesting. Dardis showed Bernstein that it came from a man named Kenneth H. Dahlberg. Woodward, in Washington, found two Kenneth H. Dahlbergs, one in Boca Raton and one in Minneapolis. A little more work and we found they were one and the same man. And a few minutes later Woodward had him on the phone in Minneapolis. He knew nothing about the $25,000 check, he told Woodward, but as a fund-raiser for Nixon he turned over all the funds he raised "to the committee." And he hung up.

Another Bingo!

A fund-raiser for the President of the United States? What's he doing putting money in a burglar's bank account?

A few minutes later, Dahlberg called back, to verify that Woodward was in fact a *Post* reporter, he said, and was more forthcoming. As a fund-raiser he had accumulated a lot of cash, and in Florida, had converted that cash to a cashier's check. Dahlberg told Woodward he gave the checks to Maurice Stans, CRP's finance chairman. And he had no idea how any of the checks ended up in Barker's bank account.*

Now we had the burglar's money traced directly to CRP.

It was three months after the "third-rate burglary" (and less than six weeks before the election). The Republican denials and counterattacks were getting louder every day, and we knew they were lying. Nothing kept us more committed to this story than our knowledge—not suspicion, not wonder, but knowledge—that they were lying.

Woodward and Bernstein got hold of a copy of the CRP telephone directory and address book, and started calling CRP employees one by one—always after work, and often five or six times.

Soon they learned that at least some of the people who worked for CRP were scared. Some were asking to be interviewed by the FBI, *without* a CRP lawyer taking notes. One of the CRP employees they talked to was Hugh Sloan, the committee's treasurer, and suddenly in September, as city editor Barry Sussman remembers, Sloan "became helpful." By now we were beginning to obsess on the Watergate story. Other newspapers were breaking new ground oc-

---

* In fact, the $25,000 check started out as a cash contribution collected by Dahlberg, from Dwayne Andreas, a Minnesota grain executive, well known for his substantial contributions to Republicans and Democrats alike.

casionally, notably the *Los Angeles Times*. But the *Post* had the story by the throat, and the story had the town by the throat. Katharine Graham was in and out of the city room two or three times a day, looking for a "fix" on each day's story. Most nights many of us would get telephone calls from friends in and out of government, unable to wait for the first edition to discover the latest development.

One morning after a particularly good story, attorney and dean of Washington insiders Clark Clifford, then at the height of his power and influence, called me, and in that dramatic, triple-breasted basso profundo of his spoke for much of Washington: "Mr. Bradlee, I would like to tell you something. I woke up this morning, put on my bathrobe and my slippers, went downstairs slowly, opened the front door carefully, and there it was. The sun was already shining. It was going to be a beautiful day. And I looked up to the heavens, and said, 'Thank God for *The Washington Post*.'"

At first the White House counterattacks had tried to laugh off the Watergate break-in as a third-rate burglary, and dismissed newspaper interest as "just politics." Kansas Senator Bob Dole, then chairman of the Republican National Committee, played the role of lead pit bull, accusing the *Post* of being Democratic candidate George McGovern's surrogate in his challenge of President Nixon. Ron Ziegler, the White House press secretary, was making the evening news regularly to deny everything, expressing his "horror" at the "shoddy journalism" being practiced by the *Post*. (Clark MacGregor, the former Minnesota congressman, soon to succeed Mitchell as chairman of CRP, grew more and more critical, even one night when his daughter Laurie was spending the night at our house, as a friend of one of my stepchildren.)

John Mitchell, Nixon's campaign manager at CRP, had weighed in with his criticism early in a uniquely vulgar and sexist way. On September 29—at 11:30 P.M.—Bernstein telephoned him for comment on a story that he had controlled a "secret fund" when he was Attorney General. Bernstein started reading out the story, when Mitchell exploded:

"All that crap you're putting in the paper. It's all been denied. Katie Graham's going to get her tit caught in a big fat wringer if that's published. Good Christ! That's the most sickening thing I've ever heard. . . . You fellows got a great ball game. As soon as you're through paying Ed Williams and the rest of those fellows, we're going to do a little story on all of you."*

Secretary of Commerce Pete Peterson, one of the few Nixon cabinet members who stayed friends with any of us, kept telling us that we were underestimating how much "they" hated us, were determined to do us in. We had no idea what they felt was their range of options. TV licenses? IRS audits? Wiretapping?

As the former Attorney General's "tit in the wringer" quote resounded through the halls of Washington, we were already working on a story about Donald Segretti, a young California lawyer, first discovered by the FBI as agents went through Howard Hunt's subpoenaed telephone records. A week after the Watergate break-in, the Feds realized that Hunt and Segretti were in some kind of business together, but they had put Segretti on a back burner when they couldn't tie him to the Watergate break-in itself. Not Woodward and Bernstein. They didn't have a back burner.

Woodward learned more about Donald Segretti from his "friend" who was known in the city room to have quite extraordinary sources. This friend was the soon-to-be legendary "Deep Throat." Managing editor Howard Simons christened Woodward's source "Deep Throat." "Deep" surely from "deep background," the terms on which he gave Woodward all information, and "Deep Throat" probably because that was the title of the year's most successful pornographic movie, starring the awesome sodomist Linda Lovelace.

In the middle of September, Woodward read Deep Throat the draft of a story saying that federal investigators "had received information from Nixon campaign workers that high officials of the Committee to Re-elect the President (CRP) had been involved in

---

* Months later an admiring orthodontist made a small, intricate model of a clothes wringer, complete with gears, rollers, and a tiny handle, and sent it to Katharine Graham as a present. She wore it on a chain around her neck for a few days. When Buchwald saw it, he persuaded a local jeweler to make a small, solid silver breast to scale, and sent it to Kay as his present. She wore both of them around her neck in the office for a few days, until we persuaded her to put them away, lest her new jewelry make the tabloids.

the funding of the Watergate operation." Deep Throat told Woodward the story was "too soft," adding, "you can go much stronger."

The next day Deep Throat offered up Jeb Stuart Magruder, deputy campaign director of CRP, and Bart Porter (Herbert L.), scheduling director of CRP, "both deeply involved in Watergate," he said, and confirmed that they had received at least $50,000 in dirty trick money from the safe of former Commerce Secretary Maurice Stans, now the finance chairman of the president's reelection campaign. Woodward was told he could be damn sure the money had not been used for legitimate purposes. That was fact, not allegation, Deep Throat said.

In late September, Bernstein took a call from an anonymous male, who described himself only as a government lawyer. He told Bernstein about an organized campaign of political sabotage and spying against the Democrats, and suggested he call Alex Shipley, then an assistant attorney general of Tennessee, for the details. Shipley told Bernstein that he had been in the Army with Segretti, and when he got out, Segretti tried to recruit him to join the sabotage effort. Woodward and Bernstein managed to get copies of Segretti's credit card records, and they confirmed that Segretti had been traveling the nation, spending a day or two in cities where the Democratic primaries would be held.

At the end of September, Clark MacGregor, campaign director at CRP, squeezed the pressure bar a bit by "demanding" an appointment with Katharine and me. With exaggerated emphasis, he would say only that the subject was "extremely important," and we set it up for the morning of the 29th. By accident I had bumped into him the afternoon before, and he had started whining to me about Woodward and Bernstein "harassing" secretaries.

An hour before our appointment, MacGregor's secretary called to say that he would be unable to keep it. She told me MacGregor felt he "had substantially accomplished his mission" during our conversation, according to a memorandum of conversation I dictated.

I asked her to tell him it had not accomplished anything, and she put him on. I asked him which secretaries were claiming what had been done to them by whom. (It would turn out that only

Bernstein was being accused of harassment above and beyond the call of duty.) According to MacGregor, Sally Harmony, a secretary at CRP, had gone home sick one afternoon, and Bernstein learned about it, and went to her apartment, "and repeatedly tried to get in." Another secretary had consistently found Bernstein waiting for her at her apartment door. Still another had been telephoned so often by Bernstein that she had been forced to move out and go live with her parents.

Bernstein had "repeatedly suggested lunch, cocktails, and so forth" to a secretary to Justice Rehnquist, again according to MacGregor.

I told him, "That's the nicest thing I've heard about either one of them in years," then murmured something about a raise for the boys, and hung up.

On October 9, Woodward and Deep Throat had their longest meeting ever, and one of their most productive.

"There is a way to untie the Watergate knot," Deep Throat started out. ". . . everything points in the direction of what was called 'Offensive Security. . . .' Remember, you don't do 1,500 interviews [with the FBI] and not have something on your hands other than a single break-in."

"Who was involved?" Woodward asked.

"Only the President and Mitchell know," came the ominous answer, without elaboration.

"That guy [Attorney General Mitchell] definitely learned some things in those ten days after Watergate. He was just sick, and everyone was saying that he was ruined because of what his people did, especially Mardian [political coordinator at CRP] and LaRue [Deputy Director, CRP], and what happened at the White House.

"And Mitchell said, 'If this all comes out, it could ruin the administration. I mean, ruin it.'

"They were playing games, all over the map . . . in Illinois, New York, New Hampshire, Massachusetts, California, Texas, Florida, and the District of Columbia," Deep Throat continued.

"What about Howard Hunt and leak-plugging?" Woodward asked.

"That operation was not only to check leaks to the papers but often to manufacture items for the press. It was a Colson-Hunt operation. Recipients include all of you guys—Jack Anderson, Evans and Novak, the *Post*, the *New York Times*, the *Chicago Tribune*. The business of Eagleton's drunk-driving record or his health records, I understand, involves the White House and Hunt somehow." (McGovern had dumped his vice-presidential candidate, Senator Thomas Eagleton of Missouri, after reports surfaced in the press that Eagleton had been treated for clinical depression.)

A Letter to the Editor, which had appeared in William Loeb's right-wing *Manchester* (N.H.) *Union-Leader*, charged presidential candidate Ed Muskie with condoning an ethnic slur against people of French Canadian descent by using the word "Canuck." It became known as the Canuck letter, and according to Deep Throat, "It was a White House Operation—done inside the gates surrounding the White House and the Executive Office Building. Is that enough?"

No. Woodward pressed for more.

"Okay, this is very serious. You can safely say that 50 people—more than 50—worked for the White House and CRP to play games and spy and sabotage."

Woodward left the meeting with a list that included "bugging, following people, false press leaks, fake letters, canceling campaign rallies, investigating campaign workers' private lives, planting spies, stealing documents, planting provocateurs."

Many people wondered then—and even now, so many years later—how the *Post* dared ride over the constant denials of the President of the United States, and the Attorney General of the United States, and the top presidential aides like H. R. Haldeman, John Ehrlichman, and Charles Colson, and stand by the guns of Woodward, Bernstein, and Deep Throat. The answer isn't that complicated. Little by little, week by week, we *knew* our information was right when we heard it, right when we checked it once and right when we checked it again. Little by little we came to realize that the White House information was wrong as soon as we checked it. That all these statesmen were lying.

Woodward was in the office a few hours later writing up his notes. We had roughed out a plan for three stories:

- A Woodstein special on the espionage and sabotage campaign of fifty agents from the White House and CRP. Surely the lead of the next day's paper.
- A Bernstein sidebar on Donald Segretti, a California lawyer recruited to play dirty tricks on selected "enemies."
- A Woodward sidebar.

Not just another day at the office, and it wasn't 10:00 A.M. yet, but all this was about to change.

Marilyn Berger covered foreign affairs thoroughly and skillfully for the *Post*, an attractive single woman, who loved being involved with the day's big story, whatever it was, like all good journalists. Bernstein was at the water cooler getting set to write the Canuck letter story—he had already sharpened every pencil at his desk and been to the bathroom three times. Berger came up to him and asked casually if "they" knew about the Canuck letter. This was an interesting question, since Woodward had only known about the Canuck letter since six o'clock that morning, and he hadn't told Bernstein until 9:00 A.M.

"What do you mean?" Bernstein asked with poorly disguised nonchalance.

"Ken Clawson wrote the Canuck letter," Berger announced, out of the blue. And it turned out Clawson had told her about it over a drink at her apartment one night a couple of weeks earlier. This was major news. First, because it confirmed part of Deep Throat's hours-old bombshell. Second, because Clawson had worked for *The Washington Post*, covering Attorney General Mitchell and the Justice Department, before joining Nixon's staff only a short time earlier. During the next eight hours, he found himself deeper and deeper in the soup, as he realized that the *Post* was about to say that he had told a *Post* reporter that he had written a fraudulent letter to the New Hampshire paper, the *Manchester Union-Leader*, and helped force Democratic presidential candidate Ed Muskie out of the race.

Clawson knew we would print his denial, but he seemed more worried that we would say where he had admitted authorship of the fraudulent letter. He was on the telephone most of the afternoon— to Berger, to Woodward and Bernstein, and to me. Clawson asked me specifically not to say he had been in Berger's apartment. The venue was of no importance to the story, but I wasn't about to let Clawson off the hook until we had everything out of him that we were going to get.

Late that afternoon (after 6:00 P.M.) we decided to combine all three stories into one big ball-breaker. It often seemed that every big Watergate story came together only late in the afternoon. However, Howard Simons and I would bet each other that as we left for home around eight o'clock, either Woodward or Bernstein would come sidling up to us and say something like, "We think we may have a pretty good story here."

One of the best "pretty good" stories they came up with in October was the first outline of the true scope of the Watergate conspiracy, showing a broad pattern of illicit behavior. It appeared in the *Post* on October 10, 1972.

FBI agents have established that the Watergate bugging incident stemmed from a massive campaign of political spying and sabotage conducted on behalf of President Nixon's re-election and directed by officials of the White House and the Committee for the Re-election of the President.

The activities, according to information in FBI and Department of Justice files, were aimed at all the major Democratic presidential candidates and—since 1971—represented a basic strategy of the re-election effort.

During the Watergate investigation federal agents established that hundreds of thousands of dollars in Nixon campaign contributions had been set aside to pay for an extensive undercover campaign aimed at discrediting individual Democratic presidential candidates and disrupting their campaigns.

"Intelligence work" is normal during a campaign and is said

to be carried out by both political parties. But federal investigators said what they uncovered being done by the Nixon forces is unprecedented in scope and intensity.

The next two paragraphs described the dirty tricks:

Following members of Democratic candidates' families; assembling dossiers of their personal lives; forging letters and distributing them under the candidates' letterheads; leaking false and manufactured items to the press; throwing campaign schedules into disarray; seizing confidential campaign files and investigating the lives of dozens of campaign workers.

In addition, investigators said the activities included planting provocateurs in the ranks of organizations expected to demonstrate at the Republican and Democratic conventions; and investigating potential donors to the Nixon campaign before their contributions were solicited.

The story then told about the Canuck letter for ten paragraphs: how White House staffer Ken Clawson had told Marilyn Berger he had written the Canuck letter that mortally wounded Ed Muskie's presidential candidacy, but now denied it. We didn't get to Donald Segretti and his dirty tricks, and the involvement of at least fifty undercover Nixon operatives who traveled throughout the country trying to disrupt and spy on Democratic campaigns, until the story jumped to an inside page at paragraph 19 (of a 65-paragraph story). The White House called the story a "collection of absurdities," but the *New York Times* had its own story on the front page, largely quoting the *Post*. There are many, many rewards in the newspaper business, but one of the finest comes with reading the competition quoting your paper on its front page.

On October 15, Bernstein and Woodward (we alternated the order of their names in bylines) revealed that Nixon's appointments secretary, Dwight Chapin, and an ex-White House aide named Donald H. Segretti were integral parts of a White House spying and sabotage operation.

On October 24, our Watergate machine blew a fuse. We had been pursuing the money, tracing it deeper and deeper into the White House and higher and higher up the White House ladder. We had followed it to the presidential appointments secretary, Dwight Chapin, but we had never been able to trace any money to Haldeman, Ehrlichman, or the president himself. Hugh Sloan, committee treasurer of the CRP, had confirmed to Woodward and Bernstein that five men controlled the White House secret fund, used to finance all political sabotage and payoffs. Woodward and Bernstein knew who four of them were when they met with Sloan on October 23: Jeb Magruder, Maurice Stans, John Mitchell, and Herbert Kalmbach, Nixon's personal attorney. They suspected Bob Haldeman was the fifth, but had been unable to confirm. Sloan was less than forthcoming. Was it Ehrlichman? No. Was it Colson? No. Was it the president himself? No. Then it had to be Haldeman. It was a question, not a statement.

As Woodward and Bernstein later recalled this back and forth in their book *All the President's Men*, Sloan said, "Let me put it this way. I have no problems if you write a story like that." Then it's correct? Woodward asked. And Sloan finally said yes.

Woodward felt Sloan's "yes" specifically included the fact that he had named Haldeman as one of the five men who controlled the secret fund to FBI investigators and in his grand jury testimony.

One source, solid, now. Deep Throat was two, but we could never quote him, and so we needed at least one more on a story this important. And this is where we got in trouble. With Woodward listening on an extension, Bernstein got an FBI agent to confirm that the bureau "got Haldeman's name in connection with his control over the secret fund," and that "it also came out in the grand jury." When Bernstein asked him if he was sure Haldeman was the fifth man in control of the secret fund, the agent replied, "Yeah, Haldeman. John Haldeman."

That was a "tilt," of course. Haldeman was Bob. And John could be Ehrlichman, though that had been denied. Carl called the agent back, and he said he never could remember names. It was Bob Haldeman. And the boys were ready to write.

As we got closer and closer to Nixon, I was becoming more and more cautious. This time, with Simons, Sussman, and Rosenfeld, we went after Woodward and Bernstein like prosecutors, demanding to know word for bloody word what each source had said in reply to what questions, not the general meaning but the exact words. Then I finally said, "Go." It was October 24, for the issue of October 25, 1972.

Meanwhile, Bernstein had gone after a fourth source, even as the story was being set in the composing room, and hit upon a gimmick that plowed new—and unholy—ground in the annals of journalism, and also could have gotten us in major trouble at just the wrong time. He tried one more source, a Justice Department lawyer, who told him he would like to help, but could not. Bernstein read the lawyer the story, and then suggested he was going to count to ten. If the lawyer found nothing wrong with our story, he would still be on the telephone when Bernstein reached ten. If something was wrong with the story, the lawyer would hang up before Bernstein reached ten. Or something.

Bernstein reached ten and the lawyer was still at the other end of the line.

All I could think of was the Sherlock Holmes tale about the dog that didn't bark. The lawyer who didn't hang up.

I watched the shit hit the fan early next day on the CBS Morning News. To my eternal horror, there was correspondent Dan Schorr with a microphone jammed in the face of Hugh Sloan and his lawyer. And the lawyer was categorical in his denial: Sloan had not testified to the grand jury that Haldeman controlled the secret fund.

No one can imagine how I felt. We had written more than fifty Watergate stories, in the teeth of one of history's great political cover-ups, and we hadn't made a material mistake. Not one. We had been supported by the publisher every step of the way, and she had withstood enormous pressures to stand by our side. Pressures from her friends as well as her enemies. And now this.

The denials exploded all around us all day like incoming artillery shells. After Sloan came Ron Ziegler, Clark MacGregor, and good

Meg Greenfield—her warmth and humor sometimes overpowered the brainy, intellectual image reflected in her Newsweek column picture.

25

Howard Simons—the great eclectic mind of the newsroom. He invented SMERSH (Science, Medicine, Education, Religion, and all that SHit).

26

27 *The pressmen's strike for five months in 1974 and 1975 killed the union and gave the Post vitally needed control of its production. That's the union president, Charlie Davis, carrying the particularly tasteless sign. He moved on to bartending.*

28

The third generation takes over in 1979 when Don Graham becomes publisher. Katharine had succeeded her husband in August 1963 and created the modern Washington Post.

In the 1980s I started moving away from my image as a bookie or a jewel thief, and started being pensive when photographed.

30

This is a meeting of our club, just after turning down Katharine Graham for member-ship. Edward Bennett Williams with his arms around Art Buchwald and me.

31

Artie and I at one of the political conventions, teasing our photographer friend Diana Walker.

Sally Quinn clowning, early in her life as a Style reporter, still an impossible dream in my eyes.

I asked artist Steve Mendelson to draw this—to give to reporters clinically unable to admit they sometimes missed a story, even part of a story.

THE DEFENSIVE CROUCH

33

Ward Just typified the new breed of smart, hungry reporters who could write like angels. We stripped his story about the patrol where he got his ass full of shrapnel over the masthead with the headline "Ain't Nobody Here but Charlie Cong."

34

The new pope was a Pole, and four days later, October 20, 1978, Sally and I were married.

*Sister Connie and brother Freddy in Leesburg, Virginia, for Marina's wedding,
October 27, 1984.*

There's no word for former stepchildren, but here they are at Marina's wedding, sandwiched between Dino and Ben, Jr.: Rosamond Casey and Andy, Tammy, and Nancy Pittman.

Quinn and his dad. It doesn't get any better than that.

39

Ben, Jr., Dino, and Quinn hamming it up at Ben's wedding in Cambridge,
November 17, 1990.

40

Harry "Doc" Dalinsky outside his Georgetown drugstore, where he dispensed wisdom, love, and bagels to his friends for almost forty years.

41

Flirting in Central Park in 1975.

42

Parenting in Georgetown, 1995. Quinn Bradlee, newly a teenager.

This is Porto Bello as we found it in 1990, on the St. Mary's River in southern Maryland.

43

This is Porto Bello in the June 1995 issue of Architectural Digest, *a glorious expression of Sally Quinn's taste and* Washington Post *stock.*

Moving out, moving on . . . with a hug from Len Downie, the new executive editor, and a fantastic send-off from the troops.

The Graham publishers and one of their chief beneficiaries.

old Bob Dole, always ready to pile on. Some of the denials sounded technical, almost hair-splitting to us. But if it looked like a denial, smelled like a denial, and read like a denial, it *was* a denial, as far as the readers were concerned. Newspapers which hadn't bothered to run the story about Haldeman's control of the secret fund head-lined the various White House denials; major newspapers like the *Chicago Tribune*, the *Philadelphia Inquirer*, the *Denver Post*, the *Minneapolis Tribune*.

Bernstein and Woodward, tails between their legs and my un-happiness ringing in their ears, started out on the long road of find-ing out what had gone wrong. I was sore . . . at them and at myself. It was a jackass scheme, and I should have caught it. All along, we had wanted to "win" without knowing what winning might turn out to be. But all along, we knew we could not afford *any* mistakes. And now we had made one. The next step was to find out where we had gone wrong, and how to get back in our stride.

Election Day was less than a month off, and the Nixon White House had settled on its ultimate defense. The night before our "mistake" ran on page one, Bob Dole, the GOP chairman, had given a speech in Baltimore with an astounding fifty-seven critical references to the *Post:*

The greatest political scandal of this campaign is the brazen manner in which, without benefit of clergy, *The Washington Post* has set up housekeeping with the McGovern campaign. With his campaign collapsing around his ears, Mr. McGovern some weeks back became the beneficiary of the most extensive jour-nalistic rescue-and-salvage operation in American politics.

The *Post's* reputation for objectivity and credibility have sunk so low they have almost disappeared from the Big Board altogether.

There is a cultural and social affinity between the McGover-nites and the *Post* executives and editors. They belong to the same elite; they can be found living cheek by jowl in the same exclusive neighborhood, and hob-nobbing at the same George-town parties. . . .

It is only *The Washington Post* which deliberately mixes together illegal and unethical episodes, like the Watergate caper,
with shenanigans which have been the stock in trade of political
pranksters from the day I came into politics.

Now, Mr. Bradlee, an old Kennedy coat-holder, is entitled to
his views. But when he allows his paper to be used as a political instrument of the McGovernite campaign; when he himself
travels the country as a small-bore McGovern surrogate, then he
and his publication should expect appropriate treatment, which
they will with regularity receive.

The Republican Party has been the victim of a barrage of un-
founded and unsubstantiated allegations by George McGovern
and his partner in mud-slinging, *The Washington Post*.

Ziegler said the *Post*'s stories "are based on hearsay, innuendo,
guilt by association. . . . Since the Watergate case broke, people
have been trying to link the case with the White House . . . and
no link has been established . . . because no link exists." And Clark
MacGregor, who had succeeded Mitchell as director of Nixon's
campaign, weighed in with a no-questions-allowed press conference, where he allowed as how "The *Washington Post*'s credibility
has today sunk lower than that of George McGovern. Using innuendo, third person hearsay, unsubstantiated charges, anonymous
sources and huge scare headlines, the *Post* has maliciously sought
to give the appearance of a direct connection between the White
House and the Watergate—a charge the *Post* knows and half a
dozen investigations have found to be false. The hallmark of the
Post's campaign is hypocrisy."

Mercifully for us, on the afternoon of October 26, Henry
Kissinger gave a press conference at the White House to announce
that "peace was at hand in Vietnam," and that gave us a little
breathing room, since it occupied both the press and the Nixon
administration. And after a long conversation with Sloan's lawyer,
James Stoner, and a few more days of digging, the truth emerged (as
Walter Lippmann so long ago promised it would): Haldeman *did*
have control of the secret fund, despite all the technical denials, but

Sloan had not testified to that effect in front of the grand jury. He hadn't told the grand jury about Haldeman's control, because the jury hadn't asked him about Haldeman's involvement.

Sloan finally told us, "Our denial was strictly limited." And so be it; they caused us anguish we had never felt before.

We had already tied Segretti to Dwight Chapin, Nixon's appointments secretary, and to Herbert Kalmbach, Nixon's lawyer, so we were keeping the pressure on. But it was lonely out there, targeted as we were more and more by Messrs. Dole, MacGregor, Ziegler and company. With only a few exceptions (*Time* magazine, the *L.A. Times*, the *New York Times*, and each of them only rarely during this period), the press was concentrating on the political race between Nixon and McGovern, seemingly content to leave us alone and "see what you guys can come up with," as one editor told me. It was discouraging as hell.

In the middle of October, my old *Newsweek* buddy Gordon Manning, vice president and director at CBS, had called with good news.

"You've never been able to do anything without me, Bradlee," he started, "and now I'm going to save your ass in this Watergate thing. Cronkite and I have gotten CBS to agree to do two back-to-back long pieces on the 'Evening News' about Watergate. We're going to make you famous."

That *was* good news, because television had been generally unable to cope with Watergate, and national acceptance of the story had lagged accordingly. Probably because it would never be a visual story until the Senate hearings five long months later, except for a few shots of Dan Rather and Nixon shouting at each other in press conferences.

"There's only one thing," Manning went on. "You've got to let us have the documents. We don't have any."

"Gordon, there aren't any documents," I told him. "Believe it or not. Of course, we'll help you, but we have information. We don't have photocopies, Xeroxes, nothing."

"Come on, Benny," he insisted. "We'll make you famous, and you guys need us. You're all alone out there."

True enough, as I saw it, but he wouldn't believe me. Instead, he sent down some hot-shot producer, and we told him what we knew and a good part of what we suspected. But he finally became convinced that Walter was not going to get nonexistent documents.

When the pieces finally ran (fourteen minutes on October 27, and eight minutes the next night), they had a powerful impact everywhere—on the *Post*, on the politicians (if not the voters), and on newsrooms outside Washington. Somehow the Great White Father, Walter Cronkite, the most trusted man in America, had blessed the story by spending so much time on it. The lack of documents had forced Gordon "Think Visual" Manning and company to use giant blow-ups of *Washington Post* logos, and front-page stories. We were thrilled. No new ground was broken, but the broadcasts validated the *Post*'s stories in the public's mind and gave us all an immense morale boost.

On November 7, 1972, the voters reelected Richard Nixon by one of the greatest margins in American history. He won more than 60 percent of the vote, and every state in the union except Massachusetts, an historic sweep. And one of the first orders of business in the second term was retaliation against the *Post* . . . most of it petty, but all of it vaguely threatening.

After the election, Chuck Colson—spang in the middle of all the obstruction of justice that eventually landed him in jail—gave a speech to the New England newspaper editors that stands by itself as a monument to lying and general dishonesty:

> Ben Bradlee now sees himself as the self-appointed leader of what Boston's Teddy White once described as "that tiny little fringe of arrogant elitists who infect the healthy mainstream of American journalism with their own peculiar view of the world."
>
> I think if Bradlee ever left the Georgetown cocktail circuit, where he and his pals dine on third-hand information and gossip and rumor, he might discover out here the real America, and he might learn that all truth and all knowledge and all superior wisdom doesn't emanate exclusively from that small little clique in Georgetown, and that the rest of the country isn't just sitting out here waiting to be told what they're supposed to think. . . .

An independent investigation was conducted in the White House which corroborated the findings of the FBI that *no one in the White House was in any way involved in the Watergate affair.*

A reporter for the *Washington Star-News* was promised by Chuck Colson that the administration would bury the *Post*. "Come in with your breadbasket, and we'll fill it," Colson is quoted as telling other reporters by city editor Barry Sussman, by then in charge of our day-to-day Watergate reporting. And sure enough, Nixon's first exclusive interview in his second term went to Garnett Horner, of the *Star-News*. He didn't say a damn thing in the interview, but we could identify a shot across our bow when we saw one. Some government officials stopped notifying *Post* reporters of bread-and-butter developments on their beats. One of the most distinguished—and unanimously loved—reporters on *The Washington Post* was Dorothy McCardle, age sixty-eight, a white-haired grandmother who had covered the Lindbergh kidnapping for the *Philadelphia Inquirer*. She covered the East Wing of the White House, the source of all information about White House social gatherings of all kinds, and she was systematically excluded from all pools, where she would have a chance to report directly, rather than accept force-fed handouts. Her exclusion actually boomeranged against the White House, after the *Star-News* wrote an editorial saying they would boycott social events rather than be used as an instrument of revenge against McCardle.

Behind the scenes, and unknown to *Post* officials until months later, Nixon himself, plus Haldeman and others, were plotting hardball revenge against the paper. The *Post* was going to have "damnable, damnable problems," according to the transcripts of the president's post-election conversations with his inner circle, when it came time for its television station licenses to be renewed.

And sure enough, we did. In those days the Federal Communications Commission (FCC) required TV license renewals every three years. By January 1973, only four challenges had been filed against all the TV stations in the United States. Three of the challenges were against *Post*-owned WJXT in Jacksonville, Florida, and the other was against *Post*-owned WPLG (for Philip L. Graham) in Miami. At least two of the challenges involved people active in Nixon's reelection effort. And the general counsel of the Committee to Re-elect the President, J. Glenn Sedam, actually traveled to Jacksonville to talk to business leaders there about how to file challenges.*

Right after our "mistake" on October 25, Woodward, Bernstein, and the rest of us had disappeared into a black hole, where we couldn't get anyone to talk, we couldn't get a smell of a story. I suggested to Rosenfeld and Sussman that they keep Woodward's and Bernstein's heads under water until they came up with something. But without success. At the same time, the Republicans—and some of our journalist colleagues—were telling everyone: "See? As soon as the election is over, the *Post* can't find anything to write about. We told you it was all politics."

Much has been made of an incident at the end of November 1972 when Woodward and Bernstein, with my knowledge and support, tried to contact grand jurors convened to investigate Watergate. I am sure we all were influenced by Nixon's overwhelming reelection win, on top of our own inability to break new ground in the Watergate story.

We had been told by our lawyers that talking to grand jurors was not illegal "per se," whatever that meant in this context, although it was possibly illegal for grand jurors to talk to reporters. And we had confirmed evidence that the Nixon administration Justice Department was not presenting certain evidence to the grand jury. We felt the playing field wasn't even to start with, given the scope of the Nixon cover-up, and the tools any administration has to cover up the truth. If key evidence was being withheld from the grand jury, we felt we had no chance to get to the truth we knew was there.

Our grand jury episode began when *Post* news editor Ben Cason was emptying the trash at his house in northern Virginia at the same time his neighbor was emptying his trash. The neighbor told

---

* Post lawyers estimated that it cost about $ I million in legal fees and audience surveys to fight each challenge.

Cason his aunt was on a grand jury, which he thought was the Watergate grand jury. His aunt was a Republican who disliked Richard Nixon—just to put a little frosting on the cake.

We went into conferences with our lawyers and ourselves. Ed Williams agreed—reluctantly—that Woodward and Bernstein could talk to the lady juror, but urged extreme caution, suggesting they merely ask the lady if she wanted to talk. I insisted that the reporters identify themselves as *Washington Post* reporters, and urged Bernstein to try to be subtle. After they left to call on the woman, we all stayed glued to the phone . . . but she wasn't home. Next morning, they rang her doorbell, identified themselves, and were invited in. They didn't mention the grand jury. They just asked her casually some questions about Watergate. Woodward quotes the lady as answering: "It's a mess, but how would I know anything about it except what I read in the papers."

She was a grand juror, all right, but on a different grand jury, not the Watergate grand jury.

Next morning, Woodward persuaded a clerk in the U.S. District Court to let him see the master list of trial jurors and grand jurors, after promising he wouldn't copy anything. He plowed through the file drawers, found the list of jurors on two grand juries sworn in earlier that summer, and picked the right grand jury by remembering that the foreman had an Eastern European name. In front of him lay twenty-three small orange cards, each listing the name, age, occupation, address, and telephone number of a Watergate grand juror. Fifteen feet away from him sat the clerk, suspicious eyes fixed on him.

Bob Woodward simply memorized the whole list. The first four names in about ten minutes, followed by a short visit to the men's room, where he copied the names down in his notebook. On his next try, he memorized five cards, and asked the clerk for directions to the chief judge's chambers. In a different men's room, he wrote down five names, addresses, ages, and phone numbers. Back for a third try—with fourteen names to go, and the clerk becoming unmanageably suspicious—Woodward memorized the contents of six cards, wrote them down during a phony lunch break, and returned to get the last eight . . . in just forty-five minutes.

The fruits of those considerable labors were nonexistent. After trying to guess which of the twenty-three might talk, Woodward and Bernstein reached "about half a dozen," they reported. One told them he had taken two oaths of secrecy in his life, one for the Elks and one for the grand jury, and wasn't about to violate either one. But several grand jurors told Judge John J. Sirica early Monday morning that they had been contacted by the *Post*, and the shit hit the fan. "Maximum John" Sirica, so called for his tough sentences, was "some kind of pissed at you fellas," Ed Williams told us after the judge had contacted him. But Sirica settled for a stern lecture from the bench, after the prosecutors recommended taking no action since no information had been given the reporters by the grand jurors. Sirica didn't even identify Woodward and Bernstein in his lecture from the bench, although he had insisted that they be brought to court and seated in the front row.

In *All the President's Men*, Woodward and Bernstein recall this episode in all our lives as "a seedy venture" and "a clumsy charade." Woodward described himself as wondering "whether there was ever justification for a reporter to entice someone across the line of legality while standing safely on the right side himself." Bernstein was described as a man "who vaguely approved of selective civil disobedience," not "concerned about breaking the law in the abstract." With him, the co-authors said, "it was a question of which law, and he believed that grand-jury proceedings should be inviolate."

I don't look at it that way. I remember figuring, after being told that it was not illegal and after insisting that *we* tell no lies and identify ourselves, that it was worth a shot. In the same circumstances, I'd do it again. The stakes were too high.

But the new year brought us the trial of the five Watergate burglars, plus Hunt, and the oddball zealot, Gordon Liddy: Liddy, an ex-FBI agent who had worked on the staff of John Ehrlichman, and was the administration's unofficial expert on dirty tricks. Hunt and the four Miami burglars pleaded guilty before the trial, and the jury found Liddy and McCord guilty. We were back in business, and because the trial was a national story, the *Post* was not alone. In fact, before the trial ended, Sy Hersh, who had broken the story of the My Lai massacre* and was now working for the *New York Times*, dropped a beauty on us and the world with a detailed account of how the defendants had been paid hush money with funds ostensibly raised to reelect President Nixon. I hate to get beaten on any story, but I loved that one by my pal Hersh, because it meant the *Post* was no longer alone in alleging obstruction of justice by the administration—as long as we didn't get beaten again.

Sentencing was set for late March, and when the day finally came, two men made sure that Watergate would never die, and that Richard Nixon himself was going to pay a fearful price for his role in it. The first was Judge John Sirica, and the second was James W. McCord, Jr. The date was Friday, March 23, 1973. The courtroom was crowded, and Sirica had whispered to a reporter that he would have a surprise for everyone. Sirica was always described as a former boxer. He was sixty-nine years old, small, scrappy, with a face you know but find hard to remember how. As chief judge of the U.S. District Court, he had assigned himself the Watergate burglary because he liked the limelight as much as the next judge, maybe a little more. He ran that trial with an iron hand, but he was frustrated by all the guilty pleas, and as sentencing approached he knew that he had been unable to get to the truth.

But now he suddenly had his chance. His "surprise" turned out to be a confidential letter received three days earlier from McCord in jail. Worried about being second-guessed, Sirica made his bombshell public as soon as the crowded courtroom came to order.

"Certain questions have been posed to me from your honor through the probation officer," McCord's letter began,

---

* Sy Hersh had uncovered the My Lai massacre, in which Lieutenant William Calley, Jr. and other GIs had brutally killed at least one hundred and perhaps as many as two hundred Vietnamese civilians in the small village. As a freelance writer, he had to sell the story from paper to paper. When he and his agent, David Obst, came to the *Post*, the more establishment editors and reporters were skeptical, but it smelled right to me. We ran it on page one, twinned with a staff-written analysis.

dealing with details of the case, motivations, intent and mitigating circumstances. In endeavoring to respond to these questions, I am whipsawed in a variety of legalities. . . .

There are further considerations which are not to be taken lightly. Several members of my family have expressed fear for my life if I disclose knowledge of the facts in this matter, either publicly or to any government representative. . . . Whereas I do not share their concerns to the same degree, nevertheless, I do believe that retaliatory measures will be taken against me, my family and my friends should I disclose such facts. Such retaliation could destroy careers, income and reputations of persons who are innocent of any guilt whatever.

But if he failed to answer Judge Sirica's questions, McCord's letter continued, he could

expect a much more severe sentence. . . . In the interests of justice and in the interests of restoring faith in the criminal justice system, which faith has been severely damaged in this case, I will state the following to you at this time which I hope may be of help to you in meting out justice in this case.

1. There was political pressure applied to the defendants to plead guilty and remain silent.

2. Perjury occurred during the trial in matters highly material to the very structure, orientation and impact of the government's case, and to the motivation and intent of the defendants.

3. Others involved in the Watergate operation were not identified during the trial, when they could have been by those testifying. . . .

Following sentencing, I would appreciate the opportunity to talk with you privately in chambers. Since I cannot feel confident in talking with an FBI agent, in testifying before a grand jury whose U.S. attorneys work for the Department of Justice, or in talking with other government representatives, such a discussion would be of assistance to me.

The Watergate dam was about to burst. These were devastating charges, by the one person involved in the break-in with some stature in his community. He was a career CIA technician, not a spy with extensive dirty trick experience like Hunt, not a kook like Liddy, not a political fanatic like the men from Miami. And here he was under oath in front of a federal judge, talking about perjury, about hush money, about cover-ups by people involved intimately with the president's closest advisers. This wasn't some press figment of the imagination, quoting anonymous sources, whose motives could be attacked. This was an insider talking, and everyone knew it.

Sirica had to recess his court for a minute because he had a serious bellyache, but when he started to feel better, he got on with the business of sentencing the defendants for what he called "sordid, despicable and thoroughly reprehensible" crimes.

First, G. Gordon Liddy, who said nothing—cool, grinning, unafraid, respected by the criminals he had met in jail, cordially disliked by the prosecutor. On six counts of burglary and wiretapping, Liddy was sentenced to a minimum of six years and eight months and a maximum of twenty years in prison, plus a fine of $40,000. He would serve fifty-two months of actual time.

Then Howard Hunt, who pleaded emotionally for mercy: "I have lost virtually everything I cherished in life—my wife [who had died with a bag of cash in a plane crash on December 8, 1972], my job, my reputation . . . except my [four] children, who are all that remain of a once happy family. . . . I have suffered agonies I never believed a man could endure and still survive. My fate . . . is in your hands." Judge Sirica was unmoved. He sentenced Hunt to thirty-five years in jail, and fined him $40,000. Unknown to anyone publicly, Hunt had just been paid off by the White House to remain silent. Hunt ultimately served thirty-one and a half months in jail.

The Miami men, also silent, got forty years and $50,000 fines. The sentences for Hunt and the burglars were especially heavy, but they were also provisional. Sirica told them he would rethink their sentences if they decided to spill the beans and tell what they knew.

"I hold out no promises or hopes of any kind to you in this matter," he told them, "but I do say that should you decide to speak freely, I would have to weigh that factor in appraising what sentence will finally be imposed in each case." None of the Miami men served more than fourteen months.

For the first time, really, I felt in my guts that we were going to win. And winning would mean all the truth. Every bit. I had no idea still how it would all come out, but I no longer believed Watergate would end in a tie. My great fear had always been that it would just peter out, with *The Washington Post* and the rest of the good guys saying it was an awful conspiracy, and the White House saying it was just the press and politics. Now, I knew there was going to be a winner. And I knew it was not going to be the president or the White House gang.

For the record, I told Woodward and Bernstein to go find out who were the people McCord said had perjured themselves, and who had put what pressure on whom. Privately, I was so damned excited I couldn't sit down. I called Kay Graham in Singapore with the news, and I had lunch with Buchwald and Williams.

That always made me feel good.

Williams and Buchwald and I had been eating lunch together so long and so often that before we knew it we had our own de facto club. First at the Sans Souci restaurant, where Buchwald had conned the owner into putting his name on a plaque over his favorite banquette seat, later at the Maison Blanche, and sometimes at Duke Zeibert's. This was an extremely exclusive and sexist club. Its only by-law (unwritten) was that no one else could join. In fact, its only purpose was to keep good friends out—Jack Valenti, George Stevens, Phil Geyelin, Joe Califano and company. Aspirants could buy us lunch and they could eat with us, but they wouldn't make it past the membership committee.

In all the years of its existence, the only exception was Katharine Graham. Once Buchwald sent her the following memo after inviting her to lunch:

This is a list of the guests at the luncheon tomorrow which will help you know who they are and what to talk about.

1. Benjamin Bradlee is the managing editor of The Washington Post, which is a very influential newspaper in the Nation's Capital. Bradlee's interests are football and girls—not necessarily in that order—but if you wish, you can talk to him about the newspaper business.

2. Edward Bennett Williams is a leading criminal lawyer in Washington who has defended such diversified clients as Milwaukee Phil, Arizona Pete, and Three-Finger George. He is a very strong Catholic, so I suggest you discuss religion with him—particularly birth control and if priests should get married.

3. Art Buchwald is the columnist for The Washington Posty. He is terribly charming and can talk on any subject. I think that of the three, you will find him the most interesting.

I doubt if there will be any toast, except to the President of the United States.

Kay would eat with us from time to time, and Williams and Buchwald would always tell her that they had proposed her for membership but I had blackballed her. Finally, on her sixty-fifth birthday, we took her to lunch and told her she had been elected, and we toasted her induction with champagne. But at the end of the meal, Williams broke the news to our new member—his prestigious client and my boss: Unfortunately, the club had an age limit, and all members had to resign when they reached sixty-five.

More normally, the three of us would eat together, and two of us would pair off on the third guy. Buchwald and I would dump on some of Ed's more unsavory clients, especially Victor Posner, the shady Miami businessman with a well-known taste for teenage girls. Ed and I would go after Art's pronouncements about what was really going on in Washington. And the two of them would gang up on me, generally complaining that anything they told me ended up somewhere in the paper. This was true, especially from Williams, but I figured he knew how I made my living, and never told me anything he didn't want me to know. He never once told me about his lawsuits, and he had the most interesting clients in town. From time to time during our meals—liberated as we all were—we would play quick games of "Wouldya" as persons of the female persuasion crossed our fields of vision.

Male friends are important to me, and the ones that I love are vitally important. These two guys, I loved. Differently. Friendship with Buchwald requires constant attention. If I didn't call Art on the phone pretty regularly, I would start hearing from mutual friends like Harry Dalinsky, who ran all our lives from behind the counter at the Georgetown Pharmacy, that Art's feelings were hurt. Art shared with me his complicated courtship with the wonderful Ann McGarry. There was some mixture of sensibility and vulnerability plus the twinkle and the humor that made Art unique. And irresistible. Then, and now.

With Williams, our friendship could survive weeks of negligence, and flourish minutes after renewed contact. From the day of our first lunch at some greasy spoon luncheonette near the courthouse, two things were quickly obvious to me about Williams: wherever Ed was, there was a good story, and whatever he did, he had a good time and it showed. He was smart, tough, funny, and soft-hearted, and he didn't take himself too seriously, while taking his jobs extremely seriously. I knew right away I wanted him by my side if I ever got in trouble. I missed him the moment he died almost forty years later, and I have missed him and his warmth and humor and common sense every day since.

After Judge Sirica's sentencing of the Watergate burglars, the Washington press corps began full-time pursuit of the story, falling all over each other like a pack of beagles, in Stewart Alsop's apt phrase, noisily barking, sometimes at the fresh scent of a new lead, but often at the scent and sight of each other.

The air was thick with lies, and the president was the lead liar. In April 1973, Nixon said he "began intensive new inquiries." That was a lie. In the same statement, he said he condemned "any attempts to cover up in this case, no matter who is involved." That was another lie. He, himself, was leading the cover-up of Watergate. Ziegler was lying so often, he had to coin the expression "inoperative statements" when he needed to find the euphemistic way to admit that he had lied. Today's statement was called the "operative statement," while earlier statements were dismissed as "inoperative." Not even George Orwell would have dared to try that in 1984.* Kleindienst even had to lie to get confirmed, when he told the Senate that President Nixon had not interfered in a 1972 Justice Department investigation of International Telephone and Telegraph (ITT).†

Henry Kissinger contributed uniquely to efforts to play down Watergate by saying that the nation had to decide whether it could stand "an orgy of recrimination," suggesting the nation might be better off by forgetting Watergate. Spiro Agnew, a man who had accepted payoffs in the Executive Office Building as a sitting vice president, found the gall somewhere to tell a bunch of students he would resign if Watergate made him unable to continue in "good conscience." The acting director of the FBI, L. Patrick Gray, destroyed two folders of Watergate evidence, given him by Ehrlichman and Dean, on July 3, 1972, and was asked to withdraw his nomination nine months later. Reporters who wrote stories Kissinger didn't want disclosed got their phones tapped. It was revealed that Liddy and Hunt had burglarized the files of Daniel Ellsberg's psychiatrist in 1971, looking for information to smear Ellsberg and get even with him for making the Pentagon Papers available. And finally Kleindienst resigned, replaced by Elliot Richardson, the incorruptible Brahmin from Boston.

The focus of the Watergate affair had shifted from Sirica's court-

---

* Ziegler later said, "I never knowingly lied, but certainly history shows that many things I said were incorrect."

† In 1972, columnist Jack Anderson published a memo, written by an ITT lobbyist named Dita Beard, stating that ITT had donated several hundred thousand dollars to the Republican cause, and for a favorable anti-trust action pending against ITT. Beard later disavowed the authenticity of the memo after she was visited in her hospital room by Hunt in a fright wig and sunglasses. It was later revealed through the Nixon tapes that the president called Kleindienst a "son of a bitch" when he ordered Kleindienst to ease off of his investigation of ITT, and when Kleindienst argued, the president asked him, "Don't you speak English?"

room and the *Post*'s Woodward and Bernstein pieces to Senator Ervin's committee, and the investigations being conducted by the committee staff, under committee counsel Sam Dash. Reporters were having a field day, simply because of the sudden multiplication of news sources. As the principals were first interviewed by committee investigators, then behind closed doors before members of the committee, the opportunities presented to each senator and each investigator for some serious leaking were proving irresistible.

Senators, on and off the Ervin Committee, were looking for high ground. Spiro Agnew announced that he was "appalled" by Watergate. Richard Kleindienst, the new Attorney General, about to be forced to resign himself, was the first to mention publicly the dreaded "I" word (Impeachment).

Nixon explained himself so many times, it was hard not to be confused. My own favorite rationale came on April 30 when the president tried one more time to con the American people in a latter-day Checkers speech: "The easiest course would be for me to blame those to whom I had delegated the responsibility to run the campaign, but that would be the cowardly thing to do." This from the man who ten days earlier, it turns out, had told his assistant attorney general in charge of the criminal division to "stay out of" the break-in to Ellsberg's psychiatrist's office because "that is a national security matter." An awesome lie.

It seemed as if reporters were just bringing their buckets to work, sure that they would be filled with the latest sleazy revelations without any great work on their part. No reporter had ever seen anything like this before.

And most remarkable of all, no one yet knew the complete story. The existence of the White House tapes, with their vivid and detailed self-incrimination, was still unknown to us—or to any investigator. At the *Post*, where reporters and editors knew more than almost anyone else, we were still trying to fit each new piece of information into the puzzle. We grew increasingly confident that this was the greatest political scandal of our time, and we still didn't know the half of it.

In the middle of all this, I got a call from my old friend Jean-Jacques Servan-Schreiber, the founding editor of the French weekly, *L'Express*, with a startling invitation. He wanted to put me on the cover of *L'Express*'s twentieth anniversary issue, to symbolize the importance to society of a free and independent press. They were in something of a hurry. (I wondered—only briefly—whether the regularly scheduled cover had just fallen through and they were in a real jam.) A photographer was on his way to take the cover photo, because JJ-SS was sure I would agree. They would fly Tony and me to Paris twenty-four hours later for the magazine's big birthday party, where "le tout Paris" would be gathered. I would have to give only a five-minute speech in French, but then we would be free to enjoy an April-in-Paris weekend by ourselves.

Without pause, I said I would do it, with great delight. And I called Tony to tell her to start packing for a roller-coaster ride, only to be told that she did not want to go. I was stunned to realize that the prospect of a unique adventure together was no longer attractive.

But I went anyway, somewhere between glad, mad, and sad.

Servan-Schreiber was an interesting man in the early seventies, not yet overwhelmed by his ego. He and his longtime friend and colleague, the spectacular Françoise Giroud, disciples of Pierre Mendès-France, had started *L'Express* in 1953, and they quickly made it the exciting weekly journal of intelligence and relevance.

Two hours after I landed in Paris, I walked into a mirrored ballroom in a downtown hotel where at least fifty four- by six-feet posters of me on the cover of *L'Express* stared out at the glitzy crowd. I was scared to death—by the pictures of me, and by the prospect of making a speech in French. I thought I had arranged for Nicole Salinger, the wife of Pierre, to help me translate my thoughts into decent French, but she missed connections and I had to write it myself.

The rest of the night dissolved into a fog of flattery. At the end of it, I found myself with an attractive escort. I didn't want to sleep alone on this night of "triumph," and wondered if she would be interested in sleeping with me. She would, she said, and she did.

And the next day, I flew back to Washington, feeling not quite as guilty as I had expected.

Life on the ladder of fame was something that all of us were still struggling with, and did not yet understand. I knew I was on it, but I didn't know how many rungs I was going to get to climb. It is one thing to have a page-one byline, but that notoriety is pretty much confined to your mother and a few friends. It is another thing to be the subject of a page-one story, as I had been when the French expelled me for contacting the Algerian rebels. But that was a three-day flash in the pan, preoccupying to me, but of limited interest to the rest of the world. Now I had been on the cover of a news magazine. Profiles were showing up in more or less serious parts of the press. Reporters were calling me for quotes. I remembered once more Russ Wiggins's importunities that journalists belonged in the audience, not on the stage, but I was plainly not following them. In fact, I felt rattled by them. All of us seek evidence of our effectiveness, and when that evidence turns public, it is hard to pretend that it doesn't feel good.

I came back from Paris to Washington to a cascade of page-one stories that would have been unbelievable only a few weeks before.

April 1973 was probably the worst month ever for the Nixon White House. The Ervin Committee, which had been created in February to investigate the Watergate break-in and related allegations, was up and running. Its members were leaking to the press like sieves as they jockeyed for headlines, even though televised hearings were still a month off. Liddy was held in contempt of court for refusing to testify to the grand jury. A *Wall Street Journal* poll showed that a majority of Americans now believed that the president knew about the cover-up. On April 12, the *Post* won a Pulitzer Prize for its Watergate reporting. Newspaper reports that month by the *Post*, the *New York Times*, and the *Los Angeles Times* showed:

- A Mitchell aide (Frederick C. LaRue) had received $70,000, to pay hush money for Watergate conspirators.

- Mitchell had been shown logs of the Watergate wiretaps.
- Magruder told the grand jury that Dean and Mitchell had approved the Watergate bugging.
- Acting FBI director Patrick Gray was revealed to have destroyed two folders taken from Howard Hunt's safe in the White House, immediately after the Watergate break-in, and was forced to resign in humiliation.
- The Ellsberg trial ended in a mistrial, after the judge reported prosecutors had withheld evidence.
- The Ellsberg judge revealed that Liddy and Hunt had burglarized Ellsberg's psychiatrist's office, while they were working out of the White House.
- And on the last day of the month, Big Casino: Ehrlichman and Haldeman were tossed over the side, and still the ship sank on, as the new Attorney General, Kleindienst, "resigned," John Dean was fired, Len Garment was named White House counsel, and Elliot Richardson became Attorney General. The press could barely keep up with the news, and the Ervin Committee hearings hadn't even started.

In the summer 1973 issue of the *Columbia Journalism Review*, James McCartney, a national correspondent for Knight Newspapers, described that last day in April thusly:

It was 11:55 a.m., on April 30, and Benjamin Crowninshield Bradlee, 51, executive editor of *The Washington Post*, chatted with a visitor, feet on the desk, idly attempting to toss a plastic toy basketball through a hoop mounted on an office window 12' away. The inevitable subject of conversation: Watergate. Howard Simons, the *Post*'s managing editor, slipped into the room to interrupt: "Nixon has accepted the resignations of Ehrlichman and Haldeman and Dean. Kleindienst is out and Richardson is the new AG."

For a split second, Ben Bradlee's mouth dropped open with an expression of sheer delight. Then he put one cheek on the desk, eyes closed, and banged the desk repeatedly with his fist.

In a moment, he recovered. "How do you like them apples?" he said to the grinning Simons. "Not a bad start."

Bradlee couldn't restrain himself . . . and shouted across two rows of desks to . . . Woodward . . . "Not bad, Bob. Not half bad!"

The day after the resignations, one of the least expected wire service stories in my lifetime was dropped on my desk by a copy boy . . . from United Press International:

White House Press Secretary Ronald Ziegler publicly apologized today to the *Washington Post* and two of its reporters for his earlier criticism of their investigating reporting of the Watergate conspiracy.

At the White House briefing, a reporter asked Ziegler if the White House didn't owe the *Post* an apology.

"In thinking of it all at this point in time, yes," Ziegler said, "I would apologize to the *Post*, and I would apologize to Mr. Woodward and Mr. Bernstein. . . . We would all have to say that mistakes were made in terms of comments. I was over-enthusiastic in my comments about the *Post*, particularly if you look at them in the context of developments that have taken place. . . . When we are wrong, we are wrong, as we were in that case."

As Ziegler finished he started to say "But. . . ." He was cut off by a reporter who said: "Now, don't take it back, Ron."

Ron Ziegler was a small-bore man, over his head, and riding a bad horse. I feel sorrier for him today than I did then, and I'll never forget his apology, but a man can fairly be judged by the quality of his heroes, by the quality of the leaders he chooses to follow.

Just after two in the morning on May 16, 1973, I got a call from Bernstein. He was calling from a public telephone nearby, to say that he and Woodward had to see me right away. In a scene right out of a le Carré spy novel, they sat down silently in my living room and handed me a memo, written by Woodward a few hours earlier after a dramatic encounter with Deep Throat. Specifically, Deep Throat had said, "Everyone's life is in danger."

That concentrated my mind for real, and I started reading the memo:

Dean talked with Senator [Howard] Baker after Watergate Committee formed and Baker is in the bag completely, reporting back directly to White House. . . .

President threatened Dean personally and said if he ever revealed the national security activities that president would insure he went to jail.

Mitchell started doing covert national and international things early, and then involved everyone else. The list is longer than anyone could imagine.

Caulfield [one time NYC cop John J. Caulfield, who had done undercover and investigative work for the White House. met McCord and said that the president knows that we are meeting and he offers you executive clemency and you'll only have to spend about 11 months in jail.

Caulfield threatened McCord and said, "Your life is no good in this country if you don't cooperate."

The covert activities involve the whole U.S. intelligence community and are incredible. Deep Throat refused to give specifics because it is against the law.

The cover-up had little to do with Watergate, but was mainly to protect the covert operations.

The president himself has been blackmailed. When Hunt became involved, he decided that the conspirators should get some money for this. Hunt started an "extortion" racket of the rankest kind.

Cover-up cost to be about $1 million. Everyone is involved— Haldeman, Ehrlichman, the president, Dean, Mardian, Caulfield and Mitchell. They all had a problem getting the money and couldn't trust anyone, so they started raising money on the outside and chipping in their own personal funds. Mitchell couldn't meet his quota and . . . they cut Mitchell loose.

C.I.A. people can testify that Haldeman and Ehrlichman said that the president <u>orders</u> you to carry this out, meaning the Watergate cover-up . . . Walters and Helms and maybe others.

Apparently, though this is not clear, these guys in the White House were out to make money and a few of them went wild trying.

Dean acted as a go-between between Haldeman-Ehrlichman and Mitchell-LaRue.

The documents that Dean has are much more than anyone has imagined and they are quite detailed.

Liddy told Dean that they could shoot him and/or that he would shoot himself, but that he would never talk and always be a good soldier.

Hunt was key to much of the crazy stuff and he used the Watergate arrests to get money . . . first $100,000 and then kept going back for more. . . .

Unreal atmosphere around the White House—realizing it is curtains on one hand and on the other trying to laugh it off and go on with business. President has had fits of "dangerous" depression.

When I asked for details about Deep Throat's feeling that our lives were in danger, Woodward and Bernstein insisted that we move outdoors. Fear began to seep in as we talked more on my lawn. I thought I knew all about hardball, but I had never yet felt that we were dealing with hitmen. I suspected our telephones were probably being tapped, that our taxes were surely getting a world-class audit, but I had never felt physically threatened. Now they were saying that our lives were in fact in danger.

I had trouble believing it then (and now). I had no idea what to do next, except—as usual—talk with Ed Williams, and with *Post* colleagues. I met with the colleagues a few hours later—in the garden court on the eighth floor of the *Post* outside Kay Graham's office to avoid any bugs. Dick Harwood, the national editor and the man I have always wanted in my foxhole, thought we were fantasizing. Howard Simons worried that we might be being set up. Ed

Williams invoked the name of the deity a couple of times, but didn't have much concrete advice. "Watch your ass, Benjy"—as if I wasn't already looking in that direction.

Woodward and Bernstein were told to do some more reporting, to see what might emerge from Woodward's memo as "storiable"— something we could put in the paper. Slowly, information from those blessed anonymous sources began to suggest that the prosecutors and the Ervin Committee were close to concluding that Nixon himself was in on the whole affair from the beginning. It is hard to describe how much energy is involved in asking hundreds of people thousands of questions—over and over again—in search of a single unknown piece of information that might shed light on other bits of information which we felt fit into the puzzle, but didn't know where.

From the day McCord told Judge Sirica that he wanted to talk on March 23, 1973, until the president's "definitive" statement of his ignorance in the Watergate "incident" on May 22, less than two months had passed, but the Watergate story had finally exploded beyond the reach of those who would deny it, cover it up, or explain it away.

There was no bottom to the Watergate scandal. In Washington, when trouble strikes, veterans know that recovery is not possible until the worst is known, until the bottom is struck, the point after which there is no worse news coming. But there was no bottom to the Watergate scandal, and the Nixon White House was working overtime to see that none of us would ever find one.

In fact, of course, the bottom was still a long way off, as the next month proved. General Al Haig was appointed interim chief of staff, the same day John Dean revealed that he had removed certain incriminating documents from the White House when he was fired. He had put them in a safe-deposit box and turned over the key to Judge Sirica. The Ervin Committee opened its hearings on May 17. Archibald Cox was named special prosecutor the next day, and on May 22, the president gave yet another official version of his involvement, a 4,000-word statement containing more lies than information.

By now we were all exhausted. We had no other life beside Watergate. Specifically, no family life. We felt as if we were in a constant, high-stakes pitched battle. If we lost, a great newspaper's reputation would suffer mortal injuries . . . and all of us would be looking for work. The first signs of paranoia were emerging. We decided that it would be prudent if we checked for taps on our office and personal telephones. A little more than $5,000 later, we were told only that while the specialists swept our telephone wires, there were no signs that our phones were tapped. But as I left my house in Wesley Heights the next morning, there was some guy on the top of the telephone pole on the sidewalk.

"What are you up to?"

"Just checking the line."

And who's paranoid?

At the end of June, John Dean testified for four days before the Ervin Committee: he accused the Nixon White House of wiretapping, burglary, manipulating secret funds, laundering money, using enemies' lists, dirty tricks, and the so-called plumbers. His testimony was dramatic, but it was based solely on his own recollection of events. He had no documentation.

In the unfolding of the Watergate drama, none was more devastating to President Nixon than the testimony on July 13, 1973, by Alexander P. Butterfield.

Reporters are always making lists of unexplored leads, or of unquestioned actors in whatever drama is being investigated. Woodward and Bernstein were no exception. In May, they realized that Butterfield, a career Air Force officer and Nixon aide who was described by White House insiders as "in charge of internal security," was on both of their lists. Woodward had stopped by his house one night in January, but no one answered the doorbell. In May, he had asked an investigator on the Ervin Committee whether Butterfield had been questioned, and was told, "We're too busy." A couple of weeks later, Woodward bugged the committee staffer once more, pointing out that Butterfield was listed as having been in charge of "internal security" at the White House. The staffer suggested a Butterfield interview to Ervin Committee counsel Sam Dash, which was to be held on Friday, July 13.

Late on the night of Dash's interview, Woodward remembers getting a telephone call from a committee investigator, offering his congratulations—off the record. "We interviewed Butterfield," the staffer said. "He told the whole story. Nixon bugged himself."

The death knell of Richard Nixon was tolling. Only the president, Haldeman, Butterfield, Lawrence Higby (Haldeman's assistant/office manager), General Haig, and the few Secret Service agents who maintained it knew of the existence of the elaborate, voice-activated taping system, which had recorded everything the president had said, and everything anyone had said to the president. It had been installed in the spring of 1971, and was still in operation, Butterfield told the committee in executive session.

It didn't take a genius to figure out that the answers to all the unanswered questions about Watergate were hidden on those tapes . . . including the vital question: what did Nixon know and when did he know it?

If it was true.

I, for one, could not believe it when Bob Woodward called with the news late that night. How could Nixon have done it in the first place? How come he hadn't destroyed them, once he saw how much trouble he was in? How could we—*The Washington Post*, and America—be so lucky?

"How would you rate the story?" Woodward asked on the phone, a question which twenty years later still seems to have been asked for the future book or the future movie. In any case I gave it a B-plus, as Woodward is fond of reminding me, one of the cloudier calls of my career.

Two days later, it seemed like the whole country was watching television when Butterfield told the Ervin Committee everything about the taping systems "in all of the president's offices."

Next time I saw Woodward, I told him, "Okay, you bastard, it's better than a B-plus." And indeed it was.

It was the beginning of the end. It was always Richard Nixon who got Nixon, not the press, but from that moment on, the courts and the Congress had the president in their sights, and he couldn't hide.

I am still half-convinced that if Nixon had not bugged himself, if there had been no record of the president's most private conversations, Nixon would never have resigned. There would have been no "smoking gun"; there would not have been enough votes to impeach; Nixon would have survived, scarred beyond recognition, but still president.

My friend Ed Williams secretly coveted Nixon as a client. He used to joke that he would collect all the tapes in a pile on the South Lawn and set them afire. While the smoke was still wafting skyward, Williams would say with drama and style, he would have the president tell the press that he had made a terrible mistake. He had wanted the tapes to preserve the vital history of his administration. Now he had been convinced that innocent people could be hurt, since most of them were unaware they were being taped. And so he had destroyed them. Pure Ed Williams-Walter Mitty fantasy, but fascinating to contemplate.

Of course, the existence of the taped conversations was the Fail-Safe revelation of Watergate. Once they were known to exist, they could probably not be destroyed, despite Fast Eddie's fantasy advice, because destruction would constitute obstruction of justice, itself an impeachable offense. And they could not be ignored—by the politicians, by the press, or by the people.

The Washington Post had played the key role in keeping Watergate on the national agenda, almost alone for the first nine months. From the break-in on June 17, 1972, until Judge Sirica revealed his "surprise" on March 23, 1973 (McCord's revelation of White House involvement), the *Post* had been the engine behind the efforts to find out the truth behind Watergate. After McCord's letter, other engines kicked in—the Senate Watergate Committee and its hearings, other newspapers, especially the *New York Times* and the *Los Angeles Times*, plus *Time* magazine, the *Washington Star-News*, and *Newsweek*, and finally the Judiciary Committee of the House of Representatives and its dramatic impeachment hearings.

What exactly *was* the role of *The Washington Post*? I have spent many hours trying to penetrate all the truths and the mythology created by the great, new American urge to celebrate the men and women involved in the news, and come up with the answer to that question.

First, Watergate happened . . . without *The Washington Post*. Men in rubber gloves, loaded down with hundred-dollar bills, sophisticated electronic-eavesdropping devices, and walkie-talkies, broke into the office of the Democratic National Committee, and the *Post* had nothing to do with the burglary.

Second, the energy of *The Washington Post* and particularly the skill and persistence of Woodward and Bernstein fixed Watergate forever in history. Together, we kept it on the national agenda. And there the arrogance and immorality of the men around Richard Nixon were slowly illuminated—first by the *Post*, and later by many other individuals and institutions.

But Woodward and Bernstein had done the heavy lifting that brought the story to that dramatic pass—with state-of-the-art support from Katharine Graham, the owner-publisher, and four of the senior editors: managing editor Howard Simons, Metro editor Harry Rosenfeld, city editor Barry Sussman, and myself. Katharine's support was born during the labor pains that produced the Pentagon Papers. Early on in Watergate, she would come down to the city room and ask us if we were sure we knew what we were doing. Once she asked me—not in jest—"If this is such a great story, where are all the rest of the press?" But before too long she was coming down before she left almost every night, and generally once or twice more every day. What did "we" have for tomorrow, and what were "the boys" working on for the next day or two?

The boys had one unbeatable asset: they worked spectacularly hard. They would ask fifty people the same question, or they would ask one person the same question fifty times, if they had reason to believe some information was being withheld. Especially after they got us in trouble by misinterpreting Sloan's answer about whether Haldeman controlled a White House slush fund.

And, of course, Woodward had "Deep Throat," whose identity

has been hands-down the best-kept secret in the history of Washington journalism.

Throughout the years, some of the city's smartest journalists and politicians have put their minds to identifying Deep Throat, without success. General Al Haig was a popular choice for a long time, and especially when he was running for president in the 1988 race, he would beg me to state publicly that he was *not* Deep Throat. He would steam and sputter when I told him that would be hard for me to do for him, and not for anyone else. Woodward finally said publicly that Haig was not Deep Throat.

Some otherwise smart people decided Deep Throat was a composite, if he (or she) existed at all. I have always thought it should be possible to identify Deep Throat simply by entering all the information about him in *All the President's Men* into a computer, and then entering as much as possible about all the various suspects. For instance, who was not in Washington on the days that Woodward reported putting the red-flagged flower pot on his windowsill, signaling Deep Throat for a meeting.

The quality of Deep Throat's information was such that I had accepted Woodward's desire to identify him to me only by job, experience, access, and expertise. That amazes me now, given the high stakes. I don't see how I settled for that, and I would not settle for that now. But the information and the guidance he was giving Woodward were never wrong, never. And it was only after Nixon's resignation, and after Woodward and Bernstein's second book, *The Final Days*, that I felt the need for Deep Throat's name. I got it one spring day during lunch break on a bench in MacPherson Square. I have never told a soul, not even Katharine Graham, or Don Graham, who succeeded his mother as publisher in 1979. They have never asked me. I have never commented, in any way, on any name suggested to me. The fact that his identity has remained secret all these years is mystifying, and truly extraordinary. Some Doubting Thomases have pointed out that I only knew who Woodward told me Deep Throat was. To be sure. But that was good enough for me then. And now.

*   *   *

Bet me that when I die, there will be something in my obit about how *The Washington Post* "won" eighteen Pulitzer prizes while Bradlee was editor. That will be bullshit, of course, on several different levels.

First, as a standard of excellence the Pulitzer prizes are overrated and suspect. My credentials for that statement are that for eleven years, from 1969 to 1980, I was a member of the advisory board of the Pulitzer prizes, which ratifies or overrules awards made by Pulitzer Prize jurors. I resigned one year before the end of my second six-year term, to make way for *The Washington Post*'s William Raspberry, the board's first black member. The powers that be wanted a black and they had agreed on Raspberry, but they obviously could not have two people from the *Post* on a thirteen-person board. So I made the deal to keep a *Post* person on the board for another twelve years, I thought. But Bill resigned in 1986; after six years he declined to run for another six-year term. It is this board, political and establishmentarian, that clouds the prizes. Mind you, it's better to win them than lose them, but only because reporters and publishers love them. In my experience, the best entries don't win prizes more than half the time.

Second, members of the advisory board, largely publishers and editors of newspapers competing for the prizes, or waiting to buy the newspapers competing for the prizes, are deeply enmeshed in conflicts of interest. Votes are subtly, if not openly, traded between advisory board members, and while lobbying is allegedly frowned upon, the crime is lobbying and losing.

And finally, newspapers themselves win only one Pulitzer a year: the prize for public service. Reporters win all the rest. By itself *The Washington Post* won only one Pulitzer Prize during my twenty-seven years, and it goddamn near didn't win that.

Pulitzer juries meet in early spring, in the Pulitzer Prize Office of the Journalism School of Columbia University. Pause for a moment to reflect on the conflicts of interest hidden in that single sentence. Pulitzer, as in Pulitzer Prize, was Joseph Pulitzer, grandfather of Joseph Pulitzer, Jr., during my time the chairman of the advisory board, and publisher of the *St. Louis Post-Dispatch*, a regular supplicant for Pulitzer prizes. Columbia University has long had a Sulzberger on its board of trustees, and Columbia Journalism School is a regular beneficiary of Sulzberger generosity. The Sulzberger family, of course, controls the *New York Times*, a regular supplicant for, and winner of, Pulitzer prizes. One of my "favorite" moments as a member of the advisory board came during a long argument about who should win in the last of the categories to be decided that day. When the board's sentiment seemed to be drifting toward one candidate, the board's paid secretary, Richard T. Baker, reminded us all: "If we do that, it would mean that the *New York Times* would be blanked this year." God Save Us All.

In the spring of 1973, the jurors met in New York and voted to award *Washington Post* reporters *three* Pulitzer Prizes, an almost unheard-of feat. The prize for commentary went to David Broder, for his column on the American political scene. The prize for foreign reporting was shared by our Moscow correspondent Bob Kaiser, now the *Post*'s managing editor, and our Belgrade correspondent, Dan Morgan, now a staff writer for the *Post*'s national desk. And the prize for local spot news—a story reported and written on deadline—went to Bill Claiborne for his coverage of a violent prison riot. The prisoners had asked for Bill to serve as an intermediary, and he walked into the jail unprotected and unafraid.

Neither Woodward and Bernstein individually, nor the *Post* itself, was on the list of five newspapers recommended by the jury in the public service category, the biggest of the Pulitzer Prizes. In other words, the public service jurors believed that at least five newspapers had produced more important public service reporting during 1972 than *The Washington Post*. The jury had deliberated early in 1973, after McCord had told all to Judge Sirica, and the Watergate defendants had already been sentenced.

I was really furious. The reporting had been extraordinary, in the face of unparalleled lying by the President of the United States and his staff. It had produced a Senate investigation, about to start, and God knows what else, and it seemed incredible that colleagues didn't agree.

But I was also in a shit sandwich, as we graduates of ancient universities like to put it. I was more than ready to try to persuade

Katharine Graham and my peers on the paper that this was worth pulling the paper out of the prize business once and for all. But I felt I couldn't in good conscience ask Broder, Kaiser, Morgan, and Claiborne to forego what the world regarded as the premier prize of our profession. For the same reason I felt I couldn't risk offending my fellow advisory board members by telling them what I thought of the jurors' decision.

As it turned out, I didn't have to. As I entered the hallowed hall of the Journalism School Library for the ritual pre-meeting coffee and danish, Scotty Reston of the *New York Times* and Newbold Noyes of the *Washington Star* came up to me with a sense of urgency. They had been thinking things over and they had concluded that they should overrule the public service jury, and give the *Post* the Public Service Award. "You damned well deserve it," Noyes said, gracefully, for as our local competition he couldn't be happy to see the *Post* get this kind of kudos.

With my eye on the three prizes and four prizewinners already awarded us by the juries, I muttered my appreciation and shut up. And the first order of business after the meeting was called to order was to vote on giving the *Post* the Public Service Award. I had to leave the room, as board members have to do if they have any connection with any paper nominated for a prize.

Three more times I had to leave the room, while the advisory board debated awarding prizes for commentary, foreign reporting, and spot local reporting.

And two out of those three times, the bastards overruled their jurors again, this time to take prizes *away* from the *Post*. Broder kept his, but prizes awarded by the Pulitzer jurors to Bill Claiborne, and to Bob Kaiser and Dan Morgan, were cruelly rescinded by the advisory board while I was in forced seclusion. Mind you, "these bastards" were all my friends, and those of them still alive are still my friends. But there I was, back in that familiar sandwich: for fear of losing the two we had won, I couldn't risk complaining too loud about the two we had lost.

For all my grousing, my spirits were soaring. Whatever the hell we had been trying to do at the *Post* was damn well working. The new hires like Broder and Haynes Johnson were proving to be the best in the business. Katharine Graham, God bless her ballsy soul, was going to have the last laugh on all those establishment publishers and owners who had been so condescending to her, and all those Wall Street types turned statesmen who warned her every day that we were going too far, were going to respect her, not use her. Fritz Beebe, who had made everything happen for me, was going to know about what we had wrought together before he died too young one month later, of cancer.

Woodward and Bernstein were pleased, of course, when I saw them next morning, but not overjoyed. They sidled into my office "to talk," and it was quickly obvious that they had more on their minds than a mutual back-scratching session. They didn't dare get to their point right away, but pretty soon it spilled out. How come the Pulitzer Prize was awarded to the newspaper, rather than to them, Woodward and Bernstein, who had done by so much the lion's share of the reporting?

The answer was perfectly simple: newspapers win the public service Pulitzer prizes, not reporters. I told them their names will be forever associated with the story and the Pulitzer. In materials submitted with the prize announcement, the Pulitzer Committee stated that *The Washington Post* from the outset refused to dismiss the Watergate incident as a bad political joke, a mere caper.

The *Post* "mobilized its total resources for a major investigation, spearheaded by two first-rate investigative reporters, Carl Bernstein, and Robert Woodward," the announcement read. "As their disclosures developed the Watergate case into a major political scandal of national proportions, the *Post* backed them up with strong editorials, many of them written by Roger Wilkins, and editorial cartoons drawn by the two-time Pulitzer Prize winner, Herbert A. Block (Herblock)."

In fact, many others on the staff played critically important roles, especially the editorial page editor Phil Geyelin, and his deputy Meg Greenfield, and the wondrous cartoonist Herb Block. Editors, especially Simons, Rosenfeld, Sussman, and Len Downie, who was to succeed Rosenfeld as the Metro editor, and twenty years later succeed me as executive editor. Reporters like Larry Meyer. None of us, least of all Woodward or Bernstein, yet had the faintest understanding of the shadow that the Watergate reporting would cast over journalism. Woodward and Bernstein themselves were going to become cult heroes in the annals of journalism, and stay cult heroes. So it was easy to forgive them their desire to maximize their own contribution. But it was already maximum.

For the *Post*, people in the know, people in power, were already speaking of the *New York Times* and *The Washington Post* in the same breath, instead of just the *New York Times*. That had been a secret, unspoken goal of mine ever since I had returned to the paper.

Refusing to bottom out, Nixon fought one of the longest rearguard operations in the history of political warfare. The taping system was shut down in the White House on July 18, 1973. but the damage was done.

After two months of government efforts to spring the tapes and the White House efforts to resist them, the month of October 1973 felt like a newspaper career all by itself:

- The vice president, Spiro T. Agnew of Maryland, resigned in disgrace after pleading nolo contendere to tax evasion, and thereby avoiding trial on charges of bribery and corruption.
- Gerald R. Ford, of Michigan, the House Minority Leader, was nominated to succeed Agnew.
- Nixon finally succeeded in getting Special Prosecutor Archibald Cox—"that fucking Harvard professor," Nixon called him—fired by Solicitor General Robert Bork, after Attorney General Elliot Richardson refused and resigned in protest, and after Acting Attorney General William Ruckelshaus also refused to fire him, and resigned. For good measure the president abolished the whole office of the special Watergate prosecutor. What General Al Haig called a "firestorm," the rest of the world called the Saturday Night Massacre.
- In the last week of October, forty-four Watergate bills were introduced in the House of Representatives, twenty-two specifically

calling for the start of an impeachment investigation. I had tried to banish the word "impeachment" from the *Post*'s city room, figuring it would look bad to read a story about how everyone at the *Post* was talking impeachment. Now, everyone in Washington was talking impeachment.

The world had known since August that the voice of Middle America, Spiro T. Agnew, was under investigation by a Republican U.S. Attorney in Baltimore, the first sitting vice president in American history to be formally placed under criminal investigation. The *Wall Street Journal*'s Jerry Landauer and *The Washington Post*'s Richard Cohen revealed on August 8 that the investigation centered on old-fashioned political corruption charges—conspiracy, extortion, and bribery. The president, about to face obstruction of justice charges himself, wanted to force Agnew's resignation, but without offending the party's right wing, whose support he would need in his own defense in the months to come.

Attorney General Richardson hoped Agnew would resign after the evidence was described to him: various Maryland contractors and engineers were ready to testify that they had made direct payments to the vice president before *and after* he took office. In plain English, they gave him green money in brown paper bags, as he was running off at the mouth about the "nattering nabobs of negativism"—the press.

But Agnew sent his lawyers to court to claim that the Justice Department was leaking information damaging to the vice president in an attempt to force him out of office. Agnew subpoenaed the notes of reporters covering his case, including the *Post*'s Richard Cohen.

It was in a motion to quash those subpoenas that our lawyers, Ed Williams and Joe Califano, developed what was known in the *Post* city room (with admiration and affection, if not awe), as "the Gray-haired Widow Defense." Namely, reporters don't own their own notes (and therefore can't produce them in answer to a subpoena), the newspaper's owner owns the notes, just as she owns other newspaper property. In our case, it was Katharine Graham, gray-haired and widowed, and a grandmother to boot, who had volunteered. In Califano's immortal words: "The judge would throw Bradlee or Cohen in jail so fast it would make your head swim. Let's see if he has the balls to put Kay Graham in the clink."

But, more's the pity, the landmark defense died before it was born. Unbeknownst to any of us, Agnew was trying to cop a plea, and the government—represented by Richardson and the state prosecutor—was ready to deal. Agnew was sentenced to three years probation and fined $10,000.

It is a measure of the darkness of the Watergate cloud that in only a few days, Agnew was history. The country welcomed the new vice president, and returned to their seats to await the start of the final act.

Many in the Washington press corps got word about the Saturday Night Massacre at the Arlington YMCA tennis courts, just across the Potomac River in Arlington, where Art Buchwald was hosting his annual mixed-doubles tennis tournament. One by one guests were called to the telephone and returned with news about the latest firing. Finally the games had to be canceled: too many players rushed back to their offices.

I was having dinner at Chez Camille's, a favorite restaurant near the *Post*, and was called to the phone four times, before I gave up and went back to the office.

At the root of the Saturday Night Massacre lay Archie Cox's determination to get the Nixon tapes and the president's determination to keep them. Two days after he learned of their existence in July from Alexander Butterfield's testimony to the Ervin Committee, Cox had requested from J. Fred Buzhardt, the special White House Watergate counsel, the tapes of nine conversations between Nixon and John Dean, Haldeman, Mitchell, and Ehrlichman. No way, came the reply from University of Texas law professor Charles Alan Wright, serving with Buzhardt as the president's counsel in the fight for the tapes. The Ervin Committee got the same answer.

Cox then subpoenaed Nixon's lawyers, asking them to produce nine tapes of presidential conversations and meetings in court. The president refused to obey. On August 29, Judge Sirica ruled that the tapes should be turned over to him. Nixon appealed, and on October 12, the Court of Appeals backed Sirica. Now, instead of appealing the decision to the Supreme Court, Nixon decided to fire Cox.

The trouble with that idea was simple: the law creating the office of the special prosecutor decreed that only the Attorney General could fire Cox, and Richardson had given his word to Cox that he would not dismiss him except for "extraordinary improprieties." Now Richardson told the White House that he would resign rather than fire Cox.

Nixon would have to persuade Richardson to go back on his word, or fire him and find an Attorney General who would fire Cox, but first he tried one last-gasp compromise, the so-called Stennis Plan. The administration would summarize "relevant portions" of certain tapes and submit the summaries to Sirica. Senator John Stennis, a conservative Democrat from Mississippi, would be allowed to listen to the tapes themselves and authenticate the summaries to Judge Sirica. And Cox would agree not to try for more tapes. This was Nixon's plan, "not . . . to intrude on the independence of the Special Prosecutor"; but neither Cox nor Richardson would play ball.

The morning after the Saturday Night Massacre, Cox held a press conference detailing how the White House had obstructed his every effort to get information, and right after that Richardson was ordered by Haig to fire Cox. He said he would not be able to do that and asked for an appointment to see the president and resign. He got it instantly, and he quit.

Haig then called Deputy Attorney General William Ruckelshaus and ordered him to fire Cox, saying, "Your Commander-in-Chief has given you an order." Ruckelshaus refused, and he quit. The third in command at Justice was Solicitor General Robert Bork. He is said to have told Richardson and Ruckelshaus that since the White House would eventually find someone at Justice to fire Cox, he would do it, and then he, too, would resign. Richardson persuaded him to withhold his resignation so there would be someone to run the department.

But the president miscalculated the reaction to the Saturday

Night Massacre. The abolition of the special prosecutor's job was greeted by a storm of public protest. Such a storm that Haig had to find a new special prosecutor, and he found the distinguished Houston attorney, Leon Jaworski. Harvard Law Professor Raoul Berger, the recognized authority on impeachment, came right out and said it: ". . . after the events of the past few days, he must be impeached," and went on to talk about the president's "attempt . . . to set himself above the law. We just cannot permit that. It's the road to tyranny, dictatorship, Hitlerism. Democracy cannot survive if a president is allowed to take the law into his own hands."

Secretary of State Henry Kissinger, juggling Middle East peace efforts and Soviet threats, warned in a press conference that "one cannot have crises of authority in a society for a period of months without paying a price somewhere down the line," and propounded a politics of faith instead of a politics of skepticism. The press countered with accusations that the administration was manufacturing tension with the Soviets to draw attention away from Watergate.

At a press conference, reporters questioned the president more aggressively than any president has ever been questioned—before or since. And finally Nixon blew up: "I have never heard or seen such outrageous, vicious, distorted reporting in 27 years of public life. I am not blaming anybody for that. Perhaps what happened is that what we did brought it about, and therefore the media decided that they would have to take that particular line. But when people are pounded night after night with that kind of frantic, hysterical reporting, it naturally shakes their confidence."

He closed by saying, "Don't get the impression that you arouse my anger. You see, one can only be angry at those he respects."

Finally Cox's successor Leon Jaworski tried to pry the tapes loose. And loose they came with the help of Judge Sirica, the Court of Appeals, and ultimately the Supreme Court itself.

In late November, the administration had to admit that there was an 18½-minute gap in the tape of one conversation between Nixon and Haldeman . . . only three days after the Watergate burglary. Experts selected by the Court and the White House found that the gap had been caused when a segment of the conversation was manually erased between five and nine times. Nixon's secretary Rose Mary Woods took the blame. Even so, edited and unedited, bleeped and unbleeped, tapes dribbled out one by one, until the smoking gun—transcripts of three conversations between Nixon and Haldeman—was revealed months later.

The editing of the tapes that were released was self-serving, and the omissions were critical, it was learned when all the tapes were finally made public. For instance, one of the passages omitted had the president saying: "I don't give a shit what happens. I want you all to stonewall it, let them plead the Fifth Amendment, coverup, or anything else, if it'll save it—save the *whole* plan. That's the whole point."

In February 1974, the House voted, 410 to 4, to establish an impeachment inquiry. On March 1, the major Watergate indictments were returned against H. R. Haldeman; John Ehrlichman; Charles Colson; John Mitchell; Gordon Strachan, staff assistant to Haldeman; Robert Mardian, political CRP coordinator; and CRP lawyer Kenneth Parkinson.* Nixon was named as an unindicted coconspirator by the grand jury (though that was not revealed until June 6). In a grandstanding press conference at the end of April, the president produced folders filled with 1,200 pages of what he called the "transcripts," but they were edited transcripts, not true transcripts—and there were no transcripts at all of eleven of the forty-two subpoenaed tapes. The *New York Times* and *The Washington Post* rushed out quickie paperbacks, adding "expletive deleted," "limited hangout," "the big enchilada" (Ehrlichman describing Mitchell) to the Watergate vocabulary, as Barry Sussman noted in his book *The Great Coverup*, but not much else. Most of the juicy stuff, and all of the smoking guns, had been edited out.

Through the spring and early summer of 1974, Nixon and his lawyer, James St. Clair, locked horns with the Watergate special prosecutor and the House Judiciary Committee over access first to

---

* Eventually, Parkinson was acquitted, Mardian's conviction was overturned on appeal, and charges against Strachan were dropped. Colson pleaded guilty to obstruction of justice in the Ellsberg case and cooperated with the government in the investigations and trials of his former Watergate colleagues.

forty-two tapes, and finally to sixty-four more tapes. The president fled town twice in June and July, first to the Middle East and then to a summit in Russia. But no sooner had he returned than the Supreme Court settled the tapes question once and for all: By a vote of 8-0 (abstaining Justice Rehnquist, who had been an assistant attorney general in the Nixon administration, and would be Chief Justice in the Reagan administration), the Court ruled the president had to turn over the tapes.

The president was now just about out of options. If he didn't comply with the Supreme Court order to turn over the tapes, he was going to be impeached. Guaranteed. But the trouble with turning over the tapes was that they would prove the president's intimate and continuous involvement in Watergate, once and for all time. The evidence had seemed overwhelming to most reasonable men, but not to die-hard Nixon supporters. They wanted a "smoking gun," before they abandoned their chief.

And they got it in spades: the tape of a 95-minute conversation between President Nixon and his chief of staff, H. R. Haldeman, on June 23, 1972—only 48 hours after the Watergate break-in.

Haldeman, talking about their own investigation into the break-in: "We're back in the problem area, because the FBI is not under control, because [Patrick] Gray doesn't exactly know how to control them, and . . . their investigation . . . goes in some directions we don't want it to go. . . . Dean . . . concurs now with Mitchell's recommendation that the only way to solve this . . . is for us to have [Lt. General] Vernon Walters [deputy director of the CIA] call Pat Gray and just say 'Stay to hell out of this, this, ah, business here. We don't want you to go any further on it . . .' the thing to do is get them to stop."

Nixon: "All right, fine. . . . How do you call him in? I mean you just . . . Well, we protected Helms from one hell of a lot of things. . . . You call them in."

Haldeman: "Good deal."

Nixon: "Play it tough. That's the way they play it and that's the way we are going to play it."

Haldeman: "OK, we'll do it."

Nixon: "Say [to Helms and Waters] 'Look, the problem is that this will open the whole, whole Bay of Pigs thing, and the President just feels that'—ah, without going into the details. Don't lie to them to the extent to say there is no involvement, just say, 'This is a comedy of errors,' without getting into it, 'the president believes that it is going to open the whole Bay of Pigs thing up again.' And, ah, 'Because these people are plugging for keeps,' and that they should call the FBI in and say that we wish for the country, 'Don't go any further into this case. Period.'"

- The tape proved that Nixon lied when he claimed that he didn't know—until nine months later—that any of his staff had been involved in Watergate.
- The tape proved that Nixon had lied when he said questions of national security were involved in this conversation.
- The tape proved that Nixon had approved the plan for the CIA to call off the FBI's Watergate investigation, and that he lied when he said he hadn't.
- The tape put the president smack in the middle of the cover-up, beginning at least with Day Two.

Woodward and Bernstein wrote in *The Final Days* that Buzhardt called Haig in San Clemente after listening to the fatal tape to say, "It's the ball game. . . . We've found the smoking pistol." Buzhardt told Haig—as he had before—he thought the president should resign. But the president fought against his lawyer's conclusion, as he fought his special counsel, St. Clair, who now advised him to turn over the tapes.

None of the tapes had yet been produced in compliance with the Supreme Court ruling, when the House Judiciary Committee started voting on articles of impeachment. But even without the smoking gun, twenty-seven members of the judiciary, including six Republicans, voted for the first article of impeachment on July 27, charging the president with obstruction of justice in attempting to cover up Watergate. There were 11 votes against impeachment, all

Republicans. On July 29, the second article of impeachment was voted (accusing the president of misusing his powers to violate constitutional rights of U.S. citizens), with one more Republican joining those in favor of impeachment; and on July 30, a third article of impeachment was approved for defying subpoenas. The vote was 21 to 17, with two Democrats voting against and two Republicans voting for it.

Barry Goldwater had never liked Nixon personally, but had tried almost instinctively to believe that there was less to Watergate than met the eyes of most of the people he did like. By July 1974, he had stopped pretending. He told his colleagues that the Nixon presidency was finished. He had finally read the real transcripts of the real tapes themselves—though not the "smoking gun" tape—instead of relying on his "expert."

Some GOP senators were urging Goldwater and Senate Minority Leader Hugh Scott to go down to the White House and tell Nixon he had to resign. Goldwater was reluctant, but he knew he had to be ready to do it. On the afternoon of Monday, August 5, 1974, Dean Burch, Nixon's political counselor, brought Goldwater a copy of the killer tape. And the senator blew his stack, angry at himself for having supported Nixon for so long.

James Cannon in *Time and Chance* freezes the moment Nixon knew he was doomed. It was July 23, when Nixon called Governor George Wallace of Alabama to ask him to persuade Alabama Congressman Walter Flowers to vote against impeachment. Wallace told the president he felt such a call was inappropriate, because he, Wallace, was no longer with the president.

"There goes the Presidency," Nixon said to Al Haig, according to Cannon.

But these historical precisions were not yet available to us daily historians. At the *Post* we were frustrated almost to the breaking point, not wanting to miss the ending of the story in which we had such a proprietary interest, but not wanting to screw that ending up by reporting rumors that had every chance of being only half-true and misleading.

About this time, I invited Senator Goldwater to a Redskins game, and he showed up with a thirty-page "analysis" of the tapes, written, he said, by "one of the smartest lawyers this town has ever seen."

Goldwater and I had become pals from the day we first met during his run for the presidency in 1963—strange bedfellows to our other friends. I didn't care for most of his judgments, nor he for mine, but I found in him basic virtues—loyalty, dignity, friendship, outspoken honesty—that I much admired. Once he persuaded me to debate him at some black-tie reunion of his conservative pals in Orange County. The Goldwater faithful showed up in droves, convinced they were going to see a pig-sticking. When Goldy started his remarks by saying something incredibly complimentary about me, his pals groaned their disapproval, and the pig-sticking never got off the ground.

After the game (Redskins 33, 49ers 9), I read the analysis, and found it just awful and dishonest, leaving out virtually all conversations that didn't fit the analyst's conclusion that Nixon was an innocent, and taking out of context bits of conversations that helped. Next time I saw Goldwater, I asked him if *he* had read the documents, and he smiled sheepishly, and said no. I didn't know then what I know now: Goldwater was poorly served by what was generally agreed to be the worst staff on the Hill.

Most of us now felt Nixon would be impeached if he did not resign, and so we concluded that he would resign, but throughout the last week facts were hard to come by. But maybe for the first time, we were feeling that we could afford to wait for the news to happen. We no longer worried that Watergate would remain unresolved. It would be resolved, and in a way that vindicated our reporting. Nixon was going to go one way or another. Goldwater was yelling as much to me. "He's going to go," he said. "I'm not sure even he knows how or when. But I know for damn sure that if you guys come out with a story that he has made up his mind to resign, he won't." Goldwater was asking us (he was asking *me*) to report whatever rumors we chose to report—and we reported plenty—but to say only that the president hadn't made up his mind.

I was really torn. First off, we did *not* know what he was going to do, or how he was going to do it. And yet, we all had had so much riding on Watergate for so long, I was going to make damn sure we did nothing to jeopardize our position.

Here are the *Post*'s page-one banner headlines from Tuesday, August 6, 1974, through resignation. August 6: "PRESIDENT ADMITS WITHHOLDING DATA; TAPES SHOW HE APPROVED COVER-UP"; August 7: "NIXON SAYS HE WON'T RESIGN"; August 8: "NIXON RESIGNATION SEEN NEAR"; August 9: "NIXON RESIGNS."

Goldwater was working privately on the GOP hierarchy, arguing that "the best thing that he can do for his country is to get the hell out of the White House." On Wednesday, August 7, Goldwater, Scott, and House Minority Leader John J. Rhodes were ushered into the president's office at 5:00 P.M. Goldwater was the group's spokesman, and he followed Haig's advice to him, and his own advice to me: play it cool, no ultimatums, no recommendations.

At first Goldwater had estimated Nixon's strength in the Senate at 12 to 15 votes. Now, he tightened the screws, telling the president that he had taken a nose count that morning. "I couldn't find more than four very firm votes, and those would be from the older Southerners," he added.*

"Some are very worried about what's been going on, and are undecided, and I'm one of them," Goldwater went on. When they met the press forty-five minutes later, Goldwater lied. He said they had taken no nose counts, and that most of the senators, including himself, had not made up their minds.

And the president had lied to the Republican leaders. He had made up his mind to resign, and gave the news to his saddened family just before 7:00 P.M. that evening.

We went to press that night saying only that Nixon's resignation seemed imminent, although we all felt he would resign next day. All day on the 8th, beginning at 9:30 A.M., when the White House reserved TV air time for 9:00 P.M. that night, the signs piled up

---

* Quoted in an interview with Woodward and Bernstein, and reported in their book *The Final Days*.

that Nixon was going to resign. A meeting between the president and the congressional leaders was scheduled for early evening. Yellow plastic lines went up around the Fords' house in Alexandria. Someone heard that a military plane was flying Chief Justice Burger back from Europe—presumably to swear in the new president. I had decided that from that morning until further notice, no television cameras, no still photographers, and for the next forty-eight hours, no *non-Post* reporters would be allowed in the city room. I wanted no stories that might have suggested elation, vindication, or anything but professionalism. Our reputation had been on the line for more than two years. We had been at the center of the most important political story of our lives, and we were all exhausted. I wanted to be sure that we didn't intrude on the story in the final moments.

We had a twenty-four-page supplement, "The Nixon Years," in type for the moment of need, and we had laid out page one with a huge "NIXON RESIGNS" across eight columns. We didn't have type big enough to fit, so we set "NIXON RESIGNS" in the largest type we had, printed the two words on glossy paper, then photographed them, enlarged them, and spaced them to fill out the 168-point type, the first since March 5, 1953: "STALIN IS DEAD."

When it finally happened, when the president said, "Therefore, I shall resign the presidency effective at noon tomorrow," I remember folding my hands together between my knees and laying my forehead down on my desk for a very private "Holy Moly."

It is no mean feat under great pressure to get the fruits of a 9:00 P.M. press conference into the first edition of a morning newspaper. A reporter must take notes and quotes from the TV screen until about five minutes before the end, when he must start his story. The pros generally complete the first edition story within minutes of the end of the press conference, and Carroll Kilpatrick performed that feat:

> Richard Milhous Nixon announced last night that he will resign as the 37th President of the United States at noon today.
>
> Vice President Gerald R. Ford of Michigan will take the oath as the new President at noon to complete the remaining two years of Nixon's term.

After two years of bitter public debate over the Watergate scandals, President Nixon bowed to pressures from the public and leaders of his party to become the first President in American history to resign.

We had no picture symbolizing the dramatic moment for the first edition, but we had White House photographer Ollie Atkins's remarkable, poignant picture of the president tightly clasping his daughter, Julie Eisenhower, before his resignation—played half the page wide and half the page deep—for the later editions.

After Kilpatrick's lead, Jules Witcover wrote a column entitled "Ford Assumes Presidency Today." Dick Harwood and Haynes Johnson wrote "A Solemn Change," an evocative piece about the mood and meaning of it all:

When the day finally came, the anger and tensions and recriminations that had so enveloped this capital for weeks had been subdued in the solemnity of change. A sense of calm and a tenuous spirit of conciliation began to emerge.

I dragged my weary bones down one floor to the composing room, not wanting to let go of the most important single newspaper edition I ever had anything to do with. George Kidwell was making up page one, and he made sure I had nothing to do except practice reading the lead type upside down.

Woodward and Bernstein, and the Metro editors led by assistant managing editor Len Downie, who had taken over day-to-day control of the story, the men who had taken us all this way almost by themselves, had gone strangely silent after writing the story three days earlier about the smoking gun tape. The National staff was the best in the business at sweep and meaning, but the Metro staff did the landmark reporting, and the whole world knew it.

From June of 1972, the night of the break-in, to August of 1974 and Nixon's resignation, the Watergate story and The Washington Post were inextricably linked. Nixon—not the Post—"got" Nixon, but the Post's reporting forced the story onto the national agenda, and kept it there until the world understood how grievously the Constitution was being undermined. Inside the *Post*, the reporting of Woodward and Bernstein was overwhelmingly important. The care and determination of the editors involved—Bradlee, Simons, Sussman, Downie, and Rosenfeld—was vital, especially in our refusal to let the story die. The support of the owners—especially under the hostile threats of the administration—was state-of-the-art, never equaled in journalism to my knowledge.

Newspapering deals with small daily bites from a fruit of indeterminate size. It may take dozens of bites before you are sure it's an apple. Dozens and dozens more bites before you have any real idea how big the apple might be. It was that way with Watergate.

The politicians involved quickly paid a terrible price. Whatever else they accomplished in their lives, the leads of their obituaries stressed and will stress their infamous roles in Watergate:

> The death of Richard Milhous Nixon, the most controversial and paradoxical of all American presidents, occurred 20 years after he became the first American chief executive forced to resign his office under threat of impeachment. . . .
> —*The Washington Post, April 23, 1994*

> H. R. "Bob" Haldeman, 67, President Richard M. Nixon's White House chief of staff and key figure in the Watergate scandal that forced Nixon to resign from his presidency, died of cancer yesterday at his home in Santa Barbara, California.
> —*The Washington Post, November 13, 1993*

Richard Nixon was disgraced and devastated, relegated to his own special Hell, forced out of office to avoid impeachment, and no one to blame but himself. The zealots—Charles Colson, John Ehrlichman, H. R. Haldeman, Howard Hunt, and Gordon Liddy—were disgraced and jailed, done in by their sense that they were above the law, and the arrogance they shared with Nixon. The amateurs—sanctimonious veterans of business, like Attorney General

John Mitchell and Commerce Secretary Maurice Stans, and the rosy-cheeked neophytes like John Dean, Dwight Chapin, Donald Segretti, Egil Krogh, and Jeb Magruder—were victims of their own indiscriminate ambition.

But for the politicians who rode the wave into Washington after Watergate, the lessons they seem to have learned have boiled down to this: Don't get caught. And they haven't learned that lesson all that well. (Nixon once told political expert Len Garment, his friend and lawyer, "You'll never make it in politics; you don't know how to lie.") In the ten years immediately following Nixon's disgrace, the number of federal officials convicted of federal crimes rose from 43 in 1975 to 429 in 1984. And that doesn't even include the Iran-Contra scandals and cover-ups.

It is on the young people of America and on the press itself—especially on *The Washington Post*—that the legacy of Watergate has been most profound.

At first Watergate pushed the press up the ladder of national esteem. The best journalists were already respected, especially the Washington correspondents and the foreign correspondents. But Watergate gave local journalists—specifically at *The Washington Post*—an almost heroic cast, especially to the youth of America. Students in high schools and colleges waiting to make those dreaded career decisions became fascinated by journalism. Journalism school enrollments shot up. It is one of the great ironies that Richard Nixon, of all people, attracted an entire generation of able, young, tough activists into journalism, a business he never understood and never liked. And with them came the reform politicians who were so appalled by the excesses of the Nixon administration in 1973 and 1974.

We were at stage center, like it or not. And our first efforts to stay pure and uncorrupted were naive, at best, and ineffective. We had banned all public discussion of impeachment for the months it was slowly coming out of the closet. I had beseeched all concerned not to do anything that might be interpreted as gloating, or even pleasure. This was hard.

After Nixon resigned, we banned all cameras, lights, and (non-

Post) reporters from the newsroom, and made it stick. Our efforts to keep our own reporters and editors off television collapsed. When one reporter declines to talk to another reporter, war is declared, and before peace breaks out, everyone is talking to everyone else. Common sense is lost in the din.

The new folk heroes, Woodward and Bernstein, became an overnight industry, profiled in magazine after magazine, giving speeches all over the country, and working overtime on their books. Carl and Bob interviewed all of us who had been involved with Watergate coverage, and one by one we were subjected to the same techniques that had so bugged Bob Dole and Clark MacGregor. You really haven't been interviewed until you have sat across from Woodward and Bernstein. Bob with his square, all-American mid-western 4-H friendliness disguising, for the most part, the relentless determination that is his trademark. Carl with his Hippy, conspiratorial, *Rolling Stone* exterior disguising his inventive, intuitive, analytical technique.

FIFTEEN

AFTER WATERGATE

Sometime during Watergate—it could have started a few months before or after the break-in—I started getting anonymous notes, maybe five or six in all, written in pencil on scrap paper. The handwriting was almost illegible, but no matter how much I tried to come up with another description, they were plainly flirtatious—short, cryptic messages suggesting a crush that was getting harder and harder to handle, not to say out of control. They were reserved, proper in every way—and rattling.

My fantasy life is healthy and vivid about persons of the opposite sex, but I wasn't ready to admit that this was a fantasy that might develop into something else. I have identified with Thurber's Walter Mitty ever since the book was published, and to this day, for instance, I am unable to walk across a bridge over the Seine River without looking down and fantasizing, however briefly, about tearing off my shoes and jacket and leaping in to save the life of some damsel in distress. It seemed unlikely that any *Post* journalist, trained as all of them were to be direct, liberated, and outspoken, would feel comfortable with anonymous notes. It felt even more unlikely that anyone would target me, still widely if erroneously assumed to be one half of a latter-day Darby and Joan couple.

And the *Post* had recently gone through a spell of unpleasant anonymous letters, to me, to Katharine Graham and others, asking insider questions calculated to sow dissent and raise suspicions. We had turned these anonymous notes over to Ed Williams, even though we thought they were the work of a secretary who had been canned.

The mild paranoia which infected us all during Watergate suggested that the people who brought you the Canuck letter, who tried to sell grass to Bernstein at 16th and K streets at high noon, and who had perfected their dirty trick skills, were certainly capable of phonying up some mash notes to the editor of the despised *Post*. And so I pretty much put them out of my mind a few days after receiving them.

But not before I spent some private time going through an alphabetized staff list for possible authors. Like Walter Mitty before me, I lingered occasionally here and there, wondering. The names are no longer important. Enough to say that when I got to the Qs, I lingered over the name of the enchanting and talented Sally Quinn, the new star of the Style Section, with whom I now realized I had been flirting. But she was too young, and the latest rumor had her quitting us to become the first woman anchor on the "CBS Morning News." CBS president William Paley was under pressure to name a female anchor for the morning news show, and he had charged my old friend Gordon Manning with finding one.

I had long since perfected the art of "hanging out" in the newsroom—schmoozing my way from one group to another, listening, gossiping, encouraging, asking reporters what the people they were writing about were really like. Hanging out was the best part of my day, maybe even the best part of my job. The Style Section was particularly fertile territory for hanging out. The reporters were brasher, less respectful of any authority, less impressed with the paper's—and their own—power. Sally Quinn and Phil Casey sat at adjoining desks and it was an especially productive place to hang out. Quinn was prettier, Casey was funnier. Together they were always intriguing to talk to, even though Sally insisted on calling me "Mr. Bradlee," and did until the day she quit the *Post* for CBS in June of 1973.

I had first met Sally when Phil Geyelin introduced her to me after he interviewed her for a job as secretary to the editorial page editor. I advised him against hiring her, and not just because she couldn't take shorthand. Speaking for myself, I suggested to Phil that anyone that attractive could make work difficult.

But a month or so later, when the *Post* was desperately looking for someone to cover the parties that form the backbone of the anthropology of Washington, Sally Quinn's name resurfaced. She was perfectly suited for the job, except for one small problem: she had never written a word in her life. She was a young Army brat who had worked as the social secretary for the Algerian ambassador, Cherif Guelal. She had worked in Bobby Kennedy's 1968 campaign, and she knew everyone in town. It was reported that I said, "Well, nobody's perfect," when she revealed her complete lack of experience. Actually, Phil Geyelin said it when I told him that this time I was thinking of hiring her.

Anyway, she was hired, and soon had patented the sassy, irreverent, insightful profile, where the interviewee provides the ammunition and the interviewer pulls the trigger. Under Tom Kendrick, and later Shelby Coffey, the Style Section had gathered under one roof a unique collection of young "new journalists," like B. J. Phillips, Myra McPherson, and Nick von Hoffman, to name just a few, who wrote with vitality, imagery, and humor. They knew their subjects, and they shared their insights with great flair.

Sally wrote some memorable profiles of people enjoying their fifteen minutes of fame, and some signature pieces about Washington institutions—high and low—with irreverence, insight, and wit. She had an amazing ability to get people to talk about themselves. Henry Kissinger once said he felt like killing Maxine Cheshire after she wrote about him, but he felt like committing suicide after Sally Quinn wrote about him.

Here are takes from some of Sally's most memorable profiles:

On stripper Sally Rand: She's a tough old broad, and she'd be the first to say so. She has a healthy respect for herself, and pride in what she does, a deep understanding and acceptance of the good and the bad, a certain simplicity that belies her sophisticated demeanor and a well-developed ability to laugh. She is tiny (size 7, junior petite) and makes many of her own clothes. She wears backless stiletto heels, short, short skirts to show off her still extraordinary legs, and a lot of make-up which doesn't quite hide the extensive face-lift scars. She is vain, exercises constantly when she is not working, and won't sunbathe except in the nude. "Otherwise my tits look like headlights."

On "Big Ruby" Folsom Ellis Austin, George Wallace's mother-in-law, after her daughter Cornelia had said, "Ah got the only bachelor in Montgomery, and ah'm scared to death Mama's gonna go after George." *Replied Big Ruby:* "Ah been lookin' for a husband for two years, ever since Dr. Austin died, but there's slim pickins in Montgomery. There ain't nothin' here. Shoooot, honey, [George] ain't even titty high."

On the Washington Affair: For the mistress there is the pleasure of having and exerting power over a man who is powerful himself. For the wife, there is the title, the social status and the money. And for the man himself, there is the satisfaction of having his needs met by two women. In the Washington Affair there is something for everyone.

On President Carter's friend and Budget Director Bert Lance: You've seen Bert Lance before. At first, you can't remember where. Then it comes to you. It was somewhere in the Middle East in the market place. He was dressed in a *djellabah* and turban, standing behind his stall. He was trying to sell you a camel. Cheap. And you were in the process of haggling with him until it occurred to you that you didn't actually need a camel. So you bought a rug from him instead. Very cheap. He was losing money, he was going to the poorhouse. His family was going to starve because of the low price he was giving you. His eyes were dancing as he rubbed his hands in mock despair. You paid him the money, much more than the rug was worth. He beamed and blessed you as you walked away. Strangely, you felt good, even though you knew you'd been had.

On ballet star Rudolph Nureyev: [He] has those high Tatar cheekbones, the slightly slanting eyes, the full cruel mouth slashed by an old scar, the taut muscular body, strong but gentle hands, tousled brown hair, and a provocative half-mischievous, half-soulful look in his eye. And, of course, there is his behind. He has a fabulous behind.

I watched her get better with each piece, surer and surer of her skills, as she became one of the paper's brightest new stars. Until on June 23, 1973, she announced that she was leaving the *Post* to take the CBS job. She would join the wonderful Hughes Rudd as the CBS answer to Barbara Walters and "The Today Show." As hard as I worked to attract the talented people to the *Post,* I hated to see any of them leave, and so I asked her if I could try to dissuade her at lunch. She agreed, still calling me "Mr. Bradlee."

It was a difficult lunch for both of us. Before I could even begin my spiel, she asked me if I knew why she was leaving . . . she was the author of the anonymous notes and she was in love with me. And I was stunned, but flattered. And vulnerable. Tony had come to feel that much of journalism was shallow, dwelling as much as journalism does on the sudden and dramatic, in preference to the meaningful and the good. She was more and more involved with The Work. I had all but lost any real hope of recapturing the delight we had shared. And I had never seen any chance to fall in love with Sally.

My efforts to persuade Sally to stay were ardent but unsuccessful. She left for New York the next day.

But her career as the "CBS Morning News" co-anchor with Rudd was doomed from the start, from a combination of her inexperience and CBS's decision to throw her into this high-profile slot without giving her that experience. The message I got was simple: The sisters want a woman anchor? Okay, here's one, and let's see how she does. I thought Hughes Rudd was superb—crusty, funny, original—and I thought the chemistry between them was great. Sally floundered a little at the start—she had a temperature of 104° the first morning—but the comfort level seemed to me to improve every day. When the plug got pulled just a few months later, their ratings were 1.6 and a 14 share. More than twenty years later, the "CBS Morning News," now called "CBS This Morning," still rates the lowest of all the networks' morning shows.

But I had reached another one of those critical forks in the road. One way involved staying with Tony, the woman I had once loved, the mother of two of my children, and trying to rekindle happiness. The other way involved recognizing that I had fallen in love, and that meant exploring a different life with Sally—a life that promised excitement, mutual enthusiasms, and all the rewards of shared goals. It didn't help much to understand that this fork in the road was not so different from the one I had faced nineteen years earlier in France. Or that people were going to be sad again. Tony had said she wished I had not come back from Vietnam and Japan two years earlier, but that didn't mean she wanted me to leave now.

My solution was to move into a hotel for a month and then into an apartment in the Watergate complex. Sally joined me there, after her CBS gig was terminated in October 1973. She had decided to turn her ill-fated tour as a network anchor into a funny book, called *We're Going to Make You a Star,* and had found another job— in the Washington Bureau of the *New York Times.* I thought this was a rotten idea; I felt the *Times* was too stuffy to take advantage of Sally's special skills. I dreaded reading her pungent social commentaries and profiles in the competition, especially that competition. But hiring a girlfriend, even rehiring a girlfriend, carried its own special baggage.

And I was right about the *Times.* When their managing editor, Clifton Daniel, hired Sally, she told him she had agreed to write one last piece on a freelance basis for the *Post,* a profile of Washington's super-quotable grande dame, Alice Roosevelt Longworth. Daniel agreed, but then just after the story appeared, he called her to say that "we at the *Times* are shocked" at what he called her lack of sensitivity for having accepted the *Post* assignment. Their relations would never again be cordial. The story appeared on a Tuesday, too long and too juicy for the *Times*, everyone agreed—Mrs. L. talked at some length about lesbianism, and "dear old men's things," meaning penises—and the town talked about nothing else for days.

That left the girlfriend problem. I told Howard Simons I had to recuse myself, but if he and Shelby Coffey, the Style editor, wanted to hire her, they could be my guest. On Tuesday afternoon, Simons called Sally in to say it was ridiculous for her to work for the *Times*, offered her her old job back, and she accepted. That solved the girlfriend problem, though she was invariably described as "Bradlee's live-in girlfriend" by the Washington newspapers, especially the *Washington Star*'s gossip column, "The Ear."

It was the fall of 1973, spang in the middle of Watergate, the most important newspaper story of the generation. I was fifty-two years old, the father of three: Ben, Jr., age twenty-five; Dino, about to be fifteen; and Marina, about to be thirteen. Sally was twenty years younger, never married, but just finishing a long-term relationship with a New York newspaperman. Once again, explaining my new situation to my children was painful beyond description. I remembered reading somewhere that the best way of dealing with children's anger in these circumstances was to encourage that anger, to expose yourself to it. And I did. Dino was the angriest. At least he expressed his anger the most, when I went out to see the children one evening. He was down in a basement workshop, making quality leather purses, briefcases, and wallets. He hammered, and cut and smoothed and oiled, almost in silence, as I tried to explain about happiness, how wonderful it was to enjoy, and how sad it was to live without it.

Dino and I worked it out in a matter of months. He was so sad, but I think he understood. Marina pretended to understand from the beginning. Friendship with Sally—true friendship—came later, but it came. It took Tony and me five years to become friends again: the day she called out of the blue to say that whatever had happened between us was as much her fault as it was mine.

But before that, Sally and I had started an exciting life. Watergate was resolved. Nixon was gone, and part of me looked at the future with some apprehension.

Sally Quinn electrified my private life the minute she stopped calling me "Mr. Bradlee." She brought a sense of excitement and a sense of humor with her, plus a refreshing, feisty conviction that life should be contested and enjoyed, as well as shared. She found the all-consuming nature of my involvement with the *Post* natural, even exhilarating. When she returned to the *Post*, she brought her unique talent to the Style Section, sweeping into uncharted waters with confidence and style.

We lived together for a year on the fourteenth floor of the Watergate complex, overlooking the Potomac River. There was something right about the address, I thought. Then Sally figured she would rather have me be a guest in her house than be a guest in my house, in case our relationship disintegrated. That sounded unthreatening, even appropriate, to me. I liked the combination I sensed of feminine and feminist at the same time. Using money earned from her book, Sally bought a great house on 21st Street, off Dupont Circle, in the middle of the neighborhood where our friend and colleague Larry Stern was the unofficial mayor.

Sally and I went quietly about our new life of discovery and excitement, and involvement in each other's work. At first there was no talk of marriage, and hence no rush to divorce. Sally had bought into that part of the feminist rhetoric that said a relationship didn't depend on a piece of paper. But eventually, the question of marriage did arise, carefully at first, then insistently. I found it harder and harder to say I would not give to one person I loved, what I had given to two other women I had once loved. And deep down, I was head over heels crazy about Sally Quinn and our life together.

As my profile had inched upward, the gossip magazines became inordinately interested in our relationship. Once, confronted for

the umpteenth time by some goddamn reporter, I said I would
marry Sally when they elected a Polish pope, which of course could
never happen. Five years later, the Polish Cardinal Karol Wojtyla
was elected pope on October 16, 1978, the first non-Italian pope
in 456 years. (And true to my word, Sally and I were married four
days later.)

Just as Sally and I began to realize that we might have an exciting
future, it began to dawn on me that my professional future would
probably not include anything as exciting as Watergate. Stories like
that show up once in a career. But how were we collectively going
to get it up for the bread-and-butter stories that newspapers must
give their readers? How were we going to keep reporters and editors
down on the farm, after they'd seen Paree. Not just Woodward and
Bernstein, or Bradlee and Simons, but the whole staff wore the *Post's*
achievements, our new eminence, on its sleeve. Now, it seemed as if
we were back to county council meetings, and Boards of Education
sessions, routine crimes and legislative actions.

I felt the need of a new project, tackling something completely
different, and during one of the many times I thought of how much
John Kennedy would have enjoyed Watergate, and my involvement in Watergate, I wondered if writing about Kennedy might
be that something completely different. I didn't have the access
or the inclination to do a scholarly account of his presidency. Sorensen and Schlesinger had done the definitive biographies, but
I did have notes of conversations with the president, dictated in
stream-of-consciousness form. Over a period of five years, but more
scrupulously during his 1,000-day presidency, I had scribbled down
notes of what we had talked about during more than 125 conversations. Some of them, one- or two-minute telephone calls, some of
them over two- and three-hour dinners with Tony and Jackie in the
White House, and some of them during weekends at Newport, Palm
Beach, or Camp David. I had dictated from these notes as soon as
possible, generally the next morning, re-creating our conversations,
and they totaled about 35,000 words. I had used most of what we
talked about in my weekly files to *Newsweek*. I had not looked at

them since the assassination. I looked at them now and I began to wonder if they might make a book.

Haynes Johnson read the notes and said encouraging things. He also put me in touch with his publisher, Eric Swenson of W. W. Norton & Co. Before too long, there was a $100,000 contract for *Conversations with Kennedy*. (Sometimes I wish I had called it *Notes for the Kennedy Biographers*, which it certainly has become.)

After Watergate, Katharine Graham had given Howard Simons and myself three months off—with pay. So, two days after Nixon resigned, I took off for the foothills of West Virginia to Seldom Seen, the log cabin I had bought in 1966, overlooking the Cacapon River 100 miles west of Washington. It was called "Seldom Seen" because it was seldom seen by anyone—two miles off a state highway down a dirt road, more than occasionally under water. There by myself and increasingly with young Dino, I had rediscovered my love of working in the woods, bush-hogging, brush-burning, and chainsawing my way to an empty mind. I didn't just unclutter my mind. I emptied it, and found peace.

Now, I was alone—even the telephone wasn't working—and I began to review my notes. I expressed my judgment of Kennedy in November 1974, eleven years after his death, in the last paragraph of the Introduction to *Conversations*.

> His brief time in power seems to me now to have been filled more with hope and promise than performance. But the hope and promise that he held for America were real, and they have not been approached since his death.

I still believe that. But thirty years after his death, and after hundreds and hundreds of revelations, and scores of assessments and appreciations, new material has convinced me

- that Kennedy screwed around. A lot. That is interesting, particularly to those of us who were unaware of this proclivity during his lifetime, and to those of us who know something about screwing around, but it is hardly disqualifying.

- that Kennedy was sicker with various stomach and back ailments than I had ever imagined.
- that Kennedy had fewer convictions than I thought. As Richard Reeves puts it, Kennedy "had little ideology . . . and . . . less emotion. What convictions he did have . . . he was often willing to suspend, particularly if that avoided confrontation . . . or the risk of being called soft."
- that Kennedy compartmentalized his life, more than I had known. No one of his friends—or biographers—knew all about him.
- that the truth about Kennedy, like all truths, emerges slowly, revealing itself more to the next generation than the last, more to the last researcher than the first. I suspect that will continue. It always has.

Alone in the woods, I fell into a simple routine: Up at six, a big breakfast of bacon and eggs, and at the typewriter on the front porch by seven-thirty. I worked straight through until one o'clock, typing so hard and fast that my fingers hurt. After a sandwich, I'd head for the woods with ax and chainsaw to attack the clearing project of the day. This was a primitive country cabin, and the clearing projects were endless. I worked in the woods until I was exhausted. Then a shower and supper about six, generally a can of corned beef hash, a glass of milk, and a fresh tomato. In the sack in full daylight, listening to Chuck Thompson, the Orioles baseball announcer, for at least a few innings.

I stayed up there for twenty-three days, the longest I had ever been alone, going a little bit stir crazy in all that silence, stir crazy enough to feel the need to go down to Melvin McDonald's country store ten miles away, even if I didn't need provisions. But I was getting four or five thousand words of prose a day out of those notes—and I was clearing a lot of land.

Halfway through one sunny work morning, I got the scare of my life, literally. Typing away, I suddenly saw something move in the woods to my left, about 50 yards away. A deer, I thought at first. But suddenly, I realized the "deer" was wearing a black Amish-looking hat, walking slowly up the hill toward me, and carrying a rifle, bro-

ken over his left forearm. I remember thinking with mild apprehension that it wasn't hunting season for any critter I knew about, as if
hunters up there gave much of a damn about hunting seasons.

He drew nearer and nearer without saying a word, until finally I
broke the silence with my most casual "Howdy." He grunted, and I
asked him what he was looking for.

"Squirrels," he said.

"Haven't seen many for a year or two," I countered, my eyes on
that gun. And then he asked:

"You Ben Bradlee?"

What the hell was he doing up there, poaching on my land? A
stranger who knew my name. There wasn't a living soul within two
miles of us, and my heart began to speed up.

"Yes, I am," I said. "I'm writing a book. It's so nice and peaceful
around here; I can get a lot of work done."

"A book about Watergate?" he asked. By now he was about ten
yards away, just standing there.

"No, it isn't. It's about President Kennedy," I told him, but I didn't
feel much better. If this guy didn't like what happened to President
Nixon, he probably didn't care for President Kennedy much.

Long silence.

"Well," he went on, "I might as well say it. I hated everything
you guys did to Nixon." And right then I felt I was going to get
drilled between the eyes. They wouldn't find my body for weeks,
and by then it would have been picked clean by the raccoons, or
the bears. (One had been seen recently, hadn't it?) I didn't own a
gun. Never had. There was nothing on the porch I could use to
defend myself except a half full cup of cold coffee. All I could do
was talk.

What did he do for a living? Just been laid off at the Mack Truck
assembly plant in Hagerstown. Know my friend (and Seldom Seen
neighbor) Bob Harden, an assistant night foreman up there? No.
Know anyone up here? The postman who owned a cabin across the
river.

He told me that he and his friends at work were members of

something that sounded a lot like the Ku Klux Klan. Not reassuring, I thought, and started talking about how so many juries had found wrongdoing. It wasn't just *The Washington Post*. All the congressmen, Republicans and Democrats, on the committee who had voted to impeach the president. He just stood there. Not moving. And then he started to walk slowly behind the cabin and on into the woods, never to be seen again.

Ten days later I packed it in, drove back to Washington, stopping off at the barber's to remove three weeks of beard, and the book was substantially done. But it hadn't been a relaxing time, and Sally and I were looking forward to a trip to the one place in the world we figured no one had ever heard of Watergate . . . the Brazilian jungle.

The editor of the *Jornal de Brasilia*, a new liberal daily in the incredible new city carved, from nothing, out of the surrounding savannah, had asked me to inaugurate a lecture series in February. He wanted the Watergate editor to talk about freedom of the press to an audience with no track record of devotion to freedom of the press. The fee was two round-trip first-class tickets on Varig Airlines, and that focused our minds on Brazil. That and the fact that it would be Carnival time. My friend Hector Luisi, the Uruguayan Ambassador to the United States, put us in touch with a remarkable professor of cultural anthropology in Bahia. He showed us his wonderful world, and we danced in the streets with strangers-turned-friends for days and nights. I think Bahia is the only place I've ever been where blacks and whites lived in what appeared to us joyous harmony. (There are more than seventy words to describe different degrees of blackness in Bahia.) We had to go to Rio to get to Brasilia, so we danced in the streets there one night, too, and were almost crushed to death.

As we came down the ramp at Brasilia, we were greeted by two men, obviously reporters. Actually, they were new Brazilians, from East Germany. Their first question was intended to explore my feelings about whether the Germanic origins of Haldeman and Ehrlichman played a significant role in the Watergate scandal. I was stunned by the question, and by their inane interpretation of

Watergate. Apparently there was to be no escape, and there never really has been.

The audience for my speech turned out to be all male, mostly the politicians who had nothing better to do at night in this sterile city. They seemed more interested in Sally, who had been reluctantly asked (she was the only female guest), than in my impassioned pleadings for any freedom which would include the possibility of bringing down a president. One of the guests was Senator José Sarney. When I saw him next on a trip to the Brazilian rain forest fourteen years later, he was president of Brazil.

From Brasilia we flew to Manaus, 3,000 miles up the Amazon River from Rio on the Atlantic coast, as far as Los Angeles is from Washington, and yet only halfway across this enormous country. Manaus had been the rubber capital of the world, until Goodyear invented synthetic rubber at the beginning of World War II. It had become a ghost town, its lovely Opera House, where the Swedish Nightingale, Jenny Lind, had come up the Amazon by boat from Australia to sing, now baking mostly empty in the sun. Manaus lies at the confluence of the crystal-clear Río Negro and the muddy Amazon, and we had hoped to board an *African Queen*–type tramp steamer to cruise up the Amazon toward Iquitos, on the Peruvian border, stopping to explore jungle villages along the way. But the *African Queen*–type tramp steamer had sunk without a trace, sometime between the day we made reservations and the day we were due aboard.

Instead, we boarded a 15-foot motorboat for a three-hour trip upriver, dodging giant teak logs, barely submerged, and giant floating islands of clotted hyacinth plants. Sally and I were still in the early stages of our relationship, and I was still learning critical truths about this relationship. All things considered, Ms. Quinn prefers to travel in a private plane, with many pilots, and many engines. Near the bottom of her list of preferred transportation would be a 15-foot motorboat, whose gunwales are only a few inches above a swiftly flowing, muddy river filled with unseen dangers (like piranhas?), untold miles from a Ritz Hotel.

And things were going to get worse. When we got to our "hotel," it turned out to be a collection of huts with thatched roofs, in the middle of a lot of short, brown people, with hair dyed orange, in grass skirts. One hut was our "room," with separate beds and an ominous rigging of mosquito netting. The toilet facilities consisted of outhouses down a path barely visible by day, but plainly impossible to follow at night. It was so bad, Sally almost laughed. But not quite. The sun was setting. There was no other "hotel" within miles. We were stuck. There was nothing to do but make the best of it: get drunk. But there was no bar; hence, no booze. There were however a dozen people sitting around a table, actually laughing. On close examination they proved to be Japanese tourists, and they were drinking Suntori Scotch whisky.

"Ask them if we can have some," Sally nudged me.

"I don't think they speak English, and I know I don't speak Japanese," I answered. In fact, I don't like to ask strangers for anything.

"Well, I do," she said, and walked over to the Japanese group, while I watched in awe. Pretty soon, the Japanese were all laughing with Sally. And in a minute they were even singing—what sounded like nursery rhymes. My wife does in fact speak some Japanese. When her father, Colonel "Buffalo Bill" Quinn, was fighting in Korea, the rest of the Quinns were living in Tokyo, surrounded by Japanese servants, and houseboys who taught the children pidgin Japanese. Good enough Japanese to return with her own bottle of Suntori which we consumed, first internally, and later externally to keep jungle-sized mosquitos big as Aichi-99s away. They were the first Japanese I had viewed without hostility since World War II. That's a fact.

But Suntori or no Suntori, we were out of there ASAP, back to Manaus, and on to Lima and Machu Picchu in Peru, then a week in Yucatán and Cancún, and back to Washington. I get nervous after more than a couple of weeks of vacation.

Soon after we returned from South America, my mother died in 1975 in a private nursing home. "Hardening of the arteries," they called it then. Alzheimer's disease, today. The last time I saw her, well before she died, she had railed at me in German. The time before that she told me she had no son named Ben, or Benny or Benjamin. And it was more than I could take, looking at this shell of a woman, who had been so beautiful, so cultured, so bright. Brother Freddy could reach her long after my sister and I, by playing records of music from the twenties and thirties.

In the final stages of editing *Conversations with Kennedy*, I got a call from Jackie, the first time I had talked to her since the funeral train bearing Bobby Kennedy's body on the way back to Arlington Cemetery. She wanted to know when I was going to let her read the book, mentioning she had heard I had shown it to Joe Kraft and some others. I told her I was waiting to get it in shape to show it to her, and I did send it off a week later. She didn't like it, it was obvious when she called a week after that. "It tells more about you than it does about the President," she said. And she didn't like the bad language. She said she thought her children would be offended. I was not sure she was coming clean with why she didn't like it.

Her criticism had hurt and baffled me. The critics would find the book interesting, but too admiring of Kennedy, not critical enough. I had no intention of writing a critical biography. I had wanted simply to tell what that president and his wife were like when they were relaxed and among friends. Someone I admired had once wished aloud for such a book by some friend of Lincoln's.

I saw Jackie twice after that conversation. Once, Sally and I were arriving at a party hosted by Arthur Schlesinger during the Democratic Convention in New York in 1976, just as she was leaving. I whispered to Sally that Jackie was coming down the street, stuck out my hand, and said, "Hi, Jackie." She sailed by us without a word. Sometime later, Jackie and her two children had the cabana next to us at La Samanna in St. Maarten. For a week we seemed to be staring at each other on the beach, but never ran into each other until one night, when we almost collided as we left our cabana to go up to the restaurant for dinner. From 12 inches away, she looked straight ahead, without a word, and I never saw her again.

One day soon after President Nixon resigned, Woodward sidled into my office to tell me that "Bob Redford is in town," and would

I like to meet him. That's how I learned that the movie of *All the President's Men* was "go." Redford was charming and professional, and he had a critical advantage over me in our first discussions: he knew he was going to make the movie and I didn't. And his wish list scared us all. First he wanted to call the paper *"The Washington Post"* With no clue as to where he was headed, never mind where the story was headed (there was no script, no director, and no cast), we said no. Next, he wanted to use all of our names. For the same reasons, plus a sense that what privacy we had was not long for this world, we said, "No way." And finally, he wanted to shoot in the newsroom, promising to shoot "only" during the five hours (4:00 A.M. to 9:00 A.M.) when a daily newspaper is not under active preparation. We said, "Out of the question."

We kept them out of the newsroom, but we lost both other battles. We asked Joe Califano if Redford could legally use *"The Washington Post,"* and while he was at it, to see if our names belonged to us, as we thought. Califano, whom we accused of secretly wanting a cameo role in the movie, surprised us by telling us Redford could legally use any names he wanted. When we told Redford, he said only that his lawyers agreed with Califano.

And thus we embarked on a strange new adventure into the fantasy world of actors playing real people in a fictional version of real history. Nothing in my education had prepared me remotely to cope with these conflicts. None of us was prepared for the mines in that field of fame.

When Woodward told us that Redford had chosen Alan J. Pakula—director of *Klute* and producer of *To Kill a Mockingbird*—to direct the movie, we said, "Big deal. How does that help him do 'Dick Nixon and the Boy Journalists'?"

We were wrong.

Alan Pakula only masquerades as a movie director. He is really a latter-day Freud. If it is the season for his reddish beard, he even looks like Freud, gently listening, analyzing the passing scene, quietly absorbing information and impressions from all around him with a glint in his eyes, and the trace of a quizzical smile on his lips. After it had sunk in that the movie was going to be made, with or without our help, it seemed smart to help wherever our help did not intrude on tomorrow's newspaper. Redford wanted Pakula to hang around the *Post* "for a while" to absorb the business. "For a while" turned into a month or so, though before long he disappeared into the woodwork. He asked for three days by my side, sharing phone conversations, news conferences, talks with reporters and editors. He sat unobtrusively on the sofa, but I was really the one on the couch. He learned more about me, my mother, father, brother, sister, hopes and fears than any shrink (five, I think) I've ever consulted. And he spent similar time with all of the other *Post* types involved with Watergate. *Post* types not directly involved with Watergate watched the filming with mixed emotions. They shared the excitement of watching headline actors, but resented being on the outside looking in.

Redford was in and out of Washington, but he became more or less Woodward's personal responsibility, once everyone realized that groupies in the Post Building made Redford's visits overly disruptive. Dustin Hoffman showed up in the city room for a couple of weeks to learn first how reporters were supposed to behave, then how Bernstein did behave. He already knew what Bernstein was like. He could become Bernstein, mimicking his voice so that even Woodward was fooled.

Once, just as we were all leaving for lunch somewhere, the police radio announced that a "jumper" had emerged outside a window on the fifth floor of a building only a short walk from the *Post*. I took Hoffman with me to show him how one of these tabloid staples unfolded. (Jumper surveys scene. Crowd gathers. Crowd yells, "Jump." Guy jumps, or he doesn't jump.) The scenario was unfolding, just as the script provided—until the crowd spotted Hoffman. Then all eyes left the poor jumper to focus on the dashing young actor. Jumper is forgotten. (He didn't jump.)

A perfect example of the newspaper variation on the Heisenberg principle, named for the German physicist who discovered that the act of measuring, even observing, subatomic particles actually changed the composition of the subatomic particles. The presence of Dustin Hoffman turned an event into a spectacle. Readers—and especially television viewers—must understand the Heisenberg principle before they can understand the news. What is actually happening that is being described by the media? Is Somalia being assaulted in the predawn dark by crack U.S. troops? Or are bewildered GIs being photographed by freelance photographers who have been waiting for them for hours? The difference is often critical.

But nothing about the making of the movie really hit me until there began to be some discussion about who might play Bradlee. There was talk about Richard Widmark, known to me only as the maniac who pushed a woman in a wheelchair down a flight of stairs in *Kiss of Death*. There was talk about Robert Mitchum, who filled up a screen pretty good—and pretty macho. And then there was talk about Jason Robards, known by all as a great actor, but something of a question mark because of his battles with the bottle. He had just come through a terrible automobile accident, where he had plastered himself against a canyon wall.

When he got the job (for $50,000), he came into Washington for part of one day. A 45-minute lunch—without even a beer—at the Madison Hotel Coffee Shop, an hour touring the *Post* city room, and a quick, early dinner with Sally and me in the kitchen of our Dupont Circle house. Again no booze, and damn little small talk. We found we were about the same age, had fought pretty much the same war in the Pacific Navy, and had the same gravelly voice. Robards and I became friends much later, but that first encounter was short and sweet.

We had fun teasing Katharine about who might play her. Names like Katharine Hepburn, Lauren Bacall, and Patricia Neal were tossed out—by us—to make her feel good. And names like Edna May Oliver or Marie Dressler, if it felt like teasing time. And then her role was dropped from the final script, half to her relief.

Jack Warden played Metro editor Harry Rosenfeld, and Marty Balsam played managing editor Howard Simons. Howard, in particular, felt that he and his role in Watergate were fatally shortchanged in the script (and that I and my role were exaggerated), and he never really got over his resentment. Our relationship, which had been such a joyous one, so congenial and close we literally could finish each other's sentences, was never the same after the film. The version of history he saw in the film made him seethe, and it was only after he left the *Post* and became curator of Harvard's Nieman Fellowship program that he regained his full confidence, and we finally regained our friendship.*

Redford re-created the *Post* newsroom in incredible detail on the Burbank, California, lot. I had promised Marina, now fourteen, a candlelight dinner with Redford (with no idea how I could deliver) if she achieved some scholastic goal, which she theoretically could never attain but miraculously did. One morning we walked onto the set together, and I was stunned. There were the same desks as we had at the *Post*, in the same colors, and the same layout. The desks were covered with the same "dressing"—which had been swept off the tops of *Post* desks in Washington and shipped to California. The radiant Hannah Pakula saved the day for me by persuading Redford to dine with Alan and her—and including Marina and me.

When the movie was completed, Redford invited a bunch of us—Katharine, Woodward and Bernstein, myself, Simons, Rosenfeld, about ten of us in all—to a special screening. Each of us sat alone, afraid to react or to be caught reacting. And when it was over, no one said a word, until finally Redford pleaded with us, "For God's sake, someone say something," and most of us mumbled our general approval.

Anyway, I thought the movie was damned good. I thought the actors were great. I thought the director was great, and I am amazed that I had no idea at the time of the shadow that movie would cast. No idea, for instance, that all that generations to come would ever know about Watergate would be in that 147-minute film.

We still faced the ordeal of the formal opening in Washington,

---

* Howard Simons died at Harvard on June 13, 1989, age sixty, after a devastating siege of pancreatic cancer.

at the Kennedy Center. "Ordeal" because the goddamn reporters and TV types were determined to follow the actors around until they cornered them with the people they played and asked us the inane and inevitable questions. "Do you think Redford (Hoffman) (Robards) was accurate in portraying you? Is that what it was really like?" I developed a slew of different answers, and then felt like a jerk trying them all out, polishing them, to see which ones played the best.

Straight: "It's hard to condense twenty-six months into two hours, but I thought it was really interesting."

Facetious: "Pretty good, except someone always answered the phones."

Self-deprecating: "It was hard to concentrate. I'd like to see it again, but you guys would spot me leaving the theater and tell everyone I was going over and over again."

The Wiggins rule about staying off the stage was in shambles. There we all were in the audience, but we were really on the stage.

All the President's Men certified star status for Woodward and Bernstein. They hadn't spent much time basking in the Pulitzer, the book, and the movie, before starting in on book two, *The Final Days*. Carl had money in his pocket for the first time in his life, and he spent it as fast as he got it, and reveled in everything about fame. Bob bought a house, and socked every spare dime into investments. Carl loved the midnight glitter. Bob loved the midnight oil.

Woodward and Bernstein were still creating their legacy, but already new reporters coming on stream were plainly looking for the same kind of stardom, using what they thought was the same kind of brash persistence they'd seen in the movie. We joked about bright-eyed, bushy-tailed young Woodsteins coming back from covering a fire in Prince Georges County, reporting that the fire chief was anti-Semitic, there was gasoline in the hoses, and a guy who looked like Howard Hunt had been seen fleeing into the woods. Some of my colleagues in the business started making speeches about the need to rein in the young hotheads before they got newspapers into trouble. I think now we worried too much about the trouble and not enough about the newspapering. After all, good editors and good copy editors can prevent the excesses of exuberance; it is not that hard to take the elbows out of a lead like:

"Despite overwhelming evidence to the contrary, the mayor today refused to admit that he had accepted sexual favors from the wife of an associate trying to sell the city a new health plan."

But there is no question that the Watergate legacy did include a major infusion of bright, young, motivated and talented men and women, who might have drifted off into other professions. Scotty Reston, the dean of Washington journalists, gave a speech about this time, urging the press not to relax their investigative pressure just because the public was leery of going through another Watergate, and just because some editors were listening to vague complaints that the press had accumulated too much power. Just the opposite, he said. Now was the time to pour it on, turn up the volume. Take a look at everything government was doing. Watergate had proved they weren't playing by the rules. He was right, but for the most part his peers were not listening.

However, it was neither the influx of hungry young journalists eager for notoriety nor the notoriety itself that made journalism forever different after Watergate. But journalism was forever changed by the assumption—by most journalists—that after Watergate government officials generally and instinctively lied when confronted by embarrassing events. "Look for the lies" replaced "Look for the woman" or "Follow the money" as the new shibboleth of journalism.

Most journalists working their way slowly up the ladder from cub reporter on small newspapers quickly learned that some public officials lie when cornered. I think back now to Jimmy O'Neil, the police chief of Manchester, New Hampshire (and later national commander of the American Legion), who lied to me rather than admit that a trap which had been set for a rapist misfired and resulted in another rape. But that involved only a small-town chief of police and, of course, the victim.

I think back now to the lies of Senator Joe McCarthy, but these were the lies of a mind gone manic.

I remember President Eisenhower authorizing lying about the U-2 incident in 1960, when the Russians shot down our supersecret spy plane, piloted by Francis Gary Powers. I didn't have any trouble rationalizing that lie, even as I wished for a world where such subterfuges were unnecessary.

And in that same category I remember Kennedy suddenly returning to Washington in October 1962, "with a bad cold," when in fact he had returned to cope with the Cuban Missile Crisis. Almost forgivable, I felt when I learned the truth, two weeks later.

But in Watergate, President Richard Milhous Nixon lied over and over again with intent to deceive the American public and thereby save his ass from the consequences of his crimes.

In Watergate, Attorney General John Mitchell, the chief law enforcement officer of the republic, lied with intent to obstruct the justice he was charged with imposing. He, too, lied to save his ass from the consequences of his crimes, and he went to jail for it. The only U.S. Attorney General in American history to go to jail.

All of these lies were on-the-record lies, before television cameras, before reporters, on the telephone, before large audiences, in front of grand juries, and in front of each other. These lies marked a generation of Washington reporters, generally considered by every generation of editors to be the finest reporters in the land.

The liars went to jail, and spent the rest of their lives trying to live down their disgrace. But the reporters went on to report tomorrow's news, with permanently jaundiced eyes.

Twenty years after Watergate, at some Twentieth Century Fund conference on journalism, I remember telling Republican Congressman Jim Leach of Iowa, a man full of common sense and compassion, that I found it easier to cope with Washington by assuming that no one ever told the complete truth in Washington. At least the first time. I was exaggerating to make my point about the new skepticism of journalists when I said that Vietnam, followed by Watergate, had changed the rules forever. Leach was appalled.

No matter how many spin doctors were provided by how many sides of how many arguments, from Watergate on, I started looking for the truth *after* hearing the official version of a truth. And it didn't make much difference whether it was George Bush telling the world that Clarence Thomas was the best-qualified Supreme

Court candidate in the land, and that his color had nothing to do
with his appointment. Or Ronald Reagan saying he knew nothing
about Iran-Contra. Or Tonya Harding saying she knew nothing
about the knee-capping of Nancy Kerrigan . . . to widen the circle
beyond governmental lies.

Journalism after Watergate changed in another important way,
more subtle and harder to define. And I realize I may be speaking about myself, here, although I believe I am speaking about my
colleagues, too. I had already declined an invitation to join the
newspaper establishment's Valhalla, the Gridiron Club. I felt that
newspaper people and newsmakers should keep a civil distance
from each other.

Watergate marked the final passage of journalists into the best
seats of the establishment. This trip had begun long before when
men such as Walter Lippmann and Arthur Krock separated themselves from the rough-and-tumble, hard-drinking journalists made
famous in the 1920s in Hecht and MacArthur's *Front Page*, and
emerged in the 1930s as leaders of a new tribe of intelligent, educated, eminently presentable newspaper people, mostly male. In
their wake came the Scotty Restons, the Alsop brothers, Marquis
Childs, Ed Lahey, Roscoe Drummond, and finally the pioneers
of television like Murrow, Huntley, Brinkley, and Cronkite, who
mixed easily with leaders of government and business. If they all
weren't making Wall Street money yet, they were well on their way
to respectability. Watergate was the last leg of this trip, bestowing
the final accolade of establishmentarianism, or the semblance of it,
on the daily press.

With membership in the establishment went a heightened sense
of responsibility. At least I began to feel subconsciously that what
the world did *not* need right away was another investigation that
might again threaten the foundations of democracy. What the
newspaper did *not* need right away was another fight to the finish
with another president—especially a Republican president, and
especially a successful fight. Without the suggestion of a formal decision, I think the fires of investigative zeal were allowed to bank.

There wasn't all that much to investigate, nor that much time to investigate it, during the Ford administration. (In the story conference room on the news floor of *The Washington Post* hangs a large framed color photograph of a smiling President Ford, superimposed with the caption: "I got my job through *The Washington Post*." It originally appeared in a skit on "Saturday Night Live," and it is cheerfully signed: "To Ben Bradlee and all my friends at *The Washington Post* . . . Jerry Ford." I can't think of another president who would have done the same thing.)

The Carter administration fascinated the Washington press corps for its regional stamp and religious quality. But except for the occasional excesses of a Bubba-like Bert Lance, the small-town Georgia banker and Carter friend who resigned in September 1977 as Budget Director in a controversy over his tangled financial affairs, there was still remarkably little smoke to suggest much of a fire to reporters.

It wasn't until the arrival of Reagan and Bush that the post-Watergate caution of editors was again visible. At last there was plenty to investigate: the scandals in public housing, the collapse of the savings and loan industry, and especially the Iran-Contra scandal. Lieutenant Colonel Ollie North's erratic zeal led the White House into some unconstitutional adventures that threatened democracy more than Watergate.

The press, to its discredit, never tumbled to the housing or the savings and loan stories, and editors have to take the blame. The press did investigate Iran-Contra to a fare-thee-well, however, and still never managed to engage the nation's attention or conscience. The public's throat was never seized by Iran-Contra as it had been seized by Watergate. Ronald Reagan was popular; there was no one to impeach him on the Hill. He was near the end of his term.

Nothing had bugged me more during and right after Watergate than the know-nothing charge that the press had gone after Nixon because he was a Republican and the press consisted of a bunch of liberal Democrats. "You guys would never have gone after Kennedy," went the dreary charge, "if he had been involved in

Watergate." Truth is, at the *Post* anyway, we were always praying for good Democratic scandals. . . and found more than our share. But that criticism, that suggestion of bias, wore me down over the years, I now think, and I know we walked the extra mile to accept the official versions of events from the White House—explanations that I doubt we would have accepted from the right-hand men of Democratic presidents. And the public was glad to go along.

SIXTEEN

WASHINGTON POST, 1975–80

After my post-Watergate leave was over, I faced some personnel problems that had been too hard to solve while we were all so preoccupied with handling that extraordinary story with its extraordinary denouement. One of these involved the Sports Section. I had been forced to make one change, but my solution had bombed. I had made another change, and that solution was plainly not working. With my reputation for picking the right people about to go up in smoke, I had a really great idea. They say you need only one good idea a day to earn your salary, but in fact you don't need that many. And a couple of really great ideas should make a career.

My great idea was to make Don Graham the sports editor. With Watergate behind us, Don had returned to Washington from a stint at *Newsweek*, and he was ready for a new challenge, as he worked his way up the ladder. He was not thrilled about working with numbers on the business side of the *Post*, where Katharine had penciled him in, nor was Katharine thrilled by my making Don an offer that he clearly preferred. He was not only a sports enthusiast, he was completely knowledgeable about sports. Everyone liked him and admired him, and selfishly, I figured that with Don as sports editor, he would have an identity with the newsroom that would benefit us—and him—forever.

I had first met Don Graham when he was a teenager and I was in *Newsweek*'s Washington Bureau. On baseball's Opening Day, various *Post* types led by Shirley Povich, the great sports columnist, plus me from *Newsweek* and Don from school, would have a lunch at the *Post* before going out to Griffith Stadium. I had seen him again at Harvard, with his fabulous girlfriend, Mary Wissler. Don was president of the Harvard *Crimson*, which was staging some celebration. I had been asked at the last minute to substitute for Bill Moyers as the main dinner speaker. It was not a great success, you could say. In fact, it was a disaster. The Harvards had been celebrating for three days, and most of them were drunk out of their minds. I don't know what subject might have satisfied them, but I gave some Boy Scout speech about teamwork and loyalty, and before I was through the bread rolls were flying across the dining room toward the head table.

Don was an instant success as sports editor, as he has been at whatever task was before him. In only a few months he calmed everyone down, got them pulling together, and set them free to produce a great Sports Section. And on top of that he tapped George Solomon to be his deputy from the *Washington Daily News* with an eye to recommending him as his successor whenever the time came. Most of his colleagues think Solomon has a special relationship with Graham when it comes time to dole out new slots and more white space, but all of his colleagues agree that Solomon was the right man, then and now.

I have never been comfortable in or with the labor movement. In 1947, I didn't understand the great rewards of trade unions—never mind the propriety as a 10 percent stockholder of being first a reluctant member, then the secretary of the smallest local in the history of the American Newspaper Guild in Manchester, New Hampshire. We were making very little money, but for most of us, half our salaries came to us under the GI Bill of Rights, and the paper was so broke it had to scratch for the other half from Day One.

At the *Post* for my first tour, I followed the path of least resistance and joined the Guild, without any forethought at all. I'm sure the Guild helped get me the few small raises I got in two and a half years. And I do mean small . . . $3 to $5 a week. There was no Guild of any consequence at *Newsweek*, although there was a small unit in the Washington Bureau, which I discovered when I fired a TWX operator for habitual intoxication without knowing she was the "unit" chairman, the word we used at the time.

When I returned to the *Post* as part of management, my dealings with the Guild and all other unions lay somewhere between scratchy and hostile.

My all-time scarring experience with the Guild unit came in the spring of 1974, at the very height of Watergate, when the *Post* and the White House were locked in a struggle for survival. The contract had expired and Guild leadership promised that if there was no contract by 4:00 P.M. one afternoon, all Guild members would walk out of the newsroom on strike—"withdraw our excellence," in their memorably pompous phrase. A few minutes before four, there being no contract, the unit chairman walked through the newsroom with four fingers of his hand raised (for 4:00 P.M.)—and out they walked meek as lambs. My friends! People I drank with. People like Bud Nossiter, Murrey Marder, Dan Morgan, Bob Woodward, Carl Bernstein, Larry Stern, Don Oberdorfer. People who were the engine behind the new *Washington Post*. People who could not be persuaded by presidents of the United States, FBI directors, Secretaries of State, or prime ministers to say "Hello" to their mothers. But for four fingers they just walked out in silence. Sheepish silence, I thought at first, wishfully, but not realistically.

One of the strikers was Sally, of course, impaled on the horns of a dilemma: cross the picket line and lose all identity except "editor's girlfriend," or join colleagues and try to preserve some independence.

It bugged me more than I could stand to realize that we friends had to pretend to go to war before we could achieve a truce, and that meanwhile we were out of business. Since Sally and I had a drink with Stern almost every night, we started talking about the strike the first day. With the permission of John Prescott, the paper's business chief executive, and very explicitly without committing the management to anything, we talked about ways of stopping the silliness and getting on with our life's work at what was plainly an historical crossroads.

Stern scheduled a meeting with Bernstein, Marder, and Bernard Nossiter, the *Post's* economic correspondent, at his house, and I joined them after a couple of hours as prearranged. But when they later tried to sell the Guild what would have been a solution, they were shouted down. Sometime after the 1975 strike was settled, all four of them were charged as scabs by the Guild and fined for consorting with management, although the striking Miss Quinn went unpunished for sleeping with management.

But if the Newspaper Guild made life miserable for those of us managers trying to make a quantum leap up in editorial quality, the craft unions (with some outstanding exceptions) at that time— printers, pressmen, and mailers especially—made life impossible. Slowdowns of various kinds in all production areas made for late press starts. Sabotaged press runs made for late off times. And late press starts and late press off times screwed up circulation of the paper. Engravings were "lost," delaying page production. Typesetting could become a joke, and an embarrassment. The dreaded F-word showed up from time to time in classified advertisements.

In the sixties and seventies, control of the production of the newspapers was in the hands of the craft unions, not management. While the *Post* was gaining on the *Star* in circulation and advertising, management had been determined to avoid a strike. And therein lay the problem: as long as the unions could close the paper down, and the paper could not print without the unions, the paper was in a no-win position.

In early 1975, ahead of the *Star* for good in circulation and advertising, the paper was determined to regain control. And step number one, under the *Post's* new president, John Prescott, who had succeeded Paul Ignatius, was to develop the capacity to print the paper without union labor. That meant, first, sending news exec-utives to Oklahoma (where newspaper owners had created a "scab school") to learn to run the giant presses, and next to establish its own training facility in Virginia to teach non-union employees the wonders of cold-type production. In the fall of 1975, the *Post* was ready: it could produce the paper without union help, under the day-to-day direction of the new young assistant general manager, Don Graham.

The showdown came in the early morning of October 1. Here's what happened as told five months later in Bob Kaiser's wonderful recap, "The Strike at The Washington Post," six full pages in the Outlook Section on February 29, 1976.

Sometime after 4 o'clock in the morning of October I, a small group of pressmen began to vandalize the press room. According to eye-witnesses, several men had lists in their hands and walked around telling others what to do.

What they did, according to the Post, was damage which eventually cost $270,000 to repair: they sliced the cushions on the press cylinders, ripped out electrical wiring, removed key pieces on the folders on almost every press, jammed the cylin-ders, cut air hoses and sabotaged other parts.

The most serious damage was caused by a fire, apparently started with gasoline on one unit of a new press. Whoever started the fire first partially disabled the automatic fire extin-guishers on that press and an adjacent one. The fire melted the lead plates that were left on the cylinders, and spread to the rolls of newsprint in the reel room below. . . .

The damage was systematic. The Post has nine presses, each with eight units. All 72 units were damaged, all within 15–20 minutes.

Minutes before the destructive rampage, the night foreman of the press room, James Hover, had been jumped by several press operators, pinned to the floor for 15 minutes with a screw-driver at his throat, and then severely beaten. It took 12 stitches to close a cut to the bone just above his eye.

"When I got to 15th Street," Katharine Graham remembered, "I saw fire engines, police cars, red lights flashing. I thought to myself, if I drive in the parking lot they'll wreck the car. I asked a policeman what to do. He said park it here. I'll keep an eye on it."

The sights and sounds were appalling, with angry pressmen now shouting and jeering on a picket line. We all were called and raced back to work, to survey the damage and begin to figure out the next steps. The first thing I did was to tour the press room, and get photographers down there to record all the destruction. The press room looked like the engine room in a burned-out ship's hulk.

The next five months were the longest five months of all our lives, as everyone in top management worked two jobs, their own and a striker's. All the craft unions honored the pressmen's picket line and refused to come to work. Crossing a picket line when your friends are picketing is tough. Crossing this picket line was a pleasure. Sally, by my side this time as we went to work, drew special, vulgar, and noisy attention, and I managed to control myself only by putting my right hand in my pants pocket—except for a conspicuous middle finger wiggling uncontrollably.

The leadership of the Newspaper Guild tried to persuade its members to honor the picket line, but the newsroom voted overwhelmingly to work, and most reporters and editors showed up for the duration. I soon settled into a routine, taking classified ads in the morning, alongside Kay Graham and other editors. I played editor or reporter (sometimes editor *and* reporter) during the day, and worked two nights a week in the mailroom.

The technical obstacles that had to be overcome before we could print a newspaper were enormous. We now had advertising salesmen and executives who could run presses, but they couldn't run badly damaged presses. None of us knew whether "winning" was a realistic goal, or even what "winning" might be. Jim Cooper, the tough and able production director, and my pal, bet me that Kay would "cave in" to the unions, because the *Post* always had caved in in a crunch. I had no idea what was going to happen, but I took the bet for morale purposes. My own morale.

But we began to realize very gradually that we had a lot going for us in this strike.

Except for the die-hard labor skates, reporters and editors were appalled by the pressmen's rampage, and wanted to work. That meant if we could physically produce any paper, it would eventually be a real newspaper, not just a strike paper.

Washington isn't, and never was, a labor town, like Boston or New York or Chicago. The people, and especially business owners, supported the *Post*. When striking pressmen poured crankcase oil over piles of clothing in the department stores, they succeeded only in doubling the businesspeople's determination to help the *Post* win by advertising in the paper.

Even the cops supported the *Post*. If I live to be a hundred, I'll never forget Police Chief Maurice "Cully" Cullinane, dressed in a sports jacket and gray flannel slacks, wading into a particularly ugly demonstration outside the Post Building. One striking stereotyper was carrying a vulgar, crudely lettered sign that read: "Phil Shot the Wrong Graham." I watched from a window as Cully walked innocently up to another striker, put his left elbow in the man's stomach, and then slammed his right fist into the palm of his left hand. The picketer dropped to the sidewalk in agony. And we all cheered.

The owners of other newspapers, in the Middle Atlantic states and everywhere else, ardently supported Katharine Graham, many of them almost gloating in their I-told-you-sos to their liberal colleague, but all of them offering any help we needed. Within forty-eight hours, six newspapers—from Chambersburg, Pennsylvania, to Charlottesville, Virginia—had offered to print the *Post*, and we had hired helicopters to fly photographs of each page of the paper—and eventually the lead plates themselves—to the six printing plants. The roof of the 15th Street building began to look like a MASH unit in Vietnam, with choppers coming in and out all day and half the night. Angry picketers on the sidewalks below shook their fists and shouted in vain.

And finally, the *Post*'s distribution was (and is) handled by independent contractors, not employees, and these contractors wanted no part of unions. That meant if we could get papers out of the press room, they would be widely distributed.

We missed one day entirely, but printed a twenty-four-page paper with no ads on the next day. The paper slowly increased in size, as our in-house skills improved. There was a sense of excitement, and it grew as we started to feel the momentum shift, as we added sections, and added outside printing plants.

On October 7, with the help of non-union machinists who got one press running, we ran off 100,000 copies of a 40-page paper, in two sections. The esprit de corps within the building was sky high. A sign on one press, run by men and women from the Advertising Department, read: "J. PRESS, printing its way into the hearts of thousands." Meals were catered for the night crews, and served by waiters in tuxedos. Everyone was exhausted, but also exhilarated. One night, there was even music after the last edition was printed, and Advertising's Lou Limber, with a flower in his mouth, danced the Greek dances he loved so much.

Many staff members slept at the office on cots scattered throughout the building. Some marriages ran aground. At least two new marriages were launched.

George Meany, the venerable head of the AFL-CIO, asked to meet with Katharine Graham in January 1976. They were old friends, and Meany did not hold the pressmen's union in particularly high regard, according to labor experts. But Meany got nowhere with the lady publisher, whose spine had stiffened every day of the strike. At one point, Meany asked Katharine what she would have done if the pressmen had ever unconditionally offered to return to work. According to Kaiser, she replied, "Slit my throat."

At one point the *Miami Herald* was printing some sections of the Sunday paper, and trucking them hundreds of miles to set up remote mailrooms. In early December, the *Post* advertised for replacements for the striking pressmen. Hundreds responded. The line of applicants stretched almost around the block right through the picket line.

In late December, the paper handlers, a union of predominantly black men who load the huge rolls of newsprint into the presses, and maintain the press room, announced that they were going to settle with the *Post*. The lily-white pressmen's union had never done anything for them.

On February 15, 1976, the mailers' union voted to settle with the *Post*, and the strike was effectively over. The February 18 issue of the paper was printed in the traditional hot-type manner, and the strike was over in fact—after 139 exhausting days. Eventually, a dozen pressmen were convicted of crimes of violence, or pleaded guilty.

The impact of this strike on *The Washington Post* has been just enormous. It leveled the playing field, so that excellence in production became an achievable goal, then a goal that was achieved. The "victory" of management gave The Washington Post Company new respect on Wall Street, which I have reluctantly concluded after these many years is a plus for the news side of the newspaper as well as for its shareholders.

This Wall Street respect may elevate some of the mountebanks in the newspaper business, like the self-aggrandizing Al Neuharth of Gannett, to undeserved heights, but it allows the best of the breed, like the Grahams in Washington, the Sulzbergers in New York, the Taylors in Boston, the Chandlers in Los Angeles, and others, to make good newspapers as well as good money.

Sally and I were married on October 20, 1978, in the chambers of my old friend David Bazelon, chief judge of the U.S. Court of Appeals in the District of Columbia, in front of my three children and my brother. Katharine Graham, Ed Williams, and Art Buchwald were our witnesses. We had invited fifty or sixty people to a cocktail party, and they arrived to find themselves guests at a wedding reception. General Quinn, who had been waiting anxiously for a Republican, an Army officer, and anything but a journalist for a son-in-law, was fatalistic about his bad luck. Bette Quinn seemed almost as pleased with me as a son-in-law, as I have always been with her as a mother-in-law.

For whatever reason, the twenty-year disparity in our ages was simply not an issue. It provided me with a slew of new friends, all younger, and after a few months of discomfort, it didn't cost me any of my older friends. "That's your problem," Buchwald had said, as he announced he had asked both Tony and Sally to his annual Easter egg hunt in 1974.

Sally was an engine of change, as she reached out for new friends, new experiences, new places. She changed me by showing me there was a life outside the confines of *The Washington Post*. There were gatherings of people—to call them parties would be true but misleading—who were bright and irreverent, who took their jobs but not themselves seriously. There were a bunch of young Brits, led by Willie Shawcross, who hung around Larry Stern, and leavened the incestuous diet of politics, national and parochial, inside *The Washington Post*. We were all vaguely anti-establishment, even as our success would seem to drive us into the arms of the establishment.

One of the new friends Sally quickly added to my life was Norman Lear. She had met Norman at a party in L.A., while she was on a promotional tour for her CBS book *We're Going to Make You a Star*. She called me up late that night, and announced, "Boy, did I meet someone you're going to love." And boy, was she right. I don't think I ever met anyone I liked so much, and so fast. The man is warm and smart and funny and generous, and loyal and kind. And the more you see him or talk to him, the more you want to see him and talk to him. And hug him. My friend Norman is an All-Pro hugger. A talk on the telephone with Norman Lear should be bottled and consumed regularly, and every shrink in the world would go out of business.

I had known—and admired—Dick Cohen and Walter Pincus for years, but Sally turned them into closest friends. I think Dick Cohen writes the best column in the country—the most thoughtful, most interesting, boldest, funniest—if Bill Safire doesn't. Walter's analytical powers as an investigative reporter are the answer to an editor's prayers. I've never known a reporter harder to shake than Pincus when he has the bit in his teeth.

Larry Stern played a key role in our lives, Sally's and my first, shared friend. We drove him to and from work every day. We had at least drinks together almost every night, and when Nora Pouillon and her pals, the Damato brothers, needed a little cash for sheet-rock to finish the walls of their new restaurant around the corner, Larry persuaded us to invest $5,000 in Nora's Restaurant. And we started eating there more often than not. When working days begin at eight-thirty and end at eight-thirty, you find no joy in cooking.

When we weren't eating at Nora's Restaurant, we did some very modest entertaining in our dining room–kitchen near Dupont Circle. One night, we were sitting around the kitchen table with Nora Ephron and Carl Bernstein, who had suggested we have sup-per together—lobsters—at our house. They had married soon after Watergate propelled Carl onto the "scene," but I hadn't noticed anything out of the ordinary about the evening until Nora—more than a little pregnant with their second child—asked, maybe a little ominously, if we had any red wine. We had been drinking white with the lobsters, but I saw no flashing lights, and opened a nice new bottle of red. Nora looked at it for a few seconds, then rose and moved to a position behind Carl's chair, and slowly poured the whole goddamn bottle gurgle-gurgle-gurgle over him—head to face to shirt to toe.

I mumbled something inane about "We all go through troubled times," and the party was over. Twenty minutes later, the telephone rang, and it was Nora, asking Sally if she wanted to know what *that* was all about. As a matter of fact, she did, and Nora returned to report that it was about an affair Carl was having with Margaret Jay, the wife of the British ambassador, unbeknownst to any of us, and to Nora until a very short time before.

Nora included this scene, substituting a pie-in-the-face for the wine-pouring, in *Heartburn*, the best-selling book (and movie) she wrote about her marriage to Carl.

Without the strike and the turmoil that went with it, I would have been starting a new life, really. A life that almost assuredly would never include events as important historically as the Kennedy pres-idency, the Pentagon Papers, and Watergate had been. Events in which I would almost assuredly never play as critical, or as public, a role. With the strike settled, that new life began, a new act in some long drama whose resolution was unknown. But journalists thrive on not knowing exactly what the future holds. That's part of the excitement. Something interesting, something important, will happen somewhere, as sure as God made sour apples, and a good, aggressive newspaper will become part of that something. Maybe not another "third-rate burglary," but something that will monopolize all the energy and wisdom at my disposal.

Like the bunch of Croatians who hijacked a plane en route from Chicago to New York in September 1976, and threatened to kill all the passengers, unless the editors of five major newspapers, including me, printed a couple of thousand words of their propaganda. On page one.

The idea of anyone—President of the United States, FBI director, storeowner, wife, or irate reader—telling me that I had to run something in the paper that I didn't want to run, much less that I had to run it on page one, was inconceivable to me on its face.

Yet I followed their instructions meek as a lamb. Once. I'm not sure I'd do it twice.

The TWA 727 was hijacked by a group of Croatian nationalists, who took the plane to Montreal, Newfoundland, Iceland, and finally landed in Paris with some sixty hostages, having freed close to thirty of the original ninety-four hostages on the way. The hijackers radioed police that their demands and complete instructions would be found in a Grand Central Station hiding place. When the cops found the hiding place, they also found a concealed bomb, which exploded and killed one of them.

The instructions were specific—and unprecedented: the five newspapers (The Washington Post, the New York Times, the Los Angeles Times, the Chicago Tribune, and the International Herald Tribune in Paris) would have to print two political screeds demanding Croatian independence from Yugoslavia . . . or else! Or else another bomb would go off somewhere, or would the remaining hostages be killed? we wondered.

The hijacking took place on a Friday morning. The first bomb exploded that afternoon, and the first hint of demands hit the city room right on first edition deadline. The first two decisions were easy: Let the first edition presses roll on time, and call up Katharine Graham, and Don, who was then the paper's executive vice president and general manager. The Grahams were especially keen on being in on the takeoff of a story, if there was a real chance there might be a crash landing. I didn't know how tough I was going to dare to be or wanted to be, but a crash landing looked like a real possibility.

Sometime after 10:00 P.M., the AP wire carried the demands, including the text of the two documents, plus demands that at least one third of each text had to appear on page one, and all "jumps" had to be in the first section of the newspaper. If we acceded to the first demand, two thirds of the front page would be devoted to the Croatians, and that seemed unacceptable.

I checked in with Abe Rosenthal and Bill Thomas, my opposite numbers in New York and Los Angeles, and found them sore as hell, but ready, however reluctantly, to publish the documents. The truth is that none of us had any stomach for reading a headline in the next day's paper that went something like this: "HIJACKERS KILL 62 AMERICANS AFTER U.S. EDITORS REFUSE TO PUBLISH DOCUMENTS." I hit on three ideas which I figured, however unrealistically, might make the decision more palatable.

First, I felt we needed an appeal from some authority that it would be in the public interest to accede to the hijackers' demands—from government authorities that we often felt free to ignore. The FBI was glad to oblige.

Second, since nothing had been said about how many copies of the *Post* had to contain the story, we didn't have to include the story until the final minutes of the final edition.

And third, since nothing had been said about what size type had to be used, we would print it in agate type, the size used for box scores and classified ads, and so minimize both the story's impact and our own chagrin.

With this bold-as-a-lion rationalization, we printed the story. And slunk home.

The hostages were released in Paris. The crisis was over as quickly as it had started. No one ever threatened to kill anyone unless we ran some screed ever again.

Right after the hijackers crawled back into the woodwork, I got my first job offer.

I don't know how common this is, but I can honestly say that I never in twenty-seven years for one second contemplated leaving *The Washington Post*. Not that I had been given many opportunities. Blair Clark had me screen-tested for Howard K. Smith's job as CBS Bureau Chief, but all by itself the makeup process quelled that job offer. And I slunk back to *Newsweek*.

Once on the telephone, a Chicago head hunter described his client only as a Fortune 500 communications company looking to widen its portfolio and improve its image. Just the words scared me, and I told the man I was married to my job and not interested in divorce. He persisted. I persisted. Finally, I was intrigued enough that I told him if he understood my zero interest in changing jobs, and he wanted to talk to me face to face, he could buy me lunch.

At lunch, he played me like a trout for ten minutes, before revealing that his client was *Playboy*, and that they were looking for a president CEO, not an editor, and I'm afraid I laughed. Probably to cover up a superfast fantasy of me and Hef swimming in the *Playboy* grotto with a couple of centerfolds. Lunch was effectively over.

For some reason, Roone Arledge thought I had "can't miss" written all over me as a TV type. In its early days, I had appeared on David Brinkley's "This Week," until I figured out that they wanted me on the show primarily as a liberal foil for George Will, a role for which I had neither interest nor talent. Like all non-CBS TV executives, Roone was looking for a weekly magazine show to do battle with the legendarily successful "60 Minutes." He thought he had the show in "20/20," and he sent former *Esquire* editor Harold Hayes to talk to me about being the host—the name of Barbara Walters was never mentioned, never mind the name of Hugh Downs. After Sally's debacle I was never tempted by television.

This time the salary was well into six figures, and for a minute I wondered how they might be right when they said I could do the job in effect on my days off. Work five days at the *Post*, rush up to New York and write for one day, perform the next day, and rush back to my real job that night. No fantasies this time. Just thoughts of nervous breakdowns.

Editors choose.

That's what they do for a living. People first, then subjects, then words. And choosing whether to print anything is often the toughest decision of them all.

In matters of national security, the question quickly boils down to this: Is the security of the nation really at stake, just because someone in authority says it is? The Pentagon Papers, for instance. I learned the answer the hard way: Almost never.

In matters of privacy, the question is this: Is there some sacred public right to know that overcomes an equally sacred right to privacy? There is no easy answer to that one.

Take national security first, two cases where the claim of national security was made. One claim was made by President Jimmy Carter himself, and we printed the story. Another claim was actually made by us, reporters and editors of the *Post*, and we never printed the story.

One morning in November 1976, Bob Woodward reported to me that although he had only one source, it looked as if a Middle East head of state was on the CIA payroll. In my book, that's close to a perfect way to start a day . . . with the promise of an important, exclusive, and vital story, and the prospect of some tough work before it was ready to print—or not to print. At this point, Woodward didn't know which head of which state was on the CIA payroll for how much, although there seemed no lack of candidates. I asked him for a full court press, and it took him two weeks to come up with the name: King Hussein of Jordan; the dollar amount: about $1 million a year for twenty years; and some further details. The money was "walking-around" money, not connected either to economic or military aid, which Jordan received regularly. The operation was called "NO/BEEF" inside the CIA. The money had been used variously . . . including to procure women, when Hussein was little more than a teenager, and to pay for bodyguards for his children when they were old enough to go to boarding school in the United States.

What we needed now was a second source. Woodward called Carter's press secretary, Jody Powell, told him everything he knew, and asked for White House comment. Less than a month in office as the spokesman for the President of the United States, Powell replied, "No shit." Next day, someone from the White House (Woodward remembers it to have been Zbigniew Brzezinski, the National Security Council director, and I remember it as Jody Powell) called to ask me whether "it would help you make up your mind [to print or not to print the story], if you could talk to the President?"

We were there the next morning for an interview I'll never forget. To be in the Oval Office of the White House with the President of the United States will always blow my mind. Carter had been president for less than a month, but looked totally comfortable, poised, friendly and hospitable. He was dressed in a pinstriped gray suit, and smiling. First, the president said, the story was true. (There was our second source.) Next, he said he had been briefed several times by the outgoing Secretary of State (Henry Kissinger), and the outgoing director of the CIA (George Bush), but neither had mentioned that we had a king on our payroll. Third, he had ordered the payments stopped. And fourth, he said he couldn't make the case that others of his staff were making that the national security was involved.

We had our story.

But, the president added gently, Jordan was vital to the Middle East settlement he had made a priority. Secretary of State Cyrus R. Vance was actually in the Middle East, scheduled to see Hussein within the next forty-eight hours. The president said he would prefer the story not be published, but added, "I can't tell you how to run your business." If we were going to publish the story, he would like twenty-four hours' notice. On the spot, I promised that we would not run the story that night, and would give him at least a day's notice, if we decided to run it. The president talked about the importance of trust. He said he wanted Woodward and me to believe in him. He said he hoped that I would come to see him on "anything." And then he ended the interview, saying, "This is your country and mine."

Back in the office, we agonized. On the one hand, the president had been so straight, so decent, that it seemed almost impolite to print anything he did not want printed. On the other hand, newspapering isn't about being polite or grateful. It's about deciding where the public interest lies. In this case, could we involve ourselves effectively in a Middle East settlement *without* our negotiators—never mind the public—knowing we "owned" a key participant in that settlement?

We had developed a policy at the *Post* to help decision making on matters of national security. We automatically delayed publication for twenty-four hours as soon as any responsible official invoked national security. Simultaneously, we reached a tentative decision to publish (so that we could arrange for the extra space normally required on a big story), and we appointed a group of reporters expert in the field at issue to talk us *out* of publishing the story.

We finally came down on the side of publishing. Because the story was true . . . we did have a king on our payroll, unknown to the public, and until very recently, unknown to the president and to the Secretary of State. Because the former CIA director and the former Secretary of State had failed to tell the new president despite hours of briefings. Because the current president would not say that national security was involved. And because effective oversight of the CIA lay somewhere between ludicrous and nonexistent. No one really knew what the spooks were up to.

The day after the story ran, I got this note from President Carter, handwritten on embossed White House stationery:

To Ben Bradlee,
I think your publication of the CIA story as the Secretary of State was on his Middle East mission and about to arrive in Jordan was irresponsible.

This is offered by way of editorial comment.

Jimmy

I could understand why the president was upset. So was I. I felt we had gone the last mile to be responsible.

When Powell told Carter that I was upset by his letter, the president replied, "Well, fuck him."

And I could understand that, too.

There were no repercussions to our publication of this story, diplomatic or journalistic. Vance never mentioned it to me. President Carter never mentioned it again.

Newspaper people spend much of their life in some kind of defensive crouch. This is ultimately deforming unless diagnosed and treated.

A clear exclusive plastered all over page one of the *New York Times* could put an otherwise outstanding *Washington Post* reporter into a defensive crouch automatically. "We had that," he would respond instinctively, within seconds. And when challenged, he would disappear into the library for an hour or so, before returning quasi-triumphantly waving a clip. Sometimes, if the reporter was lucky, there would be some vague reference in paragraph 30 to a minor bit of evidence in the exclusive.

Once in frustration at hearing "We had that" for the umpteenth time, I offered to eat any clip offered in proof, if a jury of the reporter's peers agreed that we in fact had run the same story. I never had to pay off, but the words haunt city rooms across the land.

At my request, a young *Post* artist, Steve Mendelson, came up with a marvelous drawing of a journalist deep in a Defensive Crouch, which we awarded from time to time to grievous offenders.

In the olden days, press criticism was a fairly esoteric subject. President Roosevelt once gave *New York Daily News* columnist John O'Donnell a mock Nazi medal, during World War II, to express his criticism of O'Donnell's stories about FDR's war preparations. Fifty years ago the great *New Yorker* critic A. J. Liebling periodically skewered the press in his wonderful "Annals of the Press" articles, although his target was generally hype rather than bias. Ike had decried "sensation-seeking columnists" at the 1964 convention in San Francisco's Cow Palace. In a fit of pique, Jack Kennedy canceled the White House orders for twenty-four copies of the *New York Herald Tribune*. Agnew's feelings about the press were notorious. But today everyone is a press critic. All politicians, virtually all public figures, most business leaders, and most readers.

Newspapers even have their own staff press critics, including *The Washington Post* with its own Ombudsman since 1969. They are the independent monitors of fairness, accuracy, and relevance. And there are now scores of journalism reviews devoted exclusively to scanning the press (and TV) for sins of commission or omission.

And then there are the ideological critics—people who disagree with how a newspaper covers a story as much as they disagree with what stories we cover. The chief ideological critic is an organization called AIM, for Accuracy in Media, a particular pain in the ass to the *Post*, the *Times*, the networks . . . what are generally regarded to be best of American journalism. AIM was started by a Federal Reserve Board economist named Reed Irvine, in what he claimed was his spare time, until his mom-and-pop press criticism caught the eye of some really moneyed right-wing ideologues like Richard Mellon Scaife of Pittsburgh.

With money in his kick, Irvine started burying reporters, editors, and owners under long screeds about their failure to cover obscure press conferences starring one of Irvine's protégés. About why we used the word "execution" instead of the word "massacre" to describe some horror event. Or asking why we played a story on page A8 instead of on the front page. Or why we failed to print any of his hundreds of letters to the editor. He and his cohorts started monopolizing stockholders' meetings, and then complaining when we didn't cover his contorted performances. And he often asked his readers to write letters to the *Post* which he dictated in his newsletter.

Finally, in the spring of 1978, I hit the wall, and to my everlasting regret, I put Irvine on the map for good—and helped him raise hundreds of thousands of dollars he would never have otherwise raised—by writing him a letter I never should have mailed. After some particularly offensive and tendentious criticism of the *Post* by Irvine, I wrote him a short letter, which included this sentence:

> You have revealed yourself as a miserable, carping, retromingent vigilante, and I for one am sick of wasting my time communicating with you.

God knows where I found "retromingent," but it was the perfect word for the occasion, describing that subspecies of ants (and other animals) which urinate backwards.

His supporters were outraged—Santa Barbara dentists, retired admirals, small business men lounging in the Phoenix sun—but Irvine loved the letter, and he used it for years in his annual appeals for funds from the faithful. I got a couple of hundred form postcards from AIM supporters taking me to task, but by far the most satisfying letter came from Larry Laystall in Wye, Maryland. He was having crabs and beer when he chanced to read William Buckley's column about my use of "retromingent" in the *Washington Star*, which was serving as his tablecloth.

"One of the fellows at our table was 'Big Hans,' " he wrote.

> After a couple of pitchers of beer, we all went out to the parking lot to find out whether "Big Hans" was retromingent. Hans . . . bet quite a bit of money on himself, borrowed a waitress' mirror, got himself in a funny position, and retromingented.
>
> We think that big words might be lost on Mr. Irvine anyway, since we're told he couldn't pour the end product out of a boot no matter what you called it.

Senseless critics of the press reveal their bias quickly. "Why do you Commie bastards always give away our national secrets?" for instance. That kind of stuff can be safely ignored, although every so often I would get one outrageous enough to be worth answering. Like the charming letter in 1985 to Katharine Graham from one T. J. Malone, of 444 West Wood Street, Decatur, Illinois, as follows: "Say, Cath, heard you and Ben B. were recently seen at a wild coke

party, and someone noticed you both had a hammer and sickle tattooed on your butts."

I answered him as follows: "I have a hissing snake tattooed on my
butt.* And I don't have a clue what Mrs. Graham has tattooed on
hers." Since my frat mate at college, Bill Barnes, had risen to eminence in Decatur, I added: "The president of the bank in Decatur,
Illinois, is an old classmate and friend of mine. I think I'll ask him
to foreclose on your mortgage."

Childish, no doubt, until you realize that the polls so often cited
to show public trust in the press declining include the views of T. J.
Malone, and thousands of other nut cases.

There is a need for serious criticism of the press; when it is
thoughtful and measured, it is vitally important to society, particularly to the press and to readers of the press. It was not enough for
President Ronald Reagan to start off press conference answers with
that polished grin as he told reporters, "You guys never get it right."
Or defense lawyers, or political candidates—many of them people
who have mastered the ability to use and abuse the press at the
same time. Or at least it is not enough for me to take that kind of
grandstanding criticism seriously.

There is so much to criticize about the press, but not before
recognizing a ringing truth: the best of the American press is an
extraordinary daily example of industry, honesty, conscience, and
courage, driven by a desire to inform and interest readers.

We journalists have thin skins because we are so often criticized.
Often enough, we have it coming, because we make mistakes. Lots
of them, and our mistakes hang out there for the world to see for at
least twenty-four hours and frequently longer. And I'm not talking
about the small, irritating mistakes, essentially involving wrong
names, addresses, dates, and times. Those can be first minimized,
then corrected (and routinely are corrected in good newspapers).

The best newspapers now are comfortable in the confessional,
generally collecting the day's errata on page one or three. If a mistake is so important that it must run on page one, it is never called

* And a rooster on my left upper arm.

a "correction" or any other euphemism suggesting wrongdoing. It is simply presented as a story, and the reader must be smart enough to know that the record is being awkwardly set straight.

Corrections are more fun to read than make. On the wall in front of my computer I have Scotch-taped the following front-page "story" from the *Sunday Times* of London, July 13, 1986, as an example of one editor's nightmare:

> Today's Magazine profile [of a company called Control Risks] . . . contains statements which are untrue. Contrary to what is stated, at no time has CR paid, or been an agent for paying £2 million to the IRA, nor any sum to any terrorist organization; nor was CR involved in, or aware of, the alleged attempt to smuggle £300,000 into Ireland.
>
> CR is not "persona non grata" with the Home Office and the police. The statement that CR's activities often bring it into direct conflict with local police is also untrue. We accept that CR always cooperates with the police and enjoys their confidence around the world.
>
> We are glad to make it clear that any action contemplated by the Home Secretary concerning kidnapping and ransom insurance is unrelated to CR's activities. . . .
>
> We unreservedly apologise to CR for the above errors, and have agreed to pay a substantial sum in damages to charities of its choice.

That is a front three-and-a-half grovel, with full twist . . . to be avoided at all costs by editors who believe in job security.

Every once in a while, the watchful reader will run into the very rare correction of a correction, and once in a lifetime you run into something like this: apparently the very rare correction of a correction of a correction . . . from the *New York Times* in April 1994.

> A caption in the Evening Hours pages last Sunday, about an opening at the American Craft Museum, confused the identities of several people because of a picture substitution during a production process.

The picture showed from the left, Shimoda; Dubaka Leigh; and Janet Kardon, the museum's director. (Kate Carmel and Marcella Welch were not pictured.)

Corrections in the main news section last Sunday and again on Tuesday repeated the confusion of Ms. Kardon with Ms. Carmel. In addition, the correction last Sunday referred incorrectly to Dubaka Leigh. He is a man.

Our most serious mistakes occur when we relay misinformation given us by others—presidents, spin doctors, or ignoramuses. And here lies the heart of our dilemma: we write only the rough draft of history, in the vivid words of Phil Graham. We claim to print the truth. We have led our readers to expect the truth. We have trouble with Albert Camus's realization that "there is no truth; only truths." We don't cope with the reality that the truth often escapes us.

Because our sources lie. Because our sources are themselves ill-informed, misinformed, or incompletely informed. Because deadlines force us to stop reporting, and start writing, before the truth has emerged out of the maelstrom of conflicting eyewitness accounts, clashing spin doctors, and the angers of partisan politics.

We are unable to admit any of this publicly, as I once found out, for as soon as we admit that we don't always print the truth, someone will immediately pounce on the admission and say, "See. I told you so. The press lies. Even Ben Bradlee says newspapers don't tell the truth." As former President Nixon did in his book, RN: *The Memoirs of Richard Nixon.* Nixon wrote about "rumor journalism, some true, some false, some a mixture of truth and fiction, all prejudicial," at a time when the Watergate story was gathering its fatal steam. Nixon went on:

"That it was a dangerous form of journalism should have been understood by the *Post,* whose editor, Ben Bradlee, has since observed: 'We don't print the truth. We print what we know, what people tell us. So we print lies.' "

The fact is that the truth *does* emerge, and its emergence is a normal, and vital, process of democracy. If readers are generally too impatient to wait for the truth to emerge, that is a problem. It is our problem in the press. It is far easier and more comfortable for them to accept as truth whatever fact fits their own particular bias, and dismiss whatever facts misfit their biases. It is impossible to underestimate the importance of reader bias in any serious study of press criticism.

What was the truth of the Battle of Tonkin Gulf? At the time—August 4, 1964—the Johnson administration said the truth was that North Vietnamese PT boats attacked two American destroyers, and LBJ used the attack to force passage of the Tonkin Gulf Resolution. It passed the House with no opposition and passed the Senate with only two votes against, and then was used to justify the American pursuit of the Vietnam War. Hundreds of thousands of words were written about that battle and that resolution, but were they the truth?

Twenty years later—twenty years!—Admiral Jim Stockdale revealed in his book *Love and War* that to the best of his knowledge there never was a Battle of Tonkin Gulf. His truth was that there were no North Vietnamese PT boats, and therefore no battle. He was in a position to know. On the night in question he was in a Sabre Jet fighter flying cover over the two American destroyers at the time of the "battle." He wrote that he was as sure as a man can be, after scouring the sea for more than two hours, that the destroyers were firing at phantom radar blips, not enemy PT boats. (Stockdale was shot down right after the incident, was a prisoner of war for more than seven years, and returned briefly to the limelight in 1992 as presidential candidate Ross Perot's running mate.)

What was the truth in the Pentagon Papers case, where the government tried to prevent newspapers from publishing a story for the first time in the history of the republic? In June 1971, the U.S. Solicitor General, Erwin N. Griswold, argued before the Supreme Court of the United States that publication of the Pentagon Papers would seriously threaten the national security. Almost twenty years later, Griswold described the government's case against the *Times* and the *Post* as a "mirage."

Of course the press makes other mistakes, all easier to correct:

- We do such a poor job of sourcing our information, when the source is critical to any intelligent reader, that it amounts to a mistake. "According to sources"—those three words by themselves just aren't good enough. They should be banned. Readers think we aren't coming clean here, and they are more often right than wrong.
- We can improve our sourcing 100 percent with very little effort. What kind of sources? Friends or foes? Men or women? Army or Navy? Republicans or Democrats? Young or old? Lawyers or clients? Gays or straights? Doctors or patients? In government or out? Incumbents or aspirants?

There are also, alas, the whoppers: mistakes in stories that live far longer than the stories themselves.

Such a whopper was the darkest chapter of my newspaper life, an error of judgment that put the story's byline on a special shelf of horrors.

SEVENTEEN

JANET COOKE

Janet Cooke is a beautiful black woman with dramatic flair and vitality, and an extraordinary talent for writing. She is also a cross that journalism, especially *The Washington Post*, and especially Benjamin C. Bradlee, will bear forever. At the age of twenty-six, she wrote a vivid, poignant story about an eight-year-old heroin addict who was regularly shot up by his mother's live-in lover. The story made page one, on Sunday, September 28, 1980, and held the city in thrall for weeks. The story earned Cooke the Pulitzer Prize for feature reporting on April 13, 1981.

In the earliest hours of the morning of April 15, 1981, Janet Cooke confessed that she had made it all up: there was no Jimmy, there was no live-in lover. From that moment on, the words "Janet Cooke" entered the vocabulary as a symbol for the worst in American journalism, just as the word "Watergate" went into the vocabulary as a symbol for the best in American journalism.*

---

* After leaving the Post, Cooke worked as a salesclerk in Washington. She toyed with a film script about her experiences. She married a Washington lawyer and briefly moved to Paris with him, but the marriage failed. She declined an invitation to talk with me for this book.

I had known about the story as it worked its way up the reporting and editing ladder. I had read it thoroughly the week before it ran on page one, and found it riveting. It was titled "Jimmy's World," and it started this way:

> Jimmy is 8 years old and a third generation heroin addict, a precocious little boy with sandy hair, velvety brown eyes and needle marks freckling the baby-smooth skin of his thin brown arms.
>
> He nestles in a large, beige reclining chair in the living room of his comfortably furnished home in Southeast Washington. There is an almost cherubic expression on his small, round face as he talks about life—clothes, money, the Baltimore Orioles, and heroin. He has been an addict since the age of 5.
>
> His hands are clasped behind his head, fancy running shoes adorn his feet, and a striped Izod T-shirt hangs over his thin frame. "Bad, ain't it," he boasts. "I got me six of these."

And it ended this way:

> [Ron] grabs Jimmy's left arm just above the elbow, his massive hand tightly encircling the child's small limb. The needle slides into the boy's soft skin like a straw pushed into the center of a freshly baked cake. Liquid ebbs out of the syringe, replaced by bright red blood. The blood is then reinjected into the child.
>
> Jimmy has closed his eyes during the whole procedure, but now he opens them, looking quickly around the room. He climbs into a rocking chair and sits, his head dipping and snapping upright again, in what addicts call "the nod."

In between, around a startling illustration of young Jimmy reaching his arm toward the reader, Janet Cooke promised authenticity with details such as these:

• *On Jimmy's mother:* She never knew her father. Like her son, Andrea spent her childhood with her mother and the man with whom she lived for 15 years. She recalls that her mother's boyfriend routinely forced her and her younger sister to have sex, and Jimmy is the product of one of those rapes. Depressed and discouraged after his birth ("I didn't even name him, you know? My sister liked the name Jimmy, and I said, 'OK, call him that . . . who gives a fuck. I guess we got to call him something'"), she quickly accepted the offer of heroin from a woman who used to shoot up with her mother.

- *On Jimmy's house*: Death has not yet been a visitor to the house where Jimmy lives. The kitchen and upstairs bedrooms are a human collage. People of all shapes and sizes drift into the dwelling and its various rooms, some jittery, uptight, and anxious for a fix, others calm and serene after they finally "get off."

White reporters, much less white editors, don't circulate much in Jimmy's World. I had smoked marijuana maybe a dozen times in all of the sixties and seventies. And I have never used cocaine or heroin. To me, the story reeked of the sights and sounds and smells that editors love to give their readers. The possibility that the story was not true never entered my head.

After the fact, some reporters, particularly Courtland Milloy, a streetwise black reporter, told me that they had questioned the story. Milloy had taken Cooke in his car to look for Jimmy's house. When she couldn't find it, he shared his doubts with Milton Coleman, the savvy city editor, en route to becoming a national reporter and then assistant managing editor for Metro. Coleman told others he thought Milloy was jealous, but he did pass on Milloy's opinion to Howard Simons. The story still had a long way to go, and Howard kept his feelings to himself.

The day Cooke won the Pulitzer Prize, April 13, 1981, the story—and my world with it—began to fall apart. The *Toledo Blade*, where Cooke had once worked, and the Associated Press started preparing biographical sketches about Cooke. The sketches were fatally contradictory. The AP sketch was based on a Pulitzer Committee handout, which in turn was based on biographical data submitted by Cooke herself, a few months earlier. The *Blade's* sketch was based on its own Personnel Department records, and started when Cooke went to work there some years earlier.

The contradictions that emerged were devastating. One story said she had graduated *magna cum laude* from Vassar. Another said she had been to Vassar only for one year. One story said she had a master's degree from the University of Toledo, another said she had only an undergraduate degree. One story said she had attended the Sorbonne in Paris. The other said nothing about the Sorbonne. The Pulitzer bio said Janet Cooke spoke French, Spanish, Portuguese, and Italian. The old résumé claimed French and Italian.

The exact moment when I felt as if I had been punched in the stomach came in the early afternoon, when Dixie Sheridan from the admissions office of Vassar College called to say that she thought "we had a little problem." At the very same moment Simons was on the phone to Lou Boccardi, then the AP's vice president and executive editor, who was explaining the exact dimensions of "the little problem."

At this point in my life I didn't know much about confession. Not that I had never had to confess, starting with forging my father's distinctive signature on a bad report card from Miss Bean in the fifth grade of Dexter School. But I had spent rather more time witnessing confessions from others—and enjoying it much more. But thanks to Watergate, I had learned a vitally important lesson: The truth is the best defense, and the whole truth is the very best defense.

Once we had identified the fraud, we set ourselves a simple goal: No one should ever learn anything more about the Janet Cooke case than *The Washington Post* itself revealed. The only question was how to achieve that goal. Twenty reporters on the *Post* asked me to name them as an investigative team to get the whole story, an invitation I declined quickly. This was no time for the inmates to take over the institution. I believed the investigation was tailor-made for the resolutely autonomous Ombudsman.*

The Ombudsman had a contract which allowed him to write on any subject he chose. He could not be edited; he could not

* We had created the position of Ombudsman at the Post in 1969 to monitor the paper for fairness, accuracy, and relevance, and to represent the public in whatever strains might arise from time to time between the newspaper and its readers.

be assigned; and he could not be fired. When "Jimmy's World" landed on us like a Kamikaze bomb, the Ombudsman was William Green. Bill had never been a career journalist. All told he had a couple of years on small papers in the South. He had been a public affairs officer in India for the United States Information Service, and he had worked as a special assistant to the former governor of North Carolina, Terry Sanford, while Sanford was president of Duke University. He taught a sophisticated course in journalism at Duke, and he was one wise and fair sumbitch, as the locals say, respected by the staff for his common sense and his respect for the individual.

In four days, working almost around the clock, Bill Green accomplished an incredibly difficult task: a no-holds-barred, meticulously reported account of what went wrong—18,000 words spread over the front page and four full pages inside.

How could any reporter, even someone I once described as a one-in-a-million liar, penetrate the editorial defenses of a newspaper whose commitment to truth was unequaled?

"Jimmy's World" got into the paper, Green concluded, because of the failure of the system that is called "quality control" in other industries and "editing" in newspapers. By publishing "Jimmy's World," *The Washington Post* was "humiliated," Green said in the lead of his front page story, on Sunday, April 19, because editors abandoned their vaunted professional skepticism.

Cooke had first come to my attention in a letter saying she thought she was ready for the big time, after more than two years at the *Toledo Blade*. An editor gets dozens of such letters every month. Hers stood out because she produced clips that showed she could write like a dream; she had top-drawer college credentials; and she was black. The answer to a modern editor's prayers. I passed her résumé on to Woodward, who was then assistant managing editor for Metro, with an expression of interest. Female Phi Beta Kappa graduates of Seven Sisters colleges who can write the King's English with style don't grow on trees, white or black, and we were a decade into our commitment to increase the number and quality of minorities and women on the staff. The *Post* hired Cooke six months later, after she impressed all the editors who interviewed her, myself included, except for Herb Denton, the black city editor who thought there was too much Vassar in her.

Her Vassar credentials were never checked. This was our first mistake, and it was fatal. If we had found out that she lied when she claimed she had an honors degree from Vassar, of course, that would have been the end of it. She wouldn't have had the chance to make any more mistakes.

How come we never checked? Simply put, Janet Cooke was too good to be true, and we wanted her too bad.

There is a joke in our business that every blue moon or so, a reporter runs into a story, or more likely a rumor, that is so fantastic that it's almost a shame to check it out. Check rumors like these, and you run the almost certain risk of finding quick, credible evidence that the story is just plain not true. We resist that impulse with stories, but we did not resist the same impulse in making this particular personnel decision. At a time when we were struggling to meet our commitment to increase the quantity and quality of minority and female journalists on the paper, Janet Cooke had "can't miss" written all over her. What the hell were we waiting for? Grab her before the *New York Times* does, or *Newsweek*, or television.

And she was hired.

Janet Cooke hit the ground running at the *Post*, with fifty-two bylines in her first eight months on the staff. As Bill Green wrote later: "She was a conspicuous member of the staff. When she walked, she pranced. When she smiled she dazzled. Her wardrobe was always new, impeccable and limitless."

Her immediate editor, Vivian Aplin-Brownlee, described Cooke to Green as "consumed by blind and raw ambition, but talented." "She was Gucci and Cardin and Yves St. Laurent," Aplin-Brownlee reported. "She went out on [a story from the black ghetto] in designer jeans, and came back to tell me that somebody asked her 'What kind of a nigger are you?' She thought it was funny."

Cooke was not popular with black men on the staff, perhaps

because she refused to date any of the many who asked. She did date several of the white reporters, but she was more interested in her work than in her social life. She told one friend she wanted a Pulitzer Prize in three years, and a job on the National staff in three to five years. She soon lost herself in an assignment to look into a new kind of heroin, circulating in the city, so strong it was said to ulcerate the skin.

She brought back 145 pages of handwritten notes taken during this assignment. Aplin-Brownlee thought they were good enough to show to Milton Coleman, and Coleman thought them good enough to bring Cooke in for a talk about how they should be "storified"— made into a story. It was during this conversation that she first mentioned reports of an eight-year-old addict. Coleman stopped her short: "That's the story. Go after it. It's a front page story."

Three weeks later Cooke told Coleman she had found the eight-year-old addict, had even talked to his mother. Coleman told Cooke she could promise the boy's mother confidentiality first, then anonymity. With that, Coleman felt no need to know the woman's name, at least not then.

"The jugular of journalism lay exposed," in Bill Green's great phrase, "the faith an editor has to place in a reporter."

Should Coleman have gotten the name of the "addict" and his mother? Probably. If not then, damn soon. Should he have gotten the address? In sober second thought, yes. An address is an anchor that can be checked by anyone, any time. Names of unknowns are ephemeral. But Cooke's first memo, which we all saw, was filled with such a rich supply of apparently convincing detail—eight-foot plastic sofas, blue and green Izod shirts, Panasonic stereo equipment, fake bamboo blinds, rubber trees, brown shag rugs, and much more—that doubts died before they matured. For the first time, the "addict" had a name, Tyrone, and we knew which elementary school he attended when he wasn't playing hooky. And so it moved—glacially, inevitably toward publication.

I knew nothing about Jimmy's World. There were virtually no circumstances in which I would come into contact with Jimmy's mother, or her live-in boyfriend, Ron, much less have a meaningful conversation with either of them. The same was true for Howard Simons. By the time the story was ready to publish, everyone concerned had so much at stake.

Almost 900,000 copies of the *Post* rolled off the presses early Sunday morning, September 28, 1980. The *L.A. Times-Washington Post* News Service took "Jimmy's World" to more than three hundred newspapers in the United States and around the world. Jimmy was an overnight sensation. The *Post's* phones rang off the hook. The police chief launched a mammoth search for the boy and his mother. Police threatened to subpoena Cooke and her notes, but backed off in face of *Post* resistance. Mayor Marion Barry quickly announced that the city knew Jimmy's identity. There were also reports that Dr. Alyce Gullattee, director of Howard University's Institute for Substance Abuse, knew Jimmy and his family.

It is hard for me to understand how those who later said they had doubts about "Jimmy's World" could rationalize those doubts in view of the apparent corroboration of Cooke's story by Barry and Dr. Gullattee. Aplin-Brownlee had been an early doubter and she stood by her guns. Courtland Milloy was a doubter, as soon as he took Cooke to look for Jimmy's apartment and she couldn't find it. But their doubts were more about Cooke than about her story. No one ever suggested that Cooke concocted the entire story. Worse, none of us editors thought about the life and safety of the child. If we had insisted that a *Post* doctor examine Jimmy, we would have escaped disaster. Pretty soon Cooke was working on another blockbuster about a fourteen-year-old hooker and her twenty-year-old pimp, and this time Woodward, who topped the reporting chain from Cooke up, and Coleman insisted on meeting the hooker themselves. When those appointments kept getting canceled, we thought the hooker and the pimp were getting cold feet. It did not occur to us that she had invented them, too.

By December, when newspapers nominate their best work for Pulitzer prizes, "Jimmy's World" was the *Post's* sole entrant in the category of local news reporting.

And on April 13, 1981, the worst happened: "Jimmy's World" won a Pulitzer Prize.

In destroyers, under battle conditions, one of the most important jobs is damage control: how can the damage from a torpedo hit amidships, or a Kamikaze crash, or a boiler explosion be controlled so that the ship can limp back into port, and survive to fight another day? As an assistant damage-control officer of the U.S.S. *Philip* (DD498), I had learned that damage control is one of the most important jobs on any naval vessel. As the damage-control officer—read executive editor—of *The Washington Post*, I had learned that damage control is one of the most important jobs on a newspaper.

The first lesson of damage control is to get an accurate picture of the damage as soon as possible. At the *Post*, after "Jimmy's World" exploded in the city room, we began our exercise in damage control by examining Janet Cooke's Vassar credentials, figuring that if she lied there, it was likely that she lied elsewhere. I told Milton Coleman to take Miss Cooke "to the woodshed," an old political practice described to me by Jim Rowe, once a member of FDR's Kitchen Cabinet, and a longtime Washington powerbroker. Jim Rowe had taken Hubert Humphrey to the woodshed at the request of President Lyndon B. Johnson, before LBJ decided on Humphrey as his vice-presidential running mate. When you take someone to the woodshed, Rowe told me, you get him off in a room alone and grill him about his taxes, his health, his girlfriends, his finances, his war record, his debts, his addictions, his innermost secrets. Both parties in the woodshed have to do their jobs for the process to be useful.

Coleman took Cooke to the woodshed by walking her across L Street to the bar of the Capital Hilton Hotel. At first Cooke stuck to her guns, but when Coleman called Vassar right then and there, she began her retreat. She had run into emotional problems at Vassar, she said, and completed only one year. What about languages, Coleman asked. Cooke insisted she spoke four. What about the Sorbonne? Cooke insisted she had attended the Sorbonne.

"And the Jimmy story?" Coleman asked.

"It's true," she lied.

At this point Coleman called in and we suggested he bring Cooke back into the side entrance of the *Post*, and up to the corporate offices on the eighth floor. When Woodward and I arrived, Janet Cooke was sitting on the sofa crying, Bill Green remembers, and said, "You get caught at the stupidest thing."

But Janet Cooke was practicing her own brand of damage control—admitting to phonying her Vassar records but nothing else. I suddenly felt we had been pussyfooting around too long (because she was a woman and a black?), and what followed was not a pleasant conversation.

First, I asked her to say two words in Portuguese, any two. (I myself knew only two words of Portuguese, period: O *gis* . . . The chalk.) She said she couldn't. I asked her if she had any Italian. She said she did not. I have spoken French since I was six years old, and I started asking her questions in French. Her replies suggested nothing like an ability to speak French. I told her she was lying. She was trying to cover up the truth. Just like Richard Nixon, I said, and that pissed her off. She didn't like my questioning any more than I liked her answers. I finally told her she had twenty-four hours to prove that the Jimmy story was true, and walked out.

Woodward told her he didn't believe the Jimmy story and was going to prove that she was lying if it was the last thing he ever did, and left the room.

Next we sent Coleman out with Cooke to find Jimmy's house. Coleman called half an hour later, and said she couldn't find it. He was now convinced that Cooke had made the whole thing up. The only holdout was Cooke herself. Simons and I went home, leaving Cooke in the hot seat answering tough questions from Woodward, assistant managing editor Tom Wilkinson, Coleman, and David Maraniss, the Maryland editor. Cooke complained that the questioning was "getting too cruel."

"All I have is my story," she added.

Finally, she was left alone with Maraniss, and Bill Green's report described this conversation:

Cooke, crying: "I was afraid I was going to be left alone with you. The first time I saw you today I thought, 'Oh boy! He knows and I'm going to have to tell him.' I couldn't lie to you. I couldn't tell them. I never would tell Woodward. The more he yelled the more stubborn I was. Wilkinson represents the corporation. It means so much to Milton [Coleman]. You guys are smart. Woodward for the mind, you for the heart. . . . Why are you smiling?"

Maraniss: "Because I had a tremendous surge of empathy for you, refusing to submit to the institution in an absurd situation. You were strong not to give in. The institution will survive."

Maraniss and Cooke talked for more than an hour, about their childhoods, about what she had gone through after her story was nominated for a Pulitzer Prize.

"You don't have to say anything to the others," Maraniss told her. "I'll do it for you. What do I tell them?"

And suddenly the ordeal was over.

"There is no Jimmy, and no family," Cooke confessed. She said she felt she knew enough to get away with it. She knew that Jimmy could never be found because he didn't exist. She said she had prayed she wouldn't get the Pulitzer, surely a first in the annals of journalism.

It was after 2:00 A.M. when I was called with the news that I had known for hours was coming. Once we had her written resignation in hand—and I can't explain now why I let her resign rather than fire her on the spot for the grossest negligence—I woke Joe Pulitzer up in St. Louis to tell him we were returning the prize, with apologies. And at 7:00 A.M., I called Don Graham with the sledgehammer news, and I told him that if he felt I should resign, I would do so forthwith.

Sometimes I feel sorry for publishers. The best of them, meaning the only two publishers I have worked for in my entire adult life, ask only one thing of their editors: If you want us in on the landing, please include us in on the takeoff. Don and Kay would sure as hell be involved in this landing, taking heavy flak from colleagues jealous of their success and from natural enemies on the right who would start yelling for my scalp.

Don Graham's support at this time, the lowest point in my career, was tremendous. And his support was public. Not only did he not want my resignation, he wanted us to get it behind us, get all the lessons we could out of this misery, and get on with our task.

I have always worked better, more creatively even, when I am confronted with Augean tasks—when there is a pile of it in the middle of the road, if you will, and I have a good shovel, surrounded by good shovelers.

As if the pile in the road wasn't big enough, the lions of the American Society of Newspaper Editors (ASNE)—almost one thousand strong—were in convention assembled in Washington, at that very moment. Not my favorite crowd, as I was not their favorite editor. The ASNE is composed predominantly of owners and editors of small newspapers—many of them southern—pillars of their communities whose problems and priorities did not coincide with mine. They are generally proud members of the establishment who don't like to write about their fellow establishmentarians. Anyway, my old pal Tom Winship, then editor of the *Boston Globe*, was the ASNE president, and someone had convinced him that I would make an interesting program chairman, the guy who has to line up speakers and workshops for the four-day convention. There isn't another man in the world I would have served as program chairman, especially after he prefaced his invitation by saying, "Everyone thinks I'm crazy to offer you this job." The program I had arranged was fine, maybe even good, when Tom sidled up to me at the opening reception and suggested we have some kind of panel on the Janet Cooke affair. "There's an awful lot of interest," he remarked, as if I didn't know.

Traditionally, program chairmen schedule one or two 8:00 A.M. workshops to begin each convention day, generally on esoteric topics, of interest to only a handful of editors. "Attitude Surveys . . . How Good Are They?" for instance, and good stuff like that. If you could draw a crowd of fifteen editors to one of these, you would set a new ASNE record.

I had scheduled an 8:00 A.M. session on the Ombudsman, an institution that interested me, but very few other editors. Charlie Seib, the *Post*'s former Ombudsman, and the wise and able editor of the *Washington Star* when it folded, was chairing the panel, and we spread the word that Janet Cooke would be Topic A, and that the program chairman, his very own self, would be among those present.

Well, more than 750 of my peers and their guests, plus five TV cameras, showed up at seven in the morning to watch me get raked over the coals. But the ordeal was made eminently survivable by the presence *at my side* of Don Graham. Photographers must have taken hundreds of pictures of me that day, but damn few—if any—without Don Graham's arm around my shoulder. I'll never forget it, and all these years later, his presence and his show of confidence still makes my neck tingle. And next to Graham, most of the time, was my predecessor as *Post* editor and a former president of the ASNE, Russ Wiggins, who had come down from Ellsworth, Maine, where he was editing a prize-winning weekly (and still does). Russ told everyone within earshot that he was delighted to learn of the lofty state of American journalism, a conclusion he had reached after listening to so many editors say that the Janet Cooke case could never happen on their papers. I'll never forget the generosity of his presence that day, and so many other days.

It took no great genius to make the many mistakes we made in coming up with "Jimmy's World," just as it took no great genius to learn the lessons from our humiliation.

First, there really is no protection against a skillful liar, who has earned the trust of his or her editors. That is equally true of business, law, medicine, all professions. Unfortunately, it happens, however rarely, in the best of circles. Janet Cooke had been at the paper close to two years, and after the "Jimmy" disaster a careful examination of everything she had ever written for us revealed no other questionable facts.

• Michael Daly, columnist for the *New York Daily News*, resigned in May 1981 after fictionalizing aspects of a story about British troops bullying Irish rebels.

- WABC-TV faked letters from the public. The executive producer, the program director, a reporter, and two other staff members resigned.

- In December 1981—less than a year after Cooke won her Pulitzer—the *New York Times Magazine* featured an article called "In the Land of the Khmer Rouge," describing a visit into the Cambodian hinterlands, where rebels under the deposed dictator Pol Pot were holding out. The story featured a vivid description of a battle, strongly suggesting that the author saw Pol Pot himself through field glasses on a distant hillside. Two months later, other publications (including *The Washington Post* and the *Times* itself) revealed that the author, one Christopher Jones, had never left his home in Spain, and had lifted entire passages from his own earlier dispatches to *Time* magazine and from André Malraux's novel *The Royal Way*, set in Cambodia.

And others.

Second, check job applications and references carefully. Catch a liar at that stage of the employment process, and save yourself from a disaster you can't imagine.

Third, beware of stories you want to be true, for whatever reason. And beware the culture that allows unknown sources to be accepted too easily. Double-check the one about the crooked politician, the arsonist fire chief, the philandering religious leader, the debutante madam. Then check them again.

On a really big story, find at least one naysayer, and listen to him (or her). If you can't find one, assign someone to talk you out of running the story. We did that routinely on stories involving national security.

On a really big story, look for the reporters and editors who have some reservations. Encourage people to express their reservations about someone else's story, and to listen to reservations expressed by others about their own stories.

And finally, never get discouraged by how easily things can go wrong, how hard it is to find the truth. Think of something else you'd rather be doing, if you can.

*   *   *

After all the crisis about Janet Cooke, I wrote this memo to Don Graham:

> I have held a series of meetings—with Simons and Harwood, with AMEs, with the Metro staff, the National staff, the Sports staff and the Style staff, sharing my own thoughts and searching for information. I also had the "benefit" of many conversations with colleagues in town the week before, during the ASNE convention.
>
> I have read more than 100 letters, most of them vile and hateful and vengeful.
>
> And finally, I have walked the woods of West Virginia alone, looking for answers.
>
> The frailties of our system are simple to identify:
>
> - We put too much trust in Janet Cooke, given her experience, and given the obvious lack of precision in her information. I can find no sinister reason for that—sexual, racial, or anything else. Responsibility for this is uncomplicated, and direct from Coleman to Woodward to Simons to Bradlee.
> - We failed to make even a cursory check of that part of her resume which dealt with her education. I take little comfort in the fact that I have been unable to find a newspaper (or law firm) which does make that check.
> - We failed to insist that trust is a two-way street, from editors to reporters, and from reporters back to editors.
> - We wrestled the complicated issue of witnessing a crime to a no-fall decision, probably because we got bogged down in the process of the Jimmy story.
> - We have become careless about sourcing in general, losing sight of the Style Book injunction to seek maximum precision in the identification of sources, and to retreat from maximum identification with great reluctance.
> - We have a communication problem, and a strange one: We share information down, better than we share it up. This

one bugs me more than all the others, I guess, because I had thought I was "hanging out" with the staff so effectively that I could not miss anything as apparently prevalent as the doubts about Jimmy.

The corrections we should make seem equally simple:

- We routinely check *all* information in a resume, specifically including degree verification.
- Reporters must share the identity of any source with their editor. Any exception can be granted by the Executive Editor only, and there won't be any exceptions.
- Reporters and editors must be reminded once more about the paper's position on sourcing. Perhaps an addition to the Style Book along these lines:

    "The source of information is a critically important part of any story. It gives readers the chance to decide for themselves what motives an informant may have for making information public. Accordingly, every effort must be made routinely to get information on the record with specific identification of the source.

    "It is recognized, however, that valid reasons will exist for some source identification less than specific. In those circumstances, every effort must be made to give as precise an identification of the source as possible. The so-called 'geographical attribution'—State Department, Pentagon, Congress, White House, SEC, etc.—should be the minimum acceptable sourcing. And within those geographic areas, multiple refinements are almost always possible: House, Senate, staff, military, civilian, young, old, male, female, high-level, middle-echelon, etc.

    "But it is essential that any retreat from specific identification be reluctant, grudging and precise."
- We must find a way to insure that everyone shares fears and doubts with their superiors as well as with their colleagues.
- We must work on this whole question of our role as witnesses to crime. I doubt the wisdom of etching a policy on stone,

but we need to be more comfortable before we make ad hoc decisions.

And we must not lose our nerve as a newspaper; we must not retreat into the safety of blandness. We must not give up on the role of a newspaper to have an impact on its community.

I never was any good at firing people, even after I came to understand that it was an essential management skill. I once asked Bob McNamara for advice on how to fire, since he had more top management experience—at Ford and the Pentagon—than anyone else I knew. I told him that one man I wanted to ease out was an eighty-two-year-old assistant city editor, who said he would jump off the Calvert Street Bridge if I fired him.

McNamara told me he had fired "dozens" of top managers at Ford, and almost all of them had threatened to kill themselves if he went through with it. Only one guy even tried, he said, and he made a botch of it.

I tried to delegate firing, but that never worked, either. Once a copy boy relieved himself in the desk drawer of our sports columnist, Shirley Povich, and I asked our assistant managing editor for administration, Robert E. Lee Baker, to fire him. Baker gave me a long lecture about compassion, about forgiving other people's mistakes as they forgave mine, and the guy didn't get fired . . . until some months later when he got drunk again, and passed out on the Ladies' Room sofa.

I fired one reporter for plagiarism in a feature story about an historic Georgetown House. A Georgetown neighbor of mine, who had written a story on the house for the local historical society, stopped me in the street one day and said, "I didn't know the *Post* sanctioned plagiarism."

I fired a young Style reporter, with superstar credentials from Harvard, for lifting whole paragraphs without credit from J. D. Salinger in a feature story about the new singles communities in Washington's suburbs. She found a job on one of the Detroit newspapers, but eighteen months after leaving the *Post*, she took her own life. She still haunts my memories.

I fired a political reporter for making up a quote from Robert Kennedy, a quite innocuous quote and one which Kennedy would probably have agreed to say. But between the first and second editions, he called me up to say that he had not said it; he had not even talked to the reporter.

I have never forgotten the Janet Cooke case, but the caravan does move on. Three months after the Cooke fiasco, the *Washington Star* folded. Just like that. After 129 years it disappeared, victim of mismanagement. It was already too late when the Kauffmanns and the Noyes heirs, whose forebears had founded this great newspaper in 1852, sold it to Texas businessman Joe L. Albritton. Too late, because they had let Phil Graham buy the *Washington Times-Herald* and get a morning monopoly, and they had let him keep that monopoly as reader habits shifted to morning newspapers.

The *Star* had one more go at survival, when Albritton sold the paper to Time Inc., but even the most powerful publishing force in the land couldn't save it. They put more than $85 million into the paper in little more than a year, stole a few comic strips out from under the *Post*, tried to get the *Post*'s goat with an irreverent gossip column called "The Ear" (they got mine), but in the end they just plain slunk out of town.

They left a legacy of decency and principle. Newbold Noyes was responsible for that as the editor. After reading some flattering profile of me, a man who was a friend of Noyes and of me asked me, "Do you think you could have done with the *Star* what you've done with the *Post*?"

Answer: negatory.

I could take advantage of some of the finest newspaper people in the land, however. Especially the fabulous Mary McGrory. Everyone at the *Post*—owners, editors, just friends—had been trying to lure Mary away from the *Star* for years. She never gave any of us leeway. Far too loyal. I had known her, admired her, and loved her for years. In the sixties I had been allowed to carry her bags and typewriter during the presidential campaign. (We were known as McGrory's "bearers.") She had the best eyesight of any reporter in Washington. I'll always remember a column she wrote about a Senate confirmation hearing for some pompous preppie. She never called him pompous; she just fixated on his garish argyle socks, and that was enough.

We had lunch. I said, "Now?" She said, "Yeah." I said, "How much?" She mentioned a number. We shook hands, and that was that. The Janet Cooke tide started to go out.

EIGHTEEN

NATIONAL SECURITY: PUBLIC VS. PRIVATE

———

Dealing with the Central Intelligence Agency was always dicey, at home or abroad. Mostly because the spooks like to use the press to further policy objectives known to the agency, but unknown—or disguised—to the press.

The worst examples I ever saw of this use—or abuse—of the press by the CIA used to occur regularly at *Newsweek*'s Washington Bureau in the late fifties in Ernest K. Lindley's regime. *Newsweek* used to pay reporters an extra five bucks for items that appeared in "Periscope," a collection of crystal-ball predictions which appeared in the front of the book every week. Each item was speculative at best, if not imaginative, but not hard enough to "storify." Every so often the CIA's press representative, Colonel Stanley Grogan, would show up in person in the bureau with an envelope for Lindley, containing a Periscope item actually written by the CIA. By the time I got to the bureau from Paris, Lindley didn't even open the envelopes; he just passed them on to Guy Bocell, the TWX operator, for transmittal to New York.

Believe it or not . . . but Lindley kept the five bucks for himself.
Believe it or not.

CIA station chiefs abroad—especially in Vietnam and the Middle East—could be enormously useful when both parties to the
discussions were realistic about each other's loyalties. As long as
everyone was looking for the truth, everything was fine. But as soon
as the spooks tried to make things happen, or shape foreign correspondence, the waters muddied. And the best journalists had to
decide whether they were being manipulated, and how.

A reporter's reputation could be tainted by charges that he was
too close to the CIA, or manipulatable by the CIA. Certainly, my
old friend Sy Freidin, who worked for the *New York Herald Tribune*
and *Collier's* magazine, lost most of his reputation when it was revealed that he had actually been on the CIA payroll while he was
working as a journalist. This was a shame, because he was a lovely
man, and a great traveling companion. I once watched Sy in a contest in Belgrade to determine who could eat the hottest peppers,
washed down by slivovitz. I was permanently impressed at the sight
of Friedin biting into a pepper so hot that tears poured out of his
eyes, but he never said a word.

In 1981, *The Washington Post* and the CIA were involved in an
adventure most of which could have shown up in a John le Carré
book or movie—which, in fact, they did.

It all started one day when Howard Simons and I "came into
possession"* of a manuscript, written in tiny, cramped Russian
handwriting, filled with complex mathematical computations and
diagrams. Neither of us spoke Russian, but we didn't have to: the
contents obviously involved information over our heads and over
the head of the average *Post* reader. And because we were both conspiratorial and because the Cold War was still hot, we immediately
thought this material might have great value to the American intelligence community.

Howard called Admiral Bobby Ray Inman, the deputy director

---

* I am using this euphemism at the request of the persons responsible for our possession, who
do not wish to be identified for reasons which impress me as intelligent.

of Central Intelligence, and asked for an immediate appointment. (CIA director Casey was out of town.) We told Inman what we knew, what we thought we had, and what we planned to do with it. Namely, to give it to him, pronto. We asked for two things in return, without much confidence that we would get either one.

First, we wanted first crack at whatever story might develop. If it ended the Cold War, for instance. (Walter Mitty lives!) If it proved to be a fraud, for instance. Our experience was overwhelmingly that these deals never work out, but we figured it was worth a try. Second, if there were any spare Brownie points to be earned in this matter, we would appreciate a few, to combat the constant charge from the morons that the press in general—and the *Post* in particular—regularly disregarded the interests of the country for a scoop. We didn't have much hope here either, even after I talked to CIA director Casey. But two subsequent CIA directors volunteered on separate occasions that they were aware of the *Post*'s cooperation. That awareness, plus a token, is worth exactly one ride on the subway.

Inman "put [the manuscript] into the system," as he described it to me thirteen years later. In fact, the manuscript contained the specifics of design and function of a particular new Soviet Intermediate-Range Ballistic Missile (IRBM). Combined with satellite intelligence—from the monitoring of individual Soviet IRBM test firings, for instance—these specifics proved to be invaluable.

In September 1994, a Soviet weapons expert at the Central Intelligence Agency reported, for the record, that the document "gave us the best insights we had on Soviet Strategic Force Sea Launched Ballistic Missiles, and ICBMs, on their engineering capabilities, on their propellant capabilities." At the same time Inman described the document as "unique material . . . judged to be valuable" to our country.

Well before the arrival of Josiah Quinn Crowninshield Bradlee in April 1982, Sally and I slipped into the housing business, modestly at first, and then flamboyantly. First, we built a new cabin in West Virginia high over the Cacapon River, about a mile from the original log cabin. Dino and Sally had become fast friends, but she announced one day that "you can't share a cabin with a twenty-year-old boy who smells of gasoline all the time"—at least not that boy and that primitive cabin. And discussion about a new cabin turned into a new cabin in late 1979.

Earlier that summer, we had visited Barbara Howar, the lively lady from Raleigh who had been a friend and chaperone of the Johnson daughters, Lynda Bird and Luci Baines, before her private life made that impossible. Barbara was living in Bridgehampton on Long Island, and before we left we had bought a small house in Amagansett (for $75,000). It had recently been completely renovated by a decorator, the one and only time we ever bought a house in move-in condition, and the first of some notorious real estate ventures. For as long as we have been together, we have had some real estate project going, and we have been incredibly lucky with all of them. Sally was the engine here, too. We summered in the Amagansett house for a while, financing the purchase by renting it out when we were not on vacation. I liked Long Island, especially for its beach, the most gorgeous in the world; for good tennis, often with members of the old Paris crowd: Peter Matthiessen, Peter and Mary Stone, and George Plimpton; and for old and new New York friends who were smart, funny, achieving, and great company. Friends like Howard Stringer, en route to being the head of CBS, and his wife, the doctor Jennifer Patterson; like Ken Auletta, author and political and media columnist, and his wife, the agent Binky Urban; and Nick Pileggi, the world's expert on the mob, whom Nora Ephron had managed to snag as a husband.

One rainy afternoon, Sally went looking at houses with a real estate agent friend, and came back on fire to buy Grey Gardens, the unbelievably decrepit wreck of a beautiful turn-of-the-century house owned by the Beale family, first cousins of Jackie Kennedy. For years it had been eccentrically occupied—to be kind about it—by the widow "Big Edie" Beale and her daughter "Little Edie," plus almost fifty cats.

In all my life, including years reporting about slums from Washington to Casablanca, I have never seen a house in such dreadful condition: attics full of raccoons and their droppings, toilets stopped up, a kitchen stove that had fallen into the cellar, a living room with literally only half a floor, grounds so matted with devil's walking sticks and other thorns they were impenetrable, a large walled garden which was so overgrown it could not even be seen. Over everything hung the knee-buckling smell of cats and cat excrement. Whole rooms had been abandoned when they filled up with garbage, as the Beales moved to the next room. The house had been condemned several times by the Village of East Hampton as unfit for human habitation, then rescued by friends and relatives (including Jackie Kennedy, once), who supplied the new furnace or new toilet required by authorities. A cult documentary classic, *Grey Gardens*, made by the Maysles brothers—Albert and David— had caught it all on film. The cameramen had to wear flea collars on their ankles while they filmed. "Big Edie" had passed away, and "Little Edie" was forced to sell, but willing to sell to someone who would not tear the eyesore down.

I couldn't believe myself, walking into this pigsty for a personal inspection, and I couldn't believe Sally, after I staggered out. It is alleged that I muttered something like "You're out of your fff-ing mind." But, of course, she wasn't. Rehabilitated and relandscaped, Grey Gardens has been a fabulous summer home for years, featured in *House and Garden* and *Architectural Digest*. Only Peter Stone, and only after two days of solid rain, can still detect the slightest odor of cats. The whole house had to be gutted—one side literally swayed in a good storm—and the two acres of grounds were actually bulldozed clean.

By the next summer, the hippy carpenters, with their pit bull chained in the front yard, had fixed and painted one bedroom and bath—and nothing else. Every morning at 6:30 A.M., with a warning yell of "SAL-LEE, B-E-N," they'd start hammering and sawing, but we were ensconced in our shell, Sally newly pregnant with Quinn.

Some months later, still wondering if I ever would escape Watergate, if I wanted ever to escape Watergate, we went to La Samanna, the special seaside resort on St. Maarten in the Caribbean. So did

Richard and Pat Nixon, and his pal, Bebe Rebozo. (And a couple dozen Secret Service types in the former president's security detail.)

I had been told by the management that Nixon would be there at the same time, that we would have to promise to behave. No problem. But I brought along my tape recorder, just in case, responding to a Walter Mitty fantasy that I might just bump into him, catch him in a confessional mood, and finally nail down his involvement in Watergate, his apologies to the country. Jann Wenner, the smart and energetic founder of *Rolling Stone* magazine, was also a guest at the hotel with his wife, and he bought into my fantasy—big time.

Before long we had a plan. Nixon and Rebozo, in dark blue swimming trunks down to their knees, were taking a 4:00 P.M. swim together every afternoon, followed by a stroll up the beach, passing directly in front of our cabana. Wenner would keep an eye on Nixon and Rebozo (the "Trick Watch," he called it). As soon as they started up the beach, he would call me, and Sally and I would rush out to the water's edge, looking only straight ahead, and then immediately start our own walk up the beach, maybe 50 yards in front of Nixon and Rebozo. Our plan was to walk on nonchalantly (the tape recorder was well hidden), and then suddenly turn and start walking toward them. They would be too embarrassed to turn away; we'd meet, say hello, sit down, and the historic interview would just happen. You wouldn't believe how nonchalantly we strolled, or how suddenly we turned . . . and they had simply vanished. Wenner reported Nixon had spotted us immediately, and disappeared into his own cabana.

No interview, but a great vacation.

I knew Sally and I were going to need a new house in Washington soon enough. After a new baby and a baby nurse, Sally's house would be left with no study and no guest room. What I did *not* know was what kind of a new house . . . damned near the biggest house in Washington. My brother took one look at it, and said, "My God. It looks like Chatsworth!" It wasn't Chatsworth, but it was the Todd-Lincoln House, on N Street in the heart of Georgetown, built in 1799 overlooking a field that swept down to the Potomac. Abraham Lincoln's son, Robert Todd Lincoln, had lived there in the 1920s, and Todd Lincoln's wife had died there in 1935. Actually it was two houses! Mrs. Lincoln had built an attached five-bedroom annex for one of her daughters. It was, not to put too fine a point on it, slightly more than we needed, but it was simply the most beautiful house I had ever seen. Unfortunately, it was also the most expensive house I had ever heard of—$2,500,000 (available only because of *Washington Post* stock, which seemed to be flying to record highs every day). I almost died when the *Post* ran a story about our purchase, describing it as the most expensive residential real estate purchase in Washington history, and misdescribing it as having forty rooms. It has a study for each of us, five bedrooms, living room, library, and dining room, with a housekeeper's apartment over the kitchen; and thanks to Sally, our house is delightfully warm and comfortable.

If I had the Polish pope joke to express doubt about the likelihood of my getting married again, I had no wisecrack to prepare myself for another child. By mutual agreement of the parents, it had not been a possibility. Then all of a sudden it became discussable, followed by desirable, and soon enough a reality. I could hardly believe myself at Lamaze classes (Pant-pant-blow, at age sixty), but in for a nickel, in for a dime, I was going to participate all the way to delivery, even if they thought I was the grandfather. And I did, for one of the most dramatic, magical moments of my life.

Josiah Quinn Crowninshield Bradlee—too many names really, for someone who is purely and simply Quinn Bradlee—was born on April 29, 1982, after a long, difficult delivery. For twenty-four hours he was the one in the newborn ward who lay there with eyes wide open, never crying. When Dr. Agnes Schweitzer told us the next day she had found a heart murmur with her stethoscope, we bought into the explanation that many babies have heart murmurs which disappear.

Quinn's heart murmur did not disappear, and within weeks, the murmur was redefined as a small hole in one of the chambers of his heart. Blood was pumping through his heart, and through this hole, without getting to the rest of his small, small frame. He added weight only with difficulty, and then just short of ten pounds he began to lose weight, and open heart surgery went quickly from possibility to probability to urgency.

The small hole was diagnosed as a VSD, or ventricular septal defect, and there was less and less hope that he could avoid open heart surgery. Early in July Quinn went into heart failure. Children's Hospital's brilliant Dr. Frank Midgely was telling us only an operation would save Quinn's life, and just after dawn on July 30, 1982, ninety-two days after Quinn was born, Midgely operated. The operation took five and a half hours. Ed Williams was with us as we waited and waited and waited. Finally Frank Midgely told us all was well, almost managing to persuade us Quinn was going to be fine. Two hours later we were on either side of this eight-pound infant, unconscious, inside a plastic oxygen tent. Quinn lay in the tent, one hand holding Sally's finger, one hand holding mine. His body had been unseamed, then closed with more than eighty stitches, and penetrated by more tubes and wires than I could count. He was fighting for his every breath, eyes tight shut.

It wasn't soothing talk from scared but determined parents that made our son fight. It was an instinct so awesome as to overwhelm me thirteen years later—seven years after he has last seen a heart doctor. He fought his way out of the oxygen tank, out of the intensive care unit, and finally out of the hospital, with a valor that still impresses me. How does an infant learn to fight that hard? Through tribulations that defied understanding—seizure disorders, speech difficulties, and learning disabilities—a valiant young man has emerged . . . bright, funny, athletic, energetic, and wise.

Libel is to journalism what malpractice is to medicine: both represent abuse of the public by professionals, and lawsuits for libel and malpractice are the legitimate means of public retribution.

I am no expert on malpractice, but the threat of a libel suit, and more particularly the institution of a libel suit, is bad for the digestion. Other things being equal, I'd rather be publicly whipped than sued for libel, and lose.

In November 1979, the *Post* ran a front page story describing how the president of Mobil Oil Corporation set up his son as a partner in a shipping management firm that subsequently did millions of dollars in business operating Mobil-owned ships under exclusive, no-bid contracts. The Mobil president was crusty, blunt-spoken William P. Tavoulareas, chief of the world's second largest oil company. The son, Peter, who was only twenty-four when Atlas Maritime Company started, was making less than $20,000 a year as a shipping clerk in 1974. Five years later when we published the story, Peter was the 45 percent owner of Atlas, operating seventeen ships worldwide.

It was not the most earth-shattering story ever written, perhaps, but a good, clean look into the inside workings of a major oil company.

When Bob Woodward, then the assistant managing editor for Metro, and reporter Patrick Tyler first told me about the story, it was easy to give them a green light.

If I had known that the 84-inch story would cost the *Post* more than $1,500,000 to run the story, plus thirty lousy days as a defendant on trial in District Court, plus another seven and a half years of appellate litigation, I would have told them both to go piss up a rope.

Tavoulareas, or "Tav," as the unlovable tyrannical father was known, was outraged at the story. First he called on me with his Wall Street lawyer, asking for a retraction, and demanding to know the source of certain documents that Tyler had quoted. I was polite beyond anyone's wildest hope, but I said I knew of nothing to retract, we were confident of our sources, and no journalist was going to reveal his sources. He moved on to a demand for equal space. I said we would be glad to review anything he wrote. All part of the formal, threatening pre-litigation dance.

Next, Tavoulareas sought out Ed Williams to plead his case. Williams loved it when I got in trouble, especially with some high-profile big shot. He told me he had persuaded Tavoulareas to get in the ring with me and settle the whole thing mano a mano with 12-ounce gloves. The Walter Mitty in me was intrigued, although I have hated to box ever since my childhood friend hit me on the nose during a boxing lesson and made me cry.

Anyway, Tavoulareas eventually sued, and in early July 1982—two years and nine months after the story appeared and only three weeks before Quinn's heart operation—we went to trial. Williams had been felled by yet another bout of the cancer that had plagued him for years, and so the *Post* was defended by a new partner in his firm, Irving Younger, the legendary trial lecturer on jury strategy, who had recently joined the firm from academia (he had been the Samuel S. Leibowitz professor of trial techniques at Cornell University).

We "knew" we were going to win. We had the facts. We had a top-notch lawyer, we had a jury, and we couldn't imagine Washington jurors preferring a giant oil company from New York to their hometown newspaper. Against us was a tycoon with gorilla bodyguards, a Wall Street lawyer, and a spoiled son.

The trial lasted the entire month of July, but finally, word came that the jury had reached a verdict, and I rushed down to the courtroom from Quinn's bedside.

Bradlee and Woodward: Not Guilty.

But *The Washington Post*, and reporter Patrick Tyler: Guilty, as charged. $250,000 in compensatory damages for William Tavoulareas, and $1,800,000 in punitive damages. Nothing for the namesake.

I was stunned, as I've never been stunned before, or since. I couldn't believe it then, just as I cannot believe it now, as I write.

That was rock bottom, new ground for a man as blessed with opportunity and luck as I had been. The doctors sent us home after hours in the intensive care unit. Sally and I gave a wake that night to thank and console the legal defense team and their wives, got a few hours' sleep, and showed up at the hospital early next morning to begin the long, slow climb back up the road to peace and joy.

Nine months later, the trial judge, Oliver Gasch, overturned the jury's verdict by himself, a rare decision. Judge Gasch said that the article "falls short of being a model of fair, unbiased, investigative journalism," but that there was "no evidence in the record . . . to show that it contained knowing lies or statements made in reckless disregard of the truth." I didn't agree at all with Judge Gasch's criticism. I thought it was a model of good journalism, but I thought his decision was a model of good jurisprudence. Tavoulareas appealed.

Twenty-three months after that—on April 9, 1985—a U.S. Court of Appeals panel overruled Judge Gasch by a vote of 2-1. Judge George MacKinnon, the cranky, senior judge, ruled that the *Post* story "was published in reckless disregard of its falsity," and that "clear and convincing evidence" supported the jury's evidence. In a ringing dissent, Judge Skelly Wright wrote:

> This is an extremely important First Amendment case. If this excessive jury verdict on these mundane, flimsy facts is upheld, the effect on freedom of expression will be incalculable. The message to the media will be unmistakable—steer clear of unpleasant news stories and comments about interests like Mobil, or pay the price. Thus we will have created a class of untouchables and abandoned our "profound national commitment to the principle that debate on public issues should be uninhibited, robust and wide-open."

The *Post* appealed Judge MacKinnon's decision to the full Court of Appeals, with Ed Williams arguing brilliantly in front of a crowded courtroom even though he was bleeding through the stitches of his latest cancer operation.

And finally, on March 13, 1987, almost seven and a half years after the story was written, sanity returned, when the entire Court of Appeals, sitting *en banc*, overruled Judge MacKinnon by a vote of 7-1. (Judge Antonin Scalia, who had voted with MacKinnon against the *Post* as an appellate judge, was now Justice Antonin Scalia of the Supreme Court). Writing for the majority, Judge Kenneth Starr wrote:

> The *undisputed* evidence at trial, including [Tavoulareas's] own testimony, precludes any reasonable inference that the central allegation of the challenged article—that Tavoulareas "set up" Peter in Atlas—was false. . . .

The record abounds with uncontradicted evidence of nepotism in favor of Peter. . . .

Judge Starr used language like "overwhelming evidence that the *Post* defendants published the article in good faith" . . . "plentiful, undisputed evidence of Tavoulareas' personal involvement in the establishment and operation of Atlas to Peter's manifest benefit . . ." "The contention that the *Post* engaged in a pattern of 'slanted reporting' indicative of actual malice is utterly without merit. . . ."

And finally, "After completing our task, we are firmly persuaded that the decision of the able and distinguished trial judge [Gasch] was correct. This verdict cannot stand."

There was one more river to cross. Tavoulareas appealed the Court of Appeals en *banc* verdict to the Supreme Court. (We would have done the same thing, though without much hope.) The Supremes turned this appeal down on June 11, 1987, and the ordeal was over.

The decisions to print or not to print articles that deal with privacy rather than national security involve matters of less consequence, but they are still complicated to reach. At the *Post* we developed a rule about matters of privacy: The private lives of public officials are their own business—unless and until their private behavior encroaches on performance of public duties. We had many shorthand versions of this policy. My favorite was "Drunk at home, your business; drunk on the floor of the U.S. Senate, our business."

But, not all privacy matters fit comfortably within that rule. Especially when and where privacy and sex collide, and they collide a lot in Washington, especially since the sixties, when the Counter-Culture produced sea changes in America's sexual mores.

One of my favorite (and completely irritating) examples of the privacy dilemma started with a simple schmooze in the newsroom, in the fall of 1983. A bunch of us were sitting around talking about what was Topic A in the various places we had spent our summer vacations. Jane Amsterdam, then deputy to Woodward on our investigative unit (a.k.a. the Swat Team), and later editor of *Manhat-*

tan Inc., and managing editor of the *New York Post,* told about a country club scandal she had heard about from a friend. It seemed one of the pillars of the community was well on his way to the club golf championship somewhere in the Midwest, when he was seen to "improve his lie," as the saying goes. Actually the chairman of the Rules Committee saw him kick his ball out of the rough and onto the fairway. Instead of winning the title he had coveted since he was a child, he was suspended for two years, and told he could be reconsidered for membership only if he went to a shrink to find out why he cheated.

Interesting, but no story so far, right? A nobody got caught cheating a thousand miles from Washington, and paid for it.

But a couple of peels of the onion, and it turned out this guy wasn't exactly a nobody. In fact, he was a prominent presidential appointee (President Reagan's), head of one of the many independent agencies in Washington. Not really prominent, but his agency had 125 employees, helped American businessmen, and earned money every year for Uncle Sam. Prominent enough, at least, to warrant a closer look from Ben Weiser, one of the vacuum-cleaner investigative reporters working for the Swat Team.

Weiser talked to everyone involved, including the head of the Rules Committee, the shrink, and the cheat himself. Before he was through, there was literally nothing he didn't know about the incident and the perpetrator. Nothing.

While Weiser was doing his investigating, Sally and I wound up one night at the vice president's house, where George and Barbara Bush were giving one of their periodic cocktail parties, with a lot of press guests, a lot of Reagan administration types, and some stray cats and dogs. After some characteristically gracious and jocular conversation with the Bushes in the receiving line, I was on my way to the bar for a pop, when a nice-looking chap sashayed up to me, introduced himself so fast I never caught his name, and launched into a tirade against me and the *Post.*

So you're Bradlee, he started. I've wanted to meet you for a long, long time. Just to tell you how rotten I think your newspaper is . . . how slanted, blah-blah-blah. On he went for five minutes—not even drunk. And I didn't even know his name. He did tell me he and Don Oberdorfer, the *Post's* ace foreign policy writer, had been classmates at Princeton, but that's all I knew. I had seen the vice president looking on as this man took six inches off the top of my head, and I asked him, "Who's your friend?" Bush said he'd never seen him before in his life.

Next morning, Oberdorfer came up with his name, and—you must have guessed—it was our friend, the golf cheater.

So now, our man was not only a little bit prominent, but also one of those senseless, know-nothing critics of the press who might well benefit from a lesson. Now, the decision to print or not to print was suddenly more complicated. Whatever the merits of the story, I now knew the man to be a jerk, without class or interest.

We followed our standard procedure in these tough decisions: we decided to print the story, and then formed a group whose job was to talk us out of it. There was no question of national security. There was no question of accuracy. Weiser had him cold. The only question was privacy: Was this guy important enough, was his job important enough, was his "crime" important enough to go public with the story, and subject him to the shame and derision that surely would have followed?

My answer was no, and we never ran it, despite audible grumbling that I had lost a step, gone soft, whatever. I think now, in what my Greek teacher used to call sober second thought, that the grumblers were right. Cheating by *any* public official should be exposed. The public is better served knowing a public official cheated, than by assuming that he didn't. My reasoning then involved his lack of any real importance as a public figure, the "punishment" he did receive, and his mawkish contrition—"For some crazy reason, to win a golf tournament was going to give me stature among my peers in that town," he told Weiser. "I had a mental picture of accepting the awards, and there in the audience is my wife, and my daughter, my father-in-law . . . can you imagine the humiliation of it, the shame of it all? . . . I was devastated because I had been trying to achieve recognition. I'd destroyed everything I'd worked my whole life for," and on and on and on.

I didn't understand it right away, but I think I was also worried about being considered vengeful. If he was going to cut me a new one in front of the vice president and a handful of guests, I was going to cut him a new one in front of millions.

So I was something less than completely graceful about the decision not to run the story. I wrote the protagonist of this incident a letter, enclosing a copy of Weiser's story, and told him we would reexamine our decision not to run it if he ever decided to seek political office.

Editors were always being accused of publishing vital secrets, mostly by yahoos with their own ax to grind, but often enough by people who should know better. Like Defense Secretary Caspar Weinberger in December 1984, when the Air Force and NASA imposed draconian security restrictions on shuttle flights with military payloads. Reporters would be notified of launch times and landing times. Period. Simple speculation about the mission purpose would trigger Defense Department investigations, it was announced threateningly by the Air Force's director of Public Information, Brigadier General Richard F. Abel.

The first of a new generation of these military payloads was scheduled to blast off in January 1985, and I wondered aloud one day to our national security expert, Walter Pincus, "What the hell are they carrying that has them so edgy?" Pincus was—and is—a national treasure of a journalist, in love with research, especially if it's hidden away in agate print in public documents that no one else takes the time to read. To answer my question he made exactly four telephone calls, three to the Pentagon and one to an ex-Pentagon type then working for the infamous military-industrial complex that so worried retiring President Eisenhower more than thirty years earlier. Pincus never left the office.

"The next space shuttle . . . will carry a new military intelligence satellite that is to collect electronic signals and retransmit them to a U.S. receiving station," the front page story said the next morning. It would be in a geosynchronous orbit, 22,500 miles above the western portion of the Soviet Union; and it would stay put there, because its speed would equal the speed of the earth's rotation. "It was reported to cost $300 million, weigh more than 15 tons, and carry two 75-foot-wide receiving and transmitting dishes."

That's all.

On his way to flog the Defense Department budget on an early morning TV show next day, Weinberger told CBS that the *Post* story was the "height of journalistic irresponsibility," and threw in a gratuitous bit about how it gave "aid and comfort to the enemy." Editors—and reporters, and especially owners—don't like to be accused of giving aid and comfort to the enemy, even when they know it not to be true. It riles the kooks and the woolly hats of this world, and results in a great deal of ill-tempered and unnecessary correspondence. Like this hand-scrawled note from one J. C. Turnacliffe, P.O. Box 1971, St. Paul, Minnesota:

How do I view thee? Let me count the ways. I) Dumb. 2) Smart Alecky. 3) Irresponsible. 4) UnAmerican. 5) A really poor newspaperman. What did you do during WW II?

I wrote him back:

Dear Asshole,
   I suspect I did more for my country in the war than you did. I spent four years in destroyers in the Pacific Ocean. My theater ribbon has 10 battle stars in it.

Turns out I was wrong.

"Mon Cher Con [a special French term of endearment]," he wrote back. "The salutation in your recent letter was vintage Bradlee-eze and I'm glad to have it for my memoirs. It takes one to know one." He went on to reveal that he was a Marine major, a veteran of landings at Guadalcanal, Bougainville, and Iwo Jima, where he had been decorated for heroism. I wrote him back ("Dear Pal") to tell him I took him to Bougainville, and to share my delight that Cap Weinberger wasn't in his foxhole or on my destroyer, where knowing the enemy was important.

The intelligence shuttle story would have died a miserable, un-satisfying death right there, leaving the public to choose between the Secretary of Defense and the executive editor of *The Washington Post*, had not General Abel chosen to speak to a journalism class on January 11, 1985, three weeks after the Pincus story appeared. And had not one Matthew J. Kempner, a twenty-year-old journalism major, called the *Post* on the night of January 11 to report that General Abel had just told his audience that everything in the *Post* story was "stuff that the public could have gotten in the public domain."

Was there a transcript of Abel's remarks? There was. And when we called General Abel to confirm the quotes, he first said, "Oh, shit," to a *Washington Post* reporter, and then said he thought it was improper to report remarks he made in an academic forum.

Believe it or not, journalists sometimes come into possession of information—especially national security information—that they do not feel entitled to. Information which they themselves feel would hurt the national interest, before anyone tells them it would hurt the national interest, or threatens them with jail.

If stories involving questions of national security are the toughest problems for an editor, the mother of all national security stories was the Pelton case, a classic battle in the war over national security between the government and the *The Washington Post*. I guess we won it, because we printed the story finally, May 29, 1986, but our "victory" was costly: NBC beat us to the punch, even though they had almost no details, and our negotiations with President Reagan, CIA director Bill Casey, NSA director William Odom, and National Security Council chief John Poindexter were so protracted I felt more like a lawyer than an editor, as we battled to get the story in the paper.

Pelton was Ronald W. Pelton, a low-level (less than $12 an hour) employee of the National Security Agency (NSA), and a spy who gave away the family jewels to the Russians in 1980, five years before he was identified as the traitor.

Actually, we backed into the Pelton case, courtesy once more of Bob Woodward. "Backed in" because Woodward learned of the U.S.

intelligence capability to intercept Soviet military signals before we learned that it had been compromised, or by whom. One day Woodward told me that the United States had developed the capability of intercepting cable communications between the Soviet High Command and its submarines. This capability was code-named "Ivy Bells," and it consisted of a bell-shaped contraption installed at the bottom of the ocean over a Soviet cable. Without penetrating that cable, messages sent via the cable were recorded inside the bell-shaped contraption. U.S. submarines regularly retrieved tapes of the Soviet messages and installed new tapes. The full tapes were forwarded to NSA headquarters at Fort Meade, Maryland, outside Washington. Operation Ivy Bells had the highest security classification, we were told again and again, as we began to learn the details.

I found Woodward's story appalling. First, because I could see no useful social purpose whatever in publishing news of our new intelligence capability. It was obviously of enormous value to the country, in avoiding a war, or fighting one if worse came to worst. And second, who the hell was passing on information like that to Woodward and why? Good as he was, wasn't it reasonable to assume that if Bob Woodward, investigative reporter, knew about this supersecret U.S. capability, the Soviets might learn about it one of these days? And if so, didn't we have some responsibility to tell government leaders that their secret was out?

After talking to Don Graham, by then the *Post*'s publisher, I sought and received an appointment with General William Odom, NSA director, told him what we had—limited as it was—told him we had no intention of publishing at that time, but asked him what the hell was going on. I remember wondering whether we earned any Brownie points in the process, or simply guaranteed that all our phones would be tapped, if they weren't already.

What we couldn't know then was that the Soviets knew all about Ivy Bells, and had long since removed the U.S. listening devices from their cables. The United States eventually learned that Ivy Bells had been compromised in 1985 from Soviet defector Vitaly Yurchenko, the top Soviet KGB official who redefected to the USSR a few months later, after telling the United States that

Pelton had given Ivy Bells to the Soviets. The Navy discovered the device missing, and Pelton was arrested. But Woodward found all that out soon enough, and the question of to print or not to print was back on the front burner.

If the Soviets knew all about Ivy Bells, why shouldn't the American public know about it? Before we got the answer to that question, I had some twenty conversations with all the biggest shots in the intelligence community, and Katharine Graham had one conversation with President Reagan. (Kay was called out of the shower to speak to President Reagan, one of my all-time favorite images: Katharine, who had not yet been told anything about the Pelton case, scribbling page after page of wet notes of her conversation with President Reagan, who almost assuredly had known nothing about the Pelton case much before the telephone call.)

Woodward had been joined on the story by reporter Pat Tyler, his colleague on the Mobil Oil story, who had become a top investigative reporter, and the pressure from them to print never stopped. (They found three vague but unmistakable references to Ivy Bells already in print, including one sentence in a *New York Times* story by Sy Hersh. When I now brought Hersh's story to Odom's attention, he said only, "I hoped you wouldn't find that," making it all sound like some parlor game.) Woodward and Tyler must have rewritten the story a dozen times, in an effort to meet each new objection from the intelligence establishment. Two former CIA directors—Dick Helms and Bill Colby—were consulted. One of them told us that what the Soviet leaders knew wasn't as important as what might happen when the rest of the Soviet establishment learned of the U.S. intelligence coup.

We started showing various government officials different versions of our story, something we almost never did, and that boomeranged on us. We were still convinced that our story was important and true (they had given up denying it long since), detailing an intelligence triumph in the operation itself, and an intelligence disaster in Pelton's defection. Once, aboard Air Force One, the story was shown to Secretary of State George Shultz, Secretary of Defense Weinberger, White House chief of staff Don Regan, and

Poindexter. They agreed the story was unacceptable, and concluded with evident glee that they had us on the run.

In the middle of all this, I got a request from CIA director Casey and FBI director William Webster for an immediate interview. They wanted to see me. Both of them at the same time. No subject offered. You should have seen the city-room types stare at these two big shots, as they walked from the elevators to my office surrounded by their security types. Since I didn't know for sure what they wanted to talk about (though I figured it was Ivy Bells), I had decided to start out the interview by myself, ready to call in experts as soon as they got over my head. This infuriated several of my colleagues, especially Woodward, who walked by my floor-to-ceiling glass office five times, pretending not to look in.

But it turned out they wanted to talk about Nicaragua. White House correspondent Lou Cannon had obtained a Sandinista document, which the FBI had obtained from a Nicaraguan source. Casey wanted to be sure that the document, which dealt with Sandinista lobbying plans, did not threaten his effort to get $100 million from Congress for the Contras. Webster wanted to be sure that neither the *Post*'s document nor Casey compromised the source, who worked for the FBI, not the CIA. It didn't, and the story ran much to Casey's irritation.

Casey was on our backs again on Ivy Bells the next week, this time threatening the *Post* with prosecution if we published, under a 1950 law that provides criminal penalties for anyone who "publishes" any classified information about communications intelligence. In May, Casey wanted to talk to me again, suggesting a drink at the University Club. This time I took managing editor Len Downie with me. He'd been in on all the maneuvering, and I hunched that Casey was going to muscle us—big time. And he did. After reading the latest version of the story written by Woodward and Tyler, he sipped his Scotch and water, told us he had just come from the Justice Department, and said slowly: "There's no way you run that story without endangering the national security. I'm not threatening you, but you've got to know that if you publish this, I would recommend that you be prosecuted."

Threats are truly counterproductive with me. As we waited still another couple of days, we ran a story about being threatened with prosecution. Casey called to object, saying he thought we were having a private conversation! The next day, at Casey's suggestion President Reagan made his telephone call to Kay in the shower.

On May 19, as jury selection in the Pelton case began, NBC's James Polk broadcast a story about "Operation Ivy Bells, believed to be a top-secret underwater eaves-dropping operation by American submarines inside Soviet harbors."

On May 21, our story finally ran, under the headline: "Eaves-dropping System Betrayed, High Technology Device Disclosed by Pelton Was Lost to Soviets."

On May 22, Pelton's trial began in Annapolis.

On May 26, Casey and Odom issued a joint statement cautioning against "speculation and reporting details beyond the information actually released at trial."

On May 29, Casey called to say, "I don't want a pissing match."

On June 5, Pelton was convicted and given three life sentences, plus ten years.

What lessons did the Pelton case teach me?

First, the damage to the national security was done by Pelton, not by *The Washington Post*, nor the press generally.

Second, the government tried to prevent publication to avoid national embarrassment. Once it was certain that the Russians knew everything about Ivy Bells, there was no issue of national security.

Third, the claim that publication would threaten national security is an insidious one. The public feels entitled to believe that a president, or a CIA director, or a four-star general knows more about national security than a two-stripe editor. It is a formidable task to convince the public that patriotism is not exclusively the province of administration officials. It is a formidable task to convince the public that officials often—more often than not, in my experience—use the claim of national security as a smoke screen to cover up their own embarrassment. Those of us who heard Richard Nixon claim he could not explain Watergate because matters of national security were involved will never automatically accept claims of national security. Those of us who were taken all the way to the Supreme Court for violating national security laws by publishing the Pentagon Papers got more out of that experience than an acquittal. We remember the Solicitor General of the United States *eighteen years later* writing that the national security was never threatened by publication.

In my time as editor, I have kept many stories out of the paper because I felt—without any government pressure—that the national security would be harmed by their publication.

Not all the decisions about whether to print or not to print are of earth-shattering importance. Especially those stories that might cause embarrassment, if published, but not harm.

Such a story was the non-burial of statesman W. Averell Harriman in the fall of 1986.

In July 1986, more than 750 of the nation's leading politicians, diplomats, and other friends of the mighty had attended the ninety-four-year-old Harriman's funeral at St. Thomas Church in Manhattan. More than sixty of them, including Katharine Graham, had joined an hour-long motor cortège to the Harriman estate in Arden, New York, north of the city. There, the episcopal bishop of New York (and my childhood friend), Paul Moore, Jr., performed a brief service, and sprinkled dirt on the coffin, before it was lowered into the ground next to the grave of Harriman's second wife, Marie.

Two months later, I was told by an impeccable source that Harriman had *not* in fact been buried on that day or in that place. Instead, his body had been placed in a storage crypt at the Frank E. Campbell Funeral Home, pending reburial at a new lakeside site, where he would ultimately be joined by his third wife, Pamela Digby Churchill Hayward Harriman.

For a slow news day, the story had everything: deception of the unsuspecting by the powerful, cover-up, just the suggestion of lying.

Close friends who had attended the non-burial service were appalled, including Harriman grandchild David Mortimer, and orchestra leader Peter Duchin, who had been raised by Averell and Marie Harriman. And Kay Graham. It is always rewarding to call her with news about an upcoming story; she is invariably interested and excited.

This time, I tortured her first.

BCB: "Did you go to Averell's funeral?"
KG: "I sure did. It was a madhouse."
BCB: "Were you part of the cortège up to Arden?"
KG: "All those cars. It took forever."
BCB: "Did you get to the actual gravesite?"
KG: "Of course."
BCB: "Did you see Averell go into the ground?"
KG: "Yes, I did."
BCB: "Uh-uh."

Style reporter Mary Battiata wrote the story, but I called Paul Moore before we published, and he complained that I was always causing trouble, and said the burial was "liturgically sound."

Mrs. Harriman complained first to me, then to Katharine, saying that it was a private affair and should not be published. On the day before the piece was slated to run (page one of the Style Section), she sent over our good friend Dick Holbrooke, a once and future Assistant Secretary of State, to try a little last-minute pressure to kill the story. Without success. We were all en route to Kay Graham's for a dinner honoring President Corazon Aquino of the Philippines. Pamela Harriman was to attend, but at the very last minute she backed out.

The passage of time has done nothing to dim my enthusiasm for this story. No one should be able to perpetrate a fraud on the public, and not just the reading public, and escape the modest consequences: a little sunlight.

A call from the director of the FBI or the director of the CIA was always a call to General Quarters. It meant that unidentified blips had appeared on someone's radar screen, and until they were identified, God knows what was going to happen.

Late one afternoon in the fall of 1986, I got such a call from FBI director William Webster. The timing was ominous, because dead-line was only a few hours away. The message was more ominous: He had something he wanted to talk about. Right away. Could he loop by the *Post* on 15th Street, and pick me up in his car? As optimistic as I could be—and normally am—this didn't sound promising. Was he going to take me somewhere, and where the hell might he take me?

He arrived outside the building just before 6:00 P.M., headed north because the street had already turned one-way to handle commuter traffic. He was already dressed in a tuxedo, as I joined him on the back seat, and he ordered his driver to take an early left on N Street, park the car, and wait outside until summoned. Whatever was coming, it figured to be bad. And it was.

The FBI had received information from a source it considered reliable, he began almost awkwardly, that a *Washington Post* reporter had accepted $1,000 in cash from a KGB official in Moscow.

My heart stopped. I could think of no more grievous blow. Abso-lutely nothing could be more harmful to the paper that was my life, and to the Grahams, whose courage and dedication were so vital. It was literally a long minute before I felt it just couldn't be true and asked Webster who it was, and how could he be sure his source was reliable.

Webster identified the reporter as the inimitable Dusko Doder, our cigar-chomping expert on Soviet affairs for the last twelve years, and a Yugoslav by birth, who had joined the paper as a stringer in Belgrade years earlier. He was extraordinarily well plugged in, and had filed scores of exclusive stories, ahead of the embassy and the CIA, as often as not. He had a world beat on the death of Soviet dictator Yuri Andropov, much to the chagrin of the CIA. It just couldn't be true, I said to Webster. Who was their source, and how did he get described as reliable?

The source, Webster said, was Colonel Vitaly Yurchenko, himself a former KGB official, who had defected to the U.S. Embassy in Rome in August 1985 (and redefected back to Moscow three months later). Yurchenko had told the FBI about how National Security Agency clerk Robert Pelton had betrayed his country and turned over the priceless Ivy Bell secrets to the Russians. And he had been right.

He told the FBI about Edward Lee Howard, the former Peace Corps volunteer who later defected to Moscow, but only after he received extensive CIA training in surveillance and countersurveillance.

How did the FBI know Yurchenko's hearsay charges were not simply an effort to discredit Doder, whose reporting had been head and shoulders over embassy and CIA reporting about the USSR? I asked. Had anyone bothered to look at Doder's dispatches to see if they contained anything that smelled of Soviet propaganda? The questions came pouring out.

Webster, to his everlasting credit, said his experts had in fact gone over every Doder dispatch, and found nothing more than the obvious: Doder had better contacts. He confirmed that Yurchenko had not claimed to know firsthand about any payment to Doder, had not seen any evidence of any payment. He had simply heard tell of such a payment.

Webster told me that he had decided to raise the whole thing with me now, because the FBI had heard that Doder's assignment, after returning from years overseas, had been to cover the intelligence community, which did not like to be covered by anyone, much less by someone whose 201 file now contained Yurchenko's hearsay. Webster asked me about the circumstances of the decision to assign him to that particular beat. Had Doder asked for it, or had it just happened? I did not have the answer right away, although I thought he had tried to avoid the assignment, which in fact he had. I told the FBI director that I didn't know what I was going to do, beside talk immediately to Don Graham and Ed Williams.

The conversation ended, after I told Webster he must understand we couldn't pull Doder off the intelligence community assignment on the basis of hearsay testimony from a once and future KGB agent. He said he understood, and told me I must understand the intelligence community had decreed that no one should talk to Doder, at least for now.

Ed Williams took Doder to the woodshed, as we had requested, grilling him for almost two hours, and reporting back to me: "Fuck 'em . . . he's a terrific guy . . . the charges are horse shit." Williams then went to see Judge Webster and reported him as saying, "We're really inclined to think he's clean." That left Doder uncharged, but under suspicion. Williams wanted to pursue the matter with Casey and Webster to try to "cleanse" Doder so that he could go on about his chosen business. Both the CIA and the FBI wanted Doder to take a lie detector test. Doder was ready, but Williams was vehemently against lie detectors on principle.

And there the matter lay for three or four months, when Dusko resigned to join *U.S. News & World Report*, because they would assign him to China, where the woman he loved (and later married) was to be a correspondent.

Six years later, in December 1992, for reasons that I have never understood, *Time* magazine wrote "A Cold War Tale," calling the Doder case one of "the 10 or 12 most important cases [Yurchenko] knew about," and quoting an unnamed "former CIA official" as saying that the source of the $1,000 "payment" to Doder was clear. "Of course, he knew it was the KGB. This was the Soviet Union. What else would he think?" *Time* quoted the official as saying, in as shabby a bit of character assassination as I can remember. "Where is the line between responsibly using information obtained from inside sources, and uncritically reflecting those sources' views?" *Time* asked naively and pompously. "The line is sometimes a blurry one, but it is a distinction that none the less must be heeded—whether covering the Kremlin, the White House or city hall."*

All information, whatever the source, should be used responsibly. Sources' views should never be reflected uncritically. So there is no line, blurry or clear, between the two. Doder wrote something that embarrassed the CIA, and when the agency thought they saw a chance to get even, they took their shot. It's rare to catch them in the act.

No story in the endless public-or-private debate gave me more difficulty than Gary Hart's extracurricular activities during the 1988 campaign for president.

---

* Time has been sued for libel by Doder in London, for this story, and the case has yet to be tried at this writing.

Hart had arrived on the national scene sixteen years earlier as George McGovern's campaign manager, a new incarnation of the idealistic, anti-establishment intellectual. The press found him more interesting and more fun than McGovern, and he emerged from McGovern's defeat accepted by reporters as a friend and as a man to be watched. As a senator from Colorado he became more respected for his ideas, in reporter Paul Taylor's memorable phrase, than for his ability to get them implemented.

Walter Mondale beat Hart handily for the presidential nomination in 1984, but in the summer of 1987 Hart was the front-runner, threatened only by an uneasiness about his private life. Hart had changed his name, it was revealed, from Hartpence, and he had lied about his age . . . both matters of little consequence, had he explained the discrepancies before they were discovered. And Hart was widely known to reporters as a man who fooled around.

For almost two hundred years the sex lives of politicians— especially presidents and presidential candidates—were left to the historians. However, the old rules had changed, and the new rules guaranteed scrutiny by the press if they got wind of any ongoing extracurricular sexual escapades. By 1987, the press was poking into the private lives of almost everyone, especially if they were prominent and indiscreet. And Gary Hart was both.

Many of the national reporters talked about Hart's private life among themselves at first, swapping the latest stories, and only occasionally wondering whether or when they should do a story about it. *The Washington Post*, no more and no less than any other newspaper. The relevance of these old rumors had vanished when Hart's 1984 candidacy died, but now they were back, and in retrospect, it seemed only a matter of time before one of those rumors erupted on somebody's front page as truth.

On May 3, 1987, the *Miami Herald* ended the suspense. Under a comparatively innocuous headline, "Miami Woman Linked to Hart," Miss Donna Rice began her fifteen minutes of fame as Hart's girlfriend, first with news of an overnight stay in Hart's Capitol Hill house, and later with reports of a two-day trip with Hart to Bimini, on the felicitously named motor yacht *Monkey Business*. A snapshot of the scantily clad Miss Rice on the would-be president's lap really sealed Hart's fate. There was a lot of anti-aircraft fire from Hart about the snooping press, some of it pretty much on target. But in the end the press wasn't on any overnighter; and the press was not invited to Bimini; and that wasn't the press sitting on the senator's lap.

A month earlier, I had called a special meeting of the house experts—Broder, Dan Balz, Tom Edsall and company—to discuss what we should be doing about the Hart rumors. On the one hand, if we wrote anything about them, we just added swirl to the controversy. And if we printed rumors without investigating them ourselves, we would be abandoning our principles. On the other hand, if we ignored the rumors—especially about a Democrat—weren't we courting a charge of bias? We decided to assign the sensitive and talented David Maraniss—then our bureau chief in Texas—to do a full-depth profile of Hart. But he couldn't get free from his Texas assignment until May 4, one day after the *Herald* broke its story.

On May 3, Tom Edsall, one of the best political reporters going, was given a picture of Gary Hart leaving the house of an attractive woman—not married—whose name had been linked with his for a long time. They were together: she was pictured in the doorway of her house, and Hart leaving. The picture had been taken in December 1986, by a private detective working for a former senator who suspected his wife of having an affair with Hart. The picture showed Hart leaving someone's home, not the senator's, and not his own.

The someone was a reasonably well-known woman in Washington, a former Capitol Hill staffer turned lobbyist. I knew her casually, and volunteered to find out whether her rumored romance with Hart had ever been a fact, and whether it was then a fact. I did find out, that afternoon. The answer was yes; the romance had existed and still existed. In fact, the woman had told friends she expected Hart to divorce his wife and marry her.

Or so she said.

What did the presidential candidate already flailing away at the Donna Rice fires have to say?

To answer that question we called on Paul Taylor, who was covering Hart in New Hampshire. Taylor himself had just been in the news, after asking Hart pointblank at a press conference: "Have you ever committed adultery?" Instead of telling Taylor that it was none of his damn business, Hart had said he thought adultery was immoral.

We asked Taylor to reach Hart that night, if possible, and get his reaction to the photograph and to reports of a relationship with the woman. Taylor doubted he could get any answer, and wanted to be sure we weren't asking him to negotiate anything with Hart. If Hart does such-and-such, we would do such-and-such. No one wanted any of that.

Why was this story so important?

The leading Democratic candidate for president had repeatedly told the American public that he and his wife were a solid unit, when more and more evidence was accumulating that they were not. They had "an understanding of faithfulness, fidelity and loyalty," Hart had told *The Washington Post* only a few days earlier. He had even challenged the press to follow him around, a challenge the *Miami Herald* had accepted. "I'm serious," he had told E. J. Dionne in a *New York Times Magazine* article. "If anybody wants to put a tail on me, go ahead. They'd be very bored." And the *Miami Herald* had taken him up on his offer, with results that were hardly boring.

Now, it seemed to me, our reporting plus the picture plus the *Miami Herald*'s reporting all suggested that Gary Hart was lying about his private life. The changes in the rules now gave the public a right to know, and even a need to know before Election Day. There has to be some line beyond which the truth is essential, and lying is not allowed. And it had just been drawn.

Taylor told Hart's press secretary, Kevin Sweeney, about the picture, the private detective's report, and the confirmation I had received of the relationship. Sweeney paled, and asked for time. Hart, along with his wife Lee and a few others, was actually at a Vermont hotel twenty miles from Littleton, New Hampshire. It wasn't until early next morning that Taylor got his answer. He bumped into Joe Trippi, the deputy political director of Hart's campaign, in a parking lot. "You're looking at the end of a candidacy here," Trippi said with a sigh. "Hart's going to get out of the race tonight or tomorrow."

Apparently Sweeney eventually woke Hart to tell him. "Is it a story?" Hart had asked. "Yes, it's a story," Sweeney had replied. And finally, Hart concluded, "This thing is never going to end, is it? Look, let's go home."*

The story of Hart's withdrawal was all over page one for days, of course, but we never ran a story about the private detective's report, and we never identified the other woman, even though they had specifically triggered the withdrawal. Our reasoning was simple: since Hart was no longer a presidential candidate, his private life was his own business again. And since the woman was not in public life, her private life was her own business.

Hart was furious at the press in general, and at the *Post* in particular. He just didn't get it. (In search of someone else to blame for his troubles, he even asked his woman friend, who still hoped to marry him, if she were having an affair with me. She wasn't, hadn't, and didn't.) We felt we had behaved responsibly, after determining a legitimate public interest in his private life. Our position was well stated by George Reedy, once President Lyndon Johnson's press secretary and then a journalism professor. "What counts with a candidate for president," he told Taylor, "is his character, and nothing shows it like his relationship with women. Here you have a man who is asking you to trust him with your bank account, your children, your life and your country for four years. If his own wife can't trust him, what does that say? The press doesn't invent stories about the peccadilloes of candidates." It is fair to wonder whether Reedy would have felt the same way if the press had asked LBJ about adultery.

James MacGregor Burns, a professor at Williams College and FDR biographer, spoke eloquently for those who disagreed with Reedy. "This is a tragedy," he told Taylor, "a real loss for all of us, that a really impressive man has been brought down this way. The character of candidates and presidents is crucial. But the media aren't able to deal adequately with real and total character; their judgments are based on such old-fashioned, puritanical pieces of evidence."

---

* Quoted in *See How They Run*, by Paul Taylor (New York: Alfred A. Knopf, 1990).

Was Hart a victim of a prurient press, or a victim of his own excesses? Had the rules changed, and if so, who changed them? How come Hart was the object of such press scrutiny, when LBJ, and especially Jack Kennedy, had escaped that scrutiny?

Yes, the rules had changed, without any formal agreement within the press, and without any formal notification to the candidates. Certainly, the sexual revolution that started in the early sixties had changed American society permanently by the eighties. It was increasingly normal to be interested in our own sexual proclivities, and especially the sexual proclivities of the burgeoning world of celebrities. The supermarket tabloids, with their voracious appetite for the sensational—true or not—had been joined by tabloid television with its equally voracious appetite. And the press had been accused of covering up Kennedy's fooling around, which had become increasingly well documented since his death. They had silently decided they were never going to be accused of covering up the fooling around of any subsequent candidate. If Hart was the victim of anything, he was the victim of these new rules.

I have given a lot of thought to whether Kennedy would have survived these rules, and I have concluded that he could not have withstood the pressure of publicity. If the American public had learned—no matter how the public learned it—that the President of the United States shared a girlfriend, in the biblical sense, with a top American gangster, and Lord knows who else, I am convinced he would have been impeached. That just seems unforgivably reckless behavior.

Arnold Schaeffer isn't his real name. In 1988, he was a low-level analyst for Naval Intelligence, making about $20,000 a year, when he applied for the job vacated by Jonathan Jay Pollard, who had just been convicted of spying for Israel. It seems that in his application, Schaeffer had violated security regulations when he stated what he did in his current job in electronic intelligence, since that job was highly classified and therefore should not be divulged. Schaeffer was in trouble for telling the truth, and he was pissed.

Like so many disgruntled government employees involved in

national security matters, Schaeffer contacted Bob Woodward. He was going to tell his story to columnist Jack Anderson, he said, but he just wanted to talk to Woodward first. Woodward came to me with yet another incredible story, another case of someone who wanted to give away the crown jewels. Schaeffer had code names and details for three different operations, each involving systems by which the Soviets controlled different units in their nuclear forces, each describing how the United States had been able to penetrate these systems in real time.

I'm being extra careful here, because as far as I can see those secrets are still family jewels, and I have no more business revealing them now than I did then. At the time, it was clear: it was Pelton all over again, and more. And to top it off, Woodward reported that this new source had an East German girlfriend.

The information Schaeffer was offering plainly threatened the security of this nation, and I wanted to see what a man who was ready to sell out his country looked like. At the Madison Hotel across the street from *The Washington Post* one March morning at breakfast time, he looked nondescript, cheerful, sandy-haired, on the chunky side, smiling, about thirty. A carpenter or a contractor, I would have guessed him to be. We listened as he described proudly how the United States was able to do all these vital, gee-whiz things.

"So what's wrong?" I asked him. "We can do all those things. Isn't that our job?"

"Yeah," he answered, "but I've been screwed over."

I did what I had been doing for years. I called Ed Williams and Don Graham and told them about our new hot potato. I wanted to get under the umbrella of the lawyer-client privilege, immune from questions or threats from the Feds, until we decided how we were going to handle this latest acquisition to our collection of misguided public servants. It was going to be Ed's last mission for us. Six months later he would succumb at last to the cancer he had been fighting for eight years.

We quickly agreed that there was no useful social purpose in publishing the story, and recognized a responsibility to alert the government to a potential disaster. Williams suggested that he—

not me—bring the matter to the attention of William Webster, the former FBI director, now the director of the CIA, so that I could stay out of the CIA's reach. The last time I had been involved (in the Pelton case), Casey had tied me up for months.

Ed went out to CIA headquarters and laid it on Webster, operation code names, details—the whole nine yards—and according to Williams, Webster said he was not sure any of it was true. But later that night, Webster called Williams to report that all of it was true.

The next thing we knew, two FBI agents were in my office asking us if *we* wanted to give testimony against Schaeffer, which of course we didn't. As long as we had decided we couldn't print his story, we wanted him on ice, out of harm's way. And Webster obliged. Schaeffer was rehired—and I presume permanently tapped and followed—his ego massaged, and his case was closed. Woodward recently got a postcard from him—and his East German wife.

NINETEEN

MOVING OUT, MOVING ON

Over the years, criticism had regularly forced me into thinking about our business, as well as the *Post*'s performance in that business. The press's vision of itself had changed drastically with the Vietnam War and the rise of the Counter-Culture, and with Watergate itself. The best newspapers were still involved in the pursuit of truth with conscience, and newly determined to be interesting, useful, and entertaining in the process. But at the bottom of the barrel, the stain of the tabloids was spreading with the help of television into what could be called "kerosene journalism." In this genre of journalism, reporters pour kerosene on whatever smoke they can find, before they determine what's smoking and why. The flames that result can come from arson, not journalism.

I've always had trouble developing theories of journalism that were much more sophisticated than the motto of Miss Fiske at Dexter, my old grade school: "Our best today; better tomorrow." Put out the best, most honest newspaper you can today, and put out a better one the next day. Or more productive than my old high school motto: "Age quod agis"—Do what you do. Do it right, or don't do it at all.

But theories of journalism are a pale imitation of journalism itself. Stories are for reporters and editors. Theories are for critics, and teachers. And it was occurring to me every now and then that I was spending more time on the principles and process of journalism than I was spending on the practice of journalism. And that made me tired.

Cruising through my fifties, I had thought little of retirement. Why should I quit the best job in journalism? But soon after Quinn was born, and especially after his heart surgery, I began to realize that I had already had the best story I'd ever be involved with, that no matter how many other great stories were coming, we weren't going to do better than Watergate. Sometime in early 1984, I had received a notice announcing that under certain circumstances I would soon be eligible for Social Security. I said a couple of holy shits, and talked to Sally and to Don Graham.

Fortunately, neither one was interested in my quitting—especially Sally—but Don and I agreed to talk about it every so often until the right time became the right time. When Len Downie was picked to succeed Howard Simons as managing editor, the paper finally had someone the right age to succeed me. And it became increasingly obvious that he also had the right skills, including talents that made him the first really good administrator to be managing editor in anyone's memory.

I felt great. Weekend tennis matches with Sy Hersh and Cody Shearer were still fun and satisfying, especially when I could persuade friends like Bo Jones, the Post's lawyer and a great player—now president and general manager—to be my partner. Or like reporter Art Brisbane, now vice president and editor at the Kansas City Star. Or like reporter David Ignatius, now the Post's business and financial editor. My life with Sally was exciting and full of surprises. Fatherhood had turned out to have no down side. Going home at night was as satisfying as going to work.

Then one day at our regular Tuesday breakfast when I was sixty-seven, Don asked, "How about working until you hit seventy?" and

he had a deal. Probably because Downie was so supportive of the
deal, I started looking forward to a change. Downie as my successor
was not quite a done deal, but my job was his to lose. And he won it
in a walk. The announcement of my retirement was made on June
20, 1991, effective September 1.

On July 31, 1991, the day had finally come, after almost twenty-nine
years in *The Washington Post*'s newsroom. If the first ten thousand
days or so were unrelievedly wonderful, that last day was fantastic:
the first in a memorable series of goodbyes which I have managed
to prolong as something called Vice-President-at-Large to a point
where "Forgotten, but not gone" may no longer be funny.

I don't remember much until story conference, when everyone
showed up in Turnbull & Asser shirts with the white collars I favored at the time. At almost $100 a shirt, few of them sported the
genuine article, but the Art Department had provided ersatz white
collars for the cheapos. Instead of reporting on real stories being
considered for the August 1 front page, the various editors described
stories calculated to make fun of certain prejudices they claimed I
had developed. From National editor Fred Barbash came the offer
of a story combining both the Big Bang theory of the earth's origin
and the ozone layer, about which I had been sometimes skeptical.
Mary Hadar talked about an upcoming National Gallery exhibition
on "the Phalluses of Phoenicia," reflecting my concern about what
I believed to be the Style Section's increasing preoccupation with
erotica. Business editor David Ignatius reported the "sad news" that
Turnbull & Asser had been acquired by Washington's own Mattress
Discounters. And on and on.

A little later a considerable crowd assembled around the news
desk for a "program," which lasted so long Don Graham cracked
that Liz Kastor's newborn son had grown old enough during the
speeches to say a few words himself. The proceedings still read unbelievably flattering three years after the fact.

Len Downie, who has risen to every occasion he has faced for
the last thirty years with natural grace, started things off by saying
that "Ben created the newspaper we work for now . . . he has a way

of approaching journalism and life that will remain inside all of us for as long as we work in this room. So, long after today, Ben, this is still your newsroom."

Walter Pincus, whose infamy as a convoluted after-dinner speaker is well known and well deserved, followed with convoluted but warm and emotional words about "how much fun we've all had doing what you think you love for somebody who you love doing it with." A truly Pincus sentence.

Meg Greenfield, whose humor and wisdom I had fallen for thirty-three years earlier when she was working for *The Reporter* magazine as an editor-writer, said, "The Lord made only one Ben Bradlee, and as we editorial writers say, on balance, that was a good decision, because . . . what would be left for the other Ben Bradlee to do?" I loved it deep down when she said, "The one thing Ben did that I think was the greatest . . . is that Ben made the *Post* dangerous to people in government."

Dick Harwood told the assembled crowd that he had decided he'd like us to work together when he'd first met me at a *Newsweek* cocktail party before a White House Correspondents' dinner. "Ben was in the middle of the room—standing on his head, and I thought . . . that guy's going to go somewhere," he said, before closing with something about "a great editor and a great pal."

Tom Lippman was a great general assignment man wherever he had been—from Cairo to Chevy Chase—and our resident expert on grammar and usage. He told about a day when the fabulous Debbie Regan, then my secretary, approached him after taking some dictation looking extremely uncomfortable. "She hemmed and hawed a little bit," Tom reported, "and said, 'Look, I have to ask you something. . . . Is dickhead one word or two?' "

Tom Wilkinson, in charge of newsroom hiring at the time, remembered an instance when he sent a prospective candidate in to me to be interviewed. "This guy had done well in other newsroom interviews and had good, solid clips, but he was a hesitant, softspoken, reticent type," recalled Wilkinson. "I went in after the interview, expecting a discussion about the nuances of the guy's clips, his strengths and weaknesses, things like that. What I got from Ben was: 'Ehhh. Nothing clanks when he walks.' End of the discussion."

Sally Quinn is the kind of woman who takes your breath away, mine anyway, or at least she makes you hold your breath. That's what I was doing when she got up and reminded everyone that at her goodbye party in the Style Section eighteen years early ("At that time I called him Mr. Bradlee," she revealed with only a trace of triumph), I had toasted her with "Forgotten, but not gone," and she returned the compliment, with more than a trace of triumph.

Bob Woodward and Richard Cohen added their own compliments, and then Mary Hadar got up and recited a list of my favorite Style headline ("You Can Put Pickles Up Yourself"); my favorite Style story: a spelling bee story in which we misspelled the name of the winner (topped the next year by a spelling bee story in which we listed the wrong spellings for the winning words); my favorite White House party guest list (two of the "guests" were dead). To combat my reputation as someone who couldn't keep a secret, she "revealed" that I had had triple bypass surgery "many years ago." *Not!*

By the time David Broder and Haynes Johnson, whose decision to join us had meant so much to the *Post*, got through, Don Graham was plainly worried that we would miss the Capital edition deadline. He got up and started: "In a game scheduled for 27 innings, I feel all the excitement of the guy called in to work the top of the 22nd." Then he added, "Thank God the person making [the] decisions in the last 26 years showed us how to do it with verve and with guts and with zest for the big story and for the little story, and the number one desire, the day he walked in here, of getting the best staff of reporters and editors and photographers in the United States to join him in putting out a great newspaper. It's Bradlee's paper, that's what anybody would say about us today and hopefully, Benjy, they're going to say it for a long time to come." I feel reasonably sure that if I owned *The Washington Post* I would never say it was somebody else's paper, but I loved it.

Mike Getler closed the proceedings—and brought me to tears—by reading a telegram from the valiant Nora Boustany, our great correspondent in wartorn Beirut:

Whenever I found myself alone on the streets of Beirut, I would just shrug off the shelling, the gunmen, and the dark corners, telling myself there is this distinguished eminence up there who really appreciates and understands the true meaning of courage in journalism. I always made it to my destination safely and with the story. I find myself in Beirut again. The streets are a little calmer now, but for me you will always be the grand brave man of the news who watched over me and made me want to give a little more. Thank you for giving us all something so special to believe in. (CBK: Your fan forever). Nora

Sally and I spent August in East Hampton, preparing for the official retirement ceremonies when we returned. In our absence, the stylish and thoughtful—and poetic—senior senator from New York, Daniel Patrick Moynihan, caused the following to be inserted in the *Congressional Record* for August 2, 1991:

MR. MOYNIHAN. Mr. President, It appears that Thursday was Ben Bradlee's last day as executive editor of the Washington Post. We shall not see his like again. But the standards he set, and the things he did, will be with us in song and story for ages hence.

> O rare Ben Bradlee,
> His reign has ceased.
> But his nation stands.
> Its strength increased.

I ask unanimous consent that it be ordered that a flag be flown from the Nation's Capitol in honor of Ben Bradlee and that the same be presented to him.

I am embarrassed to say how much I loved that gesture then— and now.

Readers may be getting sick of all this good stuff, and if they are they can skip ahead, but damned if there wasn't another goodbye—for all *Post* employees—six weeks later, after everyone returned from vacation. Poor Graham, Downie, and Woodward had to get up again for repeat performances. Don said he had spent his summer reading *War and Peace* and "all Bradlee's exit interviews."

Len described the closing moments of the first farewell: "After a couple of hours of raucous and teary farewells, Ben tried to walk quietly from his office to the elevator. Without planning or instigation, first a few, then more and more reporters and editors stood and applauded until everyone was on their feet joining in the ovation. . . . We would follow this man over any hill, into any battle, no matter what lay ahead."

Woodward read a letter from Bernstein ("It was the excellence, the fun, the decency, the toughness and the empathy"), noting gracefully that "Carl could always say it better."

Then Buchwald brought everyone back to earth.

First, he welcomed everyone to "the 1,756th farewell party for Ben Bradlee" and announced that American Airlines was offering frequent-flyer miles for every Bradlee farewell party people attended. He could sing Bradlee's praises, but that would be done at future ceremonies staged by the National Conference of Christians and Jews, the Burning Tree Anti-Defamation League, the Estonian-American Editors Association, etc.

My longtime hero (and predecessor) Russ Wiggins knocked me out with this: "Public opinion fastens upon the image of a public man the way people hang their hats on a hat rack. They often fasten on his idiosyncrasies, and Ben has some—pretty bizarre some of them. And they have sometimes put into eclipse the great abilities he really has as a professional newspaperman, and I will not add an extensive tribute except to say these too few words: this is a great newspaper editor."

I was more than ready to quit when I was so far ahead, but poor Katharine Graham, who had missed the newsroom bash, had to stand up and be counted. She weighed in with fantastic talk about "eternal optimism," "unyielding commitment to the highest ethical standards," "independence, outspokenness, humor and . . . most of all . . . courage."

"It's outrageous to say," she wound up, "that I was ever in love with Ben. The only editor I ever was in love with was Russ Wiggins."

What was outrageous was the not-so-secret pleasure I got from all these kind words. Man can't help but seek evidence of his own effectiveness, and there is no measure of effectiveness—not titles, nor salaries, nor prizes—equal to the esteem of one's peers.

Even before the ringing in my ears from all this had stopped, I had begun to equate "retirement" with "moving out," and "moving out" with "moving on." Maybe this was simply more of the excessive optimism which I have always shared with Pollyanna. More likely, this was more of the coping mechanism sublimation, which was identified by the Grant Study psychologists as one of the strengths that otherwise normal people use to great advantage.

In his book *Adaptation to Life*, Grant Study director and psychologist George Vaillant describes a character he named Frederick Lion, who I have been told is me in camouflage. He describes Lion variously as "someone who combined dignity and arrogance with infectious warmth," someone who learned to cope by sublimation—the expression of things that are personally unacceptable (retirement?) in constructive and acceptable forms.

In any event, as soon as I had settled for "moving on," I began to wonder about the amount of time I had spent with problems I had almost no capacity to fix. The environment, for instance. I had no real understanding of the threat to the environment until I took an incredible journey in January 1989 to the Brazilian rain forest with Dr. Tom Lovejoy of the Smithsonian Institution and a congressional delegation led by Tim Wirth. That sensitized me, but it didn't do much for the environment. I had sensitized myself to other great issues, too, like Vietnam. Overpopulation and its concomitants, abortion and birth control. Communism. Human rights, and the incredible abuses of human rights. And permeating everything that isn't right about our society, the eternal, apparently unsolvable problems of race. They resisted solution, in spite of my enlightenment.

And I began to wonder why certain milestones of a normal

Washington year were beginning to blur in my mind, run together like watercolors on cloth. When the history of the world is definitively written, what's the difference between the State of the Union message and the economic message to Congress? I could still recognize some difference in politicians' characters, but less and less in their utterances.

And truth to tell, the truth itself was getting harder and harder to find. Vietnam and Watergate had encouraged people to lie whenever the truth became uncomfortable. And no one was immune. Good people, moral people were corrupted by circumstances over which they exercised substantial control, but no responsibility. The more I looked for the truth among newsmakers, the more obfuscation I found, the more questions I had.

For all these reasons, I was drawn to thinking small, attracted to problems I could do something about, drawn to projects I could conceptualize, measure, and complete. Nothing helped me to this conclusion more than Porto Bello, a point of land on the St. Mary's River seventy miles south of Washington, across from St. Mary's City—the first capital of Maryland, the first Catholic community founded in the new world by the British (1634) and, after Jamestown, the Massachusetts Bay Colony, and Plymouth, the oldest.

In 1990, when Sally heard about it at dinner one night, Porto Bello was also the ruined shell of an eighteenth-century house, open to the elements on two sides. She was sitting next to Ted Koppel and heard him describe a ruined manor house across the St. Mary's River from the early-eighteenth-century house that he and his wife, Grace Ann, had fixed up. Unbeknownst to me, Sally and her mother drove down to southern Maryland the next morning, found Porto Bello, even found the mother and father of the owner. That night, casual as can be, she told me she had seen this interesting house and wanted me to take a look at it. No pressure, no threats. I felt we needed another house like we needed holes in the head, given Grey Gardens in East Hampton and the cabin in West Virginia, remote as it was. But I went down to see it, and I was a goner.

It quite simply blew my mind. This gorgeous wreck, looking

down the St. Mary's River, across the Potomac into Virginia, surrounded on three sides by water. Now, five years later, the manor
house has two small wings, a sunroom on one side, a kitchen on
the other. Two deteriorating buildings have been converted into a
guest cottage and a study (for me). A dock has been rebuilt. Two
crumbling barns have been given glorious new life by Amish crafts-
men; a chicken house and corncrib have been transformed into the
caretaker's house.

With Sally's creative skills concentrated on the house, my more
pioneer abilities have been spent on the land, gone literally to
seed and ruin. With all my toys—tractor, bush hog, chain saw, axe,
grub hooks, and the like—every morning I am there I take off for
the site of the day. I clear hedgerows, pull down vines clinging to
high trees, root out brambles that choke dogwoods, tulip poplars,
holly trees, pecans, walnuts, cedars, locusts, beech, and oak. I burn
mountains of brush whenever the wind and the weather are right. I
find remnants of barbed-wire fences (too often with my chain saw)
deep into wooded areas, the boundaries of old fields that have been
unplowed for twenty years. I comb half a mile of shoreline almost
every weekend, looking for the good and the bad stuff left by high
tides, just as I comb catalogues for things to plant and tools to plant
them with. I find trees to transplant whenever we are flush enough
to rent the required giant tree spade in the fall or the winter. I empty
my head—not to concentrate on anything, just to get it empty, to
free it from concerns that occupy my week. Now, more often than
not, young Quinn is working by my side, as I worked by my father's
side in the Beverly woods more than sixty years ago. We collect objects—mostly discarded from old farm equipment, like plowshares,
or harness equipment and, every now and then, an arrowhead or
hand-forged farm gadgets. We have a museum of these objects on a
barn wall.

One morning right after I left the city room, I got a call from the
gruff-talking Maryland governor, William Donald Schaefer, whom
I barely knew.

"Bradlee," he growled, "I got a job for you," but he wouldn't tell
me what it was. He made me come down to Annapolis for breakfast

the next morning. His job offer was to be chairman of something called the Historic St. Mary's City Commission, charged with promoting the development of the glories of Maryland's first capital, which, as the first Catholic settlement, was also the first experiment in religious toleration in this country. As the plain old St. Mary's City Commission, it was on its way to extinction—the legislature had abolished it, added the word "Historic" to signify meaningful change, and the governor had thirteen appointments to make. I asked Schaefer if he was going to load up the commission with a lot of folks in his political debt.

"Well," he said, "I didn't owe you a goddamn thing." And I signed on. It was a tough job for someone used to having an idea one day and seeing it in the newspaper the next day. A state bureaucracy is close enough to an immovable object for the fainthearted to faint away. As usual, my solution was to find the very best person to do the heavy lifting, and we found Sara Patton, who was running Jamestown Settlement, a heavy lifter if ever there was one. We are determined to rebuild the first Catholic church in America, on the existing foundations in the middle of our 830-acre archeological site—an intriguing challenge for a twice-divorced WASP.

The chairman of the Historic St. Mary's City Commission is, ex officio, a trustee of St. Mary's College, and that has become an exciting bonus for me. St. Mary's is a small liberal arts honors college, state supported but independent, with its own board of trustees, which includes Steven Muller, former president of Johns Hopkins University, as chairman; Paul Nitze, former Secretary of the Navy and special adviser to President Reagan; and General Andrew Goodpaster, former NATO Supreme Allied Commander and retired commander-in-chief of U.S. European Command. I have become a fan of St. Mary's College, especially during the times when Harvard is trying to raise another zillion dollars, and I think how important ten thousand dollars is to smaller, less well-known institutions.

Moving out of the city room freed me from the restrictions which prevent editors from playing an active role in pro bono causes. The theory is that editors and reporters can't be unbiased if they have to report on themselves. The treasurer of the school on whose board you sit runs off with the funds and the senior class president, for instance. For me, that meant a chance to pay back Children's Hospital, first and foremost. I was asked, and quickly agreed, to chair a capital fund drive for $40 million in five years . . . the most money ever raised for a private charity in Washington. That is really heavy lifting, but with Sally as vice chairman, we had $28.5 million pledged after the first three years. I take potential donors through the hospital, always drawn to the intensive care unit, always drawn to the bed that Quinn occupied, with five or six tubes stuck into his eight-pound body, and always in tears.

My charitable giving has changed during my lifetime. First, when I was a journalist, all gifts were anonymous. I even endowed a chair at the Kennedy School at Harvard anonymously, trying— awkwardly, I now think—to pay back *The Washington Post*, whence the funds came, and to thank Kennedy, who was so involved with my interest in the intersection of the press and public policy. But in more than five years since the gift was completed, Harvard has not been able to come up with the right professor for the chair. Similar funds given to a smaller institution with at least comparable needs would have had a far greater impact.

All that plus writing this book had pretty much filled up my dance card when the charismatic Dr. Anthony John Francis O'Reilly made me an offer I couldn't refuse. With one hat, Tony O'Reilly is the chairman and CEO of the multibillion-dollar H. J. Heinz Co. I knew him as a fellow *Washington Post* board member, along with his Irish CEO cronies: Jim Burke of Johnson & Johnson and Don Keogh of the Coca-Cola Company. With another hat, O'Reilly runs his own media company—and I joined the board— with major newspapers in Ireland and South Africa, nearly half of the *Independent* in London, plus newspapers and radio stations and outdoor advertising in Australia and a smaller share of the largest newspaper in New Zealand.

None of this has much to do with the Pentagon Papers, or Watergate, or national security, but highlights are only highlights, and these highlights are behind me. They are not a life. I miss the times when a story just plain consumes the readers, when people seem to talk about nothing else, whether it's momentous, like Nixon resigning, or simply extraordinary, like Lorena Bobbitt cutting off her husband's tallywhacker. But I don't miss the administrative meetings—budgets, diversity, reengineering. I don't miss the process stories: the President said, the Senate voted, the court ruled, the Pentagon announced.

I do hang out a little. That's part of the Vice President at Large's charter, so I don't miss that too much. But I miss the excitement of the stories that quicken your pulse.

That's when a newspaperman can get on with the job he was born to do. Not many of us were lucky enough to get that exhilarating opportunity. Again and again and again.

AFTERWORD

by *Sally Quinn*

When Ben decided to retire at age 70, I was worried. He was so young for his age, so vital, so full of life. What would he ever do with himself? I couldn't see him playing golf or tennis every day. Nor could I see us taking endless cruises. If we didn't kill ourselves we might have killed each other. I was twenty years younger than he was and we had a nine-year old son, Quinn, who had continuing medical problems and learning disabilities and who required frequent hospitalizations and special schools. I also had my work as a reporter for the *Post*, though I hadn't worked full time since Quinn had been born. We weren't going anywhere.

I also found it hard to believe that Ben wouldn't be completely traumatized at some point by having gone from such a demanding, high-powered job to, well . . . nothing. He didn't actually have a plan.

Ben, on the other hand, was his usual insouciant self, at once totally enchanting, but at the same time completely maddening. Didn't he realize what a dramatic change it would make in his life, going from being on top of the world one minute to becoming, in the cruel Washington arena we lived in, a "nobody"?

I had spent most of my career at the *Post* chronicling those who seek power, attain it, use and abuse it, then lose it. It can be devastating to watch. I didn't want that to happen to Ben.

I needn't have worried.

Ben had to be fully engaged in whatever he did, and in those last few years after Watergate he just didn't have the same passion for his work. Gary Trudeau did a famous cartoon about Ben railing around the city room, trying to rally the troops, saying, "Let's go get those great failing economy stories!" Through his glass office window one could see him relaxing with his feet on his desk, doing crossword puzzles more often than not.

When he finally told me he had made his decision to step down he said, "I want to go out at the top of my game."

He did.

Shortly after the first of many retirement parties, Ben and I went to Easthampton for August. We were sitting at dinner with the late director Sidney Lumet. Sidney leaned over to me and asked, "How could you possibly let Ben retire? Don't you realize that people all over Washington will be crossing your names out of their little black books?"

I thought about it for a minute and replied, "Sidney, anybody who would cross our names out of their little black book is not in mine to begin with."

That turned out to be true. Only one person, just one, never called or saw us again. That name will be revealed in my next memoir!

As it turned out, Ben reveled in his new role as "Vice President at Large," a title he and then publisher Don Graham deemed sufficiently impressive for his new non-job. Ben referred to himself as Chief Morale Officer and laughingly acquiesced to being what he called "a stop on the tour."

He moved his office up to the seventh floor to be with Don, and there was a constant stream of people coming in and out for advice, wisdom, and humor. Though he had vowed not to enter his beloved newsroom for six months after he left, and was true to his word, he ate most lunches in the cafeteria, surrounded by reporters who loved the banter, the insults, the stories, and the gossip of the day.

Ben was always in a good mood when he came home at night, but it was only after his retirement that I realized how much stress he must have been under during his almost thirty years as editor, especially during the Watergate time we spent together. After his retirement I kept waiting for him to miss the action, leap up from the breakfast table after reading the paper and say, "I can't stand it another minute!" This only happened once. Less than two years after he had left the job, Lorena Bobbitt cut off her husband John's penis. Ben went nuts. He apparently stormed into the newsroom and to everyone's amusement began barking orders as though he had never left. "Let's get those stories?" "Find out what kind of knife she used!" "What was the angle of the cut?" "Was he totally asleep?" "Let's find that penis!" (She had thrown the penis out the window of her car.) The entire newsroom was energized. Ben was back!

That was the first and last time he ever broke out into deadline fever.

I'd never seen Ben so happy. He was on the board of *The Washington Post* for two years after he stepped down, which he loved. He had joined the board of an Irish newspaper company, which took Ben and me and Quinn around the world on one fantastic boondoggle after the other. We were able to have two-month vacations in the summer. We would rent a villa in a different country for one month every year, always with lots of friends and lots of booze. The second month we spent at our beach house, Grey Gardens in Easthampton, which Ben described as living high on the hog. We went to St. Martin in the Caribbean where we had spent our honeymoon every Valentine's week, always with Quinn. We sold our cabin in West Virginia and bought a fabulous ruin called Porto Bello on the St. Mary's River in southern Maryland, which we restored. At Portobello Ben and Quinn would disappear into the woods with their axes and chainsaws in the morning and reappear in the late af-

ternoon, grinning from ear to ear, covered in soot. Ben would break
out a beer and the two would settle in for a late afternoon of football in front of the fire. Ben described it as "mind emptying," but
I believe working out in the woods was a form of meditation that
kept him going throughout the Pentagon Papers, Watergate, and
Quinn's illnesses. Ben was also the new commissioner of St. Mary's
City, one of the oldest settlements in the United States. This was
a job he went into with his usual gusto. They discovered the iron
coffins of members of the Calvert family buried under the ruins of
the oldest Catholic church in America, which Ben later restored.
One night at a dinner I saw Ben pull General Colin Powell aside,
and the two were deep in conversation. If I hadn't known any better
I would have thought they were talking about troop withdrawals in
Iraq. As it turned out Ben was asking the general for remaindered
army tents to use for the archeological dig around the coffins.

This was certainly the happiest time in our marriage. Both of us
were freer than we had ever been and really able to revel in our relationship. Ben was able to spend a lot of time with Quinn, more than
he ever had while he was working full-time. He gave him the love
and the confidence he needed. He helped Quinn learn to handle
his problems with courage and determination and optimism, and
never failed to show his admiration and respect for Quinn. It's such
a cliché when people say they're leaving their jobs to spend more
time with their family, but in Ben's case it was true, and it turned
out to be the most joyous time of his life. The feeling was mutual,
and Quinn later wrote the following about his father:

"The last words that my dad said to me before he died were: 'I
have a good feeling about you, Quinn' and 'I love you.' I can't imagine more perfect final words for a son to hear as he loses a beloved
father. My dad taught me that all things in life are interrelated, to
respect Mother Nature to the highest degree, and that we are all
here—and we are all who we are—because of our ancestors. He
taught me that if something bad happens, you need to learn from
it and then move on. He was the most modest person I have ever
met, and he once told me that I should "not get too close to the
royals." He hated liars, and I learned from him that telling the truth

is the most important thing in life—a person who always tells the truth has nothing to hide. But perhaps the most important thing my father taught me was to treat all people with respect no matter what, because we are all equal. Recently I opened my personal copy of my father's book, *A Good Life*, which he gave me when the book was first published. I had to smile when I reread his inscription to me: "You make me happy and proud. Love, Dad. September 1995."

One of the things that really kept Ben inspired after his retirement was writing this book. Ben was never terribly introspective ("navel gazing," he called it) yet he really threw himself into the research and the writing with enormous enthusiasm. I tried very hard to get him to write about his "feelings," to no avail. Though a total renegade, he was still an old Boston Brahmin at heart. He spent one whole summer in East Hampton writing the book in a tiny thatched roof cottage at the back of the garden on an old standup typewriter. He was totally absorbed.

Katharine Graham was writing her memoirs at the same time. After *A Good Life* came out she announced one day that she had a title for her book: *A Better Life*.

Once the book was published Ben was inundated with offers to speak, go on panels, to be honored at various events, to accept awards, etc. He refused most of them. "But for the honor of it all . . ." he would joke. He never seemed to care about personal accolades. They embarrassed him.

There were two honors, however, which thrilled him. One was the Légion d'Honneur, which was presented to him in Paris at L'Hôtel by the former French ambassador Jean-Davide Levitte. We took a gang of friends to Paris for a three-day celebration, and Ben, who spoke fluent French, was in his element.

The second was the Medal of Freedom, which President Obama presented to him the November before he died. I don't think I have ever seen Ben so excited. It surprised me. But somehow he seemed to realize that he was being honored not just for his service in World War II or his work as a journalist, but for the contribution he had made to upholding the values of his country.

Eight years before he died, Ben was diagnosed with dementia.

He never discussed it. We never discussed it. It was simply the hand he had been dealt and, as was evident by the title he chose for this book; he thought he had been dealt a pretty terrific hand.

I never once saw Ben depressed in all the time we were together. He didn't like it when I had to take the car keys away from him, he didn't like it when he became more dependent on me. But in the end he cherished the time we had together, as did I, and his disease brought us closer together than we had ever been.

Ben lived his whole life a happy man. He died a happy man. I feel grateful that I got to spend forty-three years with such a fabulous guy.

Since the 2016 election people ask me constantly: what would Ben have thought, what would Ben have done? I always tell them the same thing. Ben would have been conflicted. On the one hand he would have thought it was a fantastic story. He would, as the *Post* has done so well, have hired the best reporters and worked night and day to "get it first but above all get it right." More than anything, Ben hated lying. High on a wall at the new *Washington Post* building, outside the all-glass Ben Bradlee Conference Room where story conference is held every day, there is a quote from Ben. It reads: "The truth no matter how bad is never as dangerous as the lie in the long run."

I think Ben would have been concerned about what is happening to our country today. He would have been appalled by the total disregard for the truth in some quarters, and the acceptance of it by those who should know better. Ben was nothing if not a consummate patriot, and his love of country came before anything else.

I miss you, Ben. I think we all miss you, now more than ever.

—August 2017

INDEX

PICTURE CREDITS